W9-AFL-798

UNITED STATES FOREIGN POLICY

1945-1955

THE BROOKINGS INSTITUTION

The Brookings Institution is an independent organization engaged in research and education in the social sciences. Its principal purposes are to aid in the development of sound public policies and to provide advanced training for students in the social sciences.

The Institution was founded December 8, 1927 as a consolidation of three antecedent organizations: the Institute for Government Research, 1916; the Institute of Economics, 1922; and the Robert Brookings Graduate School of Economics and Government, 1924.

The general administration of the Institution is the responsibility of a self-perpetuating Board of Trustees. In addition to this general responsibility the By-Laws provide that, "It is the function of the Trustees to make possible the conduct of scientific research and publication, under the most favorable conditions, and to safeguard the independence of the research staff in the pursuit of their studies and in the publication of the results of such studies. It is not a part of their function to determine, control, or influence the conduct of particular investigations or the conclusions reached." The immediate direction of the policies, program, and staff of the Institution is vested in the President, who is assisted by an advisory council, chosen from the professional staff of the Institution.

In publishing a study, the Institution presents it as a competent treatment of a subject worthy of public consideration. The interpretations and conclusions in such publications are those of the author or authors and do not necessarily reflect the views of other members of the Brookings staff or of the administrative officers of the Institution.

BOARD OF TRUSTEES

WILLIAM R. BIGGS, *Chairman*

ROBERT BROOKINGS SMITH, *Vice-Chairman*

ARTHUR STANTON ADAMS
DANIEL W. BELL
ROBERT D. CALKINS
LEONARD CARMICHAEL
ARTHUR H. COMPTON
HUNTINGTON GILCHRIST
LEWIS WEBSTER JONES
JOHN E. LOCKWOOD
LEVERETT LYON

GEORGE C. MCGHEE
GILBERT F. WHITE
LAURENCE F. WHITTEMORE
DONALD B. WOODWARD

Honorary Trustees

ROBERT PERKINS BASS
MRS. ROBERT S. BROOKINGS
JOHN LEE PRATT

ROBERT D. CALKINS, *President* and *Acting Director of Economic Studies*
PAUL T. DAVID, *Director of Governmental Studies*
ROBERT W. HARTLEY, *Director of International Studies*

327.73
R

UNITED STATES
FOREIGN POLICY
1945-1955

By

William Reitzel

Morton A. Kaplan

Constance G. Coblenz

THE BROOKINGS INSTITUTION

WASHINGTON, D.C.

Wingate College Library

© 1956 BY

THE BROOKINGS INSTITUTION

Set up and printed
Published August 1956

Library of Congress Catalogue Card Number 56-11440

Printed in the United States of America
George Banta Company, Inc.
Menasha, Wisconsin

Preface

IN 1946, the Brookings Institution began a program of research and education in international relations. The program was initiated by the late Dr. Leo Pasvolsky, who until his death in May 1953 was Director of the International Studies Group at the Institution. The program was an expansion of earlier activities of the Institution in this field and continued its established policy of selecting for study problems that had a direct bearing on the national interest.

As an integral feature of the program, a series of annual surveys was inaugurated in 1947 on *Major Problems of United States Foreign Policy*. Seven such surveys have been published, of which the most recent appeared in 1954, and they were supplemented for several years by a monthly report on *Current Developments in United States Foreign Policy*. Also, a series of five national and seven regional seminars on problems of United States foreign policy was held beginning in 1947 to aid in improving the teaching of international relations.

The principal purpose of these surveys and seminars was to identify and analyze the problems of decision that confronted American policy makers as they sought to realize the objectives of the United States in the circumstances that prevailed in the world. The method used was to put the readers of the volumes or the participants in the meetings in the position of government officials who, in discharging their responsibilities, had to keep in mind the entire range of the international scene, the forces at home and abroad that would be affected by their decisions, and who had—above all—to explore the alternative courses of action that were open for the solution of particular problems. The intent was to convey something of the actual nature of the problems of public policy and something of the implications of the term "decision." This, in essence, was the "problem approach."

The present study grows out of this approach, but its scope and treatment are different than the previous annual surveys. With the close of the first decade after the Second World War, it became increasingly clear that some of the choices American policy makers

v

8838

had made during the ten years since the war had resulted in a satisfactory advance toward United States objectives in world affairs, while others had plainly not. A re-examination of the assumptions and evaluations on which these choices had been based seemed, therefore, to be prerequisite to a better understanding of the policy-making process and, perhaps, to the formulation of more effective policies during future years.

It is the purpose of this volume to contribute to such a re-examination by analyzing the official purposes and actions of the United States in its foreign policies and relations during the ten years since the war in order to try to recapture the key decisions that were made and the grounds on which one course of action rather than another was chosen. The scope of this volume is consequently much broader and its treatment is necessarily much more highly selective than the previous annual surveys. Attention has been fixed on the general pattern of United States policy as it has developed from problem situation to problem situation during the postwar decade, and general questions about the position of the United States in world affairs are raised and examined as they relate to the courses open for choice in the years that lie immediately ahead.

This study is the joint work of three members of the Brookings staff. It was planned by William Reitzel, who supervised the preparation of the preceding four annual surveys, and the basic research was done by Morton A. Kaplan and Constance G. Coblenz. The text in its preliminary form was a composite effort, which was critically read by several consultants and members of the Brookings staff to whom the authors are greatly indebted for many helpful suggestions and comments. The authors are indebted particularly to Walter S. Salant who prepared Appendix C. The text in its final form was prepared by Mr. Reitzel, under the general supervision of Robert W. Hartley, Director of International Studies. A. Evelyn Breck, with the assistance of Medora Richardson, edited the manuscript.

Finally, on behalf of the Institution, I wish to express grateful appreciation to the Rockefeller Foundation of New York for the generous grants that have supported the research necessary for this volume, as well as for the preceding annual surveys.

ROBERT D. CALKINS
President

Contents

vii

PART TWO: AMERICAN ACTION: 1946-1950

APPENDIXES

LIST OF MAPS AND CHARTS

Introduction

THE FIRST decade after the Second World War has ended. The United States is no longer concerned with the world as it was in 1945, nor is it engaged with the creation of an international system that, in 1945, seemed feasible. The United States is now participating in a system of international relations that is different both from the actual world of 1945 and from the world it was then hoped might be established in the subsequent years.

This decade may well prove to be one of the most significant in the history and development of United States foreign policy. Even before the war had ended, a deterioration began in the coalition of major powers—the Grand Alliance—that had won the war and that the United States vainly hoped would continue to co-operate in maintaining the peace. The Soviet Union and the Western allies rapidly became divided over the basic issues of aggression, subjugation, and totalitarianism with the result that a new world-wide alliance of non-Communist nations, led by the United States, was formed. In the ensuing conflict of cold, and then hot, war between the Communist-dominated nations and the free world, the United States has championed the universal struggle against communism because it has believed that success in that struggle is indispensable to the achievement of lasting international peace and security.

During these years, the United States has definitely assumed the role of world leadership in upholding those principles of international society to which the human race has long aspired but which many have always considered visionary. This role has derived unprecedented support from the faith of the American people in the espousal of moral principles, backed by their willing use of wealth and force. It has meant not only the end of the persisting American will to isolation, but also the acceptance by the American people of a role that they now recognize has been compellingly thrust upon them by the scope and pace of events.

In this world situation, intensified by the race for nuclear and thermonuclear weapons, it has been impossible to achieve many of the objectives of United States foreign policy that were envisaged at the close of the Second World War. The problems of United States

1

policy had been seen in 1945 mainly in political and institutional terms. Political adjustments were expected to come out of conferences and negotiations. But the failure of the early postwar international conferences—as exemplified by the Council of Foreign Ministers meeting in Moscow in the spring of 1947—put an end to dependence on international negotiation as a major way to carry out United States policy. This meeting made it abundantly clear that Soviet objectives for Germany and much of the rest of the world could not be reconciled with those of the West.

By 1947 the United States Government recognized that Soviet policy ruled out negotiated adjustments unless and until the Western allies had developed strength. At first the use of economic assistance was favored as the way to bring about this necessary condition. Once, however, there had been outright Communist aggression—in Korea in June 1950—the United States turned more directly to military means to build up strength. The possibility of localized Communist aggression in other parts of the world was taken more seriously. Despite this preoccupation, which meant larger military assistance programs and attention to the possibility of still further military action, such as in Korea, United States policy remained essentially defensive in concept.

In the later days of the Truman administration, however—with a cease-fire and virtual military stalemate in Korea dragging on—the American people began to look somewhat on the concept of defense as an excuse not to act. Consequently, when General Eisenhower became President in 1953, his administration undertook to restate United States policy in more vigorous terms. Out of this effort came, for example, the assertion of the policy of massive retaliation at times and in places of American choosing. This warning did not long survive in what appeared to be its original meaning: that the consequences of another aggression such as the Communists had perpetrated in Korea might be atomic warfare. The growing possibility of a Communist adventure in Indo-China contributed to the end of this concept of policy. Neither public opinion nor national policies in the free world would have acquiesced in the continued use of this form of pressure. The explosion by both the United States and the Soviet Union of thermonuclear devices emphasized the danger of resort to the use of extreme forces. An atomic and hydrogen stalemate was in the making.

The allies of the United States undertook to persuade it to return to political adjustment as the major basis for the development and execution of foreign policies. The official position, partly responsive to these pressures from abroad, began to be that the West had reached a position of strength from which it could afford to negotiate with the Soviet Union. Political negotiations between the Western powers and the Soviet Union—as carried on in the Geneva Conference of heads of government in July 1955 and in the abortive Geneva meeting of foreign ministers in October and November of that year—were beginning again to become an acceptable means of executing American foreign policy.

In spite of this change, the end of the decade found the Soviet Union and the Western world, led by the United States, still engaged in a gigantic struggle, one to impose its Communist way of life on the rest of the world, and the other to protect its traditional institutions and principles. The United States had to continue to rely on military means as well as on the system of alliances it had set up with many members of the free world. At the same time, it began to review its position and policies. The conclusion apparently was reached that the phase of outright "violence and threats of violence" in the relations between the Soviet Union and the West had diminished in intensity. It was not concluded, however, that the Soviet Union had in fact changed anything but its tactics. Responsibility for this shift was placed in part on the collective security policies of the free world and on American assistance programs. That led to the inevitability of continuing these policies and programs in some form: the American system of alliances and capacity to wage nuclear and thermonuclear war must be maintained.

Soviet actions also began to suggest that the Soviet Union did not want—at least for the time being—to reopen the violent phase. Its rulers turned to diplomacy, propaganda, and promises of economic assistance as instruments of action. In fact, the Soviet Union gave strong evidence that it was trying to reconcile its policies with the increasingly independent attitudes that the uncommitted states were taking. The direction of the development of the international system no longer conformed as closely to United States policies as it had earlier in the decade. The United States strategy of containment and the pattern of policies by which it had been developed were less successful in the context of the shift in the conduct of Soviet foreign relations. All this caused a re-examination in the

United States of alternative ways to use American resources for foreign policy goals.

This re-examination in no way invalidated the estimate of the dominating influence of the United States in the free world. Even if it were to withdraw from its system of alliances and to give up its foreign assistance policies, its decisions and actions would continue to have a determining effect on the policy choices available to other states, both free and Communist. At first glance, therefore, the position of the United States with respect to the Soviet Union or the free world did not seem to have changed greatly. This view, however, did not take account of the influences to which United States policies had become increasingly exposed. These were the influences exerted by states that could not be coerced except at the expense of the objectives that United States policies were designed to reach.

It is in the light of this re-examination that the present study has been undertaken of the evolution of United States foreign policy from 1945 to 1955. It seeks to present a picture of American purpose and action as the United States moved from a war in which it was a dominating power to a postwar situation in which it sought to shape, by agreement with other states, a particular kind of international system, and then into a situation in which it was obliged to act unilaterally as a major power in an international system that was taking quite a different form. By focusing attention on the key decisions that were made and the alternative courses that were available, it is hoped that a pattern will emerge of United States policies and actions during the period that were the consequence of an unbroken series of interlocking choices, only some of which were American. The point of view, therefore, is that of the highest levels of government, and the alternative courses examined tend to be confined to those that were significant enough to require consideration at the highest levels.

This framework imposes certain limitations on the analysis. No attempt is made fully to recreate each moment of decision, because to do so would multiply details to the point where the underlying pattern could not emerge. Similarly, no effort is made to keep up a running reference to the influence of domestic political events in limiting the choices immediately available to United States policy makers. Furthermore, questions that might be of importance only to some specialists have either been ignored or kept in strict subordination to issues involving the total position of the United States.

In accordance with these purposes and limitations, the volume is divided into four parts.

Part One considers the American goals in world affairs at the end of the Second World War. It surveys briefly the evolution of the American view of foreign affairs and of the interests of the United States and the aims of United States policy as these were officially stated at the end of the Second World War. This basic record is brought into relationship with an estimate of the capabilities that the United States had for pursuing these objectives and with an analysis of the state of the world in which these policies would have to be carried out. An examination is then made of the official reinterpretation that took place during 1946 of both objectives and policies.

Part Two is devoted to a running account of the United States policy choices that were made from 1947 to 1950 and of the considerations and guidelines that influenced these choices. It is an analytical record of key decisions made within the framework of an evolving official American interpretation of the nature of the international system. Because this interpretation was conditioned primarily by judgments about the intentions and capabilities of the Soviet Union, this part begins with an account of the strategic concept that was developed for acting on these judgments. This is followed by a record of the broad pattern of policy that was built up to execute this strategic concept. The application of these general policy lines in various areas of action is then examined, note being taken in each case of the adjustments and modifications that resulted, and the tests to which American objectives and policies were subjected by the actions of other states are considered, ending with the key test of armed Communist aggression in the Far East. The part concludes with an analysis of the changes in the priorities for American action that were made in the course of 1950 and 1951.

Part Three deals with the period since 1950. It opens with a generalized analysis of the structure of the international system as it evolved from the Second World War. It then considers the shifting framework of interpretation and purpose that guided the choices of United States policy makers as they sought to develop and maintain a secure and satisfactory position for the United States in this unstable system. This is followed by an analysis, made in terms of contingencies, probabilities, and priorities as these were seen at the time, of the problems of choice and action that arose from the key decision of 1950—to meet armed Communist aggression with collective force.

Part Four, the last one of the volume, examines the present position of the United States. It opens with an analysis of the changes that have taken place in the position and role of the United States in the international system. It then examines the case for a comprehensive review of American purposes and patterns of action, and notes the framework within which such a review might be expected to take place. The volume ends with a survey of the broad range of choices that appear to be open to the United States as the second decade of postwar history begins.

PART ONE

THE AMERICAN GOALS: 1945-1946

CHAPTER I

The Background of American Objectives

THE United States occupied a position of unprecedented power and prestige at the end of the Second World War. Its ability to influence the course of world events was immense, and its willingness to assume the international responsibilities of its position reflected the changed interpretation the American people held of their national interest. In contrast to their earlier attitude, they were prepared to have their government take vigorous and consistent action to preserve international peace and security and generally to participate in world affairs.

Behind this changed attitude lay the whole of American history and the record of a long and confused search for a satisfactory definition of the United States position in the world and an acceptable interpretation of the American national interest. The geographical location of the United States and the great wealth of natural resources within its boundaries provided the basis for the traditional interpretation of the national interest.[1] The United States lay be-

[1] The analysis that follows calls for the definitions—at least as they are used in this volume—of five terms: "national interest," "objective," "policy," "commitment," and "principle."

National interest is used to mean the general and continuing end for which a nation acts: to maintain its security and promote its well-being. This broad and omnipresent motive is, however, normally defined in a particular way to fit given circumstances. Thus the *national interest,* as it is usually found referred to, undergoes historical redefinition as the requirements of security and well-being are variously understood. It is from current interpretations of the *national interest* that national objectives develop.

Objective is used to mean a specifically defined goal, or purpose, for which national action is planned in terms of the maintenance of the national interest. Fundamentally, an *objective* is an aspect of the national interest, delimited and particularized for action in a given context. It can, therefore, be the consequence either of a widely felt threat to the national interest, or of a general conviction that a certain end is desirable.

Policy is used to mean a course of action designed to achieve an objective.

Commitment is used to mean an undertaking in support of a policy. It can be vague or precise, implied or specifically stated, depending on circumstances.

Principle is used to mean a more or less clearly formulated pattern of action that guides national decision. A *principle* tends to become a rule of conduct that a nation believes should guide its actions as well as those of other nations.

An extensive analysis of these terms and their use will be found in Appendix "A."

9

tween two oceans; it was separated from the power conflicts of Europe; it was bordered by states that were either friendly or weak; and its dominant position in the Western Hemisphere was beyond challenge. The aspect of the national interest that involved security was consequently regarded as satisfied by remaining aloof from foreign entanglements and by being ready and able to defend the American continent. The aspect of the national interest that involved well-being was regarded as satisfied by developing the resources of the continent and by insisting on an equality of economic and commercial opportunity for American citizens throughout the world.

Two wars in the twentieth century, however, in both of which the United States was militarily involved in regions far removed from its continental territory, and in both of which the well-being of the United States was affected in unanticipated ways, brought this traditional interpretation of the national interest into question. Consequently, a new interpretation of what was needed to maintain the national interest came to the fore. In shaping this new interpretation, two sets of circumstances, both products of the twentieth century, played an important part in bringing about a redefinition of what was requisite to the security and to the well-being of the United States. With respect to security, it could no longer be convincingly asserted that the strategic frontier of the United States lay in the continental waters of North America. With respect to the well-being of the United States, it became increasingly apparent that this was inseparable from the maintenance of peace and security and from the development of economic and social well-being throughout the world.

The new interpretation, by calling for constant and planned action in the whole field of international relations, inevitably led to expanded objectives and to a wider range of policies. Furthermore, policies became complexly interlocked in the continuing process of conducting foreign relations. In the end, these changes shifted the role of the United States in the world from a passive to an active one.

The United States Government could no longer, if it was to act on the new interpretation of the national interest, wait for events to take place before taking action on them. It had to anticipate events, to take the initiative, and to make positive efforts to guide international developments in directions of its own choosing. Yet, in taking the initiative, the United States policy maker could not wholly escape from the American past or from traditional concepts of the role of the United States in the world that were still an active element in American opinion. A recapitulation of earlier interpretations of the national interest and of the objectives and policies that they occasioned will give some idea of the motivations that are deeply fixed in the American tradition and hence to some extent still condition attitudes and responses.

Historical Evolution

The evolution of these motivations can be treated as taking place in three stages. In the first, the controlling motivation was to consolidate the country as a nation. This stage, which was essentially completed by 1890, was marked by continental expansion and by the increasingly co-ordinated development of the resources of the continent. At all times during this stage, the United States maintained and increased its position of dominance in the Western Hemisphere.

Initially, the problem was confined to that part of the continent that lay between the Mississippi Valley and the Atlantic Ocean, and was an aspect of the persistent struggle for dominance of the major states of Europe. This form of the problem was essentially settled by 1823. By this time the United States had secured its hold on the disputed territory. The end of the first stage came with the completion of the westward expansion from the Mississippi Valley to the Pacific Ocean. The problem during this period was one of preventing the re-establishment of European influences and of drawing sectional American interests together into a federated whole.

The second stage (1890-1945) was one in which the United States began to play a role as a world power, progressing hesitatingly toward understanding its position in the world. The period was marked by considerable public discussion, in the course of which the term "manifest destiny" was employed and disapproved, and basic and opposing concepts of withdrawal from and participation in international affairs were extensively canvassed. United States policy fluctuated between a desire to project American power and influence and a desire to avoid international responsibilities. Throughout this period, therefore, objectives and policy reflected the adjustments and the failures to adjust to the implications and requirements of being in the position of a major state. The implied uncertainties in this process came to an end during the Second World War when the United States acted throughout as a major force in world affairs.

The third and still unfinished stage is that in which the United States is acting as a major world power whose decisions fundamentally affect the whole structure of contemporary international relations. This stage was initially marked by a basic decision to exercise the influence and authority of the United States to adjust and harmonize relations with other states primarily through the medium of the United Nations, rather than to employ this influence and authority unilaterally. As will be seen later, exceptions were made to this decision in several important respects, mainly under the pressure of events, but also because the decision was still not wholly accepted by American opinion as providing an adequate method for maintaining the national interest.

Initial Interpretations of the National Interest

The history of the United States as a nation began in a network of great power relationships that involved competing European states—Great Britain, France, Spain, Austria, Prussia, and Russia. Three of these states—Great Britain, France, and Spain—had for over two centuries been especially concerned with the North American continent, and general European wars were invariably carried over to the Western Hemisphere. By the middle of the eighteenth century, Great Britain had become not only the dominant power in North America but also a predominant influence throughout the world. The policies of the European powers at whose expense Britain had achieved this position were directed to breaking Britain down.

The rebellion of the thirteen British North American colonies in 1776 was not in itself related to a European conflict, although the achievement of independence in 1783 was made possible by the assistance of European countries that saw an opportunity to profit from British difficulties. The newly independent United States of America, a very weak confederation in 1783, was a minor factor in the play of European power politics. This fact was fully recognized by the American leaders, who for several decades after reaching formal independence faced grave problems in their search for national security. The United States, surrounded by the territories of the great powers of Europe, was defenseless against their military might and ill-united against their intrigues. On the other hand, the United States was protected by their rivalries. So far as the security and even the prosperity of the United States were concerned, these conflicts were a godsend, because none of the contenders could spare the time or attention for aggrandizement at the expense of the United States.

The security of the new nation was held to require complete insulation against the re-establishment of European influences and political controls. The well-being of the new state was held to require the unimpeded development of its resources and an unremitting effort to move these resources freely in world trade. The desirable form of influence that the new state should exert in the world was held to be the model it could provide of republican and Protestant virtue, good faith, and fair dealing. These formulas, together with a realistic appraisal of the relative weakness of the new state in a world where European powers operated in great strength, furnished an interpretation of the national interest by which national objectives and their supporting policies were guided for nearly a century.

One of the classical conversions of this interpretation into a national objective was made by President Washington in his Farewell Address: "Europe has a set of primary interests which to us have none or a very remote relation. Hence she must be engaged in frequent controversies, the cause of which are essentially foreign to our concerns." This formulation touched a very deep-seated American feeling—the colonial desire to escape from Europe, then to cut ties with it, and finally to remain isolated from it. What was here stated as an objective, admirably suited to prevailing circumstances, gradually became the basic interpretation of the national interest of the United States.

Another objective, this time concerned with national well-being, was soon formulated. The prosperity of the United States was defined as being dependent on the promotion of American trade. British efforts to monopolize on this trade had been among the causes of the Revolution. Treaties of commerce and friendship with reciprocal privileges, firm insistence on the freedom of the seas and neutral trading rights, and tariffs to encourage and protect infant industries became the triple devices of policy to achieve this objective.

Concurrently with the development of these two concepts of how the national interest was to be maintained, a principle of conduct was also established. President Washington, again in the Farewell Address, sketched a picture of peaceful relations and of good faith and justice among nations: "Cultivate peace and harmony with all. . . . It will be worthy of a free, enlightened . . . nation to give to mankind the magnanimous and too novel example of a people guided by an exalted justice and benevolence." These words were pitched to a generally acceptable code and corresponded to the general wish to live alone in peace and with freedom under law that was part of the political philosophy of the Revolution. The conversion of this concept into an attitude toward international relations was rapid, and in the American conduct of foreign affairs it has been a principle more often acted upon than departed from.[2]

Cardinal methods for maintaining the national interest were thus early defined. The security of the United States did not require permanent foreign alliances, though it did require a firm defensive posture. The well-being of the United States required equality of commercial opportunity and the means to develop national resources. Finally, both the security and the well-being of the United States could best be maintained if other nations could be persuaded to share the principles of international conduct that guided American action. The success with which these courses were followed in the first half of the nineteenth century gave the United States the opportunity to develop, practically without opposition, into a continental power. The development of this position would have been in continual doubt but for the favorable situation created by British policy.

The intent of the United States to stand against intervention from Europe was firmly supported by Great Britain, which was concerned with maintaining the balance of power that had been achieved in Europe and interested in the commercial possibilities of a free Latin American market. In fact, a joint Anglo-American

[2] It is easy to point to contrary instances. Every historian will have his favorite. But the fact remains that this concept has continued to be an ideal by which much United States action has been motivated and a measure by which the actions of other states have been judged. As such it has profoundly colored the attitudes of the American people.

declaration on this point was proposed, in connection with the Monroe Doctrine, but was rejected by the United States. Some of the new Latin American republics also proposed that the doctrine be converted into a system of mutual alliances. This was also rejected. The Monroe Doctrine remained a unilateral declaration by the United States and carried no commitment to act on behalf of, or with, any other nation. British support made the position tenable, and for seventy-five years the United States was free to complete its continental expansion, to organize its continental resources, to develop its foreign trade, and to consider the possibility of there being a "manifest destiny" toward which the nation was moving. During this same period, the United States was able to determine, although the effort involved a civil war, that it would be politically consolidated as a single federal state.

The growth of American foreign trade that accompanied both the continental expansion and the development of the resources of the continent was phenomenal. With this trade came an accumulation of foreign contacts, the growth of a diversity of specific foreign activities, and the problem of satisfying domestic demands that the national influence be exerted to support and develop these activities without at the same time going beyond the requirements of the established interpretation of the national interest. The basis for policy in these matters was the traditional view of what was required to promote national well-being—reciprocal trading privileges, neutral trading rights, and equality of commercial opportunity.

At the same time, aims evolved that were less surely grounded in the traditional view of the national interest. They were concerned with such matters as the possible acquisition of territory beyond the continental United States. The reasons advanced usually blended commercial advantages with vaguely defined strategic considerations. Pressures in this direction, though they reflected a latent imperialism that was to develop toward the close of the period of internal consolidation, generally met with public and congressional indifference.

Emergence as a World Power

By 1898, however, the tone of public feeling had changed perceptibly. The United States was beginning to emerge as a world power, and there was a feeling that the American destiny consisted of more than a continental position—that it required action on the world stage as well. This was the period of the expansion of the United States into the Pacific Ocean and the Caribbean islands, of intervention and political loans in Latin America, of the concept of an American position of power in the Far East, and of President Theodore Roosevelt's steady assertion of American influence in international situations. It is noticeable that destiny led the United States west across the Pacific and south toward Latin America, not east to Europe, and that the movement was accompanied by an appreciation of the significance of sea power. The blend of commercial and strategic considerations became less vague, proposals were soon made for an isthmian canal, and the Caribbean and Hawaiian Islands were defined as its defensive outposts.

The objectives and policies that developed in response to this feeling led progressively into a world network of power relations, in which Germany was seeking footholds in the Pacific and Far East and Japan was a growing force. United States participation in great power rivalries in China began. Following from this, Japanese expansion in the Pacific was defined as a threat to both the security and the well-being of the United States. Although the courses thus embarked on implied that the traditional interpretation of the national interest was being stretched by a demand for a more active use in international relations of the power of the United States, no generally felt sense of strain appeared in American opinion. Actually, however, as will appear later, the traditional interpretation was in process of being tested by circumstances, and the groundwork was being laid for a future controversy about the interpretation of the national interest.

The power relations in which the United States thus became involved were very different from the network in which the United States had begun its existence as a nation. Great Britain, France, and Russia alone remained of the original contenders. Spanish power had declined, and the decay of the Austro-Hungarian empire was apparent. A united Germany and a modernized Japan had emerged as vigorous claimants to places in the front rank. These changes initiated a race for territorial possessions, for the command of raw materials, and for commercial advantage throughout the world. The balance of power in Europe was threatened, and for the first time Great Britain was confronted by a possible need to restore a balance in Europe and simultaneously to establish a balance in the Far East. It was becoming increasingly difficult for Great Britain to maintain single-handedly the world-wide political controls that, by means of sea power, had provided a *Pax Britannica* for over a century.[3]

Consequently, although the United States could continue to maintain, so far as the Western Hemisphere was concerned, objectives shaped by its earlier interest in expanding American territory and consolidating its continental power, it could not pursue these objectives effectively on a world scale. To do this, the power of the United States would have had to be organized and projected into the arena of international politics. Any proposals to this effect would have gone beyond the traditional concept of what the national interest fundamentally required and would have run into a profound lack of comprehension in American opinion. Thus, the Monroe Doctrine could stand because the power of the United States was directly applicable to and preponderant in the region involved. But commercial policy of the United States, American principles of international conduct, and American views of what was internationally desirable were infinitely harder to develop in situations where the United States was only one of several powerful states and for which neither American opinion nor American power was adequately prepared.

The First World War

The implications of the new position of the United States in the world did not call for comprehensive examination until the outbreak of the war in 1914. The problem that was then presented to American opinion and to makers of United States policy was to understand and act upon the significance to the national interest of the changes that had taken place in the world structure of power. This process could not be carried on without a re-examination of traditional definitions of the national interest and of the actions that had been taken in the past to maintain that interest. The examination took the form of an extended and confused public debate, during which the entire course of United States foreign relations was discussed and interpreted. But the context of the

[3] The *Pax Britannica* can be described as a unilaterally maintained world-wide system of peace and security, derived from and consonant with the real distribution of power in the nineteenth century. Its collapse became probable with the development of Germany and Japan as expanding powers, and inevitable with the reorganization of Russian power by the Soviet Union.

international power conflicts in which these historical relations had been conducted was not clearly identified as an important factor. The nature and operation of the old equilibrium of power in Europe, the essential requirements for establishing an equilibrium of power in the Far East, the role that Great Britain had played in stabilizing international relations, and finally the part that the United States might be obliged to play because of its own growing strength—an understanding of these and related questions was essential to a resolution of the debate. But these matters were not clearly brought into the discussion.

Initially, a neutral position was proclaimed, but this position was steadily undermined by events and by the fact that the scale of the war inevitably involved the American interest and impeded the achievement of traditional objectives. By 1917 German action came into clearly defined conflict with a generally understood objective— the freedom of the seas and neutral trading rights—and the United States declared war. There is no doubt that in some quarters this decision was understood in terms of national security, but, after the decision to go to war was made, it was presented and generally accepted as the defense of a principle of good faith and justice in international relations. President Wilson, in asking Congress for a declaration of war, added that the United States, in accepting this gauge of battle "for the ultimate peace of the world and for the liberation of its peoples," had no selfish ends to serve. "We are but one of the champions of the rights of mankind."

It is important to recognize in President Wilson's words a restatement of the moral conviction underlying the passage quoted above from President Washington's Farewell Address. There was, however, one significant extension. It was now asserted that only by ensuring the rights of *all* men and *all* nations freely to choose their ways of life could a pattern of international relations be shaped that would ensure the security and well-being of the United States.

This principle of conduct was developed into a group of generalized international objectives in President Wilson's "Fourteen Points." These objectives were defined as the reduction of armaments, the removal of economic barriers between nations, the self-determination of all peoples, and the establishment of an international organization to maintain world peace. The Paris Peace Conference, however, was more concerned with a rearrangement of the power relations of states. A League of Nations based on the idealism of President Wilson's "Fourteen Points" and a peace settlement based on considerations of power simultaneously emerged from the conference.

The relation between these two elements in the subsequent international situation was lost so far as the American people were concerned. The debate that arose in the United States about the basic objectives to which United States foreign policy should be directed overlooked entirely the fact that a relationship did exist between considerations of power and considerations of the requirements of an international society in which the United States could realize its aspirations and maintain its interests. Instead, the discussion became a clash of apparently irreconcilable convictions: one, placing faith in an abstract ideal, demanded a foreign policy based on the principles written into the League of Nations; the other, appealing to American historical experience, demanded a policy based on withdrawal and self-sufficiency.

The exponents of withdrawal and self-sufficiency pointed out that the economic and territorial settlements of the peace conference represented power politics at their worst and indicated no desire on the part of the major nations to co-operate in securing universal peace. The danger of fresh entanglement in European disputes was accordingly felt to exist, and the fear was widely voiced that the power of the United States would be committed by an international body to the settlement of these disputes. In addition, it was claimed that an international organization would interfere with the freedom of action of the United States in the Western Hemisphere, that the Monroe Doctrine would be implicitly abrogated, and that the United States would no longer be the sole judge of what constituted its security in a region where its unilateral freedom of decision was historically established. The simplest possible description of this critical stage in American opinion is to say that the concept of international co-operation was rejected, and that the rejection was rationalized as a return to the basic interpretation of the national interest that had long guided United States foreign policy. In consequence, after 1920, the United States was in the ambiguous position of being a major power in the world, unwilling to act as such, yet exerting on international affairs the inevitable influence of a major power.[4]

[4] The economic resources of a modern major state are such that, even when the possessor of them does not deliberately apply them to foreign policy ends, they still constitute a central element in international affairs. Thus although the

The Interwar Years

From 1920 to 1940, the ambiguous position just referred to was substantially maintained. The prosperous condition of the United States in the 1920's, and then the shock of the depression in the 1930's contributed equally to support an attitude of withdrawal— at first by seeming to justify a conviction of self-sufficient security and well-being, and later by creating an overwhelming preoccupation with domestic problems. Traditional interpretations of the national interest, traditional patterns of policy, and references to traditional abstract principles of international conduct were vigorously asserted in both contexts. The national policy line consequently fluctuated between an avoidance of commitments, an insistence on freedom of action, and an effort to establish universal principles of international conduct. In conjunction with this last purpose, the United States often attempted to universalize its national interest and even some of its long-standing objectives, ignoring the fact that these were in great part the product of its unique continental and hemispheric position. The practical difficulties of conducting the foreign relations of the United States on these premises were not widely felt. In particular, the actual structure of power in the world and the changes in the distribution of power that developed during the interwar years were not given serious consideration in the discussion of the position of the United States.

During the first half of the interwar period, until the early 1930's, the effort to obtain universal acceptance of the American formula for achieving world peace was confined to setting a good example of international conduct. This did not, however, include participation in an international organization. But the United States did express a willingness to support programs that would lead to the international repudiation of power politics and its devices. It renounced war as an instrument of policy. It disarmed beyond treaty requirements. It pointed out that the real interests of the United States lay in being surrounded by a politically stable world and in conserving, not extending, its national territory. But although the

---

United States held itself aloof, its unilateral actions forced other states to adjust their own policies. Without conscious design on the part of the United States, these adjustments weakened the relative positions of some states and strengthened those of others. These relative changes ultimately had a direct bearing on the security and well-being of the United States. Generally speaking, a refusal to exert available strength in international politics can be as dangerous to the national interest in the long run as an aggressive urge to act.

United States sometimes followed courses of action identical with those undertaken co-operatively by other nations through the League of Nations, it did so in parallel and not in conjunction.

At the same time, the United States tended, in its international economic relations, to define objectives and pursue policies that were contradictory within themselves, and at times even ran counter to the political objectives noted above. Hardly had the international gold standard been restored after 1925 than it began to disintegrate. Governments sought to free their internal economic and social policies from the restrictions imposed by too close a regard for the stability of exchanges. Large movements of "hot money" and flights of capital confused the regular processes of international investment and made the development of exchange controls inevitable. The great depression of the 1930's was the final blow. It was accompanied by a progressive collapse of agricultural prices, by defaults on international loans, and by the rapid development of protective measures. During most of this period, while insisting on the repayment of war debts, the United States led the world in successive upward revisions of protective tariffs, culminating in the Hawley-Smoot Tariff Act of 1930. The adverse effects of this policy on world trade were disguised for a time by the vast sums of American capital sent abroad in the form of loans and investments of various types. The contradictions between the commercial and war-debt policies of the United States and the actions needed to deal with the economic maladjustments of the postwar world were not revealed, however, until the depression put an end to American foreign lending.

Under the impact of the world-wide depression, economic difficulties rapidly accumulated in all countries. Great Britain went off the gold standard in 1931 and was soon followed by many other countries including, in 1933, the United States. Many other governments similarly tried to protect their national economies by restrictive devices of various kinds. An unsuccessful attempt was made at the London Economic Conference in 1933 to check these tendencies. The conference failed largely because of a short-lived policy decision of the United States to emphasize purely domestic measures of recovery, and the failure led to the triumph of regionalism, discrimination, and bilateralism in a large part of the world. An alarming drift toward anarchy in international economic and political relations set in.

The major signs of this in the economic sphere were the disappearance of an earlier system of conducting world trade and the absence of any general willingness to devise an equivalent alternative. This was due in part to the policies, incompatible with the functioning of an international system, that many states developed to ensure their internal stability. These included the special protection of agricultural products, private cartel arrangements, and the growth of regional trading agreements. Still more destructive was the acceptance of new philosophies of trade that gave rise to doctrines of economic nationalism and self-sufficiency. In this connection, new administrative techniques were developed, particularly by Germany, that turned the processes of international exchange into a form of economic warfare.

In the middle 1930's, American political leaders, confronted by an accumulation of domestic and international dilemmas and feeling the inadequacy of United States foreign policy to resolve these dilemmas, began a slow and laborious task of giving a new direction to the actions of the United States in international relations.[5] This effort by no means put an end to the basic domestic controversy about the fundamental interpretation of the national interest, but it did lay the foundation for the new attitudes that emerged during the Second World War.

The basic objective that was being sought by this new direction was clearly stated by Secretary of State Hull in an address to the nation, made shortly before the Munich Pact of September 1938. He said that: "all nations have a primary interest in peace with justice, in economic well-being with stability, and in conditions of order under law"; that "each of these objectives is today seriously jeopardized"; that "appalling manifestations of disintegration seriously threaten the very foundation of our civilization"; and that "the re-establishment of order under law in relations among nations has become imperatively necessary." He then listed the aims of the United States, noting that they constituted a program for which international co-operation was urgently needed and in which the United States should join. These were the maintenance of the basic principles of international law and of respect for an observance of treaties; the reconstruction of world-economic activity; and

---

[5] The change in direction was first signalized at the Montevideo Conference in 1933, when an inter-American system of organized political and economic co-operation was officially stated as a United States goal. The purpose was most expertly implemented in the Reciprocal Trade Agreements Act of 1934.

the attainment of the freest possible intellectual interchange between peoples.[6]

The effort to change the direction of American action came too late, however, to check the progressive breakdown of the existing structure of international relations. In addition, the United States labored under handicaps that frustrated its attempts at leadership. The domestic impediments to effective action in this respect were hard to overcome. The Trade Agreements Act was not permanent legislation, and the executive procedures that were developed under it were attacked whenever the act came up for renewal. In addition, a policy of supporting domestic agricultural prices was concurrently developed. This policy, by leading to the use of import quotas, subsidies, and surplus disposal programs, made it difficult for the United States to provide international leadership in the liberalization of commercial and economic policies.

Generally speaking, the effort itself became part of the continuing and increasingly partisan debate about the proper basic course of American foreign policy. Moreover, the concept of continuous international co-operation was not firmly enough rooted in American feeling to meet the increasingly severe tests of the years immediately preceding the Second World War. All specific proposals were befogged by a public opinion that wavered between isolationism, pacifism, cries for continental defense, and recapitulation of traditional definitions of the national interest.

As the certainty of war became obvious, the fluctuations of American opinion found a momentary point of rest. The neutrality acts of 1935 and 1937, with their clauses forbidding loans, credits, and the sale of arms to belligerents, represented the common ground on which the larger part of American opinion was prepared to stand. But these acts were also indicative of a withdrawal of opinion from a realistic contact with events and were, in effect, a refusal to act as a major nation and a world power. In consequence, because power is not a thing that its possessors can as a matter of policy refuse to exercise, the neutrality acts did not achieve their anticipated result of permitting the United States to stand aside from the current of world affairs. On the contrary, they provided no objectives, led to no adequate formulations of policy, and, in the judgment of the officials who were obliged to conduct the foreign

[6] U.S. Department of State, *Press Releases*, Vol. 19 (Aug. 20, 1938), pp. 117-19, 122-23.

relations of the United States within their limiting clauses, negated rather than protected the national interest.

The United States as a World Power

When France fell in 1940, a threat to the security of the United States was widely felt, but public opinion continued to be confused by its own unresolved conflicts. Official thinking and action, however, were sharply focused by the dangerous turn of events. The attention of the United States Government was concentrated on arranging assistance to other nations and on organizing the means of self-defense. Although these preparations were to some extent inhibited by inconclusive public debate, war plans were developed that reflected a shift from a traditional emphasis on hemispheric defense to a concept of a global war fought far from American shores. The Japanese attack on Pearl Harbor ended the public debate and imposed an objective—to win the war. The nature of this objective required the full and organized use of American power as an instrument of international relations.

From this time until the end of 1946, two separate strands can be identified in United States foreign policy. One reflected the immediate demands of the war and the shifting conflicts of allies within a military alliance. The other reflected the intent to develop methods for harmonizing the interests and actions of major powers in a system of continuous international co-operation. This second strand was designed to take care of two anticipated periods in postwar relations: an initial period in which reconstruction and the peace settlements would be the immediate objectives of co-operative action; and a subsequent period in which stability and security and peace would be organized on a long-term basis. Both strands of policy led to a reconsideration of the national interest, to a redefinition of national objectives, and to the broad formulation of relevant courses of action.

Reinterpretation of the National Interest

So far as changes in the historical understanding of the national interests and objectives of the United States are concerned, certain basic documents stand out after 1940—the Lend-Lease Act, the

Atlantic Charter, the Declaration by United Nations, and the Moscow Declaration of 1943. These contained assertions of principle and implied basic objectives. They were drafted in terms of an intent to universalize at least some of the fundamental American aspirations, and in them certain general objectives were stated clearly enough to provide a taking-off point for formulating war aims and planning postwar policy.

In the Atlantic Charter and again in the Declaration by United Nations, the political and economic objectives that were set up conformed with the statements of Secretary Hull quoted above. Essentially they were derived from the concept of "peace with justice," "order under law," and "economic well-being with stability."

By early 1943 the United States was taking the initiative in trying to build on these foundations a structure of institutions for postwar co-operation in the economic and social fields. The initial proposals by the United States were formulated in terms of separate functional agencies. The first conference was on food and agriculture. Another was devoted to co-ordinating relief activities in the immediate postwar period. The thread that linked these proposals was the American judgment that it was not too soon to consider jointly the basic economic problems that would confront the world or to apply in a concrete form the principles of the Atlantic Charter.

At the end of 1943, in the Moscow Declaration, the major allies stated their intent to co-operate in establishing an international organization for the maintenance of peace and security. From the point of view of the United States, this declaration extended the Atlantic Charter and represented a specific American commitment to accept the responsibilities of continuous international co-operation. In brief, isolation and absolute freedom of action were rejected as a basis for foreign policy. The United States, in supporting the Moscow Declaration, acknowledged that international co-operation was closely related to furthering the national interest of the American people. By this action the United States also took a major step toward acknowledging that it was in the position of a major world power whose decisions would fundamentally affect the whole structure of international relations.

Great progress was apparently made in the efforts to harmonize the postwar plans and policies of the major powers. Negotiations and conferences proceeded from Dumbarton Oaks to the drafting of the United Nations Charter on the one hand, and through a series of meetings of foreign ministers on the other. The United States also conducted bilateral negotiations, especially with Great Britain. In March 1945, steps were taken to reorganize the inter-American system at the Mexico City Conference, and on June 26, 1945, the Charter of the United Nations was signed at San Francisco. These negotiations greatly broadened the area in which the United States committed itself to a multilateral consideration of international political, economic, and social problems.

One of the major lines of action was the formulation by the United States of a comprehensive foreign economic policy, designed to free world trade from the accumulated restrictions and controls of the preceding thirty years and to provide a foundation for carrying out the economic and social purposes of the Atlantic Charter. In effect, this policy proposed to continue the prewar program of bilateral trade agreements in a multilateral form. The first step, concerned with closely related financial policy objectives, was taken at the Bretton Woods Conference in July 1944, where the Articles of Agreement of the International Monetary Fund and of the International Bank for Reconstruction and Development were drafted. In July 1945, further specific steps were taken to complete the wartime preparations for the implementation of a postwar economic policy. The Export-Import Bank was made a permanent independent agency of the government; the Bretton Woods Agreements were approved, and the United States became a member of the Fund and the Bank; and the National Advisory Council on International Monetary and Financial Problems was set up to coordinate the lending and foreign exchange policies of the government.

It must be remembered, however, that these definitions of purpose and formulations of policy were developed while the war was still in progress. There was, therefore, an ever-present and often overriding alternative objective in operation—victory. This objective could and often did require its own special policy decisions. Generally speaking, the detailed postwar plans of the government tended to develop separately from the *ad hoc* decisions of a military operational nature, and their functions of mutually supporting the national interest became at times confused. Although the postwar positions represented guideposts, the decisions and actions taken in accordance with military necessity did not always conform to them.

Consequently, as the war came to an end, the United States found itself acting in the international system on two bases that were sometimes contradictory. On the one hand, the war and the politico-military decisions of the war had left a multiplicity of specific situations for which immediate solutions were required. These were the actual conditions in which any longer-range American objectives had to be pursued. On the other hand, there was a set of long-term American goals for the better and more harmonious operation of the system. These were the outgrowth of long-standing American principles and of an American interpretation of the twentieth century experience with international relations.

Influence of Principles

The influence of principles was strongly evident in the development of American goals for the postwar period. These principles were then and since have been the source of much that is significant in American action in international relations.

The American desire for a peaceful world order has, for example, entered into the development and conduct of United States foreign policy. This desire is firmly grounded in the free way of life and the democratic institutions that were part and parcel of the earliest concepts of the United States as a republic. This goal, Americans have steadily maintained, would be most quickly reached if all states accepted and acted on a moral code of conduct in their relations with each other. This code would recognize the rights of nations and would determine their duties and obligations to each other.

An objective analysis of these rights and obligations suggests that they are a projection on a world scale of the behavior that enables people to live and work together in a democratic community: mutual respect, self-restraint, fair and equal treatment, adherence to the pledged word, and peaceful co-operation.

The right of each nation to govern itself has been the most traditional of all principles in American thinking. It embodies two other principles of equal importance: (1) every nation has the inherent right of *both* individual and collective self-defense in the event of an attack; and (2) independence or self-government should be granted to all dependent peoples who are qualified to govern themselves. In accord with the latter principle, American sympathies have always been strongly in favor of colonial peoples aspiring to independence. The former principle has been consistently maintained from the outbreak of the American Revolution to the creation of the North Atlantic Treaty Organization.

The right of a nation to govern itself carries with it the concomitant right of its people freely to choose the form of government under which they wish to live. This principle is also very close to the heart of American historical experience, and American feeling has usually interpreted it as "a right to revolution" in order to establish free and republican forms of government. The contemporary expression of the principle merely asserts that the choice should be freely and peacefully made by democratic processes; the assumption being that no people if given a free choice willingly vote themselves into servitude.

It has equally been a firmly held principle that these rights are not unlimited. They have always been held to carry with them certain minimum obligations to other states, and currently to an international community of states. It is basic in the American view that these obligations are self-denying ordinances that a state imposes on itself.

These self-imposed restraints rest on the acceptance of another principle—the sovereign equality of all nations, large and small, in their relations with each other. The major obligations that follow have been embodied in the Charter of the United Nations. They are, first, that each nation must settle its disputes with other nations by peaceful means and in such a manner as not to endanger international peace and security, and justice: and second, that all nations must refrain from the threat or use of force against the territorial integrity or political independence of any other nation.

It is obvious, however, that certain specific courses of action must be renounced if these obligations are to be reflected in national action. All states will have to give up any further territorial ambitions and accept the condition that future territorial changes will follow only from the freely expressed wishes of the people concerned. All states will have to renounce war as an instrument of national policy. Finally, all states will have to agree not to intervene in the affairs of other states.

The existence of these principles in American thinking and the projection of them into the international field have gradually resulted in a comprehensive conviction about the conduct of international relations. It is that the establishment of the rights of all states and the acceptance of the obligations necessary to maintain these rights require the continuous practice of international co-operation. The development of such international co-operation is consequently asserted to be the ultimate objective of the foreign policy of the United States, and this objective is stated broadly enough to cover economic as well as political co-operation.

The concept of international co-operation was not always accepted by American opinion. Yet the Second World War convinced a majority of the American people that a peaceful world order was possible only on the basis of constant co-operation among peace-loving states, preferably through a world organization of all states. The United States therefore became one of the foremost proponents of an organized system of international relations.

It still remains, however, for time to prove whether this change is permanent. The understanding that the American people have of what constitutes the national interest is far from constant. The willingness of American opinion to accept objectives and support policies that require the United States to exercise its power internationally is still relatively untested.

CHAPTER II

Intentions: Stated Aims

THE foreign policy aims of the United States at the end of the Second World War developed naturally out of the American position as it had evolved up to that time.[1] They reflected the strength of that position, with the vast power and prestige that it represented. They showed clearly that the United States was prepared to exercise the prerogatives and to assume the responsibilities that it had acquired because of its status as a leading power in the society of nations.

The totality of the postwar goals gives a fairly complete picture of the kind of world that the United States Government—supported adequately by the expectations and opinions of the American people—believed desirable in 1945, both for the interests of the United States and for those of other states. In like manner, the policies that the United States was prepared to execute in order to achieve the kind of world envisaged by its aims had been rather explicitly set forth. The resultant composite picture of goals and policies—as do all such pictures of political action—blends expectation, assumption, and calculation; exhortation, negotiation, and intended action; in more technical terms—interests, objectives, policies, and commitments.

In this case, the picture is more complete than usual. Throughout the Second World War, the United States Government steadily kept an eye on desirable institutions for the postwar world. Questions to this effect were constantly asked, and were constantly and conscientiously examined. In addition, these questions were put to the major allies of the United States and were discussed in various forms with members of the wartime alliance. Basic agreement was

[1] Common usage personifies nations and speaks as if a state is an entity that feels, believes, acts, and reacts as such. It is recognized that this usage is open to criticism and that to say "the United States decided" can only mean that a group of individuals, momentarily exercising the power to choose and to act "has decided." Nevertheless, it is considered better to follow common usage on the ground that it would quickly become awkward to be analytically impeccable, but that it would not be very misleading to retain a familiar form of expression.

reached on at least the broad answers, and the United States then proceeded to try to negotiate the agreements and to work out the policies that might be expected to produce the desired structure.

The American view can be summarized under four broad categories that embrace, in some form or other, all of the problems and most of the contingencies of which American decision-makers were aware in 1945. These categories are:

1. The position with respect to the politico-legal system of state relations that would best meet the American interest.

2. The position with respect to the security of states within this system, and to the maintenance of the peace and security of the system as a whole.

3. The position with respect to the goals and methods of economic relations within this system.

4. The position with respect to the immediate settlement of the war, both as concerned peace with the enemy states and the general re-establishment of international stability.

It needs scarcely be pointed out that these categories were far from exclusive. On the contrary, the American view was that they were tightly interlocked and mutually supporting. In fact, the United States position was an uncommonly neat and logical construction. The most valid criticism that can be made of it is that its very neatness and completeness may have tended to obscure the difficulties of acting on it in the specific concrete situations in which it had to be applied.

In so far as the details under these four categories go, they have a single focus in the broad statement of expectation that was expressed in the Atlantic Charter in 1941 and repeated in the Declaration by United Nations on January 1, 1942. A world was desired in which there would be "no aggrandizement, territorial or otherwise"; in which there would be "no territorial changes that do not accord with the freely expressed wishes of the peoples concerned"; in which "the right of all peoples to choose the form of government under which they will live" would be respected; in which "the enjoyment by all States, great or small, victor or vanquished, of access, on equal terms, to the trade and to the raw materials of the world which are needed for their economic prosperity" would be furthered; in which "the fullest collaboration between all nations in the economic field with the object of securing, for all, improved labor standards, economic advancement and social security" would be brought about; and, finally, a world that would rest on a peace that would "afford to all nations the means of dwelling in safety within their own boundaries, and . . . assurance that all the men in all the lands may live out their lives in freedom from fear and want."[2]

The International System

In the view of the United States, the international system would continue, and properly so, to be made up of sovereign states. The order and the nature of their relations were therefore prime considerations. The position of the United States Government was that these relations should be conducted in such a way as to maintain international peace and security and to establish the conditions that would increasingly reduce fear and want as the motivations of national policies. However, proposals to this effect had to meet certain realistic criteria. They had to leave the sovereign equality of states unquestioned; hence they could only be developed on a basis of agreement and co-operative action. They had to take into account the fact that states, although independent, were of different orders of power and influence, and that these differences implied an acceptance to some degree of guidance, leadership, and even of decision by major states. The exercise of power and influence, however, would be within a frame of law and justice. These points were clearly stated by the Secretary of State in October 1945:

> The world system which we seek to create must be based on the principle of the sovereign equality of nations.
> That does not mean that all nations are equal in power and influence. . . . But it does mean equal respect for the individuality and sovereignty of nations, large and small. Nations, like individuals, should be equal before the law.[3]

The last criterion was that the immediate settlement of the war would have to be made by the major allies acting on behalf of the smaller states. On this basis, the United States Government envisaged, first, a making of the peace and a process of reconstruction that would be decided and carried out by the United States, Great Britain, the Soviet Union, France, and China. The decisions

---

[2] U.S. Department of State, *Toward the Peace, Documents,* Publication 2298 (1945), pp. 1-2.

[3] U.S. Department of State *Bulletin,* Vol. 13 (Nov. 4, 1945), p. 711.

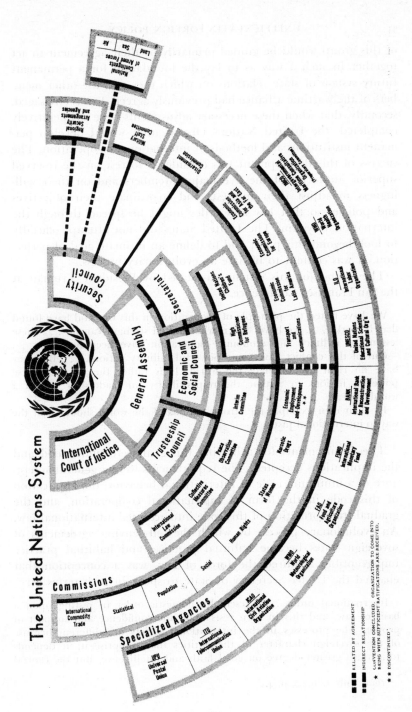

The United Nations System

of this group would be guided primarily by their agreement to act together in such a way as to lay the foundation for a permanent future system of state relations on which they and the other members of the wartime alliance had previously agreed. It was envisaged, secondly, that when these necessary adjustments were co-operatively completed, the United Nations Organization would develop permanent institutions and methods of international co-operation. The success of this development was considered to rest on the reserved superior authority of the five major Members and on their willingness to adjust their interests and co-ordinate their objectives and policies so that law and order might be spread through the international system. The United States did not attempt officially to look beyond this point and to define an ultimate goal of perfection. It was content to initiate an evolutionary process.

The essence of this system was stated by President Truman at the San Francisco Conference.

> We have tested the principle of cooperation in this war and have found that it works . . . we have shown what united strength can do . . . these lessons of military and economic cooperation have been learned. . . .
> Out of this conflict have come powerful military nations. . . . But they have no right to dominate the world. It is rather the duty of these powerful nations to assume the responsibility for leadership toward a world of peace. . . .
> By their own example the strong nations of the world should lead the way to international justice.[4]

The requirements for achieving this goal were understood and the implications accepted. The requirements were a general acceptance of a minimum code of international behavior, the application of this code in the form of international co-operation, and the gradual transformation of this code into accepted international law. An evolutionary process by which the self-denying agreements of sovereign states became habitual practice, and habitual practice imperceptibly acquired the force of law, was a conception that enabled the Under Secretary of State to speak in such terms as:

> International order . . . resembles domestic order in resting upon a basis of law, and this in turn rests upon the confidence and support of people. The processes in the international society are different because of the sovereign character of the entities that comprise it; it depends to a much greater degree on good faith and intelligence. But the central

4 *Ibid.* (July 1, 1945), p. 4.

role of the judiciary [referring to the International Court of Justice] is in both cases the same—it is to make the law a living and vital factor.[5]

The United States had taken the lead in the creation of formal and informal machinery for the development and operation of this system. Three basic channels were set up, and there seems to have been every intention on the part of the United States Government to try to get diplomatic action to flow through these channels. One was meetings of the heads of government of the major powers. These were designed to be informal, intermittent, and of immediate and short-term use. Another was a Council of Foreign Ministers of the major powers. This was designed to be formal and primarily for use in the postwar settlement. The third was the United Nations Organization, designed to be both formal and permanent.

The considerations underlying these devices corresponded with those underlying the picture of the international system of state relations that the United States had drawn. Some problems arising from the war were of such character and magnitude as to be beyond the reach of normal diplomacy. They were not, however, held to be beyond the reach of the heads of the major states. If these authorities met in confidence, in secrecy, and in the absence of small states, it was held that they could adjust interests, define common objectives, and enforce agreed decisions. This type of personal and informal negotiation, by negotiators who could enter into agreements on the broad ranges and basic ends of policy, was considered particularly important in developing the immediate peace settlements and in giving fundamental impetus to the designed system of state relations.

The Council of Foreign Ministers was thought of as operating at a more formal and technical level, where the job would be done of translating into specific accords the broad agreements of the heads of state on principles and on major objectives. It was at this level that the peace treaties were to be prepared, territorial adjustments decided, and other matters pertaining to the postwar settlement mutually examined. Although this was initially a device to achieve major power agreement in major power privacy, it could not be entirely secluded from the claims of smaller states or from the influence of the more inclusive device of the United Nations Organization. If agreement was important for the major powers, it was more important for the United Nations Organization, in which

[5] *Ibid.*, Vol. 15 (July 28, 1946), p. 154.

the major powers had demanded and had been granted privileged positions.

In principle, it was assumed that when the postwar settlement was completed, the need for the Council of Foreign Ministers would no longer exist. The technical function of adjusting relations would then be transferred to and carried on by the United Nations Organization. This logical conclusion was not, however, pressed unreservedly. As the Secretary of State stated in February 1946:

In our relations with the other great powers there are many problems which concern two or three of us more than the others of us. I see no objection to conferences between the big three or the big four or the big five.

Even conferences between ourselves and the Soviet Union alone, conferences between ourselves and Great Britain alone or conferences between ourselves and France or China alone, can all help to further general accord among the great powers and peace with the smaller powers.

But in such conferences, so far as the United States is concerned, we will gang up against no state. We will do nothing to break the world into exclusive blocs or spheres of influence.[6]

The effective use of the third basic channel—the United Nations—was, nevertheless, the logical goal of the United States position; for, in the American view, the only alternative to a drift toward another war was to plan and to develop, in co-operation with other states, a politico-legal system of state relations that would maintain international peace and security. The process of negotiating the scope and structure of the United Nations Organization had, moreover, clarified some points in the American interpretation of the role of this institution. Starting from the precept that the Organization was a voluntary association of states on the basis of sovereign equality, the United States, as well as other states, rejected any concept of intervention in matters "essentially within the domestic jurisdiction of any state." Also joined by others, it insisted not only on the specific preservation of the inherent right of self-defense, but on its extension to mean that a collective right of self-defense was inherent in regional groupings of states.[7]

In addition, and jointly with the other major powers, the United

---

[6] *Ibid.*, Vol. 14 (Mar. 10, 1946), pp. 357-58.

[7] This extension was primarily a product of the relations of the United States and the American republics as these were in process of being formalized in the Organization of American States and negotiated in security terms in the subsequent Rio Treaty. See above, p. 26.

States firmly adhered to the concept of a privileged position, including the right of veto. However, in this matter, the United States was more concerned with obtaining the approval of other nations for this position than was the Soviet Union, and more concerned to harmonize the privilege with a concept of justice and abstract right. But the view that major power unity was basic to the development of the desired system of state relations stood firm.

The position that has been described naturally represented a long-term goal. It required supporting action. In the opinion of the United States, the essential fields of action were security and well-being. The argument ran thus: if human societies were relieved of the fear of external aggression and were assured that their material needs would be increasingly met, tensions between states would be reduced and conditions favorable to the maintenance of international peace and security would be created. Thus the United States position with respect to a politico-legal system of state relations required the development of supporting positions with respect to security and economic relations.

The Security of States

The United States Government developed a position on international security that was a blend of several elements: the maintenance of its security by the unilateral use of its own resources; the maintenance of the security of the Western Hemisphere by a collective agreement of the states of the region; the elimination of any renewed threat to the security of the members of the wartime alliance by the disarmament and control of the defeated aggressor states—this action to be taken conjointly by the major allies; the development of a permanent system of collective security operated by all states within the framework of the United Nations Organization; and finally, the support of the whole by a constant attention to the maintenance of great power unity.

It was made clear that this position in its totality involved related courses of action, some of which could be given lower priority as others were successfully developed. As great power unity worked out in practice, collective security under the United Nations could be increasingly relied upon. And as collective security under the United Nations effectively evolved, the reliance of a state on its own resources could be relaxed. At the same time, when the disarmament of enemy states was completed, the co-operative regulation of armaments by Members of the United Nations Organization could proceed. In short, this was a position that permitted the United States to take into account a wide range of contingencies, while preparing to act in co-operation with other states to bring about the most desirable contingency, namely, an international system in which peace and security were maintained by political agreement within an evolving legal order.

The range of contingencies involved was also made clear. In addition to the usual run that is carried in mind by responsible policy-making officials—such as absolute bad faith, unanticipated weaknesses, or sudden shifts in political authority in other states— two were made explicit. One of these was the willingness of all states to execute the enforcement power that had been written into the United Nations Charter. The other was the willingness of the major states to harmonize their interests.

No single official statement puts the position exactly as it has been described, but its elements can be readily pieced together. President Truman, in January 1946, said: "One proposition is that lasting peace requires genuine understanding and active cooperation among the most powerful nations."[8] In April, he added:

> The United States today is a strong nation . . . with such strength, we have to assume leadership and accept responsibility. It would be a tragic breach of national duty and international faith if, consciously or carelessly, we permitted ourselves ever to be unprepared to fulfill that responsibility. . . . We must remain strong, not because we plan or want to impose our views upon the world by force, or do battle with any nation. We must remain strong in order to retain our leadership, and with all our resources, exercise that leadership on behalf of a world of peace and harmony among all nations and all peoples.[9]

The Secretary of State, in January 1946, said:

> The United Nations is not a mere pact among its members—it is an institution or a series of institutions capable of life and growth. . . . It is argued that the great states may abuse the rights given them under the Charter. There are risks in any human undertaking. . . . Great states as well as small states must come to view their power as a sacred trust to be exercised not for selfish purposes but for the good of all peoples.[10]

[8] U.S. Department of State *Bulletin*, Vol. 14 (Feb. 3, 1946), p. 138.
[9] *Ibid.* (Apr. 14, 1946), pp. 622-23.
[10] *Ibid.* (Jan. 27, 1946), p. 88.

And, in February, he stated:

We have covenanted not to use force except in defense of law as embodied in the purposes and principles of the Charter. . . . But as a great power . . . we have a responsibility to use our influence to see that other powers live up to their covenant. . . . Unless the great powers are prepared to act in defense of law, the United Nations cannot prevent war. . . . The great powers are given special responsibilities because they have the strength to maintain the peace, if they have the will to maintain the peace. Their strength in relation to one another is such that no one of them can safely break the peace if the others stand united in defense of the Charter.

The present power relationships of the great states preclude the domination of the world by any one of them. These power relationships cannot be substantially altered by the unilateral action of any one great state without profoundly disturbing the whole structure of the United Nations. . . .

We must face the fact that to preserve the United Nations we cannot be indifferent . . . to serious controversies between any of the great powers, because such controversies could affect the whole power relationship between all of the great powers.[11]

Finally, the American view of international security included concern for the problem of disarmament. The formulation of this problem was less specific than was the case with other elements of the security goal. The term meant different things to different people; meanings varied even in official statements. There was the disarmament of defeated enemy states, which meant the destruction of their present and future war-making capacity. There was disarmament in the sense of an agreed reduction by sovereign states of the resources that they allocated to the production of military equipment and to the maintenance of organized armed forces. There was disarmament in the sense of regulation; that is, a determination by agreement of the limits above which national armaments would not rise and the limits below which armaments would not be allowed to fall. The latter limit was held to be important if states were to be prepared to fulfill their obligations under the United Nations Charter. Cutting across all meanings was control, through an international organization, of armaments and their production. This question was, as it turned out, the point of greatest difficulty, in view of the development of unconventional weapons—particularly the nuclear ones—and the fact that their production was, at the end of the war, the practical monopoly of a single state, the United States.

[11] *Ibid.* (Mar. 10, 1946), pp. 356-57.

The most that can be recorded here is that these were questions that could be and were discussed, but that could not be decided because they inevitably involved still unsettled political relations. Nevertheless, the reduction and regulation of armaments was regarded as an important long-term goal by the United States and remained an important element in the official picture of the international system.

The Economic Relations of States

The relationship between the economic behavior of states and international peace and security was one that had been officially defined by the United States Government in the years before the Second World War. Secretary of State Hull had no doubts on this subject.

To me, unhampered trade dovetailed with peace; high tariffs, trade barriers, and unfair economic competition with war . . . if we could get a freer flow of trade . . . so that one country would not be deadly jealous of another and the living standards of all countries might rise, thereby eliminating the economic dissatisfaction that breeds war, we might have a reasonable chance for lasting peace.[12]

Guided by various forms of this judgment, the United States, on all possible occasions throughout the war, sought to prepare the ground for a pattern of international economic relations that would by its very nature reduce friction and eliminate tension between sovereign states and would thus make it possible for states peacefully to adjust differences that could not be eliminated. By the end of the war, the United States position in this respect was well developed.[13]

President Truman, speaking at the San Francisco Conference in

[12] *The Memoirs of Cordell Hull,* Vol. 1 (1948), p. 81.

[13] The key objectives, though expressed in a variety of ways for different situations, can be listed as follows: The reconstruction of devastated countries; the development of underdeveloped countries; the reduction of trade and financial restrictions; the maintenance of an international climate for private investment; and the promotion of international economic stability by co-ordinated national action. Another version of the objectives was adopted at the inter-American conference at Mexico City in February 1945 as the guiding principles for an Economic Charter. See U.S. Department of State, *Report of the Delegation of the United States of America to the Inter-American Conference on Problems of War and Peace, Mexico City, Mexico, February 21-March 8, 1945,* Publication 2497 (1946), pp. 120-24.

June 1945, summed up the position of the United States in terms that had already been clearly established in official thinking.

A just and lasting peace cannot be attained by diplomatic agreements alone, or by military cooperation alone. Experience has shown how deeply the seeds of war are planted by economic rivalry and by social injustice. The Charter . . . has set up machinery of international cooperation . . . to help correct economic and social causes for conflict.

Artificial and uneconomic trade barriers should be removed—to the end that the standard of living of as many people as possible throughout the world may be raised. . . . The large and powerful nations of the world must assume leadership in this economic field as in all others.[14]

In the economic field, the United States, in addition to having clearly stated objectives and carefully designed policies, was deeply committed to specific actions. In the Bretton Woods Agreements, it was committed to membership in the International Monetary Fund and in the International Bank for Reconstruction and Development—institutions designed to promote exchange stability, to facilitate reconstruction, and to prepare the way for the flow of private investment. It was a committed participant in the Food and Agriculture Organization and in the International Labour Organisation. It was pressing proposals for the establishment of an International Trade Organization, and was prepared to negotiate a general agreement on commercial practices and to enter into multilateral agreements for the reduction of tariffs. It was committed under the United Nations Charter to co-operating with other states in initiating and implementing the desired economic and social policies. Finally, it was a heavily committed participant, through the United Nations Relief and Rehabilitation Administration, and various bilateral agreements and unilateral announcements, in providing for war-devastated areas and peoples. Not only were the goals well defined; the policies were also developed and the commitments were entered into.

On many occasions, both purposes and methods were reaffirmed officially by the highest authorities.

Our objective is to enable the peace-loving nations of the world to become self-supporting in a world of expanding freedom and rising standards of living.

The cornerstone for international economic cooperation is the Bretton Woods proposal . . . concrete evidence that the economic objectives of the United States agree with those of the United Nations. . . . What we

[14] U.S. Department of State *Bulletin*, Vol. 13 (July 1, 1945), p. 5.

need and what they need correspond . . . more goods produced, more jobs, more trade, and a higher standard of living for us all. . . .

The main problem will be . . . the means of payment. . . . Unless a means of financing is found . . . countries will be unable to secure their economies and, in desperation, will be forced to carry forward and intensify existing systems of discriminatory trade practices, restrictive exchange controls, competitive depreciations of currencies, and other forms of economic warfare. That would destroy all our good hopes. We must move promptly to prevent its happening, and we must move on several fronts. . . .

We propose to do this not by setting up a super-government but by international negotiation and agreement, directed to the improvement of the monetary institutions of the world and of the laws that govern trade. . . .

The foreign economic policy of the United States is designed to promote our own prosperity, and at the same time to aid in the restoration and expansion of world markets and to contribute thereby to world peace and world security. . . .

The view of this Government is that, in the longer run, our economic prosperity and the prosperity of the whole world are best served by the elimination of artificial barriers to international trade.[15]

The Immediate Postwar Settlement

The position of the United States Government regarding the broad ends to be sought in the postwar settlement was relatively clear. The policies by which these ends were to be achieved, however, were much more subject to modification as they came up against the actual conditions that time and study revealed. Only the broad goals are considered here. The development of policies and the effects of these developments on the goals themselves are treated later in this volume.

Generally speaking, the American conception was that a speedy and effective settlement of the problems left by the war was the essential first step in the achievement of its more comprehensive and long-term purposes. The situation had three facets: settlements with enemy states; the reconstruction of liberated states; the laying of the groundwork of an international order. The first was held to be the sole responsibility of the major victorious states, to be jointly carried out for agreed ends and by agreed methods. The second was also primarily the work of the major states, on the

[15] Presidential Messages in U.S. Department of State *Bulletin,* Vol. 13 (Sept. 9, 1945), pp. 359-60; Vol. 12 (Feb. 12, 1945), pp. 220-22; Vol. 14 (Feb. 3, 1946), pp. 139-40.

grounds that they alone possessed the means and had the broad interest. But their agreed efforts required the willing support of the smaller states if international justice were to be satisfied. The third was an international responsibility, to be carried out with the maximum co-operation of all members of the wartime alliance, even though the means of executing the common purpose would still have to be furnished by the major states.

Action on these problems would be guided by the intention to establish conditions under which political democracy and economic freedom could flourish. This intention, in the American view, had been stated, negotiated, and written into a long line of international agreements, ending with the general broad statement of purposes and principles in Chapter I, Article 1, of the Charter of the United Nations.[16] Whatever difficulties might arise in detail, the guide-line for action was laid down.

The main enemy states, Germany and Japan, were to be deprived of the means of again menacing the security of other states or the peace of the world. Initially, this meant complete disarmament and demilitarization, the elimination or control of the means of production for military use, and the removal and punishment of the authorities who had deceived and misled the German and Japanese peoples into embarking on world conquest. It meant also that the political life of these states should be constructed on a democratic basis, and that they should be prepared for eventual peaceful co-operation in international life. These tasks were to be carried out by the major states acting jointly on behalf of the international community.

[16] Article 1 is as follows:

The Purposes of the United Nations are:

1. To maintain international peace and security, and to that end: to take effective collective measures for the prevention and removal of threats to the peace, and for the suppression of acts of aggression or other breaches of the peace, and to bring about by peaceful means, and in conformity with the principles of justice and international law, adjustment or settlement of international disputes or situations which might lead to a breach of the peace;

2. To develop friendly relations among nations based on respect for the principle of equal rights and self-determination of peoples, and to take other appropriate measures to strengthen universal peace;

3. To achieve international cooperation in solving international problems of an economic, social, cultural, or humanitarian character, and in promoting and encouraging respect for human rights and for fundamental freedoms for all without distinction as to race, sex, language, or religion; and

4. To be a center for harmonizing the actions of nations in the attainment of these common ends.

The minor enemy states, Austria, Bulgaria, Finland, Hungary, Italy, and Rumania, were in effect to be regarded as liberated areas. Although controls would be necessary, the aim was to re-establish these areas as quickly as possible as free and independent states with democratic governments. They were to reappear in the international sphere as co-operative sovereign entities. This implied the early preparation of peace treaties under the guidance of the major states.

With respect to the liberated allied states, the problem was considered to be mainly one of political stabilization and economic and social rehabilitation. Many channels of action existed for this purpose, including the Council of Foreign Ministers of the major states. In addition, there was the guidance of the Yalta Declaration on Liberated Europe, which had been prepared by the United States and agreed by Great Britain and the Soviet Union. The American view, recorded in this declaration, was that the major states jointly declared "their mutual agreement to concert during the temporary period of instability in liberated Europe the policies of their three governments in assisting the peoples liberated from the domination of Nazi Germany and the peoples of the former Axis satellite states of Europe to solve by democratic means their primary political and economic problems."[17]

An immediate postwar settlement on the Far East was not envisaged in quite the same way. The concept of unified major power action could not be so simply formulated for this region and was not attempted except in the most general terms. In the opinion of the United States, the future of disorganized colonial areas prejudiced the positions of Great Britain and France. Internal conflict in China prejudiced the ability of the Chinese National Government to act as a major state. The attitude of the Soviet Union was undefined except by broad international obligations. And the United States was undeniably in a position to exert considerable influence if it chose.

Certain purposes, however, were stated.

In Korea we are even now working with our Soviet Allies and with Korean leaders to create a provincial democratic government. Our aim is to speed the day when Korea will again take her place as an independent and democratic nation.

In China we are supporting a free and democratic government. . . .

[17] U.S. Department of State *Bulletin,* Vol. 12 (Feb. 8, 1945), p. 215.

We hope for the peaceful settlement of the differences which have arisen between colonial peoples and colonial sovereigns in all areas.

And, more generally,

The roots of democracy . . . will not draw much nourishment . . . from a soil of poverty and economic distress. It is a part of our strategy of peace, therefore, to assist in the rehabilitation and development of the Far Eastern countries.

A caveat was, however, entered:

We recognize that the Soviet Union, the British Commonwealth, and other nations have important interests in the Far East. In return we expect recognition by them that we also have an interest in maintaining peace and security in that area. We expect understanding on their part that our objectives are dedicated to the pursuit of peace; and we shall expect them to pursue the same objectives.[18]

Even so brief a survey as the one just given indicates the logical coherence of the goals of foreign policy that the United States presented to the world as indicative of the direction in which it proposed that the international system should develop. In support of this comprehensive formulation, it maintained that these goals could be shared by all peace-loving states and that it was in their interests to co-operate in achieving them. Finally, it should once more be emphasized that these goals represented an unusual degree of consensus, not only at the governmental level in the United States, but in American public opinion. There were admittedly sectors in government and in public opinion that rejected them as infringements on the national freedom of action or as wholly un-realistic. There were divergent interpretations of the policies needed to reach the goals. But essentially there was a formulated American position with respect to the kind of international system desired and an integrated series of policies designed to lead to this end. And the whole had been put before other states with considerable consistency.

It was summarized by President Truman in October 1945 as follows:

1. We seek no territorial expansion or selfish advantage. . . .

2. We believe in the eventual return of sovereign rights and self-government to all peoples who have been deprived of them by force.

3. We shall approve no territorial changes . . . unless they accord with the freely expressed wishes of the peoples concerned.

[18] *Ibid.*, Vol. 14 (Apr. 14, 1946), p. 623.

4. We believe that all peoples who are prepared for self-government should be permitted to choose their own form of government. . . .

5. By the combined and cooperative action of our war Allies, we shall help the defeated enemy states establish peaceful, democratic governments of their own free choice. . . .

* * *

8. We believe that all states which are accepted in the society of nations should have access on equal terms to the trade and raw materials of the world.

9. We believe that the sovereign states of the Western Hemisphere, without interference . . . must work together . . . in the solution of their common problems.

10. We believe that full economic collaboration between all nations . . . is essential to the improvement of living conditions all over the world, and to the establishment of freedom from fear and freedom from want. . . .

* * *

12. We are convinced that the preservation of peace . . . requires a United Nations Organization composed of all the peace-loving nations of the world who are willing jointly to use force if necessary to insure peace.[19]

[19] *Ibid.,* Vol. 13 (Oct. 28, 1945), pp. 654-55.

CHAPTER III

Capabilities: Political, Economic, Military

A SKETCH of the goals of American policy in 1945 is not complete until note is taken of the forms, the availability, and the distribution of the resources of power and influence that the United States had at its disposal for the achievement of these goals. National goals are no more than expectations and aspirations until they are acted upon and their validity is subjected to realistic testing in international situations. At this point, the means of execution —capabilities—and the goals and actions of other participants become significant.

A frequently repeated phrase in discussions of foreign policy proposals is that "ends and means" must be balanced if a nation is to conduct its foreign relations effectively. This generalization has acquired many of the qualities of a truism; yet states, in pursuing their objectives, have sometimes proceeded on a basis of calculated risk and have been successful in spite of astonishing disparities between their intentions and their apparent capabilities, and other states have failed even though "ends and means" were in carefully considered balance.

The notion of "ends and means" as ordinarily expressed represents far too mechanical a calculus for judging objectives. It is only in the actual execution of policies in specific situations that a calculus becomes relevant; for in these circumstances, decisions have to be made about the allocation of limited resources in measurable quantities. Here, success or failure can often be traced back to the decisions and to the calculations on which action was based. It is consequently useful to examine the capabilities of the United States in 1945 and 1946 to carry out its specifically stated intentions.

In the course of the Second World War, the potential political, economic, and military strength of the United States was developed to such a degree that the total power it deployed in the international field was far beyond that of any other single state. The United States was a major power in the international system, and there was every sign that the majority of the American people supported the intention of their government to continue to be active

47

in this role. The goals of United States policy were formulated on this tested understanding. These goals, which were comprehensive in scope and world-wide in their applications, required means. Because there was no question of insufficient resources, capability implied two sets of concurrent actions: first, the allocation of resources for the purposes that were agreed, and second, the maintenance of the necessary resources in readily usable forms.

In speaking of national power as applied to the conduct of foreign relations, a common analytical device is to distinguish political, economic, and military elements, and then to say that these elements must be in working balance because the inadequacy of any one affects the range of choices open to the policy maker and conditions the effectiveness with which a decision can be carried out. If to this is added a statement about the influence of public feeling and the distribution of domestic political power in determining what the balance between these elements will be at any given time, this breakdown is adequate for the purposes of this analysis.

Ready Military Means

By the end of the Second World War, the mobilized military power of the United States was second to none. But as victory in Europe became certain, American attention, both public and official, turned to the process of reducing this highly organized force. In general, the original government plans sought a happy medium between domestic political and social demands for a return to normal peacetime patterns and the requirements of a still unfinished war against Japan, the acknowledged need for occupation forces, and the desirability of disposing of vast stocks of equipment and stores in an orderly way. An approved demobilization plan was accepted initially both by the public and by the armed services. But what was officially proposed was, in the event, disposed of by other influences. With the early and unexpected surrender of Japan, plans for a controlled demobilization, adjusted to the estimated requirements of the international situation and of national politics, became a confused, rapid, and improvised dismantling of military power.

The essential influence was a public demand for the immediate return of the armed forces from overseas. Pressure on Congress was unrelenting. Overseas contingents demonstrated against delay. Congressional comments were vitriolic, and congressional action took the effective form of curtailing appropriations. In short, United States policy makers and responsible administrative officials were confronted by a dilemma: the American people wished their government to act affirmatively as a leading power and a major force in the world, but they would not at the moment recognize the responsibilities and accept the sacrifices that this choice implied in so far as these had to be spelled out in terms of a military establishment.

In response to the clearly demonstrated popular will, the military force in being of the United States was severely reduced. Between August 1945 and July 1946, the Army strength of 8 millions was cut back to 2 millions. What remained was organized in 15 divisions (11 infantry, 2 air-borne, 1 armored, and 1 cavalry) and in a constabulary force of divisional strength. Because the bulk of military personnel consisted of relatively untrained replacements, the combat efficiency of these units was less than 50 per cent of the wartime standard. This small and inexperienced army was scattered widely in Europe and the Far East: in Germany, Austria, and Italy; in Japan, Korea, and the Pacific Islands. The effectiveness of the Air Force was similarly reduced. Of 218 combat air groups in being at the end of 1945, only two effective groups remained in early 1947. Personnel were inexperienced and inefficient.[1]

The position of the Navy was somewhat different. It was under contradictory congressional pressures to release personnel, but to keep ships in active service for bringing men home from overseas. Yet by March 1946, naval man power was cut from 3.4 millions to 1.6 million; and, by August of the same year, the active fleet was reduced from more than 1,200 to 300 combat ships, while naval aircraft were cut from 37,000 to about 8,000. The Navy was somewhat more successful than the other services in maintaining organized forces overseas, although here, too, official warnings of a dangerous situation were made for the record.[2]

[1] The Chief of Staff United States Air Force reported to the Secretary of the Air Force, June 30, 1948: "One prefers not to speculate on what might have happened only one year after V-J Day, . . . if our Air Force had been called upon to resist a new aggression or to suppress a recurrence of combat activity from an uncontrolled element in one of the occupied countries." Quoted, John C. Sparrow, *History of Personnel Demobilization in the United States Army* (1951), p. 370.

[2] The Chief of Naval Operations in testimony before a House Subcommittee on Appropriations, March 13, 1946, stated: "I would do less than my duty if I did not point out to your committee that . . . world conditions are such as to necessitate keeping the Navy and the Marine Corps in the highest state of com-

These reductions, the effects of which were multiplied by the speed with which they were carried out and by the pressure of the public demand under which they took place, resulted in a military establishment that, by any objective standard, was inefficient and disorganized. Furthermore, in the judgment of those responsible for its maintenance and operation, it was not in a condition of readiness to support the purposes and commitments of United States foreign policy. Whether this inadequacy was, at the time, a prime factor in significantly limiting national action in the international field must be left an open question. The techniques do not exist for measuring quantitatively the adequacy of any one of the elements of national power in relation to national purposes. The most that can be said is that if United States policies had been obliged to face the test of armed opposition during this period, the test could not have been unequivocally met.

It is a fact, however, that some official circles began to develop serious concerns about the possible consequences of the rapid dismantling of American armed strength. Secretary Forrestal envisaged a period during which the military services would not have enough trained men to operate efficiently. He held the view that this implied a situation of such gravity, when the facts of international life were taken into account, that it was the duty of the President to acquaint the American people with the full significance of what was happening.[3] But this was a judgment involving a political unknown. It could be and was disputed by other official circles. No steps were taken to modify public feeling, and the Congress, reflecting public attitudes, retrenched further on military appropriations and finally, in March 1947, allowed the Selective Service Act to lapse.

Economic Power and Influence

In providing for its own war effort and in contributing to the war effort of its allies, the United States developed an enormous productive capacity and an elaborate and effective pattern of international economic activity. The economic power that was thus

---

bat efficiency; and, furthermore, that our rapid demobilization has seriously impaired the readiness of the fleets to accomplish tasks which may confront them." *Navy Department Appropriation Bill for 1947*, Hearings before the House Committee on Appropriations, 79 Cong. 2 sess., p. 32.

[3] Walter Millis (ed.), *The Forrestal Diaries* (1951), p. 102.

organized and widely deployed through lend-lease operations, loans, grants, and the provision of civilian supplies was in complete working order and available for further ready use at the end of the war. The maintenance and employment of this power in relation to national objectives and policies were, however, dependent on sustained popular support and in some degree on a system of government-operated controls.

At the end of the war, American opinion reacted to the existence of these controls in much the same spirit as it reacted to the restrictions on individual choice implicit in military service. The public demanded release from restraints and a speedy re-establishment of customary economic practices. In many respects, the government and public feeling were at one. The reconversion of the national economy from wartime to peacetime purposes had been studied, and many essential steps had been taken by 1945, particularly with respect to scaling down the allocation of resources for military consumption.

The process of reconversion, although it, too, was subjected to public pressure for speed, did not have a markedly disintegrating effect on the economic power of the United States. The productive capacity of the economy was intact, and its potential continued to be realized. By November 1945, industrial production was within 20 per cent of the wartime peak. By the end of 1946, President Truman reported to the Congress that the national income was higher than in any previous peacetime year, that the production of goods and services was 50 per cent greater than in any year prior to the start of the war, that the country had virtually full employment, and that the standard of living was higher than it had ever been in the history of the United States. Despite these obvious assets, however, the question remained open of the use to be made of the economic power that was plainly available. On the one hand, there were the claims of the American economy, particularly of domestic civilian consumption. On the other, there were foreign policy ends to be served, and these also constituted claims.[4]

---

[4] The following courses of action in the foreign field can be listed as claimants: pledges to Latin American countries in connection with contracts for strategic materials; agreements made in connection with the settlement of lend-lease accounts; participation in the operation of the Export-Import Bank, the International Bank for Reconstruction and Development, and the United Nations Relief and Rehabilitation Administration (UNRRA); the program of Government and Relief in Occupied Areas (GARIOA); financial grants to specific countries, including the British Loan Agreement, which is considered below, pp. 87-88.

This range of activities called for the specific use of economic power in the form of allocation of resources, either from current output or in the form of claims on the future. It was in this connection that confusion developed among the Executive, the Congress, and public opinion. The argument was basically a political one, for there was no short-term question of drawing on severely limited means. In general, one set of political demands for retrenchment in government spending, for a balanced national budget, for reducing the national debt, for lowering taxes, and for the maximum re-establishment of a free economy, clashed with the requirement to appropriate funds and to allocate production to carry out the commitments, obligations, and purposes of the United States in its foreign relations. The issue, however, was not brought to a final choice, for the productive capacity at the disposal of the United States was sufficient to cover most of the demands without serious strain.

Nevertheless, the fact that the argument took place made the use of economic power halting, intermittent, and improvised. Although the capability existed, maximum values in terms of national objectives could not then be realized, as they were to be more adequately realized later under the Marshall Plan and under subsequent assistance programs. In this sense, the economic power of the United States, though not reduced in its totality, was weakened by dispersed application.

On the one hand, lend-lease operations were abruptly stopped after V-J Day. On the other hand, assistance programs were set up for the relief and rehabilitation of allied and occupied countries. Again, the Congress was slow in appropriating funds for the United States contribution to the United Nations Relief and Rehabilitation Administration and was quick to terminate American participation in this organization; but at the same time, funds were made available for a wide range of more limited and specific actions in the foreign field. In brief, and regardless of the principles and values variously asserted, the United States, between mid-1945 and early 1948, engaged its economic power in programs of assistance in Europe and Asia to the extent of $14.5 billion. There was obviously no question here of a refusal to employ economic power in the conduct of foreign relations. The only question was to what extent the use was co-ordinated and effective.

Political Position

In addition to the military and economic power that the United States had in mobilized form at the end of the war, the United States had also taken a very active part in the establishment of an array of politicial organizations and arrangements. All of these provided channels through which the influence of military and economic power could be exerted in the form of political power. In 1945, after a long period of study, planning, and negotiation that ran from the drafting of the Atlantic Charter to the San Francisco Conference, the United States became a leading member of the United Nations Organization. This was the keystone of a large structure of international agreements, activities, organizations, and groupings to which the United States had committed itself for the purpose of forwarding its objectives and of working toward the kind of international system believed most likely to ensure the peace and security that were essential to the realization of those objectives.

Public opinion, the Congress, and the Executive were broadly at one in approving this pattern of political action. In principle, there was no drawing back from this position at the end of the war, no demand that the United States should disengage itself from these devices for collective action and regain its freedom to act unilaterally. In detail, however, there was a partial dismantling of the elaborate structure of wartime co-operation, although this did not take place in response to any consistent public demand. It was instead a by-product of changes in the character and use of military and economic power and a consequence of a desire not to impede the operation of the key organization—the United Nations.

The various Anglo-American agencies, starting with the Combined Chiefs of Staff and running through the combined boards, were either disbanded, completely reorganized, or allowed to fall into disuse on the grounds that they had either served their purposes or would interfere with the growth of a more general and multinational pattern of agreement and co-operation. Alternatively, however, the United States implemented its stated adherence to the principle of co-operation. The Congress approved the Bretton Woods Agreements and provided the funds for American participation in the agencies they had set up. The Executive continued work begun during the war on an International Trade Organization. No objections were made to extremely detailed joint planning and action in the occupation and control of defeated enemy states. There was complete agreement that the United States should exert its full influence in the Council of Foreign Ministers, especially because this was held to be related to the necessary co-operation of the major powers in the Security Council of the United Nations.

But in another direction, there was a tendency to reassert unilateral action in other areas. The government exercised its right to terminate the lend-lease agreements, giving no consideration to the fact that this action broke up a useful pattern of international co-operation and closed a possibly valuable channel of political action. In much the same spirit, the Congress later placed restrictions on United States participation in co-operative relief and rehabilitation activities, preferring to recover political freedom of action in these matters. In spite of this, however, the United States had left at its disposal an extraordinary number of channels, multilateral, bilateral, and unilateral, through which political influence could be exerted.

In addition to the extent to which military and economic power could be expressed as political influence through these channels, the United States possessed a considerable degree of political power separate from these more tangible and measurable forms of strength. This derived from the obvious good intentions of United States policy as a whole; from the relative consistency with which American actions reflected humanitarian motivations and an advocacy of personal liberty and political freedom, and a strong conviction about the benefits and the universal applicability of the democratic way of life; and from the expectations generated in all parts of the world by the stated goals of United States foreign policy. Such a stock of good will is one of the components of prestige in international politics, although it is an uncertain element and soon dispersed by inconsistencies. Nevertheless, this intangible form of power was also at the disposal of the United States at the end of the war.

The Balance Sheet

As of late 1945, the United States had laid out a range of broad goals. These represented the general direction, and in some instances the specific ends toward which the United States intended to influence the course of international events. For the most part, these objectives had been agreed in principle by the members of the wartime coalition, particularly by the major powers. In the American view, it was understood that they would be sought by co-operative and collective action.

Measured against these broad goals, the capability of the United States to execute these purposes in company with other states appeared adequate. Its economic resources and potential were supreme. Its political power was high, and there were channels available for its ready employment. As for its military power, although the force in being was seriously depleted and dispersed, the potential had been demonstrated during the war and was well remembered. Furthermore, the interlocking international agreements that were presumed to be coming into operation did not call for the extensive maintenance of military power in being. They required only that military strength should not fall below the levels needed to carry out obligations for collective action. Finally, the consensus in the United States was that the available means should be used by the government to effect the accepted purposes. In other words, the United States had the will and the capacity to participate with other nations in giving direction to the total international situation within a framework of agreed principles of action.

The question of possible disparity between ends and means apparently did not arise on this high plateau of purpose. It arose at lower levels, in concrete, immediate, short-term situations. It was here that basic principles and purposes were confronted by the need for action. The actions taken at this stage had at least as much influence in shaping and reshaping policy as did the objectives that guided their general formulation. Furthermore, it was at the lower levels that broad international agreements were continually subjected to testing—in terms of the behavior of states, in terms of interpretation and application, and in terms of national objectives and good faith. Here a disparity between intentions and capabilities could quickly become significant. For example, at any given time, the value of economic strength or of political influence may have to be measured against the value of military strength in the handling of a concrete situation. As these values are not comparable, their relative weights cannot be estimated in advance. This is determined by the outcome. In this sense, the United States could find itself at a disadvantage from the deterioration of its military power even if its economic strength were obviously superior; for if another state chose to exert its military strength, it would thereby alter the character of the particular situation and confront the United States with a new set of circumstances.

What is implied here is that there is no formula by which a disparity between national intentions and national capabilities can be determined in the abstract. It does not help to say that the American people failed to see the need for maintaining military strength at the end of 1945. It is useful, however, to say that, as the international situation developed in 1946, a real disparity became apparent between the intentions of the United States and its capability in respect to the military element of national power.

CHAPTER IV

The State of the World

THE GOALS of United States policy had, of course, to be pursued in the circumstances that prevailed at the end of the war. Given the interrelationship of the goals—the more specific and short-term ones concerned with the method and the nature of the immediate postwar settlement, and the more general long-term ones concerned with the nature and operation of the international system—two ranges of action were mutually supporting and mutually limiting. The pursuit of the short-term goals naturally had a higher priority, not only because the immediate situation demanded action, but also because the achievement of these goals was an essential first step toward the longer-term ones. Yet the short-term solutions could not be permitted to foreclose progress toward more distant objectives. Conversely, the pursuit of the ultimately desirable goals could not be allowed to require dangerous sacrifices in the handling of current situations. Balances and compromises were consequently the order of the day—the weighing of alternatives, the determination of priorities, the discussion of competing values, the search for courses that would not sell either the present or the future down the river.

In illustration of the contingent nature of United States decisions at this time, certain significant concrete situations can be examined, but always with the understanding that the basic objectives of the United States required for their achievement the continuation of major power unity, particularly the willingness of the Soviet Union to honor its wartime agreements. However, neither this unity nor this willingness was proved. The only certainty was that a relationship had been negotiated that might become a concert of interest and a basis for co-operative action. The existing evidence did not justify a final conclusion one way or the other, and there were, in the United States Government, supporters of both possible judgments. Although the over-all position of the United States remained unchanged, this did not mean that an assumption of great power unity was treated as a fact and as a sole basis for policy decisions. The immediate postwar settlement became a kind of testing ground, where intentions could be estimated, good faith judged, and surer grounds for decisions uncovered.

The Enemy States

The enemy states were clearly indentified by the United States in the early stages of the war. By the end of the war, however, the picture had become blurred: the enemies were Germany and Japan. Italy was a co-belligerent. Austria was regarded as a liberated state; so were the Axis satellites of Eastern Europe—Bulgaria, Hungary, and Rumania. Finland had never been an enemy of the United States. These differences of status implied differences of purpose and method in determining their futures. Yet, in every case, a peace treaty had to be negotiated by some member of the victorious alliance. Pending the peace treaties, controls, assistance, or guidance, as required by the varying situations, would be concerted and applied by the major allies in accordance with wartime agreements.

The agreements were both general and specific. The general pattern called for the conversion of the enemy states into peace-loving nations with democratic institutions and for their preparation for reinstatement in the international community. It was assumed that the major allies would carry out these purposes by their own means and in accordance with their own judgments, and that the smaller allies would have no influential voice in what was done.

Specific patterns had been developed by the major allies for their own use. These were embodied in the four-power declaration at Moscow in 1943 and in the agreements reached at the Teheran and Yalta conferences. Machinery had been created to work out concerted policies: the European Advisory Commission, the device of allied control councils, the Council of Foreign Ministers, and, somewhat later, a Far Eastern Advisory Commission. These patterns of purpose lacked substantive detail, however, and the methods were still untested in actual situations. Nevertheless, this was the framework within which the United States began to deal with the concrete problems of the enemy states.

Germany

Germany was, from the start to the finish of the Second World War, regarded as the major enemy by the United States, Great

Britain, and the Soviet Union. German aggressive power was both feared and respected, and it was not assumed that military victory of itself would necessarily eliminate the German potential for future aggressive action.

The Nazi authority that controlled this force was regarded as a competent and widespread organized conspiracy to achieve world domination at the cost of all human values. It was considered both right and essential to root out this conspiracy. Plans for settlement with a defeated Germany were, therefore, developed in emotionally hostile terms, and the United States view did not differ appreciably from that of its major allies.[1] The more extreme proposals did not in the end prevail—not so much because the principles underlying them were rejected, as because they failed on analysis to make political and economic sense to the officials and expert advisers of the United States and British governments. In their view, the existing German population could not be supported by an agrarian economy, a German industrial economy was in many respects essential to the economy of Europe as a whole, and an unviable Germany would be a future political liability.

Compromise objectives, agreed by the major allies, emerged as the solution to these problems. The outlines were drawn at the Yalta Conference: the occupying forces would "take such steps, including the complete disarmament, demilitarisation and dismemberment of Germany as they deem requisite for future peace and security."[2] It was also decided that Germany would be divided for occupation purposes into zones, each under the authority of the respective Allied Supreme Commander. These commanders would also act collectively as a Control Council for co-ordinating the administration of Germany as a whole. The decisions of the Council had to be reached unanimously. These agreements were still to be spelled out.

In spite of the work that was going on in the European Advisory Commission and in the official bureaus of the major allies, nothing resembling an accord on substance was reached until the Potsdam Conference of August 1945. By then, Germany had surrendered unconditionally; zones of occupation had been established; and the commanders in each zone had been acting for some months

[1] The most fully developed destructive proposal was the Morgenthau plan by which Germany was to be reduced to the level of a subsistence economy on an agricultural base. Henry Morgenthau, Jr., *Germany Is Our Problem* (1945).

[2] U.S. Department of State, *Foreign Relations of the United States: The Conferences at Malta and Yalta 1945,* Publication 6199 (1955), p. 936.

on an *ad hoc* basis under national directives that interpreted unilaterally the previously agreed surrender terms. Germany was completely destroyed as a state. There was no governmental apparatus in being through which the Allies could operate. The piecemeal occupation by force of German territory had required the setting up of military government authorities, and sovereign responsibilities fell by default to the commanders of the occupying armies.[3]

At the Potsdam Conference, some of the needed substantive agreement was negotiated out of the existing diversity. It was agreed that Germany should be completely disarmed and demilitarized, and that all German industry that could be used for military purposes was to be eliminated or controlled. Germany was to be denazified. The allied administration in Germany was to work for the decentralization of the political structure and the development of local responsibility. For the time being, no central German government was to be established. However, certain essential administrative departments, headed by state secretaries, were to be established centrally. Under the Allied Control Council, these would act in the fields of finance, transport, communications, foreign trade, and industry.

In order to eliminate the German war potential, the production of arms, ammunition, and implements of war, as well as of all types of aircraft and seagoing ships, was to be prohibited and prevented. At the earliest practicable date, the German economy was to be decentralized for the purpose of eliminating excessive concentration of economic power. During the occupation, Germany was to be treated as a single economic unit.

Allied controls were to be established over the German economy, but only to the extent necessary: (1) to carry out programs of industrial disarmament, demilitarization, reparation, and approved exports and imports; (2) to ensure the production and maintenance of goods and services required to meet the needs of the occupying forces and displaced persons in Germany and essential to maintain living standards in Germany not exceeding the average of the standards of living of European countries; (3) to ensure, in the

---

[3] Guidance for the American commander was given in April 1945 in the Joint Chiefs of Staff paper, JCS 1067, a document drafted primarily by the civilian departments of the United States Government. The tone of this directive was considerably more punitive than the actual occupation practices of the military government. U.S. Department of State, *Germany, 1947-49: The Story in Documents,* Publication 3779, pp. 21-33.

manner determined by the Control Council, the equitable distribution of essential commodities between the several zones so as to produce a balanced economy throughout Germany and reduce the needs for imports; (4) to control German industry and all economic and financial international transactions including exports and imports, with the aim of preventing Germany from developing a war potential and of achieving the other allied objectives; and (5) to control all German public or private scientific bodies, research and experimental institutions, laboratories, and other groups connected with economic activities.

It was decided that the reparation claims of the Soviet Union would be met by removals of capital goods from the Soviet zone of Germany and from appropriate German external assets. In addition to reparation from its own zone, the Soviet Union would be permitted to remove from the zones of the Western powers 25 per cent of such capital equipment as would not be required by the intended German peacetime economy. However, in return for three fifths of the removals thus made, the Soviet Union would make available from its zone supplies in equivalent value of food, coal, potash, zinc, timber, clay, and petroleum products. A two-year limit was placed on these removals. Furthermore, the exaction of reparations would not be permitted to be carried to the point at which the German people would lack the means of subsisting without external assistance. The United States noted that it did not intend to pour into Germany resources that the Soviet Union could remove in other forms.

There was much in the detail of these substantive agreements that was unsatisfactory from the American point of view. The process of negotiating even this minimal co-ordinated policy had the effect of raising doubts about the purposes of the Soviet Union. But generally, the course approved at Potsdam contradicted neither the immediate United States objectives for Germany nor the longer-term and broader United States objectives with respect to a peaceful and secure international system. The American view was that the initial steps in Germany were to be punitive but not destructive. They were to be carried out by severe unified allied controls. Finally, these were to lead rapidly to a reconstructed and modern Germany with which a peace settlement could be made that would restore it to the community of nations.

It was expected that these objectives could be reached in a relatively short time, and that the military occupation of Germany would not be a long, drawn-out affair. Firm action, based on the unity of the occupying powers, was the primary need. Complete satisfaction with substantive detail could be sacrified to this end. There were two reasons to justify this choice. The first concerned Germany itself. Unless allied unity was maintained, it was argued that the Germans could play one side off against the other and nullify the political and economic aims of the victors. The second concerned the broader range of objectives that the United States had formulated. These, whether they related to the immediate postwar settlement or to the development of general peace and security, also required a basis of major power unity.

Japan

When stated in general terms, United States objectives with respect to Japan were similar to those for Germany. Japan would be occupied for the purpose of destroying the Japanese war-making potential. The conduct of the occupation would be such as to reform Japanese political, economic, and cultural institutions and to enable the Japanese to establish a peace-loving democracy free of aggressive intentions. These objectives were not pursued with the same intensity as was initially the case in Germany, for the highest levels of the United States Government never regarded Japan as a comparable threat to American security. Nor were the problems of postwar control and settlement considered of equal difficulty or of equal significance. Both political and military high echelons, as they looked to the future, were impressed more by the existing industrial capacity of Europe than by the theoretical potential of Asia. Europe would carry weight in forwarding American objectives, and the co-operation of European states was not only more essential but also was more likely to be granted willingly.

Between the date of victory in Europe and the end of the war in the Pacific, immediate political considerations began to have a modifying effect on these objectives for Japan. The concept of unconditional surrender was softened. Japan would be allowed to remain an independent nation and to retain a viable economy limited only to the extent that would prevent it from undertaking another war of conquest. There would be no immediate interference with the Imperial institution. On the contrary, it would be used as one of the devices for control. Thus when the end came, the surrender was formal. There was a government to treat with and the structure of the Japanese state was intact. The victors did not fall heir by default, as they did in Germany, to the attributes and responsibilities of sovereignty.

Before this moment came, however, the United States Government was experiencing the difficulties that arose in Germany from the division of the country into zones and from the practical limitations on maintaining allied unity. The opinion developed that the United States should unilaterally control the occupation of Japan. The importance of allied unity as a principle was not played down, but a structure of occupation was proposed that would prevent the principle from interfering with practical necessities. In August 1945, the establishment of a Far Eastern Advisory Commission was proposed. Its function would be to oversee and advise. The Soviet Union demurred, preferring a Control Council with strong powers. The United States stood firm.

The matter was finally settled at the Moscow conference of foreign ministers in December 1945. There would be a Far Eastern Commission, with authority to formulate principles for the control of Japan. Its decisions, which would be reached by a majority vote, including those of the United States, Great Britain, China, and the Soviet Union, would be incorporated into the directives of the United States Government to the Supreme Commander for the Allied Powers (SCAP). Pending agreement by the commission, the United States was free to issue urgently required directives with only three reservations: (1) changes in the control of Japan as set forth by the surrender terms; (2) fundamental changes in the Japanese constitutional structure; and (3) changes in the Japanese Government as a whole.

There was also set up an Allied Council for Japan, a four-power body under the chairmanship of the SCAP. This body was to advise and consult with the SCAP, but the decision of the council would be final in all except the three reserved matters.

As the Secretary of State reported, these arrangements made it "clear that we intend to cooperate with our Allies and we expect them to cooperate with us. But at the same time our agreement safeguards the efficient administration that has been set up in Japan. . . . We were determined that . . . [this] . . . should not be obstructed."[4] In short, the United States was in a position to act freely,

---

[4] U.S. Department of State *Bulletin*, Vol. 13 (Dec. 30, 1945) p. 1035.

even while preserving a formal framework of allied agreement and great power unity.[5]

This position, however, was not felt to jeopardize the principle of allied unity. It was argued that the Soviet Union did not regard Japan as a real security threat, as it did Germany; that the special United States security interest in the Pacific was understood and accepted; and that the concessions already made to the Soviet Union in the Far East were sufficient to provide a basis for the development of major power harmony and co-operation.

Another consideration must be mentioned here although it gets somewhat ahead of the story. Peace in Europe had brought to the surface political disagreements between the allied democracies and the Soviet Union, and United States official circles were re-examining their views of the future role of the Soviet Union in world politics. This was not leading to any fundamental revision of basic American objectives, but it was beginning to introduce more precise reservations into the formulation of particular short-term objectives and to influence the direction and development of specific policies. The end of the war in the Far East consequently found political and strategic considerations sharply to the fore. This shift in emphasis was reflected in the occupation structure for Japan and in the conciliatory interpretation made of the objectives of the occupation.

Austria

The four power Moscow declaration of 1943 had stated that Austria should "be liberated from German domination," and that a free and independent Austria would be re-established and the way thereby opened "for the Austrian people themselves, as well as those neighboring states which will be faced with similar problems, to find that political and economic security which is the only basis for lasting peace. Austria, however, is reminded that she has a responsibility which she cannot evade for participation in the war."[6]

Within this formula of an indeterminate status, the stated aims of the United States became the elimination of the political influences that were opposed to democratization; the re-establishment of

---

[5] In a sense, the formula developed here was a variant of the formula employed by the United States and Great Britain in Italy in 1943, and by the Soviet Union in Bulgaria, Hungary, and Rumania in 1944. See below, pp. 66-67.

[6] U.S. Department of State *Bulletin,* Vol. 9 (Nov. 6, 1943), p. 310.

Austrian borders as they had been before the *Anschluss* with Germany in 1937; the establishment of an elected central government; and the restoration of an Austrian economy freed from dependence on Germany. But, when Soviet forces entered Vienna in April 1945, none of the major allies had yet converted these intentions into agreed and concerted proposals for action; nor is there evidence that even their separate national views had become precise. In fact, the first official and specific allied agreement was reached in June 1945 in the European Advisory Commission, and by then events had overtaken intentions.

Representatives of three Austrian prewar political parties had met and proclaimed a democratic republic according to the constitution of 1920. The Soviet Union recognized the government thus set up as the Provisional Government of Austria. The United States, Great Britain, and France withheld recognition, and it was not until Austria was completely occupied by Allied troops in four zones as in Germany, a Control Council was in place, and a congress of political leaders from all parts of the country had been held that the regime was recognized and authorized to govern "under the guidance and control of the Allied Council."

Austrian elections were held in November 1945, and the government then chosen was recognized by the United States in January 1946 in accordance with a resolution of the Control Council. The act of recognition, however, emphasized that the supreme authority of the Allied Council was in no way affected. A Control Statute was negotiated in June 1946 between the occupying powers and the Austrian Government. The authority of the government was extended fully throughout Austria, except that it was required to carry out directives of the Allied Council, and could not, without authorization, take action affecting the security needs of the occupation forces and the allied objectives concerned with the redress of Nazi wrongs. Finally, the Control Statute reaffirmed the rule of unanimity with respect to decisions taken in the Allied Council. By this date, none of the four powers would dispense with its veto right in the absence of a peace treaty protecting its political and strategic interests. Efforts on the part of the United States to proceed to the negotiation of a peace treaty were either evaded or blocked by the Soviet Union from late 1945 until early 1947.

In October 1946 the United States made a declaration of its position, mainly for the record, as it was obviously not a statement of the facts of the situation: "The United States Government recognizes Austria for all purposes, including legal and administrative, as a liberated country comparable in status to other liberated areas and entitled to the same treatment, subject only to the controls reserved to the occupying powers"[7]

Axis Satellites

The situation in the three satellite states of Eastern Europe—Bulgaria, Hungary, and Rumania—was the most significant of all those that confronted the United States at the end of the war in Europe because, although not perhaps of the highest practical importance, it became a tacitly admitted test of the validity of some of the basic assumptions on which American objectives rested. There was a formula applicable to the situation as it would exist when the satellite states were defeated. It has been quoted above as part of the Moscow Declaration on Austria and is repeated here. The objective was to open the way for the Austrian people, "as well as those neighboring states which will be faced with similar problems, to find that political and economic security which is the only basis for lasting peace." This statement, it will be remembered, was put in the context of Austria as a state to be liberated from German domination.

The European Advisory Commission had not specifically been charged with preparing proposals for the surrender of the satellites before the Soviet armies began to move into these states. When Rumania capitulated before the end of 1944, it was on the basis of an armistice agreement negotiated with the Soviet Union. The United States and Great Britain protested this unilateral action, and the armistice was recast in tripartite terminology with the notation that the Soviet commander had been authorized to act on behalf of the United Nations.

Under pressure from the United States and Great Britain, the other satellite armistices were formally brought within the framework of major power unity. Allied control commissions were established, with a Soviet president and with British and American members. These commissions did not function harmoniously. The Soviet Union displayed every intention of calling the tune, and at least in these areas, of paying rather less than minimal attention to the

---

[7] *Ibid.*, Vol. 15 (Nov. 10, 1946), p. 865.

thesis of allied unity. Consequently, the issue came up for discussion at Yalta in February 1945.

At the Yalta Conference agreed objectives were set forth in the Declaration on Liberated Europe. Reasserting the principle of unanimity and harmony, it was stated that the three major powers would "jointly assist the people in any . . . former Axis satellite state in Europe . . . to form interim governmental authorities broadly representative of all democratic elements in the population and pledged to the earliest possible establishment through free election of governments responsive to the will of the people."[8] The Soviet Union, however, continued to follow courses of its own devising—courses that, by the end of the year, left the Communist parties of the three states firmly entrenched in the three governments. The United States Government protested, but was apparently unwilling to take a firm line while the war against Germany was in progress, while the Soviet Union had to guard long lines of communication to the German front, and while the agreement of the Soviet Union to enter the war against Japan had still to be executed.

By the start of 1946, the situation was for all practical purposes irreversible, and the United States was confronted by the difficult necessity of choosing between mutually exclusive objectives. The objectives with respect to the three "liberated" satellites obviously could not be realized except by the employment of means that would endanger the longer term objective of major power unity. The United States had to decide whether it was willing to breach Allied unity and to forego the goals that unity would make possible in order to attempt to insist on the application of an agreed course in what seemed a relatively remote region. It was decided with considerable unanimity that the vigorous pursuit of principle in this situation would impede the pursuit of more important objectives.

Italy

Italy was in an anomalous position at the end of the war. It had passed through all of the stages from defeated enemy, through cobelligerency, "working its way back," and liberation, to something very much like being a step-child of United States and British

[8] *Ibid.*, Vol. 12 (Feb. 18, 1945), p. 215.

policy. The United States, supported in principle if not always in detail by Great Britain, was prepared to make a nonpunitive peace treaty, to provide assistance in re-establishing Italian economic life, to stabilize Italian political institutions on a democratic base, and to accept Italy as a participant in the international community.[9] It was not, however, possible to proceed rapidly on this final step. Yugoslavia backed by the Soviet Union, the Soviet Union itself as far as reparations were concerned, and France and Greece resisted the realization of so broad-minded and generous a purpose. The ability of the United States to press for its ends was limited by the veto that the Soviet Union could employ in the Council of Foreign Ministers.

Therefore, instead of achieving a quick settlement by Allied agreement, the United States found itself engaged in a hard bargaining process. Its aims for Italy were weighted against its opposition to Soviet aims for the satellite states, while the smaller allies complicated the issue by introducing extensive claims against a defeated enemy.

The Liberated States

Belgium, France, Greece, and the Netherlands presented situations that were widely different variations of a single theme. Belgium and the Netherlands can be left aside. Their exiled governments were prepared to reassert political authority and were acceptable to their liberated peoples. Their problems of reconstruction were reasonably well envisaged, and plans and means for attacking them were in hand.

The other cases were not so straightforward. In the case of Greece, the exiled government had lost touch and a vigorous competition for political control was under way, with Communist partisan resistance groups in strong political positions. In the case of France, although the provisional government of General de Gaulle was generally acceptable, it was not heartily supported by the United States, and the Communist party, with a favorable resistance record, was claiming a share of political power. In both cases, immediate relief and rehabilitation were a first priority.

[9] There were reservations with respect to the disposition of the Italian colonies. Initially, this problem was not regarded as serious, although both it and the reservations became important when Soviet claims were entered to participate in their disposition.

The general United States objective was the political stabilization of these states and the revival and reconstruction of their economies in order that they might quickly co-operate as free and sovereign states in carrying out the purposes of the United Nations. Pending this, they were to be restrained by the major powers, kept from confusing the peace settlements by exorbitant nationalistic demands, and assisted to regain status by concerted great power efforts. The general guide to major power action had been laid down in the relevant sections of the Yalta Declaration on Liberated Europe. No particular objectives were formulated by the United States. Policy took the form of adopting broad courses of action to meet particular circumstances as they arose in particular states.

The one important exception was in the case of France. Official American attitudes had been ambivalent, some groups arguing that France was a reduced power in the world and should be so regarded, others that a strong France was essential to the operation of the international system.[10] The policy of the United States, pressed by French insistence, by British arguments about the need for a French counterweight on the continent of Europe, and by the wish of the United States to withdraw its forces from Europe, gradually accepted France as a major state. It was admitted to the European Advisory Commission, given a zone of occupation and a place on the Control Council in Germany and Austria, and made a permanent member, with a veto right, of the Security Council of the United Nations. But, because the position of a major power was not one that France could support with its available resources, the United States found itself moving toward a policy of underwriting the French status.

Poland, Yugoslavia, and Czechoslovakia were still other cases. The Germans were driven out of Poland by the Soviet army and a Soviet-controlled government—the Lublin Government—was set up and the authority of the Polish Government-in-exile was deliberately undermined. Native partisans, controlled by the Communist, Tito, freed Yugoslavia. A government was formed, in which the exiled authority was initially given a small share but from which it was soon excluded. Czechoslovakia became free in consequence of allied military operations designed to destroy the German army in

[10] Roosevelt's initially strong views on the position of France and on the necessity for anticipating the breakdown of the French Empire are a matter of record. See William L. Langer, *Our Vichy Gamble* (1947).

Germany. When these operations were completed, American forces were withdrawn to Western Germany. The Czechoslovak Government-in-exile resumed control, having earlier entered into a bilateral treaty with the Soviet Union.

Developments in Poland had been strenuously resisted by the United States and Great Britain, and the issue was discussed at length at the Yalta Conference and again at the Potsdam Conference but without getting satisfactory action from the Soviet Union.[11] In the end, Poland became, for United States policy, part of the Eastern European satellite picture and hence more or less beyond the reach of immediate action. In the case of Yugoslavia, the actions of the new government placed this state also in the satellite context so far as over-all United States policy was concerned; but here there was a sovereign state clearly asserting its freedom of action, and the United States had no dormant international agreements to refer to for the record. In the case of Czechoslovakia, no policy problem arose. The relations of the Czechoslovak Government with the United States and with the Soviet Union were apparently running in a normal course, and the possibility of a Communist *coup d'état* was not in sight.

China

The United States goal in China was basically set at the moment of Pearl Harbor. The destruction of Japan as a dominating power in the Far East was established, and China was designated to assume the leading role at the close of the war. It was a goal that satisfied both political and strategic requirements and that furthermore derived naturally from the traditional American attitude toward China. In the view of the United States, therefore, China was defined as a major power and, at American insistence, although with British reluctance, was treated as such. In the course of the prolonged discussions about the postwar world, China was built into the proposed structure in this capacity.

With this as the goal, United States policy was directed to giving China the attributes of a great power. The territories that China

---

[11] Churchill was prepared for a show-down with the Soviet Union on the matter, but could not persuade the United States to force the issue. His proposals to this effect were rejected on the grounds that the United States did not wish to appear to be "ganging-up" on the Soviet Union. See Winston Churchill, *The Second World War,* Vol. 6, *Triumph and Tragedy* (1953), Chaps. 6 and 20, pp. 418-39 and pp. 647-67 respectively.

had lost to Japan over decades were to be restored. The central governmental authority was to be assured, and resources were to be made available for stabilizing the Chinese economy and reducing political confusion. As is often the case in policy making, there was little argument about the end, but plenty of controversy about the means. One issue stood out above all others: the need to create a unified central authority from divergent Chinese Nationalist and Chinese Communist groups. To this issue, United States policy addressed itself.

No effort was spared to negotiate a coalition government. But no extension of good offices, no patience as mediator, and no application of influence could adjust differences as profound as those that separated the Nationalist Kuomintang and the Communist groups. The effort of the United States to make China conform to the image that had been constructed of a China that would fulfill American purposes was further weakened from within by two considerations. The United States was unwilling to furnish the National Government with further military equipment prior to the formation of a coalition, fearing that, if it did so, the issue would be settled by force. Secondly, there was a view, taken by some American Far Eastern experts, to the effect that the Chinese Communists were a more viable and significant political force than the Kuomintang, that the latter was corrupt, without a real hold on the peoples it governed, and doomed to lose even the little authority it still possessed.

When the Chinese situation was examined in light of United States relations with the Soviet Union and of larger American goals, it appeared even more complex. In order to ensure that the Soviet Union would come into the war against Japan, commitments were made with respect to Soviet claims in the Far East that infringed on the status of China as a sovereign major power. At the same time, a guard had to be set up so that the Soviet Union would not throw its weight behind the Chinese Communists and thus prejudice a coalition and the chances of political peace by agreement in China. This implied, so far as American action in China went, that the United States would equally avoid unconditional support of the Nationalist regime—at least until its base had been broadened. These arrangements were made at Yalta. They required for their execution, however, that the United States persuade the National Government to enter into a treaty with the Soviet Union by which

Soviet claims would be confirmed. The United States agreed "to take measures to obtain this concurrence," and in due course did so.[12]

With this agreement confirmed, by a Sino-Soviet treaty in August 1945, in the background, the United States continued on the course it had previously fixed: the creation of a broadly representative unified Chinese government. When Japan surrendered, however, and the shaping of a postwar world began, the Chinese Communists refused to accept the subordinate role in which they had been cast. They demanded to be treated as a governmental force. United States pressure on both parties—Nationalist and Communist—to continue to negotiate was redoubled. The Kuomintang was told that it would not have unqualified American support unless an agreement were reached; the Communists were told that they could not hope for backing unless an agreement were reached. Meanwhile, the Communists captured stocks of arms from the Japanese. The United States assisted in the transportation of Nationalist troops northward to accept the Japanese surrender. The Chinese Communists denounced this activity bitterly, as well as a proposal to land United States Marines in Chefoo in August, pointing out that there were no Japanese in the area. The United States refrained from taking this step.

The situation began to deteriorate for the Nationalist regime, and United States policy was confronted by a need for re-examination. The Soviet Union was giving the Chinese Communists at least passive assistance. They permitted them to infiltrate Manchuria. They refused to permit Nationalist troops to use the port of Dairen on the pretext that it was an open commercial port. The promised American airlift to the north was so slow in materializing that Chiang Kai-shek agreed to extend the deadline for Soviet troop withdrawal from Manchuria until January lest the Chinese Communists

[12] This agreement has been the subject of bitter controversy. It was reached in a period when the policy of unity among the main powers was viewed as the indispensable means of achieving United States world objectives. The pact seemed, indeed, to limit Soviet objectives in Asia and to strengthen the Nationalist regime. Moreover, American means were not available to protect the Manchurian rights of the Nationalists if the Russians had the intention of aiding the Communists. While many believed wholeheartedly that the Soviet Union would co-operate, even less sanguine interpreters of Soviet aims might well have justified the agreement as a gamble to safeguard United States objectives in Asia. The Soviet Union, as required by dominant military thinking in the United States, had entered the war against Japan, and, as required by political thinking in the United States, had pledged support for a coalition based on the existing Nationalist regime.

have the area entirely to themselves. By November 1945, the United States Government began to regard the problem as one of holding liberated areas for the Nationalists and to debate whether the Marines should be kept in North China. It was officially reported to Washington that Chiang Kai-shek could not bring stability and democracy to China because he was surrounded by selfish and unscrupulous men. If the Marines were to interfere and aid the Nationalists, it would take forces and shipping "far beyond those now available or contemplated in the area."[13]

Another attempt at mediation was made, and the Marshall mission was despatched to China in late 1945. Its instructions were that the Nationalists were to be told that American aid would be withheld if an agreement with the Communists was not sought; the Communists were to be told that if they were not reasonable, Nationalist troops would be air lifted northward by American planes. However, because the United States objective was a unified and stable China, General Marshall was orally informed that the United States would continue to aid the Nationalists even if they refused to be conciliatory.[14]

Throughout, the United States objective in China remained unchanged. The United States sought a strong, unified China that could act as a major power in the Far Eastern sector of a peaceful and secure international system. Events, however, threw the policy into flux. The Soviet Union, the Chinese Communists, and the character of the Nationalist regime were realities. The Communists were a strong force. The area they controlled was contiguous to the Soviet Union. Unity and stability were obtainable only with their co-operation, or by breaking their power. The latter choice was not a real one. The United States could not readily project its power onto the Asiatic mainland for this purpose, even if its larger objectives had permitted such a choice to be made. No matter how pessimistic a view might be taken of Communist intentions, no matter how willing policy makers might be to use force, the choice was foreclosed by the fact that the demobilization of the United States armed forces was in full swing. Yet the United States was clearly not prepared to abandon its basic aim in China. As the government saw it, even if the policy of conciliation had only a slight chance of success, it was the only policy that the United States was in a position to pursue.

[13] Herbert Feis, *The China Tangle* (1953), p. 402.
[14] *Ibid.*, p. 420.

Korea

At the Cairo Conference in November 1943, the United States, Great Britain, and China declared that "mindful of the enslavement of the people of Korea," they were "determined that in due course Korea" should "become free and independent."[15] The Soviet Union, on entering the war against Japan, subscribed to this declaration. Beyond this, the United States had no objectives with respect to Korea that were not comprehended by general American aims for international peace and security.

But on the surrender of Japan, the United States found itself a co-occupying power in Korea along with the Soviet Union and hence obliged to develop specific policies for reaching the broadly stated goal of a free and independent Korea. Owing to the need for making practical arrangements to accept the surrender of Japanese forces, responsibility had been divided with the Soviet Union on the line of the thirty-eighth parallel of latitude. As events soon demonstrated, occupation also appeared to mean partition, and the objective of the United States accordingly became to unify Korea as well as to make it free and independent. Action to achieve this goal brought the United States into direct negotiating contact with the Soviet Union on a bilateral basis. Differences of purpose were quickly revealed with a sharpness more clearly marked than at other points of contact. Diplomacy failed to bridge the differences, and the matter came before the Moscow meeting of foreign ministers in December 1945. They agreed on the establishment of a Joint Commission, charged with assisting in the "formation of a provisional Korean government," with helping "the political, economic and social progress of the Korean people," and with working out "an agreement concerning a four-power trusteeship of Korea for a period of up to five years."[16]

The commission met in January 1946 and immediately disagreed about its terms of reference. Generally speaking, the United States interpreted them as requiring Korea to be treated as a whole without reference to the division at the thirty-eighth parallel. In contrast, the Soviet Union interpreted the terms of reference as calling only for the co-ordination of activities north and south of this line. These differences were never resolved. The occupying powers,

[15] U.S. Department of State *Bulletin,* Vol. 9 (Dec. 4, 1943), p. 393.
[16] *Ibid.,* Vol. 13 (Dec. 30, 1945), p. 1030,

driven by the necessity for governing, improvised controls and initiated Korean governments. The two conflicting positions gradually hardened into South and North Korean systems of authority, backed respectively by United States and Soviet military commands. Differences became so pronounced that further discussion was useless. The Joint Commission adjourned *sine die* in May 1946, and there the question rested until the United States brought it up in the United Nations Organization over a year later.

It is significant that until this point was reached, the United States apparently regarded Korea as a low priority nuisance in the total field of its foreign policy. It was given peripheral attention only and then always within a context of considerations that were regarded as of much greater moment. The basic initial objective was rigidly repeated for the record. General policy consisted of merely standing firm on a position. Specific action tended to be improvised and to leave an accumulation of practical consequences that kept the situation unstable. In the final showdown, the ultimate goal became infinitely more difficult to reach.

Latin America

The position of the United States as well as its standing policies with respect to Latin America seemed clearly established at the end of the war. Inter-American relations had, with the exception of the Argentine, been tightened up, and this closer-knit system had been fitted into the structure of the United Nations.[17] Arrangements had been made for controlling the impact of declining wartime demands on the raw material productive capacity of Latin American countries. No problems other than those traditionally inherent in inter-American affairs were anticipated, and the new forms that these might take were felt to be well within the range of general United States policies.

Although events have not quite turned out in this way, and the relations have been attended by uneasiness and even crises, it is nevertheless generally true that the problems of Latin American relations have tended to be off to one side of the main stream of the evolution of United States foreign policy over the past decade.

[17] The collapse of the Peron regime at the end of 1955 eliminated the Argentine as an exception. This state is now being built back into the existing structure of inter-American relations.

This is not to say that these problems are not real; for those who deal with them, they are continuous and time-consuming. It is only to say that they have been on the outer edge, not at the focus of United States attention. Consequently, this pattern of relations will be treated at this point in its broadest and most general form. It should be remembered, however, that the requirements of the inter-American system were always present at the elbow of the American policy maker.

The governing principle of these relations was laid down in the Monroe Doctrine, and the exclusionist features of that doctrine are still considered applicable and, as much as any other single factor, have been responsible for keeping inter-American relations astonishingly self-contained. During the formative years, United States policy ranged from the recognition of revolutionary governments to open intervention in Latin American affairs. American attempts to justify intervention on the ground of mutual benefit were not acceptable to the Latin American countries. But as time went on, and in particular as the United States outpaced all of the Latin American countries in its economic growth and in the rate at which it achieved major power status, the tone of relations changed. Secretary of State Stimson said in 1931: "The Monroe Doctrine was a declaration of the United States versus Europe—not the United States versus Latin America."[18] This attitude culminated in the Good Neighbor Policy of the first term of Franklin Roosevelt. Essentially, this is the relationship that was finally embodied in the Charter of the Organization of American States—good partners in exclusiveness.

Prior to the approval of the Charter at Bogotá in 1948, various steps had been taken to bring the whole pattern of inter-American relations into consonance with the security demands of the modern world. The first of these was taken early in the Second World War, when the American states conferred on means to protect the Western Hemisphere from the consequences of a possible German victory. During the war, a number of economic and military agreements were made. The last of these steps followed from the conference at Chapultepec in February 1945 and took the form of the Inter-American Treaty of Reciprocal Assistance (Rio Treaty) of September 1947.

[18] *The United States and the Other American Republics,* Address before the Council on Foreign Relations, Feb. 6, 1931, p. 2.

This treaty provided for collective action within the hemisphere, bound the signatories to consult in the event of aggression either from within or without the Americas, and provided for enforcement measures, which, if approved by a two-thirds majority, would become binding on all parties. But no state was required to use armed force without its own consent. The Rio Treaty established a precedent for the North Atlantic Treaty and provided a model for other regional collective security arrangements.

The whole of this process of adjustment was finally formalized at the Tenth Inter-American Conference. The purposes of the Organization were stated as:

(a) To strengthen the peace and security of the continent;

(b) To prevent possible causes of difficulties and to ensure the pacific settlement of disputes that may arise among the Member States;

(c) To provide for common action on the part of those States in the event of aggression;

(d) To seek the solution of political, juridical, and economic problems that may arise among them; and

(e) To promote, by cooperative action, their economic, social, and cultural development.[19]

Thus equipped with respect to their own exclusive relations, the United States and the states of Latin America entered the postwar decade.

From the point of view of the United States, here was a very special regional structure that, in terms of the world situation, contributed directly to the security of the United States. Although the military strength of Latin America was not great, the Latin American republics as sovereign entities were significant in the system of collective security for the free world that the United States sought to construct. Their territories were important for communications and shipping, and as air and naval bases. In addition, these states controlled valuable strategic materials that were within fairly certain reach. From the point of view of the Latin American countries, however, their dependence on the United States was immediate and particular and involved their economic aspirations and the political stability of their governments. This difference in need between the Latin American countries and the United States gave rise to the specific problems that have been alive in inter-American relations throughout the last decade.

---

[19] See *United Nations Treaty Series*, Vol. 30 (1948), pp. 55-116.

The United States was concerned with the stability of Latin American regimes and intent on ensuring that the Communist movement should not gain a foothold in the inter-American system. The states of Latin America were concerned with their own economic growth and could not see why the United States, as it set up programs of economic assistance elsewhere in the world to check communism, should not meet the needs for economic improvement in Latin America. Policy, negotiations, agreements, programs, and action gravitated between these two poles of interest.

The traditional pattern of United States economic relations with the Latin American countries had developed mainly through trade, private investment, and public loans. In the last ten years, United States private capital has gone into Latin America at an average yearly rate of about $250 million, and the private earnings of American companies have been reinvested at an average rate of about $190 million each year.

But in addition, the United States Government has furnished investment funds to further the social and economic advancement of the Latin American countries. Through the Export-Import Bank and the International Bank, loan funds have been provided at the rate of about $93 million each year since the end of the Second World War. Limited technical assistance programs were also set up. In the fiscal year 1955, for example, the United States furnished about $28 million in direct support of such programs.

From the Latin American point of view, this was definitely unsatisfactory. There was resentment in many Latin American quarters at being expected to be content with so little from the United States when so much was going into the large assistance programs for Western Europe, the Middle East, and the Far East. The Latin American states were unwilling to believe that the vast economic resources of the United States could not be stretched to cover Latin American needs, while still providing billions of dollars elsewhere in the world. They wanted to rise from the category of underdeveloped countries, and for this purpose required capital in volume to undertake rapidly both industrial and agricultural development.

A dilemma appeared when this desire for increased foreign capital, public and private, was viewed in the light of the political instability of the Latin American republics. The erratic nature of Latin American politics has been called one of the most serious impediments to hemispheric solidarity, and, despite improving economic and social conditions, the danger of revolution remained a real one in many Latin American countries. Furthermore, it was not beyond possibility that nationalism and communism might at any time join hands to frustrate political goals that were being pursued by economic means.

Communism in the Latin American republics has generally appeared in the guise of nationalist parties. Communist leaders have generally tried to exploit poor economic and social conditions, usually by holding the government and the United States jointly responsible for their existence. The United States, looking at the threat of Soviet-Communism in terms of a strategy of containment, has been inclined to take the Latin American Communist parties seriously. It has tried to get the Latin American republics to deal with the matter through joint action. Most of them have outlawed the Communist party and terminated diplomatic relations with the Soviet Union; but they have remained reluctant to agree to take joint action. Joint action, as they represent it, would involve interference in their domestic affairs, and this smacks too much of United States intervention.

At one inter-American conference after another, these two themes have appeared: a resolution, presented on United States initiative, to take joint action against communism and a resolution, supported by virtually all the Latin American republics, favoring greater economic co-operation. The principles are always admitted to be unimpeachable, but they prove extremely difficult to translate into specific agreements to act.

For example, the long-delayed meeting of the ministers of finance and economy of the American republics, which was held in Rio de Janeiro in late November and early December 1954, was disappointing to the Latin American countries.[20] The Secretary of the Treasury, who headed the United States delegation, offered only two concessions to the Latin American countries. He said that the

[20] The agenda items were: (1) international trade, including the establishment of stable and equitable prices and markets, the question of disposing of surplus production of raw materials, elimination of trade barriers, and stimulation of trade; (2) economic development, including plans for future progress and co-operation on financing development and increasing technical assistance; (3) transportation, with the emphasis on expansion and co-ordination of international facilities; and (4) other subjects, including procedures for consultation on economic and financial matters, codification of standards of economic co-operation, and a report on the reorganization of the Economic and Social Council.

United States would increase its financial support by an intensification of loans. He referred to three media for increased loans, the Export-Import Bank, the International Bank for Reconstruction and Development, and a proposed International Finance Corporation. He also promised that the United States, under proper safeguards, would be prepared to recommend a formula for relaxing double taxation on private investments. In making these two commitments, he stressed again and again the necessity for free enterprise in solving long-range economic problems. Many of the delegates, however, felt that the United States was not approaching the economic problems of the hemisphere in a broad or useful way. They pointed out that the United States proposals offered no solution for such problems as extreme fluctuations in the price of the raw materials on which the economies of many of the Latin American countries were based.

Again, as an illustration of the other theme, the United States Secretary of State, at the Tenth Inter-American Conference at Caracas in March 1954, proposed the adoption of a new resolution on communism. The reaction of the conference was far from enthusiastic. A number of counterproposals were made, one of which would have limited collective action to instances in which an extracontinental power actually invaded the Western Hemisphere. The Secretary considered this approach "unthinkable." It was the purpose of the United States resolution, he said, to prevent such an invasion. The Secretary assured the delegates, moreover, that they need not fear that the proposed resolution could be "interpreted as intervention, or justifying intervention in the genuinely domestic affairs of an American State." He believed this fear was based on historical reasons rather than on "any language in the U.S. proposal."[21] The following resolution finally emerged:

That the domination or control of the political institutions of any American State by the international communist movement, extending to this hemisphere the political system of an extracontinental power, would constitute a threat to the sovereignty and political independence of the American States, endangering the peace of America, and would call for *a meeting of consultation to consider the adoption of appropriate action* in accordance with existing treaties.[22]

[21] U.S. Department of State *Bulletin,* Vol. 30 (Mar. 22, 1954), p. 423.

[22] *Ibid* (Apr. 26, 1954), p. 638. The words in italics above represent a Colombian amendment and replace the words *appropriate action* in the original United States draft.

Quite apart from these grounds of difference, the security policy of the United States has regularly called for the extension of military assistance to Latin America on a limited scale. Consequently, the United States had never had any real difficulty in obtaining resolutions acknowledging the common security interests of the Organization of American States. At the Fourth Meeting of Consultation of Ministers of Foreign Affairs in Washington, in March and April 1951, held when the Korean War was in full swing, the Final Act directed the Inter-American Defense Board to prepare military plans for common defense, and recognized that the member states should "orient their military preparation in such a way that, through self-help and mutual aid" they could develop armed forces best adapted to collective defense and could co-operate to increase the collective strength of the continent.[23] To assist in carrying out these decisions, the United States Congress appropriated $38.15 million (in the Mutual Security Act of 1951) for direct military assistance to Latin America. In 1952, the Congress appropriated an additional $51.68 million. These funds were furnished to the Latin American republics under bilateral military assistance agreements.

Taken as a whole and seen in a long-time span, inter-American relations have obviously been a kind of give-and-take affair, traditionalized in concept, formalized in broad agreements, and conducted by familiar routines. The substance of these relations consists mainly of a multiplicity of private contacts and exchanges, occasionally enlivened by crises, and punctuated at intervals by recurring negotiations on well-explored differences. On this basis, the United States has been able to keep regional political problems in the hands of the countries of the Americas. Essentially, this is all that the interests of the United States have required.

United States policy has been somewhat less successful in handling the economic and social aspirations of the Latin American countries. It has offered economic and technical assistance on a limited scale. It has stressed the role of foreign investment—primarily private. However, it has insisted that the major share of investment capital must come from the Latin American countries themselves. It has maintained that the principal United States contribution to the development of the Latin American republics must be through normal trade. These decisions, however sound they

[23] *Ibid.*, Vol. 24 (Apr. 16, 1951), p. 607.

seem to American policy makers, fall short of the expectations and requirements of Latin American policy makers.

Nevertheless, the framework of treaty, economic necessity, and the habit of maintaining good rather than bad relations that holds the inter-American system together has provided mutual if somewhat disparate benefits since the Second World War. The Latin American states have acquired a security that would not have been obtainable by their own efforts or with their own resources. The United States has been able to engage in world affairs on a scale that would have been risky in the extreme, but for the assurance that it operated from a secure base in the Western Hemisphere. There is, however, an opposite side of this coin that must be noted in conclusion. Certain unanticipated strains have developed. The United States, intent on resisting the expansion of Communist influence, has occasionally demanded that a very broad interpretation be made of its doctrine of non-intervention.[24] The action of Great Britain to dismiss an elected but Communist-bent government in Guiana gave rise to outcries against a European intervention in Latin American affairs. And, finally, the easy American assumption that the votes of the Latin American republics in the General Assembly of the United Nations were always and freely at the disposal of United States policy has been subjected to increasing disproof. In short, while the United States position in respect to Latin America is still a tenable one at bottom, its indefinite continuance without re-examination cannot be taken for granted.

[24] The removal of a Communist-oriented government in Guatemala in 1955, although ultimately regulated by the Organization of American States, left a considerable feeling in Latin America that the matter had been directly engineered by the United States.

CHAPTER V

Reinterpretation

PERHAPS the most striking feature of the pattern of United States goals and actions is the extent to which they rested on an assumption about state relations and the social nature of man. The nature of this assumption can be described as an optimistic expectation that peace, prosperity, freedom, and justice could be given a universal meaning, that when so defined these goals would be sought by all men, and that the only requirement for their achievement was that governments—and, of course, governments meant human beings—should work together harmoniously and co-operatively.

It has often been said of the American conduct in international affairs that the nation voices millennial hopes and moves to realize them, not by employing instruments of policy, but by embarking on crusades. There is no doubt that the Grand Alliance of the Second World War was publicly presented as an example of international harmony. There is no doubt that a sincerely calculated risk was taken in projecting this picture of a successful military alliance as the foundation for an international politico-security system. There is no doubt that the optimistic idealism of this effort, focusing as it did on desires and expectations that were almost universal, was a potent political force during and immediately after the war.

It is only too easy to dismiss the intellectual content of this projection as naive, self-deceptive, and unrealistic. There is no historical difficulty involved if anyone wishes to point out that the divorce of military strategy and political goals by the United States had no counterpart in the behavior of other states. This can be called a myth, but even if only a myth, it sustained the Grand Alliance and damaged the enemy, and there is no way of judging its ultimate effects on popular attitudes toward state relations.

For the decade with which this volume is concerned, however, the optimistic idealism that the United States wrote into the Grand Alliance and then translated into the Charter of the United Nations and into its own pattern of objectives and policies did not become an exclusive and powerful motivation for state action in international affairs. The wartime agreements, which, it was hoped, would lay the ground work for changing the rules of international life, never got beyond the talking stage. A reinterpretation of the United States position was, consequently, inevitable. The United States either had to adjust its position to fit the situations that were being brought about by the actions of others; or it had to exert its strength to make its view of what was desirable prevail. The latter course implied so considerable a reorganization and expenditure of national effort as to be almost out of the question in terms of domestic politics. Adjustment consequently became the order of the day.

With a hindsight fortified by the experience of the past ten years, it can now be seen that the process of adjustment was fundamentally conditioned by judgments about the motivations, intentions, and capabilities of the Soviet Union. The process was slow. Its stages are by no means clear. The chronology of the shift in judgment is neither neat nor logical. Governmental positions resist changes. There seems to be a law of inertia decreeing that it takes more energy to change a policy than to continue to implement it against mounting obstacles. Over a period of time, changed ideas give rise to changes in policy, even to shifts in objectives, but the process cannot readily be pinned down to dates.

Before and throughout the Second World War, the place of the Soviet Union in the international system was the unsolved riddle. Expert as well as popular opinion was perpetually uncertain. Relations with a state that was both powerful and committed to changing the international *status quo* tended to rest on either improbable hopes or exaggerated fears. The continuing political intent of the United States during the war was to draw the Soviet Union into international life as a normal participant. So far as this could be done by written agreements, it was presumed to have been accomplished. Initially, much was staked on acting as if it had been accomplished. Because, in policy matters, action is often taken on similar "as if" grounds, this judgment, made in the year 1945, cannot be legitimately condemned from the point of view of subsequent years.

Enough uncertainty remained, however, so that the Soviet Union continued to be watched with suspicion. Soviet actions were scrutinized closely in terms of whether they were to be regarded as acquiescing in or disregarding wartime agreements. After all, American attitudes had at various times shifted to all points of the compass with respect to the Soviet Union. The Rooseveltian re-establishment of relations, accepted at the time with reservations, was negated in popular feeling by the tricky Soviet-Nazi pact of 1939. This judgment was officially, although not popularly, reversed when the Soviet Union was attacked by Germany in 1941. With the entry of the United States into the war, official and popular views largely came together in a picture of a heroic nation fighting fiercely in a common cause. The constantly experienced difficulties of dealing with the Soviet Union—the blunt demands, the refusals to reciprocate, the ungraciousness, the almost psychopathic suspicion and secretiveness of Soviet officials—were given the most favorable possible interpretations by the United States Government and by American opinion. In those governmental circles most deeply concerned with building a postwar order for which Soviet co-operation would be required, interpretations of this kind were psychologically compelling.

But these views were not unanimous. A certain residue of "crossed-fingers" remained in official circles and in some sections of public opinion. This skepticism was either quiescent or ineffective during the war. Nevertheless, its existence meant that the basic assumption of harmony on which the American view of the future shape of international society rested continued to be regarded as something that still had to be proved before it could be accepted as an exclusive basis for action by the United States. Naturally the required proof could only be found in the actions of the Soviet Union.

In the closing stages of the war, doubts began to develop in administration quarters, where of course evidence was bound to accumulate most rapidly. As 1945 progressed, these doubts started to cohere and to form the groundwork for an alternative assumption about Soviet objectives. Few persons, however, were ready to challenge the overriding objective of allied unity. At no time, did official statements give the public any reason to question Soviet co-operation in the postwar era. Yet, a close review of official discussions and actions makes it clear that by the end of 1945 United States policy makers, while continuing sincerely to pursue the goal of great power unity as a primary purpose, were exploring contingent policies for protecting the United States against the possible failure of this effort. Still, for the greater part of the period from V-J Day to the end of 1946, a gap remained between these official explorations and a public awareness of the development of a new direction in the policies of the United States Government.

Change of Direction

The process of changing direction can be most easily examined from two separate points of view: official experience and the conclusions that were derived from it, and the public discussion of both the experience and the conclusions.

Between the formal surrender of Japan (September 2, 1945) and the announcement of the Truman Doctrine (March 12, 1947), the officials of the United States Government, guided as they were by a coherent set of objectives and policies respecting the postwar world, went through a harrowing eighteen months of frustration and hasty *ad hoc* adjustments. On a high level, these involved four meetings of the Council of Foreign Ministers,[1] and a meeting of the foreign ministers of the United States, Great Britain, and the Soviet Union in Moscow in December 1945. These also involved at a lower level, meetings of the General Assembly of the United Nations in London in January and February, and in New York in October-December 1946; and a Peace Conference in Paris (July 29-October 15, 1946). Finally, they involved diversified working contacts with Soviet officials and Soviet policies, widely dispersed through the world—in Europe, in the Middle East, and in the Far East.

The details of this experience need not be gone into here. They are matters of history and are now adequately recorded. The general pattern of the experience and the conclusions to which it led are the immediate concern.

It was gradually revealed that, behind the documents by which the Grand Alliance had been cemented and in which the outlines of an international system of state relations had been recorded, the major powers had from the start pursued objectives whose divergence was obscured by their having been expressed in such general terms that contradictory interpretations were always possible. What these differences were and the extent to which they had

---

[1] London (Sept. 11-Oct. 2, 1945); Paris (April 25-May 16, 1946); Paris (June 15-July 12, 1946); and New York (Nov. 4-Dec. 12, 1946).

to be accepted as fact and adjusted to, became clear only in connection with the immediate postwar settlement, and only as respective national postwar policies were developed in action. Then, however, it became apparent that while the attainment of American objectives depended on a prolonged, co-operative, international effort, the Soviet Union was gaining immediate and concrete advantages by unilateral action.

In brief, the Soviet Union was, by its actions, presenting itself as an expansionist state, unremitting in its efforts to seize every opportunity that opened to create fresh advantage for itself. It appeared unreliable in its interpretation of its international pledges, and to be fostering disintegration in the international system while advocating the need for great power unity. Above all, it appeared to be renewing the thesis of world revolution that its wartime allies hoped had been abandoned.

Communist regimes were maintained in Bulgaria, Hungary, Poland, and Rumania. The self-installed Communist regimes of Albania and Yugoslavia were supported. Local Communist parties in France, Czechoslovakia, Italy, and Korea were encouraged in political sabotage and in Greece and China were indirectly supported in open civil war. Direct pressure was brought to bear on Turkey and Iran. The anticipated joint control of enemy states was being made unworkable, and occupation policies were becoming divergently national.

At the end of the war, it seemed to many American officials that Great Britain and the Soviet Union were the main protagonists and that the areas in which their differences arose were Europe and the Middle East. In this situation, the role of the United States was obviously that of mediating the necessary adjustments by referring always to the ultimate and higher claims of an organized, peaceful, and secure international society. In the course of 1946, however, the United States and the Soviet Union passed a point of no return in Germany, and the United States indicated the importance it attached to the position and influence of Great Britain as a world power by providing credits on favorable terms in the amount of $4.4 billion.[2] By the start of 1947, the Soviet Union was con-

---

[2] What is generally called the British Loan Agreement consisted of three related negotiations: (a) commercial policy, (b) lend-lease and other related settlements, and (c) a financial agreement. The amount finally available to Great Britain comprised $3.75 billion under the Financial Agreement and $650 million under the Lend-Lease Settlement. An analysis of the prolonged debate in the

fronted by an informal revival of Anglo-American wartime association, and the area in which differences arose between what can now be called the West and the East was world-wide.

Generally speaking, however, this development did not lead directly to an official formulation of an extreme alternative assumption, namely, that the Soviet Union constituted a threat to the security of the United States. Even less was such a conclusion understandable to public opinion. But the signs of Soviet intransigence were not ignored, and they gradually became common knowledge. A range of interpretations of Soviet behavior was built up. Consequently, the characteristic American political process of publicly debating a national position was initiated. A working consensus was not reached until 1947. The various positions developed in the course of this debate are germane to the policy choices that were later made by the United States.

Three easily identifiable positions were sketched out. The most important, because it came closest to being official, was one that continued to look to the United Nations Organization and its purposes as the end to which United States policy should be directed. In this view, the Soviet Union, by its demonstrated expansionist tendencies and aggressive foreign policies, was preventing a rapid and exclusive pursuit of the course. Priority, therefore, had to be given to checking the Soviet Union as a prerequisite to any further progress toward international peace and security. The practice of sacrificing particular positions in order to maintain the general thesis of great power unity had, according to this line of thinking, reached a dead end. A "tough line" toward the Soviet Union was called for, but this toughness was to be used only in specific issues as they arose. There was no coherent and steadily maintained notion of pushing the Soviet Union out of international society, or of organizing an international opposition to Soviet policy. On the contrary, the idea was that the Soviet Union could be disciplined

---

Congress on the loan shows that the political significance of the proposed action gradually displaced the economic arguments. Not, however, that the economic policy objectives should be overlooked. The conditions attached to the agreement were designed to lead toward the kind of economic world that the United States desired because, as the National Advisory Council (NAC) assured the Congress: "No other country has the same crucial position in world trade as England. . . . The early realization of the full objectives of the Bretton Woods program . . . requires an immediate solution to Britain's financial problem." *Report of the National Advisory Council on International Monetary and Financial Problems*, H. Doc. 497, 79 Cong. 2 sess. (March 1946), p. 17.

into seeing the value—even if only the value in terms of its own national interest—of carrying out its international pledges in the sense in which these obligations were understood by the United States and by most of the nations of the West.

The position was summarized by President Truman in his State of the Union Message of January 1947: "Whatever difficulties there may have been between us and the Soviet Union, however, should not be allowed to obscure the fact that the basic interests of both nations lie in the early making of a peace under which the peoples of all countries may return . . . to the essential tasks of production and reconstruction."[3]

This position meant to most of its exponents that the Soviet Union had to be induced by firmness to play the game in the American way. There was no consistent official suggestion that the United States should begin to play a different game. Such a suggestion was, however, made by others as they developed more extreme positions.

Two of the more extreme theses have become connected with the names of Henry Wallace, then Secretary of Commerce, and Sir Winston Churchill, then speaking as a private citizen in Fulton, Missouri.

The Churchill thesis asserted that: "Nobody knows what Soviet Russia and its Communist international organization intends to do . . . what are the limits, if any, to their expansive and proselytising tactics. . . . From Stettin in the Baltic to Trieste in the Adriatic, an iron curtain has descended across the Continent." The Soviet Union, in this view, did not necessarily want war, but it did want what was usually only to be had by force—the indefinite expansion of its power and influence. The thesis went on to conclude that "neither the sure prevention of war, nor the continuous rise of world organization will be gained without . . . a special relationship between the British Commonwealth and Empire and the United States."[4] In effect, this position challenged the idea that the United Nations must operate on a

---

[3] U.S. Department of State *Bulletin,* Vol. 16 (Jan. 19, 1947), p. 123.

[4] Winston Churchill, "Alliance of English-Speaking People," *Vital Speeches of the Day,* Vol. 12 (Mar. 15, 1946), pp. 329-32. It should be noted that this position, although attacked on the grounds that it would inevitably lead to a head-on collision with the Soviet Union, was never wholly lost sight of in American calculations. It later furnished the argumentative basis for the North Atlantic Treaty, for the concept of atomic deterrence, and, as its most extreme development, for the concept of preventive war.

basis of great power unity and called instead for an organized confrontation of the Soviet bloc. In short, Soviet power would expand until halted by a force capable of matching it. If not so checked, it would acquire world hegemony.

In contrast, the view to which Secretary of Commerce Wallace gave the fullest expression can be called the "soft" interpretation:

. . . Enemies of yesterday and false friends of today continually try to provoke war between the United States and Russia. . . . On our part, we should recognize that we have no more business in the *political* affairs of Eastern Europe than Russia has in the *political* affairs of Latin America. . . . Under friendly competition the Russian world and the American world will gradually become more alike. . . . Russia must be convinced that we are not planning for war against her and we must be certain that Russia is not carrying on territorial expansion or world domination through native communists.[5]

In a later and fuller development of this position, it was pointed out that 80 per cent of the United States national budget was applicable to military use, that the atomic bomb tests at Bikini were generally interpreted as American saber-rattling, and that technological developments were in any event outdating the state-craft of threat and bluster. Some form of adjustment and of friendly agreement was the only solution to the situation. The implications of this interpretation were that American-Soviet relations were a two-way street. Some blame fell to the United States: its high military budget, its collaboration with "British imperialism," and its support of reactionary elements abroad. The Soviet Union would respond, not to "toughness," but only to a breaking of the vicious circle of suspicion. Agreement would be possible once an atmosphere of confidence was re-created.[6]

With this range of interpretations of Soviet intentions before it, and with a corresponding range of recommended courses of action, American opinion wavered uncertainly. Only two points were

[5] Henry A. Wallace, "The Way to Peace," *Vital Speeches of the Day*, Vol. 12 (Oct. 1, 1946), pp. 738-41.

[6] While this position brought Secretary Wallace an unusual amount of fan mail, and continued to be restated in various forms for at least eighteen months, it was not the position of the administration or the basis on which the Secretary of State was then negotiating at the Paris Peace Conference. Secretary Byrnes insisted that the position of the United States was being undermined by apparently divided counsel at the center of authority, and Secretary Wallace was asked to resign on September 20, 1946. See James C. Byrnes, *Speaking Frankly* (1947), pp. 239-43.

clear. The first was that the Soviet Union came sharply into focus as the major obstacle to the continued successful pursuit of the basic objectives of the United States. The second was that extreme solutions, calling for the complete abandonment of these objectives and for the radical redirection of policies, were not generally acceptable. Consequently, the middle ground, developed and followed by the administration, was widely supported. In addressing the United Nations General Assembly in October 1946, President Truman adequately stated this middle course.

> The war has left many parts of the world in turmoil. Differences have arisen among the Allies. It will not help us to pretend that this is not the case. But it is not necessary to exaggerate the differences.
>
> For my part, I believe there is no difference of interest that need stand in the way of settling these problems and of settling them in accordance with the United Nations Charter. Above all, we must not permit differences in economic and social systems to stand in the way of peace either now or in the future. To permit the United Nations to be broken into irreconcilable parts by different political philosophies would bring disaster to the world.[7]

The Middle Ground

Factors other than a natural democratic preference for the middle position, however, played a part in holding the administration to this line. Although the government was becoming seriously concerned with the Soviet problem and public opinion was beginning to react unfavorably to Soviet behavior, the area of possible policy choices was being narrowed by domestic political considerations. A $275 billion national debt was felt to require a very careful scrutiny of any proposals that would increase the tax burden. Strong foreign policies, especially if they called for supporting appropriations, would not get a sympathetic hearing. With the end of the war, the executive branch of the government was no longer as free to make policy decisions as had been the case earlier. The Senate was eager to resume its traditional watchdog role over the conduct of the foreign affairs of the nation. The Executive conception of the possible policy choices that might be open was becoming more obviously limited by the adjustments that had to be made to the temper of the public and of the Congress.

In this connection, the deterioration of United States military

[7] U.S. Department of State *Bulletin*, Vol. 15 (Nov. 3, 1946), p. 810.

power that was discussed above became of practical significance. In 1946, the Soviet Union had about 6,000,000 men in its army, and its aircraft industry had been extensively retooled. In July 1946, the United States Congress had specified that the size of the army should not exceed 1,550,000 and that this number should be progressively reduced to 1,070,000 by July 1947. Briefly, except for the atomic bomb, the United States was without the military capability to pursue a bold diplomatic course. And the greater number of those who advocated the "toughest" line showed no eagerness to pay the monetary and human costs of following their own advice.[8] When to this reluctance was added the further pressure of the considerable segments of opinion that accepted the thesis of walking softly, making adjustments, and removing suspicions, it is not hard to understand why the middle course was not only the one chosen, but probably the only one available. In spite of its shortcomings, it did not foreclose on either the present or the future, and it could be followed without rigidity.

The President, in his State of the Union Message of January 1947, tried to express these mixed values.

We live in a world in which strength on the part of peace-loving nations is still the greatest deterrent to aggression. World stability can be destroyed when nations with great responsibilities neglect to maintain the means of discharging those responsibilities.

This is an age when unforeseen attack could come with unprecedented speed. We must be strong enough to defeat, and thus to forestall, any such attack. . . . When a system of collective security under the United Nations has been established we shall be willing to lead in collective disarmament, but, until such a system becomes a reality, we must not again allow our weakness to invite attack.[9]

This middle course, however, could provide little more than a broad guideline of temporary validity. When confronted by concrete Soviet action in specific situations, it produced an impression, against which United States officials struggled with a growing sense of frustration, that the United States, while holding to admirable

---

[8] General Marshall, recounting his experiences as Secretary of State, said: "I remember . . . I was being pressed constantly, particularly when in Moscow, by radio message after radio message, to give the Russians hell. . . . At that time, the facilities for giving them hell . . . was $1\frac{1}{3}$ divisions over the entire United States. That is quite a proposition when you deal with somebody with over 260 and you have $1\frac{1}{3}$." Quoted, John C. Sparrow, *History of Personnel Demobilization in the United States Army* (1951), p. 282.

[9] U.S. Department of State *Bulletin*, Vol. 16 (Jan. 19, 1947), pp. 124-25.

long-term goals, was in fact becoming involved in disjointed re-actions to a determined, coherent, and immediate Soviet policy of domination.

The middle course was consequently an unstable basis for a consistent and effective reordering of United States objectives and reshaping of United States foreign policies. It was accordingly sub-jected to gradual modification both from within and without the government. Within the government, an awareness was widely developed of the importance of relating intentions and capabilities. Either objectives had to be defined in more limited terms, or capa-bilities had to be brought to a greater condition of readiness for use. Also within the government, a balance sheet of American-Soviet relations was being drawn up. The conclusion was forcing itself that the international position of the United States, and hence the position of the West as a whole, was steadily deteriorating.

There was a growing shift in judgment toward the view that the Soviet Union could not be trusted. It was increasingly believed that the Soviet Government would not co-operate with the United States in world affairs. This, however, did not lead to the view that the Soviet Union was a major threat to world peace. Furthermore, a large minority of the American people rejected the idea of an Anglo-Amer-ican alliance, but there was a general desire for unspecified action. In sum, in late 1946, a large majority of Americans appeared to favor the position of the government as it was being acted upon by the Secre-tary of State; only a small minority favored Wallace. Simultaneously, a large number of the American people favored keeping American occupation troops in Europe. There were evidences of waverings of judgment with respect to specific questions. These were accompanied by a slow change in the basis of judgment.

One point that stands out is that both official judgment and pub-lic feeling were shifting in the same direction, even though the rates of speed were different. Accordingly, there was no fundamental pulling in opposite ways. The proof of this was demonstrated early in 1947 when the administration proposed to aid Greece to resist Communist insurrection and Turkey to resist Soviet pressure. This proposal, which was presented in terms that implied a con-sidered intention consistently to check further Soviet expansion, was accepted by the American people.

It is justifiable, therefore, to confine the rest of this analysis to a more detailed review of the forms in which an official view of Soviet intentions finally crystallized. This crystallization is of primary importance for understanding the new pattern of purpose and the new policies that the United States began to shape in 1947.

Judgments of the Soviet Union

The essential change was from a judgment that the Soviet Union was a typical, if somewhat heavy-handed, stubborn, and suspicious nation-state, to a judgment that the Soviet Union was an aggressive state, which, by virtue of its control of the Communist party, enjoyed the benefits of an international trouble-maker. The first judgment had furnished a reasonable basis for assuming that, as a typical nation-state, the Soviet Union could enter into agreements with other typical nation-states in good faith, because it would be obvious that Soviet national interests could be forwarded by acting correctly within the traditional framework of the nation-state system. Even if differences developed, this view assumed that there was always a point reached in the give and take of state relations at which adjustment and accommodation could be expected. The second judgment, however, did away with all such expectations. Instead, it involved the assumption that both because of its political and social philosophy and its structure of power, the Soviet Union and its instrument of international communism were at war and would always be at war with the United States and the West. Even if agreements were reached, they could not be relied upon; for, in the Communist view, agreements were temporary expedients to be rejected when circumstances permitted.

Communist writings provided ample texts to support such a judgment, and these writings were studied in order to explain Soviet moves and to justify the American stand. An analysis, published in July 1947 by *Foreign Affairs* under the title of "The Sources of Soviet Conduct," summarized the results of this search.[10] The substance of the article had been shaped in the preceding year. In a dispatch from Moscow in February 1946, George Kennan said:

. . . The Kremlin's neurotic view of world affairs is the traditional and instinctive Russian sense of insecurity. . . . Russian rulers . . . have learned

[10] By X. "The Sources of Soviet Conduct," *Foreign Affairs*, Vol. 25 (July 1947), pp. 566-82. The article was written by George Kennan, formerly the United States Chargé d'Affaires in Moscow, and had official blessing; hence its significance.

to seek security only in patient but deadly struggle for the total destruction of rival power, never in compacts and compromises with it.[11]

Consequently, it was concluded that the Soviet Union would exert constant pressure on the international system, using the apparatus of the Communist party to infiltrate, disrupt, and paralyze; using diplomacy to exploit the opportunities created by covert action; and participating in international organizations only to increase its influence or to reduce the influence of other states. Conventional or normal international relations could not be established with a state of this kind.

In particular, this analysis maintained that the Soviet Union was

. . . committed fanatically to the belief that with the United States there can be no permanent *modus vivendi*, that it is desirable and necessary that the internal harmony of our society be disrupted, our traditional way of life be destroyed, the international authority of our state be broken, if Soviet power is to be secure. This political force has complete power of disposition over the energies of one of the world's greatest peoples and the resources of the world's richest national territory. . . . In addition, it has an elaborate and far-flung apparatus for the exertion of its influence in other countries. . . . Finally, it is seemingly inaccessible to considerations of reality in its basic reactions.[12]

A rationale was thus provided to explain the concrete Soviet acts that were being reported from all areas of actual contact between the United States and the Soviet Union. Soviet pressure on Turkey had as its object the establishment of Soviet power in the Eastern Mediterranean. Native Communists were using every possible means in France, Italy, Greece, Japan, and China to prevent those states from achieving political and economic stability—with the goal of seizing power out of chaos always in mind. The Soviet Union was determined to dominate Eastern Europe regardless of Western protests and local resentments. Soviet pressure was increasing throughout Asia.[13] A consistent picture began to take shape in governmental circles and to be transmitted to the public as a necessary basis for action.

In August 1946, Turkey was confronted by new Soviet demands. In the view of the Department of State, these indicated an intention

[11] Walter Millis (ed.), *The Forrestal Diaries* (1951), p. 136.
[12] *Ibid.*, pp. 138-39.
[13] *Ibid.*, pp. 135-40.

to control and dominate. If the Turks gave in, it was officially argued that Greece would be infiltrated and subverted, and that the end result would be Soviet control of the Middle East and a fundamental threat to the world position of Great Britain. The President was advised to take a firm stand in spite of the possibility that the Soviet Union might not back down, and that armed conflict might follow. The recommendation was accepted.

PART TWO

AMERICAN ACTION: 1946-1950

CHAPTER VI

Emergence of a Strategic Concept

IN THE HIGH level conduct of foreign relations, as in the high level conduct of war, a pattern of objectives and policies cannot be reoriented without the development of a corresponding strategic concept. This means an agreed view on how to proceed: in which places, by what means, at what times, and in what order. The term "strategic concept" is a familiar one in military usage. It can be equally well applied to political action although in the political field, the formulation of a strategic concept is likely to be both a slower and a more unregulated process.

The policies of states are not developed in a vacuum. They are at least in part designed to take account of the fact that, in the international system, all states are engaged in trying to achieve objectives and that some of these efforts will coincide, some will proceed quite unrelatedly, and still others will come into conflict. In connection with this last possibility, there is an element in policy making that is concerned with applying policy in a situation in which an opponent can be presumed to be seeking conflicting objectives. It is for this type of situation that a "strategic concept" tends to be developed. In a world as large and complicated as the one in which we live, it is usually not possible to protect against every use that potential enemies may make of their resources. A set of policies that protects against the most dangerous and most probable uses that the presumed opponent can make of its resources usually provides the maximum protection practicable. Therefore policies are partly determined in light of the capabilities and probable intentions of an opposition. Consequently, the assessment of Soviet capabilities that was made in the course of 1946 was an essential element in examining the alternatives that were available to the United States.

Soviet Military Capabilities

In 1946, the Soviet Union had an estimated 6 million men under arms. A system of compulsory military training was in operation, so

99

that the Soviet Union was able to maintain large reserve groups at a high level of training and effectiveness. It was presumed in March 1946 that large numbers of Soviet troops were massed in the Balkans within easy reach of the Turkish borders. The Soviet air force was in a state of readiness, and it was reported that the Soviet aviation industry was retooling to produce new and up-to-date planes.

Given this military strength and the weakness of the forces that could oppose it, it was officially considered in 1946 and 1947 that the Soviet Union, if it chose, could over-run all of Europe (except Great Britain), the Middle East, and North Africa in a few months. Soviet aid to the Chinese Communists was considered capable of producing military victory in China and possibly also in Southeast Asia. Because of Soviet weakness in amphibious military operations, the American occupation forces in Japan were considered capable of holding out for a period of time. The island strongholds in the Pacific were held to be defensible, and no consideration was given to a possible successful Soviet assault against the Western Hemisphere.

It was not officially believed, however, that the Soviet Union would pursue these military courses. Its scavenging of resources from Manchuria, Eastern Germany, and Eastern Europe was generally taken to mean an eagerness to rebuild the Soviet economic machine that had been so badly damaged during the war. It was also believed that the American monopoly of atomic weapons had produced a kind of equilibrium of armed force.

Soviet military objectives were considered to be limited to a defensive holding of the line that had been reached in 1945. Use of the Red army permitted the Soviet Union to manipulate the political situation in the satellite areas and in Eastern Germany. The perimeter that the Red army held through the center of Europe would permit an excellent defense-in-depth of the Soviet Union and would also make it correspondingly difficult for the West to wage more than a delaying retreat in case of Soviet assault. This was particularly true with respect to air power. Western Europe was within easy range of Soviet air bases for tactical operations, while the vital areas of the Soviet Union were at considerable distances from Western bases for strategic bombing operations—especially given the shift of Soviet industry eastward. Moreover, the man-power situation was becoming increasingly favorable to the Soviet Union. The populations in the Soviet orbit were increasing rapidly, and the age level was declining. Western populations, in contrast, were increasing at a slower rate, and the age level was rising.

It was assumed, therefore, that the Red army would be quiescent, except in the defense of the areas it already held, at least until Soviet economic activity was restored and improved, and until the Soviet Union produced the atomic bomb and built a stockpile of atomic weapons. Soviet politico-military objectives, however, would probably become more ambitious as these goals were reached, unless the West constructed a countervailing force. Soviet politico-military objectives could thus be viewed as a function of future Western military strength. While Soviet objectives probably did not include an early overt aggressive move, signs of an increasing Western weakness, or even of a failure to increase Western strength, might change this situation.

Soviet Political Capabilities

The basic instruments of Soviet strength in this respect were considered to be the monolithic political structures of the Soviet Union and of the states in which Communist regimes had been installed, and the centrally directed apparatus of the international Communist party. These two instruments, used in conjunction with military power, were generally regarded as able to produce a pattern of controlled political action unlike anything with which the states of the West were familiar. In fact, there was a tendency in the public mind to attribute extraordinary effectiveness to these instruments. Professional observers, however, noted that beyond the actual limits of the monolithic authority of the Soviet state itself, the effectiveness of the instruments began to diminish somewhat, and concluded that, at least, their use had to be significantly modified to fit the particular conditions prevailing in specific areas. In this way, Communist parties in France and Italy worked to remain within the national governments and to gain parliamentary majorities. When forced into opposition, as they were in mid-1947, their political effectiveness was reduced. However, these same observers noted that the Soviet Union, working through diplomatic as well as other channels, would and did exert pressures on France and Italy to impede co-operation with the United States and made use of the national Communist party instrument for this purpose.

Soviet political capabilities in Germany and Austria were officially held to be limited. Communism, at least in its Soviet guise, was not politically attractive. The uncontrolled behavior of the Soviet army of occupation, the economic stripping of Eastern Germany, and the policy of playing on the anti-German sentiments of the French and the Eastern Europeans made force a necessary instrument. The establishment of Communist rule in East Germany was not considered the result of political capability.

In the Far East, the party instrumentality was used effectively in Korea, where it would be combined with Soviet military power. In China, the same instrumentality could be controlled with certainty only to the extent that the Soviet Union was willing and able to supply the means for the party to act, or was prepared to accept the Chinese Communist goals as satisfactory.

In colonial areas generally, the Soviet political capability was highly rated. The Soviet Union supported the aspirations for freedom of the colonial peoples. This position served to benefit the Soviet Union in two ways. It helped to weaken the Western powers by reducing their empires and dislocating their economies. It gained good will for the Soviet Union, for it could pose as the champion of colonial liberation. In areas that had not yet won their independence, the prestige gained by the Soviet Union as a champion of self-determination generally aided the recruiting campaigns of local Communist parties.

Although the Soviet Union was in the minority in the United Nations, its use of the veto in the Security Council and the vigor and skill with which it used the Organization as a forum for building popular support for its international position and for impeding action by other states gave it a significant supporting political instrument. Furthermore, as the United States Government was quick to realize, this was an area of political action in which it could easily be put at a disadvantage in view of its consistently stated position of seeking to develop the United Nations Organization as the foundation of an international system of peace and security.

In general, these various political capabilities were officially believed adequate to enable the Soviet Union to consolidate its authority in the areas that it had occupied during the war, to establish control in certain contiguous areas, and to engage in subversive opposition in countries where the seizure of political power was not immediately possible.

Soviet Economic Capabilities

The postwar five-year plan of the Soviet Union aimed at restoring prewar rates of production by 1948. As of the end of 1947, however, these goals were still on paper.

In order to rebuild the Soviet economy, the Red army was used in occupied areas to collect equipment and materials. Billions of dollars in industrial equipment was removed from Manchuria and Eastern Europe. It was noted, however, that the benefit to the Soviet economy was not in proportion to the monetary values involved, for much of the equipment was lost, destroyed, or made useless by removal. In addition, skills were not always available in the Soviet Union for making proper use of the removed equipment.

In the immediate postwar years, the Soviet Union had negotiated with the satellite countries economic agreements that could only be called exploitative. Under the agreements, these countries were often obliged to subsidize the sale of their products to the Soviet Union. The deflation of the Soviet currency toward the end of 1947 was officially interpreted as an effort to raise the consumption levels of the Soviet people. Therefore, production of goods for consumption was emphasized relatively at the expense of capital goods production. The harsh economic plans foreshadowed in 1947 for Poland and Czechoslovakia and the new trade agreements with those countries gave evidence of a Soviet effort to recoup its capital goods losses by imports from the satellite economies. This could be accomplished only by diverting satellite sales of wheat, bread grains, timber, and manufactured products from the West to the Soviet Union. Because trade with the West was traditionally advantageous to the satellite economies as well as to the nations of Western Europe, the purposes of the plans could be accomplished only by depressing severely the standards of living in the satellites. The Soviet Union, with specific exceptions, could not supply the quantities of raw materials and other resources required. This situation probably required tighter political controls in the satellites as a response to the tensions that lowered standards of living induce.

These reported developments were widely interpreted as evidence of the weak competitive position of the Soviet economy. Therefore, it was considered that the economic growth of the Soviet and satellite areas would have to be almost self-generated, at least for the immediate future. The broad conclusion was, therefore, officially drawn that the limited Soviet economic resources would be mainly allocated to rebuilding the Soviet economy. It was also believed that the economies of the states of Eastern Europe would be exploited for the same purpose. It was held to be unlikely that resources would be applied to sustaining an aggressive military action, even of a fairly local character. It was believed, however, that they could and would be diverted to the maintenance of a defensive war. Finally, the relative weakness of the Soviet economy was considered to imply that Soviet political capabilities would be used to impede at every turn the reorganization and expansion of the economic capabilities of the Western nations, and that the military capability would be used as an implied threat, in order to avoid an increasingly unfavorable position.

A Concept for American Action

In addition to the process of reorientation that went on in American thinking through 1946 and to the new judgment of Soviet intentions and capabilities that accompanied this reorientation, a changed view of the structure of the international system developed. This became the basis for a concept of action. It was in this period that the term "bipolar" came into use. Whatever may have been thought and said about "one world," the demonstrated fact, it was held, was the bipolarity of the international system.

The world was split into two power groupings, in each of which a single state—in one case, the Soviet Union, in the other, the United States—played a predominant role. In the pre-First World War system of alliances, there had been two opposing coalitions, but each had consisted of a number of states of relatively equivalent power, any one of which might play a major role in determining policy or in changing the line-up of states. In the post-Second World War situation, the Soviet Union and the United States formed powerful centers of attraction, both for the allegiances of states and for the determination of their policies. Minor states became captives of their geographic or economic situations. While neutral and independent powers continued to exist, their roles were restricted. They were less important both in number and influence than at any other period of modern history. Finally, the focal points of power, the United States and the Soviet Union, were considered to have basically irreconcilable philosophies and fundamentally different types of political communities.

Much can be said in criticism of this view of the political structure of the world. Its shortcomings as a description of the international system and as a basis for action were gradually revealed by events, and will be taken up in their proper place later in this volume. What is important here is that the view had sufficient validity by the end of 1946 to make it widely acceptable as an account of the international scene and as an adequate basis for setting fresh objectives and designing relevant policies. It provided a formula for the exposition of a strategic concept of the United States.

The concept was given unusually concise statement in the article in *Foreign Affairs* in 1947.[1] In this article the strategy of containment was first publicly presented. A preliminary analysis of Soviet motivation led into an examination of the courses of action that the Soviet Union could be expected to follow and that the United States should develop in opposition.

The essence of the concept was that single and sporadic efforts to counteract Soviet policy would fail. The Soviet-Communist doctrine of historical inevitability inclined Soviet policy to patience and to tenacity. There was every doctrinal ground for Soviet policy to be flexible: to retreat in the face of strong opposition; to advance whenever and wherever no countervailing force was present. The policy and action of the United States, therefore, had to be long-term, patient, firm, vigilant, and consistent. Nothing would suffice but steadiness and consistency of purpose. Threats, bluffs, and mere outward displays of "toughness" would fail. Whatever the substance of United States policy toward the Soviet Union, the strategy of its application should be to contain Soviet power "by the adroit and vigilant application of counter-force at a series of constantly shifting geographical and political points, corresponding to the shifts and manoeuvres of Soviet policy."[2]

The strategic concept went on to consider the exploitation of the opportunities that it could be expected to create. There were weaknesses in the Soviet Union. It was believed that police supervision, forced industrialization, and the toll of war had left the Soviet people tired, disillusioned, and skeptical about the goals of the Communist state. The Soviet economy was deficient. There was a growing diversity of outlook and expectation in the ruling strata of the Soviet Communist party. The monolithic authority of the state

[1] By X. "The Sources of Soviet Conduct," *Foreign Affairs*, Vol. 25, (1947), pp. 566-82.
[2] *Ibid.*, p. 576.

was only a thin crust over the amorphous mass of the Russian people. Any serious break in the crust would produce chaos.

Consequently, it was argued, effective containment by counteraction at every point at which there were signs of encroachment on the interests of a peaceful and stable world would have a long-term frustrating effect on the Soviet state, which in turn would work on the points of weakness of the Soviet system. The hopes of its adherents would wane. Strains within the Soviet Union would increase, and it would be forced to adjust, in one way or another, to the new state of affairs. As this process continued, the United States could look forward to the "break-up or the gradual mellowing of Soviet power."[3]

The strategy thus formulated called for drawing a ring of power—political, economic, and military—around the area of Soviet control. It assumed the indefinite prolongation of some form of conflict. It ruled out any search for accommodation and aimed at bringing the Soviet Union to the point where it would be obliged to do the adjusting.

The extent to which this concept was adopted by the United States Government as an exclusive basis for the development and execution of national policies cannot, of course, be measured. However, the available evidence suggests that it was a fairly accurate, although more formally worked out, record of a pattern of ideas that was being given great credence, gained wide acceptance, and was used as a general guideline.

As a concept, however, it had certain limitations. It was a long-range strategy, not a program of action that could produce immediate results. It was a conservative strategy advocated for what was by definition a conflict of indeterminate length. It required a constant tactical maneuvering of a kind difficult for democratically organized states, whose control over their instruments of policy was relatively weak. They were consequently at a disadvantage as compared with the Soviet Union in conducting a strategy of this kind. It was a strategy from which it was extremely difficult to deduce specific objectives and relevant policies. All that was predicated was that pressure should be consistently applied, everywhere, all the time. This purpose could not be readily translated into the provision and allocation of resources. Consequently, objectives could not be arranged in any sort of priority of importance. Because each

---

[3] *Ibid.,* p. 582.

was of equal significance, no clue was given regarding what should come first if a choice had to be made. As a concept, it tended to rule out a very important alternative course of action: the testing of situations to see if compromise were possible in specific policy areas. Finally, it was a strategy of reacting, and left the initiative to the Soviet Union. Evidence of the degree to which the strategy of containment was acted upon officially is to be found in the way in which these implicit limitations were dealt with in concrete instances, and caused the concept itself to be modified and reformulated.

Alternative Ways of Containing

Inasmuch as the strategic concept of containment did not automatically set up objectives or indicate definite courses of action, a considerable field for discussion remained open. The concept could be agreed upon while the ways of executing it could continue to be controversial. The next step in this analysis is, accordingly, to examine the alternative ways of containing the Soviet Union that were recognized and advocated within the United States Government. This is an essential preliminary to tracing the course that actually was developed under the confused and confusing impact of events and current problems.

The basic alternatives were indicated by the means at the disposal of the United States—military, economic, and political. Various possible courses could be conceived that differed from one another in respect to which of these means was selected as predominant—the other means falling into supporting roles. In addition, a course could be envisaged in which all means were thought of as usable in a fluid and changing relationship. The full range of the governmental and public discussion of ways of containing falls within this set of possible courses, although many other combinations were suggested at some time or other. The preference of any particular advocate or group of advocates was likely to be conditioned by the values they cherished or the expectations they held. The common ground, however, was the judgment that the Soviet Union was the predominant obstacle to the accomplishment of the goals set by the United States, that this obstacle would become a threat to the United States unless it were dealt with, and that any further expansion of Soviet-Communist power—whether by force, threat of force, or subversion—had to be prevented.

Moreover, certain elements in the situation were generally accepted as given. The United States was obligated to regard the United Nations Organization as an institutional basis for maintaining the peace and security of the world, and it was committed to provide military forces for and to participate in measures approved by the Security Council for this purpose.[4] The United States was also obligated, by the Inter-American Treaty of Reciprocal Assistance, to maintain the security of the Western Hemisphere. This treaty was linked with the United Nations Charter. Thus in the view of important and well-organized bodies of opinion, the implementation of a strategy of containment had to recognize the superior claims of these international instrumentalities. The emphasis desired by this line of reasoning was primarily political. Political action, it was argued, would be most effective if it were taken through these organized international channels. In effect, this body of opinion said: do what obviously must be done, but do it under the aegis of the world organization.

The United States, however, had other actual or implied interests and obligations that did not come within this framework. These were military-strategic in nature and were widely dispersed in Asia, in the Western Pacific Islands, in Great Britain, in Iceland, in the Azores, in Europe, and in North and West Africa. They were the concomitants of base rights and occupation responsibilities. These were duly emphasized by those who were inclined to look to military means as the key to containment. This view also looked to the re-establishment of American military power, to military alliances, and to the exploitation of positions already held or obtainable on the circumference of the area to be quarantined.

Furthermore, the United States was actively embarked on a foreign economic policy that sought, quite aside from strategic considerations, to maintain economically and politically healthy states in the areas involved in the strategy of containment. A considerable portion of its resources had been put into relief and rehabilitation programs. More was flowing into international financial agencies, and still more was being made available in the form of grants and loans. A good case could be made for increasing these actions and using them to implement a strategy of containment. The argu-

---

[4] It was, of course, understood that such measures could not be initiated without the express agreement of the United States. This was ensured by the right of veto.

ment here ran that communism thrived and Soviet authority expanded in areas where social instability followed from economic uncertainty and from underproduction and underconsumption. The restoration of a stable, expanding, economic activity in Europe and the improvement of economic and social standards elsewhere would result in the establishment of a belt of solid, reliable, healthy states around the Soviet Union and its satellites. These states in their own interest would be increasingly committed and increasingly able to play their part in the containment of Soviet-Communist power.

Finally, the United States had a monopoly of atomic weapons. While it is virtually impossible to determine whether there was a generally accepted estimate in 1946 of the significance of the monopoly, it is probable that this fact exercised considerable influence in producing an agreed course of national action out of a multiplicity of stoutly advocated possible courses. However, the conception of the atomic bomb as "the great deterrent" came at a later date and appears to be a product of hindsight. In 1945 and 1946, there was no consensus. Judgment fluctuated between descriptions of "the absolute weapon" and opinions that sought to deflate its importance. Except for an immediate effort on the part of the United States to negotiate in the United Nations for the international control of atomic energy, the existence of the new weapon did not appear comprehensively and consistently in official thinking. Although war plans might be based on the use of the bomb, this was not the same thing as an agreed understanding of how it might be used as an instrument of policy. Consequently, an atmosphere of uncertainty and ambiguity prevailed that would have made it hard to treat the existence of this monopoly of nuclear weapons as a deterrent on either the objectives or the policies of the Soviet Union; at least not as a deterrent separate from, and of more significance than, other restraints.

Deterrence, however, was not the main point. The main point in the period under consideration was the value placed on the exclusive possession of the atomic bomb as an item in a balance sheet of United States and Soviet intentions and capabilities. For example, the Secretary of Defense noted:

As long as we can outproduce the world, can control the sea and can strike inland with the atomic bomb, we can assume certain risks otherwise unacceptable in an effort to restore world trade, to restore the balance of power—military power—and to eliminate some of the conditions which breed war.[5]

In so far as the basis of a policy can be reconstructed from the evidence of the actions ultimately taken, the possession of the atomic bomb seems to have influenced judgment generally in much the way it worked in the case of the Secretary of Defense: that is, as an insurance against risk and as an indeterminate hedge against contingencies. With it in pocket, it was felt to be possible to follow less extreme courses, such as one that would give primacy to ready military power; that is to say, to develop policies that required the minimum rather than the maximum adjustments of the domestic social economy of the American people. As a matter of fact, policies of the middle range were better suited at the end of 1946 to the temper of American opinion and to the international values that the United States continued to place high in its order of objectives. A common understanding and a working consensus had not yet been reached either among the American people or within the United States Government. Certainly one did not yet exist between the people and the government, but the material for reaching consensus was present.

Choice—The Truman Doctrine

The necessity for making a choice and for developing a pattern of action out of a range of alternatives began to become pressing by the end of 1946. The specific situation in which action had to be taken was the civil war in Greece, where Communist forces were making a serious bid to overthrow a duly and popularly elected government that was being sustained economically by Great Britain.

The question of aid to Greece and Turkey first arose at the Cabinet level in a meeting of September 25, 1946, at which a Department of State paper, advocating aid to friendly countries, including Greece and Turkey, was discussed. The paper was generally endorsed. A related paper on military aid was, however, considered too restrictive by some, and the advisability of including military aid to Turkey was urged. Although the Department of State paper advocated a general policy of aid to countries subscribing to principles similar to those of the United States and of withholding aid

[5] Walter Millis (ed.), *The Forrestal Diaries* (1951), pp. 350-51.

from countries that, because of adverse will or helplessness, opposed the principles of the United States, the purpose of the specific programs of aid that were developed from this base appears to have been the containment of Communist power.[6]

No action was taken on this proposal for some time. Meanwhile, the basic discussion of alternatives continued. Early in 1947, however, the British Government gave the United States notice that it would be unable to continue to give economic and military support to Greece and Turkey beyond the end of March. Viewed against the events and interpretations of the preceding twelve months, this was seen as giving the Soviet Union a free hand in the Turkish Straits and, in the end, as permitting the intrusion of Soviet influence into the Eastern Mediterranean and the Middle East. With this, two questions that had been gone over in principle were presented in a concrete form. Here was a situation to which the concept of containment was applicable. Was it to be applied? If this was to be the point at which the direction of American action was to be changed, what form was containment to take?

Decisions were made with remarkable speed considering their implications. It must be recalled, however, that the substance of the issue had been pretty thoroughly argued, and that the alternative general forms of action had been identified and examined at some length. At any rate, by March, the United States had decided to take over the British role in Greece and Turkey, and the President had asked the Congress for $400 million for direct aid to those countries. The proposal was justified in terms of the national security of the United States. It was supported on the grounds that "it must be the policy of the United States to support free peoples who are resisting attempted subjugation by armed minorities or by outside pressures," and that the United States "must assist free peoples to work out their own destinies in their own way." With respect to means, it was recommended that the assistance should be given "primarily through economic and financial aid which is essential to economic stability and orderly political processes."[7]

Other parts of the President's message made it clear that the administration proposed to be explicit about its resistance to Soviet

[6] See Joseph M. Jones, *The Fifteen Weeks* (1955) for an account of the genesis of the Truman Doctrine.

[7] U.S. Department of State *Bulletin*, Vol. 16 (Mar. 23, 1947), p. 536.

expansion, intended to produce a favorable psychological reaction in Europe, and worked to emphasize that it was prepared to commit its resources to the containment of communism. It must be noted, however, that economic means were given primacy, political means followed closely, and military means were strictly subordinated. Furthermore, although the decision did not involve the use of United Nations channels, the existence of the international organization was not ignored. The President stated:

We have considered how the United Nations might assist in this crisis. But the situation is an urgent one requiring immediate action, and the United Nations and its related organizations are not in a position to extend help of the kind that is required.

Nevertheless, the President added,

To insure the peaceful development of nations, free from coercion, the United States has taken a leading part in establishing the United Nations. The United Nations is designed to make possible freedom and independence for all its members. We shall not realize our objectives, however, unless we are willing to help free peoples to maintain their free institutions and their national integrity against aggressive movements that seek to impose upon them totalitarian regimes.[8]

Such objections as were voiced to the proposed policy were based on its by-passing the United Nations and on the fear that it would lead to war. The bedrock of public feeling, however, accepted the decision and was inclined to be relieved by concrete signs of action. A majority of the American people appeared to be in favor of aid to Greece. In brief, the selected course, pieced together as it was from diverse considerations and various possibilities, would seem to have been well adjusted to the circumstances of the moment. It identified a new objective, not by abandoning former goals, but by setting more realistic priorities. The goal of a peaceful and secure international system remained valid, but an obstacle to its realization had appeared. This obstacle had to be dealt with as an unpleasant but necessary prerequisite to further movement along the desired road. The new course defined a policy for reaching this new objective that employed the most readily available United States resources in the manner most acceptable to the American people.

[8] *Ibid.*, pp. 535-36.

CHAPTER VII
Broad Lines of Policy

THE THREE YEARS between the proposal to aid Greece and Turkey (March 1947) and the outbreak of fighting in Korea (June 1950) were marked, so far as United States foreign relations were concerned, by a steady and even more extensive development of policies conditioned by the strategic concept of countering the power of the Soviet Union. It must be emphasized again that these broad lines of action were not developed and implemented in a vacuum. They rested on the assumption of a bipolar world, one part of which—the Soviet bloc—was organized and equipped for action, and the other part of which—the United States and such nations as it could bring into some sort of association with itself—was unorganized and, although potentially strong, in a condition of dangerous unreadiness. In these circumstances, the official analysis ran, the strategy of containment required two complementary motivations: the first was a willingness on the part of the United States to oppose the Soviet Union as and when necessary by any and all means; the second was a willingness on the part of the United States to assist other nations to oppose Soviet-Communism as and when necessary by any and all means, and thus to distribute the burden of containing the Soviet Union more widely through that part of the international system that was soon to become known as the free world.

In effect, this was understood to mean two things. The United States had to accept the risk of war with the Soviet Union and to bring itself to a condition of readiness for meeting this risk, And the United States had to accept the burden of creating an organization of the free world that would be, no matter how different in structure and purpose, at least equivalent in power and in determination to the organization of the Soviet bloc.

Finally, while the broad outlines of policy could be determined by the United States, their solid substance and the claims they would make on American resources would have to be measured by the strength of the reactions of the Soviet Union. This followed inevitably from the bipolar view, in which a strategy of expansion and a strategy of containment were seen as the reciprocally interacting grounds of policy. Although both the United States and the Soviet Union could propose, neither was master of the ultimate disposition.

As the United States developed its policies for confronting the Soviet Union and the Soviet Union continued to maintain its policies of expansion, the scope of American action tended to broaden as Soviet pressures seemed to mount. At the same time Soviet action tended to shift to areas where the United States had not yet built up obstacles. There is a certain symbolic significance in the fact that this particular three years of conflict and adjustment of power relations start in Europe and the Middle East and end in the Far East and Korea.

The Truman Doctrine Opens the Way

It is a matter of some interest that what was proposed to the Congress and emerged as Public Law 75, "An Act to provide for assistance to Greece and Turkey,"[1] became known at once as the Truman Doctrine. It was quickly and generally recognized, and the feeling was encouraged by the administration, that more was involved in the way of policy than an *ad hoc* appropriation of $400 million to meet an emergency. A new direction had been set, and, however varied the interpretations of the purpose and the policy, no one seems to have doubted that a fundamental change had been made.

Much was made at the time of the way in which the proposed action dismissed the United Nations as an effective instrument for the conduct of state relations. The best reasoned objections to the proposal were based on the argument that the United States was abandoning a principle of collective security under international control and turning to the outworn practices of "power politics." On the face of it, this was a substantive criticism. In effect, the proposal was the first action after the war in which American opposition to the Soviet Union was put into a channel other than the United Nations.

The real significance of the proposal was not, however, so generally grasped. It lay in the fact that a genuine rearrangement of values and priorities had been made in the decision-making circles

---

[1] 61 Stat. 103.

of the United States Government. It was tacitly accepted, even though not explicitly stated, that a world community of law did not exist and was not likely rapidly to emerge from the Grand Alliance of the war or from the United Nations, the institutionalized shadow of that alliance. The achievement of this world community, formerly an objective of high priority, was now given a lower order of importance. The corollary of this was that the United States, in framing objectives and policies, acted more as if it were a participant in a conventional system of nation-states, in which the achievement of national purposes was to be gained by the well-tested processes of power. From this point on, the primary United States objective, as revealed by policy, was to build a coalition of states in order to contain Soviet-Communism. As things worked out in fact, even the United Nations Organization itself was used as an instrument for this purpose.

But this is not the only element in the situation to which attention should be drawn. The President, in presenting his proposals, had shaped his remarks in a way that lifted their application above the situation of Greece and Turkey and converted them into important generalizations. Note should be taken of the following:

. . . A militant minority, exploiting human want and misery, was able to create political chaos which . . . has made economic recovery impossible.

The peoples of a number of countries of the world have recently had totalitarian regimes forced upon them against their will. The Government of the United States has made frequent protests against coercion and intimidation, in violation of the Yalta agreement. . . .

At the present moment in world history, nearly every nation must choose between alternative ways of life. The choice is too often not a free one.

. . . it must be the policy of the United States to support free peoples who are resisting attempted subjugation by armed minorities or by outside pressures. . . .

. . . we cannot allow changes in the *status quo* in violation of the Charter of the United Nations by such methods as coercion, or by such subterfuges as political infiltration. . . .

The seeds of totalitarian regimes are nurtured by misery and want. They spread and grow in the evil soil of poverty and strife. They reach their full growth when the hope of a people for a better life has died.

We must keep that hope alive.

If we falter . . . we may endanger the peace of the world—and we shall surely endanger the welfare of our own Nation.[2]

[2] U.S. Department of State *Bulletin,* Vol. 16 (Mar. 23, 1947), pp. 534-37.

These phrasings opened questions larger than events in Greece and Turkey by treating those events as typical and not as isolated instances. By doing so, they furnished a basis for more comprehensive answers than were necessarily required by the immediate situation. Future developments make this clear, but it is also important to grasp that these generalizations had been built up in the course of a year's experience of international life as affected by Soviet policies. At any rate, the Truman Doctrine was rightly called a "doctrine" because it initiated a new pattern of American action.

In spite of the fact, however, that this new pattern had a stated security motivation, the means that were proposed for its execution were those of economic assistance. The choice of economic means as primary was significant in several ways. It linked the present proposals with the whole structure of relief, reconstruction, grants, and loans that had been developed during and after the war, and in this respect appeared to be merely an extension of past practices, modified only by the concept of containment. The playing down of political action avoided questions of seeming to interfere in the domestic affairs of other states, or of entangling the United States unduly. The playing down of military means avoided even more delicate questions of the state of the American military establishment and of seeming to make counter threats of force and endangering world peace. In fact, except for overtones of generalization, the proposals were moderate and tentative. The United States remained relatively uncommitted, but the Soviet policy makers now had something to think about.

The congressional enabling act was passed on May 22, 1947, and the required agreements with Greece and Turkey were signed on June 20 and July 12, respectively. By this time, however, the field of vision had been enlarged, not because of any significant Soviet or Communist reaction to the Truman Doctrine, but because the United States Government had been taking a new look at its own foreign economic objectives and policies. A re-examination of these matters was needed for several reasons. In and of themselves, the foreign economic policies were not producing their designed results. Furthermore, the relation was ambiguous between this pattern of action, which after all had been worked out in terms of international co-operation in "one world," and the strategy of containment, which was based on a presumption of a bipolar world and a cold war.

In the period since the war, the United States had extended credits to Great Britain of $3.75 billion, had furnished France well over $2 billion, mainly as loans and credits for particular needs, and had put about $1.5 billion into Italy. The return on this capital expenditure, either in terms of progress toward basic economic objectives or of the basic reconstruction and stabilization of the economies of individual countries, had been unsatisfactory. Great Britain was drawing on its assets at an alarming rate and, as the British withdrawal from Greece and Turkey showed, was not likely to be able to pull its weight beside the United States in reshaping a world economic system. France, where the Communists were then out of the government but were fomenting strikes and impeding economic recovery, was obviously living from hand to mouth both economically and politically. Italy was in an equally precarious condition.

On strictly economic grounds alone, the situation was ripe for review, and the technical experts were already at work. One thing was becoming clear: the pattern of foreign economic policy was an amalgam of separate programs and procedures—odds and ends as well as large chunks of assistance reaching individual countries through a confused assortment of channels. In addition, although this was nontechnical, political events—Soviet-Communist actions— were reducing the effectiveness of existing economic policies. On this point, the economist, the political expert, and the military came together, and found a common ground in a strategic concept of confronting the Soviet Union.

The Marshall Plan

Even while the Congress was debating the Greek-Turkish proposals, the economic condition of Europe was deteriorating visibly, and existence of a Soviet-Communist threat to European political stability was becoming more generally accepted. Consequently, the Truman Doctrine did mark a first step on a new path and was not merely one more *ad hoc* proposition. The next step was the European Recovery Program—the Marshall Plan—a much longer and firmer stride.

The Secretary of State, speaking on June 5, 1947, suggested that the countries of Europe should plan their economic recovery in common. He said that any governments willing to co-operate to this end would get encouragement and help from the United States. The speed with which the suggestion was acted upon in Europe and the rapidity with which it was worked out in the United States indicate that it was probably not made without careful consideration of the effect it was desired to produce.

The Secretary was very careful to avoid positive commitments: "It would be neither fitting nor efficacious for this Government to undertake to draw up unilaterally a program designed to place Europe on its feet economically. . . . The initiative, I think, must come from Europe." On the other hand, no opening was given to American opinion, to European opinion, or to Soviet policy to say that the United States Government was splitting the world into two camps. "Our policy is directed not against any country or doctrine but against hunger, poverty, desperation, and chaos. Its purpose should be the revival of a working economy in the world so as to permit the emergence of political and social conditions in which free institutions can exist."[3]

The United States, in opening up this proposal, had to find its way through a variety of considerations. The magnitude of the demands on American resources that might result would probably not be acceptable to American opinion if presented solely as further economic assistance to foreign countries. But precisely the same demands might be accepted as part of a strategy of resisting a Soviet threat. Conversely, however, the proposal could not be presented to the states of Western Europe as a means of implementing an American strategy. There was a definite tendency in these states to seek an adjustment and to improve economic and political relations with the Soviet Union and its satellites. Yet, it was necessary, if European initiative were to be generated, to give some sign that the United States was thinking in broad terms and was seeking to set up a relationship that would have both continuity and coherence.

The Secretary of State, feeling the way through these multiple considerations, indicated at a subsequent press conference that his remarks were applicable to all European countries that were willing to co-operate, and that the Department of State had estimated that $5 billion or $6 billion a year for several years was the order of magnitude. This left the door open for the Soviet Union and the Communist regimes of Eastern Europe to come in, although this was a bold position to take so far as the temper of the United States

[3] *Ibid.* (June 15, 1947), pp. 1159-60.

Congress and people were concerned. However, if the Soviet bloc did not come in, the onus of rejecting a fair offer lay with the Soviet Union. If the Soviet bloc did come in, it would mean one of two things: either there had been a shift in Soviet policy toward co-operative goals, or the Soviet Union wanted to sabotage the proposal from within. The latter possibility could be countered in the event, but not without some difficulties and dangers. The former could be countered by equivalent American policy.

The unanswered questions were quickly settled. Great Britain and France called a preliminary conference. France, solicitous for Soviet good will, informed the Soviet Union that British representatives were coming to Paris on their own initiative and also indicated a desire to have bilateral discussions with the Soviet Union. Both Britain and France then invited the Soviet Union to a preliminary conference of the three powers. Great Britain showed less sensitivity than France about Soviet participation. Foreign Secretary Bevin announced that Europe would proceed to consider the Marshall Plan with or without Soviet participation, and that no long delays or prolonged discussions would be tolerated because speedy action was essential.

There were indications that at least two countries in the Soviet sphere of influence—Czechoslovakia and Poland—would co-operate. On June 16, however, *Pravda* attacked the Marshall Plan as a disguised Truman Doctrine, which would apply political pressures through dollar aid, and asserted that the United States could not seriously want Soviet participation.

Nevertheless, the Soviet Union attended a preliminary three power conference with Great Britain and France in Paris on June 27. The Soviet Foreign Minister soon created a deadlock by proposing conditions that were plainly unacceptable. All efforts to break the impasse failed, and the Soviet delegation withdrew. This decision simplified the situation for the United States by removing an obstacle to congressional approval. On July 3, 1947, invitations to a general conference were sent to all European countries, including the Soviet satellites, but not including Spain. Fourteen Western European countries accepted.[4] All the Soviet satellites rejected the invitation, although the decisions of Poland and Czechoslovakia were in doubt for a time. The conference opened on July 12 and

---

[4] In addition to Great Britain and France, representatives were present from Austria, Belgium, Denmark, Greece, Iceland, Ireland, Italy, Luxembourg, the Netherlands, Norway, Portugal, Sweden, Switzerland and Turkey.

established a Committee of European Economic Cooperation (CEEC) to gather information on European requirements and on the availability of supplies. The committee report, completed at the end of August, envisaged a four-year recovery program requiring supplementation by $29 billion in American assistance. Detailed technical reports followed two months later. The emphasis throughout was on voluntary co-operation through the co-ordination of national policies and actions. Each country agreed to make every effort:

(i) to develop its production to reach the targets, especially for food and coal;

(ii) to make the fullest and most effective use of its existing productive capacity and all available manpower;

(iii) to modernize its equipment and transport, so that labour becomes more productive, conditions of work are improved, and standards of living of all peoples of Europe are raised;

(iv) to apply all necessary measures leading to the rapid achievement of internal financial monetary and economic stability while maintaining in each country a high level of employment;

(v) to co-operate with one another and with like-minded countries in all possible steps to reduce the tariff and other barriers to the expansion of trade both between themselves and the rest of the world, in accordance with the principles of the draft Charter for an International Trade Organization;

(vi) to remove progressively the obstacles to the free movement of persons within Europe;

(vii) to organize together the means by which common resources can be developed in partnership.[5]

Meanwhile, in the United States, three governmental bodies examined the American role: the Committee on National Resources and Foreign Aid (the Krug Committee), the Committee on Foreign Aid (the Harriman Committee), and the Council of Economic Advisers. These committees agreed that American resources were more than adequate to support a large program of economic assistance. The Council of Economic Advisers said that 2 or 3 per cent of the gross national product could be safely allocated for this purpose. It fell to the Harriman Committee to set forth the non-economic considerations that were involved.

The interest of the United States in Europe . . . can not be measured simply in economic terms. It is also strategic and political. We all know that we are faced in the world today with two conflicting ideologies. One is a system in which individual rights and liberties are maintained. The opposing system is one where iron discipline by the state ruthlessly stamps out individual liberties and obliterates all opposition.

Our position in the world has been based for at least a century on the existence in Europe of a number of strong states committed by tradition and inclination to the democratic concept. . . . If these countries by democratic means do not attain an improvement in their affairs, they may be driven to turn in the opposite direction. Therein lies the strength of the Communist tactic; it wins by default when misery and chaos are great enough. Therefore the countries of Western Europe must be restored to a position where they may retain full faith in the validity of their traditional approaches to world affairs and again exert their full influence and authority in international life.[6]

Out of this activity, American and European, came in June 1948 the Economic Cooperation Act. It provided for the establishment of the Economic Cooperation Administration (ECA), with headquarters in Washington, to administer the new foreign assistance program. The new agency was to be directed by an administrator appointed by the President and confirmed by the Senate. The act also provided for the establishment of the Office of the Special Representative in Paris, and missions were set up in all of the participating countries except Iceland and Switzerland. To represent the participating countries collectively, the Organization of European Economic Cooperation (OEEC) was created. This organization prepared and executed measures of economic co-operation, reviewed the actions of individual countries, and assisted United States authorities initially by recommending the distribution of funds among the participating states.

For its part, the United States Government, while acknowledging the security aspects of the program, made it clear that it believed that some such program for Europe would have been necessary support for American objectives even if there had been no threat from the Soviet Union and from international communism.

Up to this point, except for the already mentioned political and security context in which the program was placed, the policy was formulated and developed in economic terms and by technical experts. In 1949, a new political objective was superimposed. In the amendments of April 1949 to the Economic Cooperation Act of 1948, it was recorded by the Congress that: "It is further declared to be the policy of the people of the United States to encourage the

[6] President's Committee on Foreign Aid, *European Recovery and American Aid* (1947), p. 4.

unification of Europe."[7] This purpose had not been mentioned in the original proposals or during the discussions that attended their conversion into the original act of Congress.[8] Its appearance in early 1949 can probably be explained by the course of events in 1948, and particularly by the fact that the strategy of containment was also being worked out along another course—the negotiation of a military alliance in the North Atlantic Treaty.

Once the objective of European unification was stated, however, it began to assume great importance in American eyes. Politically, the history of the United States seemed to demonstrate the value of bringing sovereign states together in a higher unity. Economically, American strength seemed to be traceable to the absence of the economic barriers that so often accompany political sovereignty. Militarily, a coalition of too many sovereign authorities was inefficient. At any rate, the ECA began to press its European correspondents in this matter. The ECA Administrator stated in a speech in Paris, in October 1949, that it was an American purpose:

. . . to move ahead on a far-reaching program to build in Western Europe a more dynamic, expanding economy which will promise steady improvement in the conditions of life for all its people. This . . . means nothing less than an integration of the Western European economy. . . .

The substance of such integration would be the formation of a single large market within which quantitative restrictions on the movements of goods, monetary barriers to the flow of payments and, eventually, all tariffs are permanently swept away. The fact that we have in the United States a single market of 150,000,000 consumers has been indispensable to the strength and efficiency of our economy. The creation of a permanent, freely trading area, comprising 270,000,000 consumers in Western Europe, would have a multitude of helpful consequences. It would accelerate the development of large-scale, low cost production industries. It would make the effective use of all resources easier, the stifling of healthy competition more difficult.

This was not intended as mere exhortation because there was an implied threat in the closing remarks:

I have made a number of references of the urgency of starting immediately on this program of integration. My conviction on this point is based, in the first place, on the acute realization of the very short time still remaining during which American aid will be available to cushion the

---

[7] 62 Stat. 137, as amended by 63 Stat. 50.

[8] It has, however, been claimed by some that the purpose was implicit. See Donald C. Stone, "The Impact of U.S. Assistance Programs on the Political and Economic Integration of Western Europe," *American Political Science Review,* Vol. 46 (December 1952), pp. 1106-16.

inevitable short-run dislocations which a program of integration will involve. There is another very important reason for speed. The people and the Congress of the United States, and I am sure, a great majority of the people of Europe have instinctively felt that economic integration is essential if there is to be an end to Europe's recurring economic crises.[9]

With this end in view, economic means began to be subordinated to political means; for integration or unification, whichever term was preferred, could only be a product of political action. It could not be created by economic technicians. Whether deliberately, the program of economic assistance was increasingly adjusted in conception and execution to the growing requirements of the strategy of containment.

As this volume is not concerned here with the Marshall Plan in its technical aspects, there is no need to do more than state that it achieved much of its original purpose. The vital margin of aid supplied to Europe provided an important leverage for the mobilization of European economic and political resources in behalf of United States objectives. Their expanding economies became assets to the military coalition that was simultaneously being built. Moreover, this leverage could work without bringing pressure to bear on specific issues, and the distasteful, and often self-defeating, consequences of too dictatorial a policy could largely be avoided. If the Western European countries were not ready politically, economically, or psychologically to develop policies designed specifically to contain communism, their economic recovery, assisted by the Marshall Plan, was nevertheless an addition to American strength, or, at least, partially remedied American vulnerability. Furthermore, it made it possible for the United States to make more effective use of its own resources in opposing Communist expansion. In short, this action, although fitted within the strategy of containment, implied more. In various ways it worked toward what was soon to be called a "position of strength"—that is to a situation to which Soviet policy might conceivably be forced to adjust.

Concurrent Security Action

The states of Western Europe were not indifferent to their security or to the security aspects of the American aid program. The same Soviet actions that changed American views in 1946 and

[9] Paul G. Hoffman, "An Expanding Economy Through Economic Integration," *Vital Speeches of the Day,* Vol. 16 (Nov. 15, 1949), pp. 68-70.

1947 weighed equally on the minds of European statesmen, and the effect of the Communist seizure of power in Czechoslovakia at the end of February 1948 caused even more alarm in Europe than it did in the United States. In particular, the British and French governments took such initiative as was possible and attempted to create a defensive coalition by treaty, although knowing full well that it would be a paper alliance in the absence of participation by the United States. Furthermore, if American opinion came to regard the political unification of Europe as a desirable and necessary end, the idea had already been set in motion in Europe and by Europeans.

In January 1948, the British Foreign Secretary, following the abortive meetings of the Council of Foreign Ministers in London at the end of 1947, and after talks with the United States Secretary of State, proposed an alliance of Great Britain, France, Belgium, the Netherlands, and Luxembourg. He referred to "the conception of the unity of Europe and the preservation of Europe as the heart of western civilization."[10] He proposed that the existing Anglo-French Treaty of Dunkirk (signed in March 1947) should be made the nucleus of a larger alliance that might in time be extended to include "other historic members of European civilization." The proposal became the Brussels Pact in March 1948, a fifty-year treaty of economic, social, and cultural collaboration and of collective self-defense. Article IV provided that: "If any of the High Contracting Parties should be the object of an armed attack in Europe, the other High Contracting Parties will, in accordance with Article 51 of the Charter of the United Nations, afford the party so attacked all the military and other aid and assistance in their power."[11]

By April, a permanent consultative organization had been established, consisting of a Council, a Permanent Commission, and a

[10] Hansard, *Parliamentary Debates*, 446 H. C. DEB 5 S Col. 396-97 (Jan. 22, 1948).

[11] "Treaty Between Belgium, France, Luxembourg, the Netherlands and the United Kingdom of Great Britain and Northern Ireland," *United Nations Treaty Series*, Vol. 30 (1948), pp. 53-63. Article 51 of the United Nations Charter reads in part: "Nothing in the present Charter shall impair the inherent right of individual or collective self-defense if an armed attack occurs against a Member . . . until the Security Council has taken the measures necessary to maintain international peace and security."

This article, as well as Article 52, authorizing regional arrangements for the maintenance of peace and security, were frequently referred to from this time on as demonstrating that the development of alliances was not undermining the authority of the United Nations.

Permanent Military Commission. American and Canadian observers were associated with the work of the Military Commission from its inception. The treaty was highly approved by the United States. The President, addressing the Congress said:

Its significance goes far beyond the actual terms of the agreement itself. It is a notable step in the direction of unity in Europe. . . . This development deserves our full support. I am confident that the United States will, by appropriate means, extend to the free nations the support which the situation requires.[12]

While this purely European development was under way, the European Recovery Program was being debated through the United States Congress. Official testimony at the committee hearings increasingly emphasized the security implications of the proposed legislation and noted with approval the evidence of a unified defense policy in Europe. This emphasis, however, was not allowed to override the fact that it was economic and not military means that were being recommended. Yet, the United States Government was seriously concerned about its military future. Its intelligence agencies were reporting that a Soviet attack on Western Europe was a real possibility.

At the end of April, President Truman called a high level conference to consider the threat to the United States. John Foster Dulles, at that time a consultant to the Department of State, describing the conference later, said that there was fear in Western Europe of Communist uprisings, particularly in France and Italy. "All of this interfered greatly with economic recovery," he said, and "it seemed that only a decisive pronouncement by the United States would check the fear that was inspired by Moscow." Agreement was reached, therefore, "to proceed along the lines of a North Atlantic regional pact." Senator Vandenberg, who was present, indicated that "he felt that the Senate liked the idea of regional associations and would be disposed to approve in principle a further developing of such associations for collective defense."[13] In May Senator Vandenberg introduced a resolution, which was passed on June 11, 1948, that among other advices, encouraged the Executive to proceed to the:

Progressive development of regional and other collective arrangements for individual and collective self-defense in accordance with the purposes, principles, and provisions of the Charter [of the United Nations].

[12] U.S. Department of State *Bulletin*, Vol. 18 (Mar. 28, 1948), p. 419.
[13] John Foster Dulles, *War or Peace* (1950), pp. 95-96.

Association of the United States, by constitutional process, with such regional and other collective arrangements as are based on continuous and effective self-help and mutual aid, and as affect its national security.[14]

In other words, the Congress went on record as agreeing in advance to the entrance of the United States into military alliances. This, in effect, smoothed the way for extending the strategy of containment beyond reliance on economic means. As an Undersecretary of State later stated: "The contents of this resolution . . . became our guide in the discussion and subsequent negotiations which led to the conclusion of the North Atlantic Pact."[15]

The North Atlantic Treaty Organization

With both the Economic Cooperation Act and the Vandenberg Resolution in hand, the executive branch began exploratory talks in July 1948 with the signers of the Brussels Pact and Canada about a regional defense arrangement for the North Atlantic area. The number of interested parties was later increased to twelve. By January 1949, President Truman reported in his inaugural address that negotiations were proceeding and that:

The primary purpose of these agreements is to provide unmistakable proof of the joint determination of the free countries to resist armed attack from any quarter. . . .
If we can make it sufficiently clear, in advance, that any armed attack affecting our national security would be met with overwhelming force, the armed attack might never occur.[16]

The North Atlantic Treaty was signed on April 4, 1948, and ratified by the Senate in late July, after extensive hearings and considerable debate.[17] Both the hearings and the debate suggested that the policy makers were, however much they judged their proposals to be required by circumstances, beginning to press against the

---

[14] *Congressional Record*, Vol. 94, Pt. 6, 80 Cong. 2 sess., p. 7791.

[15] *North Atlantic Treaty*, Hearings before the Senate Committee on Foreign Relations, 81 Cong. 1 sess., Pt. I, p. 237.

[16] U.S. Department of State *Bulletin*, Vol. 20 (Jan. 30, 1949), pp. 124-25.

[17] The original signers were Belgium, Canada, Denmark, France, Great Britain, Iceland, Italy, Luxembourg, Netherlands, Norway, Portugal, and the United States. Sweden was strongly pressed by the United States to join, but refused to do so. Greece and Turkey, at American insistence, were admitted to the organization at a later date as was the German Federal Republic.

outer limits of American opinion as it was then constituted. Various senators attempted to enter reservations to the treaty—against stationing American troops in Europe, against acknowledging a moral or legal obligation to furnish or supply arms, armaments, military, naval, or air supplies, including atomic bombs and information relating thereto. These were defeated. But in addition to these attempted hedges against precise military commitments, public feeling became restive at the implication that United States policy was abandoning the United Nations, was organizing a military coalition against the Soviet Union, and was moving toward developing military means to achieve its objectives. The margin of success for the administration was narrower than had been hoped for, but the choice seemed unavoidable, and policy was able to move one more step in the preferred direction.

Articles 3 and 5 of the treaty were the key operative ones. In Article 3, the signatories agreed, separately and jointly, "by means of continuous and effective self-help and mutual aid," to "maintain and develop their individual and collective capacity to resist armed attack." Article 5 set forth the primary obligation incurred:

The Parties agree that an armed attack against one or more of them in Europe or North America shall be considered an attack against them all; and consequently they agree that, if such an armed attack occurs, each of them, in exercise of the right of individual or collective self-defense recognized by Article 51 of the Charter of the United Nations, will assist the Party or Parties so attacked by taking forthwith, individually and in concert with the other Parties, such action as it deems necessary, including the use of armed force, to restore and maintain the security of the North Atlantic area.[18]

For the rest, the signatories reaffirmed their faith in and their obligations under the United Nations Charter; undertook to strengthen their free institutions to promote conditions of stability and well-being, to eliminate conflict in their economic policies, and to encourage economic collaboration; and, finally, to consult together whenever the territorial integrity, political independence, or security of any one of them was threatened.

Ratifications were completed, the treaty came into force at the end of August 1949, and representatives of the signatory states began to set up a North Atlantic Treaty Organization (NATO) to execute

[18] For text of North Atlantic Treaty, see *United Nations Treaty Series,* Vol. 34, No. 541 (1949), pp. 244-55.

the agreement. Out of the work of this group came the announcement of the first meeting of the North Atlantic Council in Washington in September. The Council set up a defense organization: a Defense Committee (composed of the chiefs-of-staff of each of the treaty powers) and a Standing Group (a subcommittee composed of representatives from the United States, Great Britain, and France) to provide continuing guidance for five regional military groups. The Defense Committee met in Washington in October and set up a Military and Supply Board to organize industrial mobilization in Western Europe. At a second meeting of the North Atlantic Council in November, a Defense Financial and Economic Committee was established. By the time the Council held its third session early in January 1950, it was in a position to approve recommendations for an integrated defense plan for the North Atlantic area.

The reference to "an integrated defense plan" opens up a related subject, that of military assistance as distinct from economic assistance. The expansion of policy into the provision of military assistance will be examined separately below. No more need be done here than to note that this particular policy growth had been anticipated in the discussions leading to the North Atlantic Treaty, it being clearly understood that if the defense intent of the treaty were to be realized, this could only be done in the first instance by the allocation of American resources. The administration was accordingly forearmed with supplementary proposals, and the Mutual Defense Assistance Act, providing military assistance for members of NATO, went through the legislative process and became law by early October. Nearly $1.5 billion was appropriated for the first year of operations. The act, however, made it mandatory that the NATO members agree on an integrated defense plan and that this plan be approved by the President before any major funds became available.

This constituted what can be called the paper formulation aspect of the policy. The hard executing part, and the problems that arose, as well as the adjustments that were made, came later. One comment, however, is in order in connection with this preparatory stage. The extension of the strategy of containment to include the concept of a defensive military coalition opened up a whole range of implications that were not clearly envisaged when the basic strategy was adopted.

The most important of these was the practical consequence of shifting support of the United Nations from a primary to a subordinate place in the order of United States objectives. No mere repetition of the phrase, "in accordance with the purposes of the Charter of the United Nations," could conceal the fact that American power and influence were being diverted into channels that were by definition regional, and hence less comprehensive than those provided by the United Nations Organization. This shift, no matter how justified by circumstances, and no matter how satisfactory to the recipients of American assistance, left many states unhappy.

Two problems quickly arose. The first was the tendency of smaller states to group themselves together in various informal ways and to voice, especially in the forum of the United Nations, their unwillingness to be drawn into a bipolar international system. An idea of constituting a neutral bloc, a "third force" in international politics, began to take shape. The second was whether the United States —recalling that containment was containment everywhere, and that remarks about the free world had been extensively made—would extend its commitments beyond the area of the Western Hemisphere and the North Atlantic region.

An important question developed concerning the actual military readiness of the United States itself. The more military power was specified as the instrument of policy, the more explicitly were posed such queries as: To what extent would European states be willing to rebuild their own military forces without a corresponding reestablishment of American forces? And, in this case, how would the American people respond to the practical and personal consequences of being called on to provide the military means?

A general consequence was that entrance into a military coalition fundamentally altered the nature of the American participation in international politics. Although there had been no withdrawal to a position of detachment and isolationism at the end of the war, as some had feared and predicted, the American interest in the shaping of an international system was dispersed through internationally organized channels. United States policies, by being aimed at a universal target, had a somewhat detached quality—overlooking detail in the interest of the larger purpose. This detachment disappeared in the face of Soviet policy and the development of a strategy of containment. The United States was now perforce an active participant in a struggle—gaining in intensity of purpose as its objectives were more specifically stated, but losing detachment as it worked to persuade other nations to support these specific objectives. When consequences of this change in United States relations with other states began to be felt, they caused a good deal of restiveness in American opinion and raised many practical problems for United States policy makers.

The last consequence that will be mentioned arose from the organizational requirements of the new pattern of policy. These requirements were felt by the United States Government, by European governments, and at all points where the United States and European governments had to collaborate on actual programs. The wartime experience of large-scale joint operations was a guide, but no final answer. During the war, the operational problems were mainly concrete and could, for the most part, be treated as puzzles to be solved. Now the operational problems tended to be intangible and political. For the most part, they constituted difficulties that had to be surmounted or side-stepped, but could not be solved with finality. Consequently, each new step in policy was accompanied by a proliferation of new organizations, both within governments and between governments.

In the American system of government and administration, this led to considerable overlapping of authority and to confusion of responsibility, particularly as between military, economic, and political agencies. It also led, in an effort to escape the resulting confusion, to constant attempts to reduce the complex organizational structure to simpler forms. But the problem was not, and has not yet, for that matter, been settled to the satisfaction of all concerned.[19]

Nevertheless, it is a fact that men and governments do become accustomed to living and working quite happily and effectively in intricate organizational atmospheres. They develop habits and skills to compensate for what appears to a theoretician to be an almost

---

[19] It should be remembered that the basis for such rationalization had been established by the National Security Act of 1947, 61 Stat. 496, by which the National Security Council, the Central Intelligence Agency, and the National Security Resources Board were set up. The intent of the law was "to provide a comprehensive program for the future security of the United States; to provide for the establishment of integrated policies and procedures for the departments, agencies, and functions of the Government relating to security."

unbearable administrative complexity. Furthermore, overlapping authorities, especially in multinational organizations, often result in the growth of co-operative techniques and attitudes that are actually more effective in producing a detailed and daily interlocking and integration of effort than could be achieved by a more mechanically perfect organization.

Military Assistance Programs

It was mentioned above that the United States policy makers were ready to follow the ratification of the North Atlantic Treaty with a proposal for providing military assistance to members of the treaty organization, and that this had resulted in the Mutual Defense Assistance Act of October 1949, with an initial appropriation of $1.5 billion. On the face of it, this was a justifiable extension of the course on which United States policy was set. If foreign governments were being aided to rebuild their economies, in part as a contribution to their own and to American security, their military establishments should also be rebuilt in order that they might be able to defend their reconstructed economies. The logic of containment certainly did not admit creating economic strength only to have that strength gathered in at a later date by the Soviet bloc because there was no military strength available to protect it.

Initially, the administration had maintained that there was no essential connection between the North Atlantic Treaty and the military assistance proposals; they were separate, although related instruments of policy. The Secretary of State, in connection with hearings on the Treaty, said, that "even without the existence of the North Atlantic Treaty, the need for assistance for defense of these countries would be the same."[20] This position, however, and the original proposals, did not stand up to congressional criticism. Some members objected to the mounting costs of an "open-ended" policy. Others objected to the "blank check" nature of the authority to aid that the President requested. Still others, taking the administration at its word, argued for the inclusion of China as a recipient. There was a general questioning of the absence of any specified machinery by which the United States could be sure of getting its money's worth. Running through the whole debate was a reluctance

[20] *North Atlantic Treaty*, Hearings, Pt. I, p. 12.

to shift the emphasis of American policy with finality from economic recovery to the building of military strength.[21]

The preamble to the act, as finally passed, indicates the level at which the differences were resolved.

The Congress hereby finds that the efforts of the United States and other countries to promote peace and security in furtherance of the purposes of the Charter of the United Nations require additional measures of support based upon the principles of continuous and effective self-help and mutual aid. These measures include the furnishing of military assistance essential to enable the United States and other nations dedicated to the purposes and principles of the United Nations Charter to participate effectively in arrangements for individual and collective self-defense in support of those purposes and principles.

The preamble further specified that

. . . Economic recovery is essential to international peace and security and must be given clear priority. The Congress also recognizes that the increased confidence of free peoples in their abilities to resist direct or indirect aggression and to maintain internal security will advance such recovery and support political stability.

And, finally, the Congress kept the way open for still further expansion of the strategy of containment, by favoring

. . . the creation by the free countries and the free peoples of the Far East of a joint organization, consistent with the Charter of the United Nations, to establish a program of self-help and mutual co-operation designed to develop their economic and social well-being, to safeguard basic rights and liberties and to protect their security and independence.[22]

The act also reflected a growing feeling that too many programs were coming into operation and that their consolidation within a unifying framework of objectives and policy was necessary. Consequently, the act became a package in which old, new, and future desirable programs of different kinds of military assistance were combined and given a single, all-embracing purpose. Title I related the North Atlantic Treaty to a program of military assistance for Western Europe. It required that assistance had to be requested, and that assistance should be given only on the basis of bilaterally negotiated agreements with individual governments to ensure that

[21] A detailed account of the legislative history of the act can be found in William Adams Brown, Jr. and Redvers Opie, *American Foreign Assistance* (1953), pp. 457-63.

[22] 63 Stat. 714.

integrated defense planning, integrated military effort, and unified direction would be achieved to the satisfaction of the United States. Title II authorized the continuance of assistance to Greece and Turkey. Title III authorized the continuance of assistance to Iran, the Republic of Korea, and the Republic of the Philippines, and earmarked part of the funds appropriated for use in the general area of China. Three types of assistance were involved: financial disbursements in Western Europe, arms and equipment, and technical and training assistance.

In a precise sense, the Mutual Defense Assistance Act of 1949 can be regarded as the implementing legislation needed to activate the North Atlantic Treaty. But, even in this limited interpretation, it represented a supplementary policy choice of considerable significance: the decision to complete a policy by converting an agreement in principle into an operation in concrete reality. In passing this act, the Congress defined an American obligation to act in concert with a group of eleven states to prepare, and, if necessary, to carry out mutually agreed plans for military action.

It is worth noting, however, that this decision was awkwardly hedged by an unwillingness to accept its full implications. NATO was a voluntary association of sovereign and equal states. Its course as an alliance could, therefore, be determined only by negotiation, adjustment of views, and compromise. The United States, although superior as power resources are measured, was only one of twelve when it came to the determination of basic political questions. The Mutual Defense Assistance Act introduced a new note. By defining the terms on which assistance would be given—that is, by unilaterally stipulating conditions—the United States Government was obliged to work both as a leading influence in an alliance and as a final and sole judge of the purpose of the alliance. The Executive, responsible for the conduct of foreign relations, was in fact embarrassed in dealing with fellow members of NATO.

The military assistance program was very slow in getting under way. Negotiation of the required bilateral agreements was difficult. The work of the treaty organization was impeded. The development of the specified "integrated defense plans" was halting and haphazard. Furthermore, the specification that economic recovery was to be given clear priority allowed prolonged discussions about first principles. These took place within the United States Government between the Economic Cooperation Administration, which was a large, successful, going concern, and the officials responsible for planning and executing programs of military assistance, who were simultaneously engaged in trying to set up a new organization. These unresolved discussions permitted the intended recipient states of NATO to negotiate at great length in order to make sure that their recently achieved economic recovery would be directed toward military ends to the minimum extent possible.

It is probably not going too far to suggest that these difficulties might have dragged on interminably, if the Soviet Union had not tested its first atom bomb in September 1949, and if Soviet-Communist policy had not been set on a crescendo course at this time— a course that reached its critical point in the attack on the Republic of Korea in June 1950. But even with this stimulus, the military assistance program did not become effectively operational until early 1951.

The Point Four Proposal

President Truman, in his inaugural address of January 1949, listed four major lines of policy that the United States would follow to achieve its international objectives. Three were familiar because they were already in operation. The United Nations would continue to be supported. It was the key to the ultimate objectives of international peace and security. Programs to strengthen the free world, both those of economic assistance and those of military assistance and collaboration, would be maintained. These, although applicable to creating conditions of peace and security, were basic to achieving the more immediate objective of containing communism. The fourth item was a proposal to the effect that a program of economic development for underdeveloped countries should be initiated on a broad scale.

> . . . We must embark on a bold new program for making the benefits of our scientific advances and industrial progress available for the improvement and growth of underdeveloped areas.
>
> More than half of the people of the world are living in conditions approaching misery. Their food is inadequate. They are victims of disease. Their economic life is primitive and stagnant. Their poverty is a handicap and a threat both to them and to more prosperous areas. . . .
>
> The old imperialism—exploitation for foreign profit—has no place in our plans. What we envisage is a program of development based on the concepts of democratic fair-dealing. . . .
>
> Greater production is the key to prosperity and peace. And the key to

greater production is a wider and more vigorous application of modern scientific and technical knowledge.

Only by helping the least fortunate of its members to help themselves can the human family achieve the decent, satisfying life that is the right of all people.

Democracy alone can supply the vitalizing force to stir the peoples of the world into triumphant action, not only against their human oppressors, but also against their ancient enemies—hunger, misery, and despair.[23]

Multiple, and in some respects contradictory, motivations underlay this proposal. One of the strongest was a feeling in American opinion that the policy lines of the two preceding years had got too far removed from the fundamental interest of the United States in developing an international system of peace and security. Although it might be necessary to prepare defenses against the Soviet Union, the United States should not be diverted entirely from the actions it could simultaneously take to keep moving in the direction of its long-term and more highly principled objectives. Many states in the world, notably the countries of Latin America, the Middle East, and the new nations that had emerged from colonial empires in the Far East, were not within the compass of the major efforts of current American policy. These were areas in which the United States could act through United Nations channels, and thus support the United Nations and serve its own interest in a more stable international system at one and the same time.

Another almost equally strong motivation was a more official judgment to the effect that the strategy of containment had to be extended to cover those regions in which a struggle to escape from a colonial status was mingled with a demand for economic and social betterment, and in which consequent political instability was providing communism with a happy hunting ground. Evidence was accumulating that the Soviet Union, by directing local Communist parties, was putting considerable effort into turning weak, underdeveloped countries against the West and, at the least, was scoring triumphs in a propaganda struggle. The Communists were gaining strength steadily in China, and in other parts of the Far East were the spear head of active rebellion. In this view, a requirement to contain was as justified in Burma and Pakistan, or for that matter in South America, as in Western Europe.

This motivation became coupled with another set of considerations that was beginning to make itself felt. The areas in question

---

[23] U.S. Department of State *Bulletin*, Vol. 20 (Jan. 30, 1949), p. 125.

were, by and large, the producers of raw materials for industrialized countries. As the Economic Recovery Program began to produce results, and as the requirements of the Mutual Defense Assistance Program began to be worked out, the relation between the industrial needs of these programs and the stability of the states that produced raw materials became a source of genuine concern. Furthermore, underdeveloped but newly-independent states, as they took their places in international forums, had begun to press for assistance. They, too, desired progress and stability.

Finally, however, it became apparent to the administration that any comprehensive proposal to these ends would meet with increasing resistance in the Congress on the grounds that the United States was over-extending itself, that the costs would be too high, and that the American people could not carry the world on their shoulders. Whatever was proposed would have to be small-scale and largely symbolic.

By mid-1949 the executive proposals were sent to the Congress. They blended a humanitarian impulse to aid the poor and the weak, a policy of promoting a sound and expanding world trade, a recognition of the need to increase supplies of raw materials, an intent to counter Communist activity in the underdeveloped countries of the world, a wish to act to the greatest possible extent through the United Nations, and the intention of doing all of this with the minimum of financial commitment.

Some important sectors of public opinion saw in the proposals evidence that United States policy was getting back onto the proper track of international co-operation for social betterment, and called for a greater diversion of resources from military to peaceful use. The Congress, however, modified the proposals in ways that diminished their value in relation to the strategy of containment. The debate in the Congress brought to the fore the points on which the legislative branch was beginning seriously to diverge from the executive branch: the unspecified duration and cost of the policies and programs of the administration; the tendency of these programs to be government-operated rather than left to private enterprise and to be multilateral and international rather than bilateral and national; and the feeling that there were so many programs in operation that they were interfering with one another.[24]

---

[24] The Economic Cooperation Administration was engaged in technical developmental programs. The Greek-Turkish aid authorities were engaged in capital investments for long-term development. The United Nations and its spe-

When the Act for International Development was finally approved in May 1950, it reflected these congressional views. Five conditions, all of which combined to emphasize that action would be primarily unilateral United States action, were laid down: the President had to be satisfied—that is, the Executive had to be prepared to demonstrate to the Congress—that the recipient country was paying its fair share of the costs, that it was publicizing the role of the United States, that it was co-ordinating all such programs, that it was making effective use of the American contribution, and that it was co-operating with other participating countries. Because most of these conditions were matters of judgment and opinion rather than of fact, much controversy developed both domestically and abroad.

Generally speaking, because the goal of this last segment of policy —technical assistance—was essentially long-term, it was the least effective adjunct of a short-range purpose. The immediate public relations benefits that attended the President's initial proposals in the form of widespread welcome from underdeveloped countries were largely dissipated as the congressional debate slowly developed and as the proposals were reduced to a small-scale operation. It is true that official warnings against exaggerated expectations had been given. It is equally true that these warnings were wholly disregarded by the governments and peoples of the small states of the world. They all assumed that the United States was at long last ready to live up to the thesis of removing economic rivalry and social injustice from the international system, of bettering standards of living, and of thus laying the basis for a peaceful world. The multiple motivations that were built into the final form of the program made it a very inadequate device for meeting the extensive hopes and the demands that it naturally generated. The program initiated in part as a complementary course of action in a strategy that was being vigorously furthered in other and more extensive ways, quickly receded to a minor and supplementary course of action, to which much devoted service was given by groups and individuals, but which remained on the fringes of operational attention.

The objectives of the United States and the broad patterns of policy that were developed between the end of 1946 and the start of

---

cialized agencies, to which the United States was contributing funds, had many developmental projects in hand. And, finally, many American private agencies of religious, charitable, or commercial kinds were channeling American resources into comparable activities.

1950 were basically conditioned by the conviction that any further expansion of Soviet-Communist influence by force, by threat of force, or by subversion had to be prevented. This conclusion meant an acceptance of the fact that the objectives of the United States as formulated during the war and the operative goals of policy in 1945 had to be relegated to a lower order of importance; or, to express it another way, had to be regarded as more remote than had originally been the case. Containment of Communist expansion and the creation of opposing "situations of strength" were defined as the strategy. A fundamental decision was early made to the effect that the United States would pursue this strategy in collaboration with other states rather than by its own unilaterally developed efforts.

Thus the essential policy line became one of building a coalition, strengthening the individual members of the coalition, and emphasizing collective effort and mutual obligations. This line was developed into specific policies and programs: economic assistance, military assistance, joint military planning, and general developmental programs; all interlocking and all designed to be the complementary instruments of a political purpose. The political purpose, as it came finally to be expressed, was to organize the "free nations" of the world into a loose coalition, composed of various regional groupings, in each of which the United States would be a participant. The whole would be backed by American resources and maintained by comprehensive American commitments. This association of like-minded states was, in principle, to be developed within the framework of the United Nations Charter. Military, political, and economic means would be utilized although in the period covered here, the emphasis was placed on economic measures.

By virtue of its inherent economic and its potential military strength, the United States inevitably became the activating power in the free world and thus lost some of the advantages of the more detached but not isolated position in which it had stood in 1945. Its more specific objectives required more concrete policies, and more concrete policies required more constant and active participation in the give and take of current situations. In this new position, and in consequence of the courses of action it had advocated and initiated, the United States Government was increasingly called upon to give guarantees of military assistance to independent governments threatened by armed force, to supply armaments and material to governments involved in civil war or threatened with

Communist-directed guerrilla tactics, and to grant economic assistance to governments that were willing to join in the pursuit of American objectives.

The basic motivation of this extensive reformulation and redirection of United States action was never more adequately expressed than in the Secretary of State's report on the failure of the London meeting of the Council of Foreign Ministers at the end of 1947.

There is another and I think even more fundamental reason for the frustration which we have encountered in our endeavor to reach for realistic agreement for a peace settlement. In the war struggle Europe was in a large measure shattered. As a result a political vacuum was created, and until this vacuum has been filled by the restoration of a healthy European community, it does not appear possible that paper agreements can assure a lasting peace. Agreements between sovereign states are generally the reflection and not the cause of genuine settlements.

It is for this very reason, I think, that we encountered such complete opposition to almost every proposal the western powers agreed upon. The Soviet Union has recognized the situation in its frank declaration of hostility and opposition to the European Recovery Program. The success of such a program would necessarily mean the establishment of a balance in which the 16 western nations, who have bound their hopes and efforts together, would be rehabilitated, strong in forms of government which guarantee true freedom, opportunity to the individual, and protection against the terror of governmental tyranny.

The issue is really clear-cut, and I fear there can be no settlement until the coming months demonstrate whether or not the civilization of western Europe will prove vigorous enough to rise above the destructive effects of the war and restore a healthy society. Officials of the Soviet Union and leaders of the Communist Parties openly predict that this restoration will not take place. We on the other hand are confident in the rehabilitation of western European civilization with its freedoms.

Now, until the result of this struggle becomes clearly apparent, there will continue to be a very real difficulty to resolve, even on paper, agreed terms for a treaty of peace. *The situation must be stabilized. Western nations at the very least must be firmly established on a basis of government and freedoms* that will preserve all that has been gained in the past centuries by these nations and all that their cooperation promises for the future.[25]

But even the clear statement of purpose, the development of a strategic concept, and the initiation of comprehensive patterns of action were not the whole story. Policies were more than the un-

[25] U.S. Department of State *Bulletin*, Vol. 17 (Dec. 28, 1947), p. 1247. Italics supplied.

conditioned generalizations, presented as proposals for acceptance by the Congress and the American people. They had to be carried out in actual situations. They had to be adjusted to the realities of daily operations. They were confronted by every obstacle and impediment that their opponents could devise. It is this aspect of United States foreign policy that must now be considered; for it was in this connection that the real problems of choices and decision continually arose.

It has already been noted that the strategy of containment was based on a view of the international system as bipolar. This view was never as valid in fact as it seemed to be in theory. And, actually, as the broad lines of United States action began to be developed, the more complex structure of the international political system was gradually revealed. The United States and the Soviet Union came into direct contact at only a limited number of points: in Central Europe (in the four-power occupation of Germany and Austria), in the Far East (in China, Japan, and Korea), and in the Security Council of the United Nations. In all other respects, the United States and the Soviet Union were in reality competing by indirect means for final and authoritative influence in regions where third party sovereignty was still a fact. Consequently, the United States strategy of containment wore very different faces as it was applied in areas of direct contact or in areas of indirect influence on a third party. In the latter case, there was considerable variation in the pattern of effective influence as between Western Europe, the Middle East, and the new nations of Asia.

CHAPTER VIII

Areas of Application: Central and Eastern Europe

THE BROAD patterns of revised United States policy were, of course, applied in actual situations between 1946 and 1949. These situations were of two general kinds: those involving a modification of the postwar settlement that the United States had originally envisaged, and those involving an American effort to organize a coalition of free nations. The first kind of situation developed in Central Europe, in Eastern Europe, and in the Far East; the second in Western Europe, in the Mediterranean, in the Middle East, and among the nations emerging from colonial status. There were important differences between situations in which the United States and the Soviet Union were in physical confrontation.

From the American point of view—and perhaps equally from the Soviet—the common element in both kinds of situations was the over-all relationship of the United States and the Soviet Union. The main lines of action by the United States were roughly guided by a strategic concept of how to conduct these relations in a way that would advance American and check Soviet purposes. Accordingly, what is being examined here is a double process of policy development and policy adjustment. What had been worked out in the form of general proposals was confronted at every stage of execution by resistive fact, by the existence of contrary purposes, and by the deliberately created obstacles of opposing policy operations. The process of development, consequently, is not a clear line; it is a fluctuating, winding course of minor and major adjustments. What emerges at later stages of the double process is not always what was anticipated or desired by the designers of policy.

Germany

There was at the start no governmental machinery in Germany except that set up by the four occupying military forces. The country was divided into four zones, and in each zone supreme authority rested with a national military commander. This authority was subject only to the higher authority of the four

141

commanders—American, British, French, and Soviet—acting unanimously in matters affecting Germany as a whole. Behind these four commanders, there was little in the way of agreed four-power guidance, except an undertaking that the power of Germany as an aggressor state was to be reduced and controlled once and for all. This understanding was not developed in specific policy terms until the Potsdam Conference in August 1945. During the intervening period, each commander, however, received a good deal of guidance from his national political superiors both with respect to the exercise of authority in his zone and with respect to the maintenance of national policy when he acted quadripartitely in matters affecting Germany as a whole.

The situation in the western areas of Germany was initially complicated by the fact that the top military authority was a combined command, Supreme Headquarters Allied Expeditionary Force (SHAEF), and a specific American responsibility did not emerge until July 1945 when this command was dissolved. After this, the United States machinery for exercising authority continued to be complex. It was not until October 1945 that an Office of Military Government (OMGUS), as distinct from the operational theater command of the Army, was set up and assumed the function of executing United States occupation policy.

Even then, the picture of United States policy is obscure because of the number of institutional channels through which it was formulated. The occupation itself was run by the Army under policy guidance from the Department of State. There were, however, inevitable conflicts and disagreements concerning not so much the objectives to be pursued as the priority to be given to various objectives. The Army was primarily concerned with the security of its forces and with mastering its administrative responsibilities. Moreover, the occupation command tended to develop its own bureaucratic objectives. It had the job of conducting the occupation successfully, and it was more concerned with achieving this purpose than with the relation of the occupation to United States global foreign policy objectives. On the other hand, the Department of State was delegated the specific function of relating occupation policy in Germany to American global objectives. In addition, the Department of State was in physical communication with the representatives of other nations and was both more cognizant of, and more susceptible to, the needs of these nations.

Finally, neither the Department of State, nor the United States Army, nor the occupation command was free of internal conflict either in conceiving or in carrying out policy. Differences within organizations are inevitable when policy decisions are involved, but the strong emotions investing German policy exacerbated this factor. The combination of occupation responsibilities and governmental functions was a sore point with the Army, which continually pressed for complete separation of the two functions. The Department of State steadily resisted taking on operational responsibilities. The separation did not take place until 1949, and by then, most of the essential features of United States policy had been set.

Initial Purposes

In the opening stages of the occupation of Germany, the problem was seen primarily in terms of the future security of the victors. Implicit in this interpretation of the problem, however, was the consideration that major power unity was essential to prevent the potential strength of Germany from being reorganized and used once again for aggression. If the wartime allies fell out, the conditions were provided for Germany to regain great power status. There was one important open question involved in this consideration. It was whether the broad agreement on a punitive policy would be accompanied by a supporting agreement to share the costs of such a policy. The United States and Great Britain were not prepared to ignore the gap that would develop in the economy of Europe if Germany could not rebuild a productive economy, and they were concerned with the probable costs to themselves of plugging this gap. France, on the other hand, was not worried by this prospect, and envisaged a situation in which it would replace Germany as the predominant state in Europe. Soviet policy, in marked contrast, was focused on somewhat different ends: reconstruction of Soviet productive capacity at German expense and the vigorous reduction of Germany as a security threat. The Soviet Union had no interest at all in the reconstruction of the European economy. In fact, as events were to prove, it was desirous of seeing this economy permanently weakened.

These were the circumstances in which the United States began to deal with the German problem. Given the responsibility for administering the affairs of a wholly disorganized society, immediate practical tasks bulked large—the re-establishment of police and other public services, the provision and maintenance of minimum living conditions, and the creation of local authority. These could be, and for the most part were, handled by improvisation and without reference to other than practical considerations.

Other tasks, however—the purging of the population for "crimes against peace," "crimes against humanity," and "war crimes"; legal and educational reforms; reorganization of the press and radio; the breaking up of industrial cartels; and the rebuilding of labor unions —were undertaken either on the basis of a punitive concept or on the grounds of a political concept of democratization.[1] There were also administrative burdens that required at least some consultation and negotiation with the authorities of other zones. These involved an occupation currency, interzonal movement, and the handling of expellees, refugees, and displaced persons. Generally, the Soviet authorities were not co-operative in these matters, and agreement was usually confined to the United States and Great Britain.

Although none of these matters could ever be regarded as finally resolved, working agreements were reached. Then the real problems of policy had to be faced. In essence Germany had survived, and since neither time nor life stood still, the issue of the German future arose as a concrete problem. The problem had three aspects: the German economy, German political institutions, and the degree of consensus among the major powers with respect to the future economic and political structure of Germany.

The time scheme is important. In late 1945 the basic objectives of American policy were still linked with the maintenance of major power harmony. The process of re-examining this thesis had scarcely begun. Yet the actual give and take of occupational operations in Germany had gone some way toward weakening the thesis.

The established positions for Germany were the elimination of Nazi military and industrial controls, the political tutoring of the German people, the return of a refurbished German state to the community of nations, and the execution of these tasks by combined four-power action under a unified approach. Slight disagreements and passing failures to reach accord, even if they did not put

---

[1] General guidance in those matters existed in the directive on United States occupation policy contained in JCS 1067. It must be repeated, however, that the detailed execution of these instructions by the military authorities was more realistic and less punitive than was strictly called for. This directive was replaced in July 1947 by a new and non-punitive one.

the Germans immediately in a position to bargain for favors, obliged the zonal authorities to proceed unilaterally because the questions that arose invariably required an action-decision of some kind. The process of making a continual series of small policy choices within the framework of broadly stated purposes that was steadily being more and more strained by the pressure of events can be followed by seeing what took place in connection with the German economy and political institutions.

The allied intention had been to dismantle all German industries designed to produce arms or armaments and to reduce the capital goods production of Germany to a level inconsistent with the maintenance of a war machine. Other proposed modifications in the industrial and transportation structure of Germany were designed to attain the same objective. This implied, of course, that Germany would be treated as an economic unit. In practice, however, the Soviet Union resisted all proposals to this effect. In addition, it dismantled industrial plants and shipped them out of the country without reference to any future plans for a German economy. French objections prevented the establishment of centralized transportation and communication agencies in Germany. The French also objected to centralized trade unions. They pressed for the economic integration of the Saar with France and for some form of international control of the Ruhr industrial complex.

Nevertheless, the fiction of the economic unit was adhered to, and studies continued to be made on this basis. American experts assigned to OMGUS concluded toward the end of 1945 that a German steel production capacity of 7.8 million ingot tons would satisfy the American objective of enabling Germany to play a satisfactory role in the European economy without sustaining a war economy. French experts proposed a ceiling of 7 million tons, the Soviet Union 4.9 million, and Great Britain 9 million tons. The Department of State, however, communicated to OMGUS the conviction of its experts that an annual steel production of 3.5 million tons would suffice to meet Germany's minimum requirements. Late in December, after prolonged four-power discussion, it was agreed to permit Germany to retain a capacity of 7.5 million tons, but to restrict actual production to 5.8 million tons until the Allied Control Council decided otherwise. The Department of State again indicated its displeasure, holding that its estimate was adequate.[2]

[2] See *Germany 1947-49*, The Story in Documents, U.S. Department of State Publication 3556 (1950), pp. 348-56.

The concept of Germany as an economic unit was further invalidated by the continued dispute between the Soviet Union and the other occupying powers over reparations. The Soviet Union insisted on $10 billion as the sum it was to receive—claiming that this amount had been approved at Yalta—while the Western powers felt that so great an amount could be extracted from Germany only if financed by the West. The Soviet Union also refused to account for the capital and consumer goods that it was removing from its zone of Germany. The United States contended that the Potsdam agreement to provide a balanced economy for Germany as a whole was not being fulfilled. The United States representative on the Control Council insisted on an equitable distribution of essential commodities throughout the several zones. The Soviet Union, however, refused to pool resources until the economy had first been balanced. OMGUS therefore in May 1946, ordered removals on reparation accounts to be stopped. Similarly, OMGUS, confronted by resistance in matters of restoring transportation and communication facilities, proceeded unilaterally in the American zone.

The picture that gradually emerged was of an American administration of competent technicians whose primary job was to restore and manage a functioning economy. This administration—as it saw the problem—was hampered by existing allied agreements, harassed by unrealistic directives and by the requirement of trying to obtain the agreement of other powers to what it found necessary. Above all, it grew increasingly indifferent to the concept of a punitive policy, concentrating instead on efficiently constructing a viable socio-economic order in the American zone. If this course of action ran counter to the concept of a unified control of Germany, OMGUS pointed to Soviet and French recalcitrance as having forced its hand.

A somewhat similar pattern of unilateral action was followed in connection with the re-creation of German political institutions. There was no agreed four-power basis for action, except that of tearing apart the state that the Nazis had constructed and putting something else in its place. The United States military authorities perforce restored German county and city government at the earliest possible date. Regional administrations to supervise several counties were also established. Although military government officials still retained final control, local German governmental functions were again in operation. Later in 1945, three states, based partially on the previous state systems, were established in the American zone.

These states had administrations headed by minister-presidents appointed by OMGUS. These administrative apparatuses were made responsible for postal, telegraph, rail, and highway transport.

Soon OMGUS found it desirable to co-ordinate the activities of the states in its zone. On October 5, 1945, a council of states, or *Laenderrat,* composed of the minister-presidents of the three states, was established. In order to avoid the appearance of setting up a separate German government in the American zone of Germany, no capital was chosen, and the *Laenderrat* was not given executive powers. Nevertheless, a permanent secretariat was established in Stuttgart, and working committees were formed to consider such problems as refugee resettlement, the collection and distribution of food, the allocation of transportation and communication facilities, denazification, the redress of Nazi wrongs, land reform, and social measures. Moreover, decisions of the *Laenderrat,* when approved by OMGUS, were issued as decrees by the minister-presidents of the states.

In August 1945 OMGUS encouraged the formation of democratic political parties within the counties. In November, these were permitted to organize on the state level. Elections were permitted in villages in January of the next year, and in counties and larger towns and cities in April and May.

In January 1946, state advisory parliamentary assemblies were established with members selected by the various political parties. OMGUS decided to transform these advisory bodies into assemblies with definite political powers. Early in 1946, the ministers-presidents were required to prepare preliminary drafts for state constitutions and to arrange for the election of constituent assemblies to consider those drafts. These assemblies completed their work in October; the constitutions were ratified in the course of the following year. Generally speaking, they embodied democratic principles as understood by Americans, and each recognized the supreme reserved powers of the occupation authorities. OMGUS retained a guiding influence on the form of political developments even in the fields in which German officials were authorized to act.

Shift in Purpose

Up to this point, it is possible to see these developments in economic and political reconstruction as the almost inescapable outcome of efforts by administrative technicians to deal with the concrete responsibilities that confronted OMGUS in the American zone of Germany. By early 1946, however, the technicians had done all that they could within the limits of their authority, and their achievement now had its own momentum. Either further steps were required to permit what had been created to become self-sustaining, or it would have to be maintained artificially as a charge on American resources. But further steps meant attempting to extend what had been done in the American zone beyond the boundaries of this zone. This confronted OMGUS with two sets of obstacles: the United States policy of punitive four-power control of Germany, and the demonstrated fact that four-power control did not mean the unified control of Germany as a whole, but merely the control of an area in terms of four distinct zones and four national policies.

In these circumstances, something had to give way. It might be the importance that was still officially attached to major power harmony. But if this policy were reduced in importance, so drastic a shift of American purposes would be implied that the consequences would be global and not confined to Germany. Or, the emphasis on a punitive policy—still present in Soviet thinking, in French thinking, in the attitudes of small states bordering Germany, and in many sections of American and British opinion—might weaken; but if this policy were abandoned unilaterally by the United States, it could easily lead to the disappearance of even a semblance of major power unity.

Consequently, the situation was cautiously tested. Early in 1946, when it became clear that neither the industrialized British zone nor the American zone could be made economically viable as separate units, OMGUS recommended bizonal economic fusion. The proposal, made primarily on technical grounds, was denounced by the Soviet Union and rejected by France as undermining four-power unity. Nonetheless fusion—for purely economic reasons—was completed by the end of the year. However, operations could not be kept on the strictly technical plane. Often the state governments, which the United States and Great Britain had permitted, resisted the rulings of the bizonal economic agencies, and the military authorities found it necessary to force the state governments into line. Thus still further co-ordinating action seemed called for, and the proposal was born for a German Economic Council with essential political authority throughout the two zones.[3] Economic fusion therefore generated a requirement for political co-ordination and consolidation. As 1946 came to an end, this trend was not resisted. On the contrary, the course of events led to its encouragement.

Attention must again be called to chronology. The pressure against existing policy of the developments that have been recounted coincided in time with the re-examination of Soviet objectives and policies in general that was taking place at the policy-making levels of the United States Government. Reports from Germany contributed their weight to this re-examination, and the accumulating piecemeal conclusions that were being reached in Washington were fed back to OMGUS by various channels. Although these conclusions were not yet firm enough to produce full-dress policy guidance, positions held firmly earlier were weakening, and the American authorities in Germany had greater freedom to proceed on an *ad hoc* basis than would otherwise have been the case. Until the end of 1946, therefore, when a new frame of action began to be clearly fixed, there was an interim period during which the possible limits of further American action in Germany were in part defined by on-the-spot decisions.

Furthermore, the general review of Soviet policy, when related to the developments that had already been brought about in Germany by United States action, led American policy makers straight to the key question. If Germany could not be, first, controlled, and, second, brought back into the community of nations as a democratic state by the four major powers acting in agreement, what was the alternative? The generally accepted answer was not one that American opinion, public or official, had much pleasure in contemplating. It was that if Germany as a *potential threat* could not produce major power accord, then Germany as a *potential prize* would certainly be a bone of contention between the major powers. Once this answer was faced, however, the evidence undeniably

---

[3] This council was established in May 1947. It was composed of fifty-two delegates, one for every 750,000 persons. Subject to the approval of the bi-partite control board, it was given the functions of adopting and promulgating ordinances in the fields of transport, finance, communications, food, and agriculture, and for the regulation of its own civil service. These functions were accompanied by the power to adopt measures binding on the state governments. The establishment of the council can be regarded as the first step in the direction of a separate West German national government.

suggested that the four powers had failed to develop a common policy for Germany, and that policy for this area had to be based on the contingency of a power struggle with Germany as the prize.[4]

The reality of this contingency became steadily more apparent through 1946. French policy showed growing resistance to all proposals that might restore a German national state with a central government. The Soviet Union, content that France should appear to be the obstacle to four-power unity, played on French security fears of a revived Germany and attacked American courses in Germany as undermining agreed positions. These attacks were phrased to suggest, on the one hand, that it was the policy of the United States to destroy all possibility of a national German state and, on the other hand, that the United States was restoring Germany at the expense of France.

An official American view developed that these attacks represented the genesis of alternative lines of possible Soviet policy. If the attacks got a sympathetic response either from France or Germany, the Soviet Union could emphasize those aspects that accorded with the response and base Soviet policy on them. In any case, the Soviet Union could confuse the issue, gain time to reconsider its position, and take advantage of any new or unforeseen developments. In the meantime, it could concentrate on organizing its own zone in Germany.

Meanwhile, Soviet attacks on American policy were vigorously pressed within Germany. In these circumstances, OMGUS urged that a strong policy statement be made to counteract the Communist appeal. At Stuttgart on September 6, 1946, in the presence of members of the United States Senate and German notables, including the four minister-presidents of the American zone, the United States Secretary of State satisfied this request.[5] He initiated what was, in the event, a policy of confronting the Soviet Union in Germany. While expressing faithfulness to the Potsdam accord and

---

[4] It should be recalled that in April 1946, at a meeting of the foreign ministers, Secretary of State Byrnes formally offered the Soviet Union a four-power treaty designed to keep Germany demilitarized for twenty-five years. It was his thesis that, if Soviet activities in Eastern Europe were security measures designed to protect the Soviet Union from future German aggression, the treaty would solve the problem for the Soviet Union in a satisfactory fashion.

[5] The full text of this speech will be found in U.S. Department of State Bulletin, Vol. 15 (Sept. 15, 1946), pp. 496-501.

to the program for demilitarizing Germany, he stated that the time had come to consider a revision of the economic program for Germany. Insisting that revision was necessitated by the Soviet breach of the reparation agreement, he held out to the Germans hope for a higher standard of living as a consequence of American resistance to Soviet claims on current production and American support for higher levels of industry.

The Secretary favored the economic unification of Germany and stated that "the German people throughout Germany, under proper safeguards, should now be given the primary responsibility for the running of their own affairs." Although some high level controls had still to be maintained primarily for security reasons, the occupying powers should do no more than lay down the rules under which German democracy could govern itself. He then served warning to the Soviet Union that, so long as an occupation army remained in Germany, American forces would be among them.

The Secretary stated clearly that the German territory under Polish administration had not been formally ceded to Poland. Although the United States, in pursuance of its wartime agreements, would support a revision in favor of Poland, the extent of the area to be ceded to Poland would not be determined until a German peace treaty was negotiated. Moreover, he informed France that, if the Saar were integrated economically with France, it would have to readjust its reparation claims. The United States would favor control for security purposes over the whole of Germany, including the Ruhr and the Rhineland, but it would "not favor any controls that would subject the Ruhr and Rhineland to political domination or manipulation of outside powers." He then restated an earlier offer of a security treaty directed against German militarism and extended the time period of the offer to forty years.

The position developed by this speech rapidly became the foundation of a key shift in American objectives. The implications of the new position were markedly distasteful to France, and subsequent developments from this basis had the effect of reducing French policy in Germany to a series of stubborn rear guard actions against proposals that had always to be accepted in the end. But this consequence may have been considered and treated as less important than the crisis that was building up in Greece and the breakdown of American hopes in China. There were, in influential circles in the United States, the stirrings of the idea that German man power and industrial capacity had to be conserved and kept from Communist hands. Still, no matter what the intention, the result was that the United States and the Soviet Union came into defined opposition in Germany. By the end of 1946, reciprocal action and reaction within this frame of reference were the policy order of the day.[6]

The Security Motive

Chronologically, United States policy making was now at the point where the strategic concept of containment began to provide a guide to policy decisions. Its first full-scale application in Greece and Turkey was only a few weeks off. It should be noted, however, that events in Germany had helped to produce this concept and that American policy in Germany fitted into its framework with the minimum of strain. The only difference was that what had previously been set in motion on technical and administrative grounds was now rationalized on security grounds and was carried on with increased energy and a clearer sense of direction. Consequently, the stages in the development of over-all policy—the Marshall Plan, the North Atlantic Treaty, and military assistance— were readily adaptable in principle for use in Germany in relation to Soviet actions. Any difficulties in applying these policies to Germany arose in other connections, most particularly in the field of United States relations within the coalition of free nations.

One vital question, however, appeared very quickly in connection with Germany itself. Nothing could be done about Germany as a whole except by four-power agreement. Significant action by either side was, therefore, confined to the parts of Germany in which its influence and authority could be made to be felt. The operation of different policies in Western and Soviet areas could have only one end result: the creation of two German political communities in two different images. Yet, the more successfully conflicting policy operations proceeded, the more remote became the possibility that

[6] Early in 1947 the Soviet Union announced increases of 200 to 300 per cent in the economic production level of "peacetime industries" in its zone. It also invigorated its denazification program in a manner that led to charges of "political purge." The integration of the Soviet zone into the Soviet power bloc was unmistakably under way.

the United States and the Soviet Union would be able to negotiate an agreed settlement of the German problem.

Concurrent international developments could not be regarded as auspicious for agreement. The Truman Doctrine had been announced to the world on March 12, 1947, two days after the Moscow conference of foreign ministers opened. The Brussels pact, encouraged by the United States, was signed on March 17. Opposing coalitions were being organized. It was unlikely that either could accept a German solution that would permit a reunified Germany to enter the opposing coalition. It was equally unlikely that either side could withdraw its forces from Germany and thus relinquish its authority. Therefore, while it is difficult to say with assurance that neither side genuinely desired agreement, it is perhaps accurate to suggest that neither side was likely in the near future to permit the German problem to be solved except on its terms.[7]

The German problem was split into two levels of action: the zonal level, at which national policies were carried out and the face of Germany was slowly but surely altered to fit the pattern of American-Soviet relations; and the quadripartite level of the meetings of the foreign ministers at which the discussion of the future of Germany as a whole went on fruitlessly in an atmosphere of unreality.

From March 10 to April 24, 1947, the Council of Foreign Ministers met in Moscow. With reference to the problem of Germany they discussed five major topics: reparations; a provisional and permanent German government; the American proposal for a quadripartite treaty providing for the controlled demilitarization of Germany; territorial changes; and coal. The four powers were unable to find a major area of agreement on any of these items. Britain and the United States were almost invariably in opposition to the Soviet Union, and the position of France was shifting.

Following this meeting, the functioning of the Allied Control Council in Berlin bogged down. A propaganda campaign against United States policy was waged by the organs of communication

---

[7] It should be noted that a new situation was created when a part of Germany acquired status as a sovereign state. United States policy moved the West German Republic to this point, and the implications of the new situation were revealed when its Chancellor, Konrad Adenauer, negotiated with the Soviet head of state in September 1955. However, in 1947, no policy maker seriously discerned this still remote contingency.

in the Soviet zone. During October, the information director of OMGUS was ordered by authority in Germany to resist communism throughout the United States zone. Charges were exchanged, each side accused the other of failing to demilitarize its zone or to carry out the denazification program properly; the existence of former Nazis in high places was freely alleged.

Meanwhile, the basic directive under which OMGUS had operated, was replaced. The new directive stated that the basic objective of United States policy in Germany was the "creation of those political, economic and moral conditions . . . which will contribute most effectively to a stable and prosperous Europe."[8] It further stated that the stability and prosperity of Europe and Germany were intertwined. Demilitarization and disarmament were still given as objectives to be pursued, but the economic unification of the Western zones, improved economic conditions, and the development of political institutions were to have high priorities. France officially protested the increase in the German war potential that would result from the policy, but finally gave grudging consent to bizonal actions. The Soviet Union and Poland also delivered vigorous protests.

The foreign ministers met again in London at the end of 1947. No agreements were reached, and tension increased when the conference abruptly broke up. During the meetings, the arguments of the Soviet Union, Great Britain, and the United States were directed primarily to the Germans. Each posed as the champion of German production, economic recovery, and political unity. France, committed to the decentralization and demilitarization of Germany, found itself in danger of being the orphan of the meeting and shifted closer to the Anglo-American line than had hitherto been the case. The French Foreign Minister, when later defending this shift, argued that the Marshall Plan had created an unbridgeable gulf between the United States and Great Britain and the Soviet Union. Consequently, the wartime alliance was not going to hold together to control Germany, and France had to protect itself by acceding to the position of its logical allies.

The reference to the Marshall Plan was revealing, even if not entirely accurate. It will be remembered that this extensive pro-

---

[8] JCS 1779 U.S. Department of State *Bulletin*, Vol. 17 (July 27, 1947), pp. 186-93.

posal of economic aid had been made in June 1947, and had been very promptly acted upon both in Europe and the United States. From the American point of view, the proposal implied that the three western zones of Germany were a part of the Western Europe that was to be aided. The Soviet reaction to the proposal will be recalled. It did not require very clear vision to see that, as the various strands of United States policy were more clearly woven, a German state would be called for. France was concerned with avoiding an end situation in which it would be economically prostrate and politically isolated in Western Europe, while a German state was restored and strengthened.

Great Britain was less sanguine about the implication of the American policy for Germany than was the United States. But it was not as fearful of a reborn Germany as was France and, therefore, could accept the new American policy with better grace and equanimity. Also the administration in the United States for its part, was under strong pressure from the opposition party, which held majorities in both houses of Congress, to implement vigorously the policy it now advocated. The United States, in any event, was now much more concerned with the actual danger arising from Soviet policies than it was with the potential dangers that might rise from a revived Germany.

Toward Sovereignty

In January 1948, the Secretary of State announced to the press that the Department of State was prepared to take over the functions of military government from the Department of the Army.[9] It now became United States policy to move toward the formation of a Western German government. In preparation for this development, six nations—the United States, Great Britain, France, Belgium, the Netherlands, and Luxembourg—met in London in February to consider security measures, political and economic reorganization, and provisional territorial arrangements for Germany. When the conference recessed, a joint communiqué of March 6 stated that agreement had been reached in principle on an international control of the Ruhr, a federal form of government for

---

[9] The change-over was connected with returning major governmental responsibility to the Germans because the Department of State lacked the personnel to administer the United States zone.

Western Germany, and measures for economic co-operation between the three Western zones of Germany.[10]

The six-power meeting was protested vigorously by the Soviet Union as a violation of allied agreements. It is impossible to estimate the influence of these developments on the Communist decision to stage a *coup d'état* and seize power in Czechoslovakia in February. But it is certain that as the confrontation of opposing purposes in Germany sharpened, the Soviet Union took vigorous action to consolidate its controls in Eastern Europe.

The Prague conference of the foreign ministers of Czechoslovakia, Yugoslavia, and Poland strongly deplored the policy of the Western powers in Germany. Soviet Marshal Sokolovsky introduced this declaration on March 20, 1948, at a meeting of the Allied Control Council in Berlin. A bitter debate developed, and neither side seemed to desire to conciliate the other. Sokolovsky, who was Chairman of the Control Council at the time, terminated the meeting abruptly. It soon became apparent that none of the four powers was prepared to request a resumption of Control Council meetings and that the last pretenses of a quadripartite control of Germany were being abandoned.

Before this point was reached, however, the United States had ceased to consider the concurrence of the Soviet Union as something to be sought in the development of its German policy. The main lines were set in opposition to the Soviet Union, and possible Soviet counteractions became factors to be taken into account. The real area of concern had shifted to negotiating the goals, the scope, and the timing of the German policy with Great Britain, France, and other interested free nations. This ground will be quickly covered before going on with the account of American-Soviet relations.

The broad points of difference that exacerbated these negotiations were as follows:

---

[10] See U.S. Department of State *Bulletin,* Vol. 18 (Mar. 21, 1948), pp. 380-81. The decisions of this conference illustrate a characteristic response to a well-known dilemma in state relations. A victorious coalition, confronted by the need to make adjustments to the new situation that victory has created, tends to rebuild defeated states in order to meet presumed elements of threat in the new situation. At the same time, the process of strengthening a defeated enemy is restrained by a fear that it may be put in a position to revive the very threat that victory has recently put an end to. Germany presented this kind of dilemma to both Soviet and Western policy, although here the concern is mainly with the American interpretation of the problem.

1. While the United States and Great Britain agreed on the goal of a viable German state made up of the three western zones, France sought reservations, in the name of French security, against future German aggression.

2. The French concept of security was so broadly formulated that it ran counter to American and British proposals for political centralization, for economic growth, and for the integration of Western Germany into the political and economic structure of Western Europe.

3. While Great Britain and the United States did not accept the French position in principle, they did, in the interest of presenting a common Western front to the Soviet Union, try to meet French objections as they were raised individually. In this respect they stood on common ground, but they differed on the general character of the German state that they had agreed to create. The British sought to establish institutions that would reflect the political, economic, and social concepts of the British Labour Government. The Americans sought to establish institutions that would reflect the patterns of a "free enterprise" society.

4. The United States was primarily concerned with its position *vis-à-vis* the Soviet Union. Great Britain was also concerned with its relations with the Soviet Union but, in addition, was interested in maintaining a superior British influence in Western Europe. France was primarily concerned with ensuring that Germany would not become the predominant state in the Western European community of states.

The interplay of all these motivations made the development of American policy slow and laborious. It also strained the process of carrying out policies of economic aid, of forming a coalition of free nations, and of furnishing military assistance. All the negotiators had strong cards to play. France had its geographical position and a clearly understood nuisance value. Great Britain had global interests and strategic holdings throughout the world that were important to the American strategic concept. The United States had the surplus resources. The ability to force a decision was, however, limited by the fact that the prolonged negotiations took place under the shadow of Soviet power. Consequently, the negotiations were marked by adjustment, compromise formulas, and a great deal of backing and filling. In general, the United States got agreement on the principle of what it wanted in Germany. Great Britain, unable to find resources to carry its share of the burden of administering jointly the United States and British zones, gradually relinquished the deciding voice to the United States. France, unable to support any but a negative position, was generally obliged to follow the American-British lead in order to avoid risking the loss of American aid or the possibility that Western Germany might replace France as the European kingpin of American policy. The results were only attained after the processes of persuasion and compromise were approaching exhaustion.

When the details are eliminated, a line of progression emerges that stretches straight from the first bizonal economic agencies that the United States and Great Britain had set up in 1946 to the establishment of the Federal Government of Germany in late 1949. At every stage economic decisions required supporting political arrangements, and agreements respecting German political institutions led to the reformulation of economic arrangements. And at every stage after early 1948, the underlying purposes of the Economic Cooperation Act and the North Atlantic Treaty entered into the development of German policy. Finally, the rate of advancement and the kind of emphasis—economic, military, or political—given to the negotiation of a solution for Germany were conditioned by the actions of the Soviet Union.

These Soviet actions took three general forms: direct action against the other occupying authorities—as in the Berlin blockade (June 1948 to May 1949); the conversion of the Soviet zone into a German national state; and political appeals to the German people, designed to embarrass the Western powers by creating expectations of the ultimate unification and freedom of Germany and by generating fears that Germany would be the *corpus* for which a war might be fought. These patterns inevitably produced equivalent reactions: the Berlin airlift; the speeding up of the creation of a West German Republic on the most favorable possible terms; and the political appeals to the German people designed to embarrass the Soviet Union. There is little doubt at this date that the basic Soviet aim was either to force the United States to alter its German policy, or to disrupt plans and timing of the execution of that policy, or to return the German issue to the four-power control level where it could be kept fluid and unsettled.

As a technique the Berlin blockade gradually became useless to the Soviet Union, and secret talks were started in April 1949 to bring it to an end. However, the implications of this kind of direct action were such as to have finally persuaded the United States and a considerable body of German opinion, that a West German government had to be formed prior to an agreement to lift the blockade. There was genuine fear in American official circles that a premature return to four-power arrangements might well divide the Western powers and disrupt their negotiations with each other and with the Germans. There was also fear that if four-power controls were revived, the Soviet Union might accept proposals for a government of Germany as a whole and then work to put the German Communists in effective control of this government. The United States wished to take a *fait accompli* into any renewal of discussions in the Council of Foreign Ministers. A critical decision was reached on the German problem when the Basic Law for a Federal Republic of Germany was approved on May 12, 1949, the very day on which the Berlin blockade was formally lifted.

This was followed by a meeting of the Council of Foreign Ministers (May 23-June 20, 1949). The United States came to the meeting with a firm plan for a German state; with a developed program of economic aid to restore and strengthen Western Europe: with a defensive treaty that was designed to co-ordinate the military and economic power of the United States, Canada, Great Britain, and the states of Western Europe; and with proposals to put teeth into this treaty by means of a program of military assistance. The Soviet Union came to the meeting with a plan for a possible German state: with its control of Eastern Europe firmly established; and in a state of military readiness far surpassing that of the United States and the Western coalition. A four-point agenda was adopted: (1) German unity; (2) Berlin; (3) a German peace treaty; and (4) the Austrian state treaty.

With regard to the unity of Germany, all powers agreed on the need for unity and on the principle of four-power control. However, whereas the Western powers desired the Soviet zone to accede to the Federal Republic of Germany, the Soviet Union wanted new central organs created. Each side denied the democratic nature of the solution offered by the other. Moreover, the United States opposed a merger unless it could be demonstrated that the Soviet zone would not constitute an economic drain on the other zones.

The Western powers desired greater autonomy for the national government. The Soviet Union espoused a plan less clearly delineating the powers delegated to the German organs and permitting any one of the occupying powers to withdraw a function from the German organs and to return it to four-power control. In addition, the Soviet Union desired the rule of unanimity to operate in the occupation control organ, while the American delegation insisted that issues be determined by a majority vote of the occupying powers.

When the Soviet Union desired to discuss a peace treaty and suggested that all occupation troops be withdrawn within one year of the signing of a treaty, the United States insisted that it was useless to discuss the treaty in the absence of agreement on matters concerned with the government of Germany. When the ministers adjourned, they issued a statement promising to continue their efforts to reach agreement on the restoration of the economic and political unity of Germany. Following this, the three Western powers proceeded with the establishment of the Federal Republic of Germany (September 1949), and soon afterwards the Soviet Union proclaimed the German Democratic Republic.

These developments appear to indicate that neither the Soviet Union nor the United States was prepared to agree to a settlement for Germany that permitted the other power to integrate a free and reunited Germany into its power bloc unless sufficient concessions were offered elsewhere to counterbalance this loss; or one of the powers became so weak that it could not oppose a solution imposed by the other; or long-range strategic plans made a tactical retreat in this area advisable. In the period under review, none of these alternative conditions existed to any significant degree.

The economic attractiveness of the United States in this period—the United States could assist the German economy whereas the economy of the Soviet Union required the "exploitation" of German resources—made it impossible for the Soviet Union to accept the American solution of a federal Germany organized according to Western democratic principles. If the Soviet Union had made this choice, it would have lost all Germany to the West.

Similarly, the Soviet plan of a centralized German state, over which the occupation authorities retained extensive and loosely defined powers and operated according to the veto, could not be accepted by the United States because it would have given the Soviet Union unlimited time and opportunity to interfere with the economic recovery of Germany and to frustrate all attempts to integrate Germany with Western Europe. Given the weakness of the West on the continent of Europe in terms of territorial maneuverability and man power, the United States policy of organizing a Western coalition against the potential Soviet threat would have been seriously undermined by an acceptance of this plan, and the international position of the United States would have been significantly modified in relation to the Soviet Union.

In view of the mutual hostilities, fears, and suspicions of the United States and the Soviet Union and of the security objectives each had formulated and was acting upon, no common ground existed for agreeing on a solution to the German problem. Consequently, the partition of Germany promised to be of indefinite duration; for the longer it was maintained and the more closely the two halves of Germany were integrated into opposing blocs of power, the more difficult it became to undo the process or to develop an alternative solution for Germany.

Eastern Europe

In the course of 1946, the general situation in the states of Eastern Europe was apparently frozen in a form that frustrated any further effective progress toward specific American goals.[11] The process by which this rigidity came about directly contributed to the reinterpretation of the American position in the world and to the definition of new American goals. But before new directions were set and new policies formulated, peace treaties had been negotiated for Bulgaria, Hungary, and Rumania and, in those three states as well as in Poland, Soviet-supported governments containing strong Communist elements were in control.

The three peace treaties had included clauses guaranteeing human rights, limiting armed forces, and guaranteeing the free and open navigation of the Danube River. The United States, however, did not have the means to enforce the treaties except with the concurrence of the Soviet Union. Within a relatively short period, the United States was obliged to watch governments with which it had established diplomatic relations purge the last elements of Western influence, enter into exclusive relations with each other and with the Soviet Union, and generally remove themselves beyond the range of American action.

[11] The states concerned were Bulgaria, Hungary, Poland, and Rumania. A similar development took place in Czechoslovakia in February 1948.

The United States protested treaty violations only to have the protests consistently rejected by the Soviet Union as one of the allied signatories. At a later stage, in early 1949, the United States and Great Britain, referring to increasing violation of human rights, attempted to enlist the United Nations and did succeed in getting the General Assembly to ask the International Court of Justice for an advisory opinion. The Court ruled that disputes existed and that the states involved were required to abide by the settlement procedures of the treaties, but it also ruled, in reply to a subsequent request, that the United Nations had no power to appoint commissioners to settle the disputes except by agreement of the parties concerned. Neither compliance nor agreement was achieved, and no further progress could be made in this direction.

The essence of the situation was that the United States lacked the means to maintain its interests in Eastern Europe and was conspicuously unable to furnish support to groups that might have acted on its behalf. American action was soon reduced to maintaining and protesting the record.

When, however, the direction of United States policy was altered, and the guidance of a strategic concept was felt, Eastern Europe fell into a different category of interest. Although obviously such policy developments as economic and military assistance had no application in the states of Eastern Europe, these states had a place in any strategy of containing the Soviet Union. They constituted the outer fringe of Soviet power in Europe. This did not give the United States a basis for immediate action, but it did permit the governments of these states to be regarded as holding power against the popular will and as satellites of the Soviet Union; and peoples could be addressed as separate from governments and could be spoken of as candidates for ultimate liberation.

Direct United States relations with the Eastern European states fell to the level of propaganda charges, disputes about the espionage activities of diplomatic personnel, and the like, but indirect and peripheral pressures were developed by the United States in order to weaken the position of Communist regimes and to undermine Soviet influence. Here, too, the United States was unable to push such activities vigorously. In short, Eastern Europe became a subsidiary objective for the United States, but continued to have a high priority on the Soviet scale.

The question of the Danube River is interesting in this connection. In addition to the unhonored clause in the peace treaties, an agreement had been made to call a conference on the administration of its commerce and navigation. This conference finally met in Belgrade in July 1948. The voting-members were the Soviet Union, the Ukraine, Czechoslovakia, Yugoslavia, Rumania, Bulgaria, Hungary, the United States, Great Britain, and France. No effort was made by the Communist states to discuss or to resolve the issues. They rested their case on a voting majority in the conference and on an effective physical control of the Danube basin. On this basis, the conference adopted a new convention despite the legal objections from the Western delegates. The lesson of the inability of the West to change the facts of the situation was relentlessly driven home. A restoration of Western influence in Eastern Europe plainly could not take place except as part of some larger settlement.

Austria

For different reasons, there is as little to be said at this point about the application of American policies in Austria. Less so than for Germany, but more so than for Eastern Europe, significant and effective movement toward the goals of the United States depended on the results of action elsewhere. For the period 1946 to 1950, American actions in Germany and Western Europe and Soviet actions in Germany and Eastern Europe made the Austrian question of secondary importance.

The Austrian situation lent itself to being thus put to one side. A properly elected government, whose authority extended throughout the country, was functioning. The relations of this government with the quadripartite control authority, although sometimes confused in detail, were clear enough in principle. Legislation and international agreements had to be submitted to the Allied Council, and approval could be assumed if the Council did not object within thirty-one days. Constitutional changes, however, required the written approval of the Council. Decisions of the Council had to be unanimous and it was generally understood that none of the occupying powers would dispense with its veto power in the absence of a peace treaty that protected its strategic interests and that did not foreclose on its long-range objectives.

The United States and Great Britain tried to get their drafts of a treaty with Austria considered when the treaties for the former

Axis satellites were being negotiated in 1946. The Soviet Union steadily refused. Not until January 1947 were the deputies of the foreign ministers authorized to proceed. Between that date and March 1948, over one hundred meetings were held, after which the United States announced that the sessions had been suspended in order to determine whether a real basis for further negotiations existed. Meetings were resumed in 1949, but with no better success.[12] The United States interest in maintaining so fruitless and wearing an activity was, of course, to keep its position of seeking a free and sovereign Austria constantly on the record and to throw the onus on the Soviet Union for preventing the accomplishment of what had been from the start an agreed purpose. Given the relationship between Soviet rights in Austria and the maintenance of Soviet troops in Hungary and Rumania, whatever embarrassment the Soviet Union may have been subjected to was covered up by a flow of stubborn argument about the details of a final settlement. As the actual background was one of unmentioned differences of political and strategic purposes, specific issues, such as the complicated one of the disposition of German wartime acquired assets, could be and were used to cause endless delay.

Within this framework of stalemate at a high level of policy, the United States and the other three occupying powers went about their daily affairs with a minimum of conflict. The German scene was by no means duplicated. The Soviet Union thoroughly exploited its zone in the early stages, but the pressure was gradually reduced. No consistent effort was made to detach the area. Similarly, although the United States brought the western zones of Austria within the scope of its economic aid programs to the fullest extent possible, it did not press its policies to the point of calling forth vigorous Soviet reaction.

None of the parties was satisfied with the situation, but none was so discontented as to seek to take strong action to change it. Questions of high strategy, both political and military, generally determined the attitudes of the United States and the Soviet Union toward Austria. As these issues were never presented in a purely Austrian form, some care was taken not to raise them. In the absence of

[12] In March 1955 the Soviet Union took the initiative and completed unilaterally the negotiation of the treaty with Austria that had been mainly prepared by the four major powers. This was then submitted to the other three powers concerned, was approved, and came into force in July 1955.

a strong Communist element in the Austrian Government, the Soviet Union would have lost a forward position if it had accepted a peace treaty. It therefore had the most to lose by a settlement and the most to gain by prolonging the *status quo*. On the other hand, although the United States would gain from a settlement, the gain would not be important enough to justify strong measures. A free and sovereign Austria had little to contribute to the execution of the American strategic concept of containment that could not be extracted from the existing situation in any event.

CHAPTER IX

Areas of Application: The Far East

THE OVER-ALL situation in the Far East differed both in kind and degree from that existing in Europe. It broke down into three rather disparate areas—Japan, China, and Korea—and the short-term aims of American policy for these three areas, as well as the immediate problems that confronted the executors of policy, could not be easily or clearly related to one another. China was to to be built up into the dominant Far Eastern state. Japan was to be reduced to a secondary role and re-educated as a peace-loving, democratic nation. Korea was to be restored to sovereign status. Although there were obvious relationships between these purposes, the courses of action undertaken to achieve them tended to remain distinct. Nor did the actions of the Soviet Union have the effect of forcing problems into a coherent whole as in Europe. And, although the strategic concept of containment would in time become operative in the Far East, the initial programs of economic aid, coalition building, and military assistance could not be effectively developed there in their original forms. In any event, variants of some of these programs were already in operation as grants to China, subsidies for Japan, and relief appropriations for Korea.

Japan

The occupation of Japan was planned and executed as an American responsibility. Enough frustration had developed in the early months of the German occupation to produce an exasperated determination on the part of the United States not to repeat the experience. The struggle against Japan had been predominantly American in every sense—mass of material, numbers of men, and freedom of decision. The contributions of others had been tokens, offered and accepted for political reasons rather than for any tangible difference they made in the ultimate conclusion. Even the entrance of the Soviet Union was quickly seen to have been unnecessary in fact and awkward in its possible consequences. Furthermore, important influences in American thinking regarded the

166

Far East as an area in which fundamental change was in progress. Empires would disintegrate, new nationalisms would emerge, and new forces would stir. The interest of the United States in this historical process was considered vital, and there was no official intention of relaxing the power to guide this process that victory in Asia seemed to have brought.

The Japanese people and the structure of Japanese society responded with surprisingly little strain to the initial demands of the occupation, and attention was quickly shifted to the business of reforming, reorganizing, and re-educating the Japanese nation. The details are of no moment, but the over-all intent is significant. Japan was to remain a nation—to become in time a sovereign state— but it was to be reduced in the international hierarchy of states. Japanese institutions were to be altered to fit this purpose, and the Japanese people were to be tutored into accepting this purpose as natural. The major efforts of the Supreme Commander Allied Powers (SCAP) were directed to these ends as soon as immediate control and security matters were safely in hand. Given the extent to which SCAP managed to insulate itself against outside influences, even against those emanating from superior American authority, it was on these ends that action was concentrated for a considerable period of time. Therefore, the range of questions concerning economic structure and activity, political institutions, and social institutions that in Germany had to be dealt with in relation to the purposes of other states were in Japan dealt with in a more uncompromising way.

Occupation Targets

The purge of militaristic influences worked, at least in appearance, to eliminate many of the traditionally controlling groups in Japanese life. All career officers, active militarists, militant nationalists, and influential members of ultranationalist, terrorist, or secret patriotic societies were ordered removed from participation in public life. These categories were not clearly defined, and were somewhat indiscriminatingly interpreted. By 1949, the purge had become so unpopular, and the focus of United States policy had so changed, that a reversal became inevitable. Although SCAP promptly checked an attempt to re-examine all cases in which the holding of an office had been the only ground for disqualification, over five thousand educators and publishers were reinstated. Because of the growing Communist danger, the Japanese Government was permitted to set up a purge appeals committee to reinstate those who had been treated unjustly. The purge thereupon lost its force, and by 1952 many high service officers and political figures had been restored to full political rights.

Another target of the occupation was economic authoritarianism. Occupation policy regarded the *Zaibatsu*, the group running the large interlocking holding and operating companies that dominated the Japanese economy, as an integral part of the conspiracy for waging aggressive war. The dissolution of these economic empires was an early goal, and a directive to this effect was issued in late 1945.

The *Zaibatsu* were not capitalistic in the ordinary sense of the word. Their enterprises could not be equated with the German cartels as great agencies of production. They were both bureaucratic and paternalistic institutions. Many of their operations were conducted at a loss. Loyalty was more important than efficiency, and promotions were determined largely by seniority, although certain management positions tended to "harden" along hereditary lines. Many more employees were retained than could be effectively used, but they were poorly paid. Each *Zaibatsu* concern controlled widely diversified holdings and covered every important aspect of the Japanese economy.

In general, the American intent was to destroy the war-making capacity of Japan and to reduce Japanese economic activity to the level called for by this aim. The dissolution of the *Zaibatsu* was part of this policy, along with reparation and plant dismantlement, as well as part of the policy of reforming the structure of Japanese life. But the Japanese economy was scarcely viable except in terms of its own peculiar structure and institutions. Consequently, what was broken down by occupational policy, in addition to what had been disrupted by war and defeat, could not be put together quickly in some other and more desirable form by any action of SCAP.

Second Thoughts

Japan was not even remotely self-supporting in the new circumstances. Industrial production in 1947 was only 45 per cent of the 1930-34 average, although the population of Japan proper had increased by about 20 per cent. Exports were only 10 per cent of the prewar average and imports only 30 per cent. The United States, because it had sole authority in Japan, had also sole responsibility. The alternatives were clear and few. The United States could subsidize the existence of Japan, could let the country sink toward chaos through ever declining living standards, or could drastically revise its economic occupation policy and permit reconstruction in what eventually would be Japanese forms. With some protests from interested states, such as Australia and the Philippines, the United States chose the last course, combining it, however, with interim aid.

Given this shift, the policy of breaking up the *Zaibatsu* ran into resistance in American opinion. SCAP was required to permit industrial organizations to remain intact unless it could be shown that they restricted competition. Under the controls existing in Japan at that time, it was almost impossible to demonstrate this. Moreover, the control of a considerable number of non-related lines of endeavor was not considered to be in restriction of competition, and this type of control had been characteristic of the *Zaibatsu* combine.[1]

In the course of 1948, the downward economic trend was checked. Japan was encouraged to restore its international commercial links. Iron and steel production were allowed to expand. American survey missions produced plans for stabilizing currency, prices, and wages, and for increasing production. American financial aid was an essential part of the improvement. A little later, fiscal reforms were carried through. The allocation of raw materials was controlled, and credit restraints were tightened. As a result, the currency issue declined by 20 per cent from the postwar high, and inflation virtually ceased. Nevertheless, there were still significant shortages in consumer goods. The situation was far from satisfactory, and many adverse factors lay beyond the direct influence of American policy.

A high proportion of Japanese imports came from the United States, but the United States absorbed a relatively small share of Japanese exports, especially as nylon became a substitute for silk. Because of the inconvertibility of currencies, Japan could not close the gap by its earnings from trade with other areas. More-

---

[1] By the end of the occupation, most of the holding companies had been restored under the control of the old managerial elite, if not of the *Zaibatsu* families themselves.

over, many of the previous enemies of Japan restricted the expansion of trade with Japan, or refused to accept Japanese products. The United States had no way of altering these attitudes without jeopardizing other American objectives. The burden of supporting the Japanese economy might be reduced, but there was no sign that it could soon be wholly lifted from American shoulders. However, by the time this became apparent, American-Soviet relations had deteriorated, and the strategy of containment was the guide to policy. To support Japan by grants-in-aid, while directing the revival of Japanese strength, was not considered out of line with what was now the basic pattern of American action.

Another important lever of change to which SCAP addressed itself was constitutional reform. There was no American directive to SCAP that called for the revision of the Japanese constitution. The declaration on Japan that was made at the Potsdam Conference merely specified that the Japanese Government should remove all obstacles to the survival and strengthening of democratic tendencies. However, there emerged at an early date the idea that a new constitution would crystallize and symbolize the democratic society the American occupation aimed at creating. When, late in 1945, SCAP demanded action on freedom of the press, civil liberties, woman suffrage, and broader educational privileges, the Japanese understood this as the preliminary in the process of producing a new constitution, and constructed a number of model drafts accordingly. The Japanese Government and the occupation officials did not see eye to eye on the substance of these drafts, and finally SCAP produced its own draft.[2] The new constitution went through the machinery of Japanese approval and was promulgated in November 1946.

The articles of the constitution that were designed to break traditional controls over the Japanese body politic and to release the democratic potential of the Japanese people are of little concern now. It is enough to note that the design was as comprehensive with respect to human rights, police, freedom of press, education, and other such matters as the American drafters could have desired. There is one section, however, that is germane in view of the fu-

---

[2] SCAP was anxious to get the matter under way before the Far Eastern Advisory Commission, which had been agreed by the foreign ministers at Moscow in December 1945, became operative; for no fundamental changes in the Japanese constitutional structure could be made without the approval of the commission once it was in being.

ture development of United States policy. Chapter II of the constitution, which is entitled "The Renunciation of War," reads:

Aspiring sincerely to an international peace based on justice and order, the Japanese people forever renounce war as a sovereign right of the Nation and the threat or use of force as a means of settling international disputes.

In order to accomplish the aim of the preceding paragraph, land, sea, and air forces will never be maintained. The right of belligerency of the State will not be recognized.[3]

This article, while compatible with part of the original intent of occupation policy, became an uncommonly big stumbling block when American policy for Japan began to shift in relation to a strategy of containment and to a policy of strengthening states to oppose Soviet-Communist expansion. This shift took place with some speed at the end of 1946 and in early 1947, under double compulsion: a drive to reduce the economic burden of Japan on the United States, and a drive to utilize the geographic position and the man power and industrial potential of Japan as an element in the general policy of checking the Soviet Union.

The essence of the situation was that the unilateral position of the United States in Japan had developed quickly into autonomy for SCAP, and that SCAP seemed to be following a policy line increasingly divergent from that of the United States. The introduction of other states into this situation—even on a limited scope—had the effect of forcing a review of this ambiguous relationship. The establishment of the Far Eastern Advisory Commission (FEAC) in Washington and the initiation of Allied Council meetings in Japan served this purpose. Although the United States Government showed no intention of permitting these bodies to impede American action, the administration was not averse to using at least the FEAC as a check on SCAP. At any rate, differences began to develop, not only between the United States and the Soviet Union, but between the United States and its other wartime allies, between them and SCAP, and between important sectors of American policy making and SCAP.

Security Motives

The issue, at bottom, was the question of the place of Japan in the politics of the postwar world, and views were bound to be sharply

---

[3] A. J. Peaslee, *Constitutions of Nations* (1950) Vol. II, p. 308.

divergent. In fact, there are grounds for thinking that serious differences between the United States and some of its closest allies were only kept under control because of the more significant hostility between the United States and the Soviet Union.[4]

At any rate, by the autumn of 1946, SCAP had decided that Japanese economic recovery could not take place in the absence of a peace treaty. Public statements were made, declaring that a spiritual revolution had occurred in Japan, and that it was on the road "to real democracy." The Department of State, however, apparently felt that, given the then current degree of international friction, the negotiation of a treaty was premature, and the proposal was rejected. The Supreme Commander contended, in press conferences, that the military work of the occupation was completed, that the political task was nearing completion, and that the economic job was being impeded by a needlessly prolonged occupation. If Japan was felt to require continued control or guidance, it was suggested that the United Nations was the proper agent.

Apparently the hand of the government was forced, for several days later it was announced officially that the United States was preparing to open negotiations on a peace treaty with Great Britain, the Soviet Union, China, and possibly Australia and that the other members of the Far Eastern Advisory Commission would be permitted to participate in the negotiations at a later stage. However, the failure of the Moscow Conference of foreign ministers in April 1947, made the timing seem inauspicious. The United States shifted responsibility for the peace talks to the FEAC, where a larger number of nations would mediate disputes and slow down action. This move was satisfying to the smaller nations represented on the FEAC. The members of the British Commonwealth called a conference at Canberra in Australia to consider Pacific questions prior to the formal discussion of a Japanese peace treaty. The conference approved the idea of a speedy settlement, but called for the creation of an allied agency to supervise the execution of the treaty.

In the meantime, the Soviet Union insisted that the original proposal for a four-power conference be adhered to, while the United States insisted that its new plan for an eleven-nation conference be

---

[4] The Philippine Government disagreed with respect to reparations claims. The Pacific nations generally disagreed with policies that strengthened Japan and hence served a threat to their security. Great Britain was sensitive to the reappearance of Japan as an international trader in Far Eastern markets.

accepted. There were some suggestions that the United States might proceed with a separate peace. However, in September, China warned against separate peace moves, and stated that it would boycott any conference that did not include the Soviet Union. In November 1947, the Soviet Foreign Minister proposed that a four-power meeting be held to work out the problems of a Japanese peace treaty. China and Great Britain rejected this proposal. Great Britain then suggested a meeting of the eleven members to discuss the question, but by this time the United States had decided to let the matter rest for the time being.

In early 1948, after the Communist *coup d'état* in Czechoslovakia, the United States became still more resistive to the idea of a peace treaty for Japan. But the hardening was accompanied by directives to SCAP to tone down the policy of re-educating the Japanese and modifying Japanese institutions. However, with the situations in China and Korea deteriorating, this shift could not be smoothly made. If the United States wished to restore Japan, it had two choices. It could underwrite the Japanese recovery program, or it could, by relaxing its exclusive position in Japan, obtain the co-operation of other states to this end. But the co-operation of other states, even of those friendly to the United States, could only be had at the price of a Japanese treaty that protected their varying interests. This condition might conceivably have been met, except for the attitude of the Soviet Union. There could be no hope that the Soviet Union would not use a peace conference to veto any treaty that would enable Japan to contribute to an American strategy of containment. To complete the circle however, it gradually became clear that the new American policy for Japan, if it were to be brought to fruition, would sooner or later require a treaty of peace.

By the end of 1948, the concrete question of Japan had not been clearly set forth within the context of broad United States policy. Although a modification of original objectives had been made, and a new purpose had been formulated, the necessary policies had not been developed. It was agreed among American policy makers that the struggle between the Soviet Union and the United States had reduced the importance of the effort to change Japanese society, and that it was of greater significance to rebuild Japan as a useful base for American power and to reduce the strain on American resources. In such a program, the release of the old and conservative sources of power appeared likely to be more instrumental in achieving the desired results than the further democratization of Japanese institutions. Moreover, because the situation in Japan did not easily conform to the economic, coalition, and military assistance policies being developed for Europe, the Japanese question tended to be exclusively presented in military strategic terms—a tendency that was strengthened by the unfavorable turn of events on the Asiatic mainland.

It is almost impossible to weigh the pros and cons of the strategic estimates of 1948-49. The victory of communism in China made the defense of Japan look militarily impracticable. Given the limits of American economic and military resources, it could be argued that the United States should channel all its available resources to Europe. If massive aid were essential to maintain Europe in the face of a Soviet threat, it could be held that it was probably unwise to make extensive commitments in Japan. If, on the other hand, the Soviet threat to Europe was largely economic, political, and psychological, then the maintenance of United States military power in the Orient would serve to deter Communist action and to force a wide dispersion of United States military resources over the continent of Asia.

While a debate on these terms went on at the policy-making levels, SCAP, in accordance with its most recent directives, was restoring to the Japanese much of the machinery of governmental power and was withdrawing into the higher reaches of policy guidance. All that remained was to sign a peace treaty. However, if American forces were to be withdrawn as part of a treaty, it was important that a strong Japanese Government be re-established. The United States consequently encouraged the development of a Japanese army —the national police reserve, trained and equipped by the American Army—despite the anti-war provisions of the American-drafted Japanese constitution. The United States now favored a peace conference in which a veto could not be employed or, failing this, even a separate peace, provided that the postwar allies of the United States would go along.

These allies, however, were not enthusiastic. Their memories of the Pacific war were more bitter than those of the United States, and they still feared a resurgence of both Japanese military and commercial strength. Some, moreover, doubted the wisdom of a treaty to which the great bordering Asiatic powers—Communist China and the Soviet Union—might not be parties. The Japanese themselves, fearful of the withdrawal of American economic and military support, were not overly eager for a treaty that would leave them in a technical state of war with the Soviet Union and China and lacking the Chinese markets that they considered necessary for their economic viability. Thus in the period ending in 1948-49, the United States had an ambiguous policy with reference to Japan. It was apparently not certain of the policy best adapted to its global objectives, both because popular and congressional pressure were forcing a rethinking of its Asiatic policy and because it was difficult to estimate the results for global policy of the various alternative allocations of American resources. Moreover, any policy that could get from other nations the support necessary for its adoption and effectiveness would almost certainly fail to satisfy American purposes. Although there had been a clear and consistent decision to give highest priorities to the European policies and projects of the United States, subsidiary decisions affecting the Far East could not be derived with mathematical precision from this decision.

Korea

Korea was the one area in the Far East in which United States and Soviet authority, influence, and power met on an agreed line, and that—at least initially—constituted a joint responsibility. The situation, therefore, resembled in principle the situation in Central Europe. However, it developed differently and, like other situations in the Far East, did not respond readily to the application of basic United States policy.

It will be recalled that the initial effort to co-ordinate American-Soviet responsibility in Korea was by the establishment of a Joint Commission. It will also be recalled that this commission adjourned *sine die* in May 1946, after a prolonged discussion of wholly divergent objectives. The resulting impasse put an end to the original conception of the postwar status of Korea as a nation restored to sovereign statehood. There was no specific United States policy to stand in place of this original purpose.

But while the impasse was developing, and in the year that followed the adjournment of the Joint Commission, the Soviet authorities devoted themselves to constructing an indigenous political and military structure in the north, and the United States, although with much less directness and intensity of purpose followed a policy of co-operating with non-Communist groups in the south. The group headed by Syngman Rhee gradually emerged as the most powerful such group.

By the time the Joint Commission was reconvened in May 1947, both the United States and the Soviet Union were in effect committed to the support of local but opposing forces. The impasse continued unbroken. However, as the detailed implications of the strategic concept of containment were beginning to be developed in American circles, especially in military circles, Korea and the Korean situation were examined in strategic terms. One view was that Korea was of great importance because of its geographic relation to Japan. Others felt that Korea had little or no strategic value for the United States. Although it is not certain that a final judgment concerning the strategic importance of Korea was reached at this time, an interim decision was made to resist Soviet maneuvers on the Joint Commission.

During the summer of 1947, General Wedemeyer reported on the situation in Korea. He noted the strength of the indigenous forces that the Soviet Union had organized. He warned that an American withdrawal could only lead to a Korea unified under Soviet-Communist direction. He concluded that such a development would impair the American strategic position in the Far East. He recommended that the American objective should be to ensure the military neutralization of Korea, and that the United Nations seemed to be the appropriate medium through which a provisional Korean government, functioning under a four-power trusteeship, could be set up for this purpose.[5]

In September an American policy decision was made to transfer the Korean question to the United Nations, resting the case on the fact that the implementation of a wartime agreement concerning the future of a friendly people was being delayed by the failure of bilateral negotiations, and asserting that the matter called for the impartial judgment of others. The motivations of this decision are not clear, but the willingness of the United States to submit its case to the United Nations suggests several things: the possibility of world opinion forcing a reasonable compromise from the Soviet Union, the absence of any American objective of suffi-

---

[5] *Report to the President, Korea,* Senate Committee on Armed Services, Committee Print, 82 Cong. 1 sess. (1951), p. 8.

cient priority to be pressed for unilaterally, and a background judgment about the relatively minor importance of Korea when weighed against the value of maintaining a clear United States position in the United Nations. At any rate, the case was accepted by the General Assembly, and from this point on, the position of the United Nations Organization and the development of American policy in Korea could not be disentangled.

The Assembly passed a resolution recommending elections not later than the end of March 1948, to be followed by the convening of a Korean national assembly, and the formation of a national government with its own security forces. After this, arrangements would be made for the withdrawal of American and Soviet troops. The Assembly also established a United Nations Temporary Commission for Korea to prepare for and to supervise elections and to be available for consultation in connection with the establishment of a national government and the withdrawal of foreign troops.

The commission reached Korea in January 1948 and set to work. It was refused permission to enter North Korea. Nevertheless, it reported to the General Assembly that the people of Korea desired self-government, that they were able to govern themselves, and that they relied on the United Nations. The commission then observed that, because it could not report on the northern part of the country, it could only make alternative recommendations: elections to establish a government for South Korea, elections to select representatives of the South Korean people who could then consult with the commission, the exploration of other possibilities for establishing a national government of Korea, or to report its inability to carry out its mission in the circumstances prevailing and to return its mandate to the General Assembly.

Although doubt was expressed about the legality of the action, the General Assembly instructed the commission to proceed with elections in those parts of Korea to which it had access. Elections were held in May 1948. The elected Assembly of South Korea then convened and chose Syngman Rhee as temporary chairman. Rhee took the position that the Assembly represented all of Korea. He said that seats were being reserved for North Korean representatives, and that he would open negotiations with the Soviet Union for a solution of the Korean problem. He expressed the hope that United States troops would remain in Korea for security reasons until the country had been unified. The United Nations would not recognize the claims of the Rhee regime to be the Government of Korea; and the Rhee regime, for its part, refused to consult with the commission, although required to do so by the resolution of the General Assembly. The United States, however, gave the regime at least partial recognition as a government and terminated the American military government.

The General Assembly of the United Nations met in Paris in December 1948, and, by a large majority, declared that the Rhee regime was "a lawful government" with "effective control over . . . part of Korea," and that it was "the only such Government in Korea."[6] The General Assembly did not, by this act, recognize the Republic of Korea government as *the* government of Korea, although the United States took the resolution as grounds for granting full recognition in this sense in January 1949. The same resolution also recommended that a new seven-nation commission be established to continue the work of the Temporary Commission. It was instructed to proceed to lend its good offices in negotiating unification, the integration of all security forces, the removal of economic barriers, and to supervise the withdrawal of occupation forces.

In the meantime, a Korean Democratic People's Republic had been established in the north. General elections, which were not supervised by the Temporary Commission, were held in August. The North Korean Government also professed to represent the whole of Korea and stated that certain members of its parliament had been elected in the south and in "underground" fashion. The Korean Democratic People's Government regarded the Rhee Government as illegitimate and pledged itself to remove that government. This attitude was reciprocated by the South Korean Government.

In September 1949, the Soviet Government announced that all its military forces would be withdrawn from Korea by the end of December at the request of the Supreme National Assembly of North Korea. Two days later the Department of State announced that it agreed, in principle, to the withdrawal of occupation forces at the earliest practicable date, but added that the question had to be considered within the larger problem of the unification and independence of Korea. It was pointed out that this question was under consideration by the General Assembly of the United Nations. Behind the announcement was the belief of the United States

[6] Res. 195 (III), Dec. 12, 1948.

Government that the South Korean Government would not prove viable—given the superior armed forces of the north—should American forces be completely withdrawn.

Actually a decision to withdraw American forces had been made by the United States as a result of a high level study carried out some time in 1948. The recommendation had been made on economic grounds and because the United States Army had a total complement of only 630,000 men, distributed in four under-strength divisions in Japan, slightly more than one division in Europe, and five under-strength divisions in the United States.[7] In these circumstances, it was noted that the country could not afford military commitments in Korea. On this basis, the United States had gone along with a United Nations recommendation for a general withdrawal of troops from Korea.

By this time, it was very hard to distinguish the determining element in Korean policy: the United States, the United Nations, or the South Korean Government. Even within the United States Government, it was difficult to identify either the basis for or the source of American policy. The new United Nations Commission reached Korea, but was frustrated in the south and was unable to establish contact with the north. It did, however, note that there was a good deal of military "posturing" by both governments. In fact, each side was threatening to invade the other, and frequent border clashes were taking place. There was every indication that the United States was finding it almost impossible to fit the Korean situation neatly into its over-all pattern of policy. It had apparently come to the conclusion that Korea was not a sufficiently important strategic asset to warrant the commitment of scarce American man power and military supplies. But in terms of its strategic concept and in view of the general situation in the Far East, the United States could not wholly let go. It was not indifferent to the fate of the Republic of Korea and attempted to bolster its international prestige, its economic viability, and its capacity to defend itself; but these were subsidiary objectives of American foreign policy. Yet the United States was committed by its own choice to decisions of the United Nations. Moreover, the United States Government was disturbed by the hostile treatment accorded the United Nations

[7] *Military Situation in the Far East,* Hearings before the Senate Committee on Armed Services and the Committee on Foreign Relations, 82 Cong. 1 sess., p. 2327.

Commission by the Rhee Government, and fearful that this government might engage in hostilities against the north that would either lead to its collapse or to American involvement.

China

When 1946 opened, the United States was already in a dilemma with respect to China. The American objective was clear: a strong, unified, and democratic China able to act as a major power in the Far East. The dilemma arose from the discrepancy between the realities of the Chinese situation and the policy of mediating between the contending forces in Chinese politics, to which the United States had committed itself unreservedly. As the United States Government interpreted the situation, a policy of conciliation to produce unity was the only course that it was in a position to follow. No alternative way of reaching the desired end was in hand; no alternative goal was envisaged. Consequently, the United States approached the China question without freedom of choice.

The National Government of China did not have the military resources—troops, equipment, or leadership—to maintain itself south of the Great Wall and to establish its authority in Manchuria. Therefore, unless the United States were willing to commit an army to the mainland of China and to fight a war with the Chinese Communists, there was no possibility of establishing Nationalist rule over a unified China unless the Chinese Communists agreed. Conciliation by a third party consequently could only take the form of persuading the Nationalists to extend their maximum offer to meet the minimum Communist offer. Such pressures as the United States could, or chose to, bring to bear fell more frequently and more heavily on the established National Government.

The United States Government recognized that to obtain a working adjustment between the major Chinese groups involved a fundamental compromise of the political objectives of these groups. There is little evidence to indicate how the United States evaluated the probabilities of achieving this goal, when each of the groups was of comparable strength, was centrally organized and controlled, and when both would continue to exist within the same territory— for China was to be unified. In effect, this course involved the political neutralization of China vis-à-vis both the Soviet Union and the United States, and it could succeed, so far as the Chinese were concerned, only if the costs to the contending parties of fighting through to a decision appeared so great as to destroy the value of victory, or if each side were confident that a present compromise would not rob it of the power to assert itself at some future date.

In spite of these drawbacks, the basic alternatives were still less desirable. The United States could have considered dropping the vision of a unified China and supported instead a real consolidation of the National Government in the area in which it was actually exercising authority. The United States could also have considered intervention in force. Or, finally, it could have considered its China policy at a dead stop and ended all further effort to direct the outcome of events. For reasons that need no arguing here, none of these courses was acceptable in 1946, and all became even less acceptable as time went on. Almost by default, the United States remained committed to the search for a *modus vivendi* between the Nationalist and Communist groups.

The Marshall Mission

The mission on which General Marshall was sent to China at the end of 1945 consequently became involved in a long drawn out game of Chinese checkers, in which each contestant jumped the other, play by play, and gradually eliminated from the board all the means by which the United States might have influenced the end result. General Marshall was chairman of a committee of Nationalists and Communists, set up to discuss a cease-fire and related matters. Almost at once, the committee reached the crux of the problem: the reorganization of the Nationalist and Communist armies. These constituted the real issues of power and control, for here was concentrated the means of enforcing compliance with any political agreements that might be reached.

The details of the endless circling around this key point are no longer significant. It is enough to note that agreement was not reached, and that meanwhile the cease-fire that had been agreed on broke down. By April 1946, both sides had violated the terms of the truce. The Communists had infiltrated troops into Manchuria and taken over Japanese equipment, and the Nationalists had initiated military actions in Manchuria in an effort to establish their authority. In spite of a superficial appearance of success, Nationalist military circles continued to advocate a policy of force that could not have been carried out, even assuming logistical support from the United States.

General Marshall lectured both sides. He told the Nationalists that their actions had given the Communists reason to be suspicious and accused them of breaking the truce without gaining any military benefits. He pointed out that the Communists, feeling their strength, were now demanding a better ratio of Communist to Nationalist troops in Manchuria. On the other hand, General Marshall told the Communists that they were now being offered reasonable terms, that it had been agreed that governmental authority should be restored in Manchuria, and that this could not be accomplished unless the National Government controlled key cities. He said that the Communist attack on Changchun, for example, had taken the matter out of his hands, and that he could no longer act as a mediator.

The demands of the Nationalists increased rather than diminished. The Nationalist thesis now was that the Communists could be crushed by force. An expressed Communist willingness to end hostilities in Manchuria seemed to confirm this point of view. The arguments and the advice tendered by the United States fell flat when they met this conviction. By the end of June 1946, Nationalist demands had been raised so that they maintained that political matters could not be gone into until military adjustments were completed. Both sides now unleashed a barrage of anti-American propaganda. The Nationalists demanded military rather than economic aid, and the Communists claimed that unconditional American aid was encouraging the Nationalists to follow a war policy. The ground was softened under the Marshall mission and, at the suggestion of the General, a new ambassador, Dr. John Leighton Stuart, President of Yenching University, a man of unquestioned integrity and long experience in China, was appointed in order to exert as much official United States influence as possible.

The Nationalists were then told that their recalcitrant policies could only result in their loss of China. No matter how favorable circumstances seemed at the moment, it was inevitable that the Nationalists would sooner or later be forced to appeal to the United States to save the regime; and by that time American opinion would have been alienated by their present actions. In fact, the National Government was creating the conditions that would result in what it most feared—a Communist regime in China. At the same time, President Truman informed the Nationalists that their policies were creating an unfavorable impression on American opinion and that the government might be obliged to re-examine its China policy. A later re-enforcing message added that only the prompt ending of the civil war and the attainment of unity would justify American aid for the economic reconstruction of China. In addition, Chiang Kai-shek was personally told that in the American view he did not have the means to force the Communists to sue for terms—his forces were so overextended that they could not cope with guerrilla tactics, and their success in capturing cities was no measure of their ability to dominate militarily.[8]

Under these pressures, the Nationalists agreed in August 1946 to reopen conversations with the Communists through the medium of an informal committee of which the United States Ambassador was chairman. However, the discussions soon bogged down in a new maze of demands, conditions, charges, and countercharges, while the real test of relative strength continued in open hostilities. The Nationalists continued to find grounds for optimism and were warned not to push the Communists to the point at which they might ask the Soviet Union for assistance.

As neither side found any real reason for being conciliatory, the United States representative found them both increasingly troublesome to deal with. Much American attention had to be given to avoiding the support of proposals of dubious integrity. General Marshall finally asked to be recalled. The Nationalists then softened their demands slightly, and the Communists became truculent. Nothing, however, checked the incidental fighting.

Minority Chinese groups began to enter the negotiations as third parties and seemed to be exercising some influence. The United States representatives encouraged this new force, hoping to find in it a lever for shifting the rigidly fixed Nationalist and Communist positions. For a time, the third parties seemed to be producing this effect, but, after a few months entanglement in the negotiations, the third parties lost their force and ceased to have any value as a mediating agent.[9]

By the end of 1946, General Marshall was nearly persuaded that the impasse could not be broken. In a long conversation with the Nationalists, he insisted that the Communists could not be destroyed

[8] See U. S. Department of State, *United States Relations with China*, with special reference to the period 1944-49, Publication 3573 (August 1949), pp. 652, 654.

[9] *Ibid.*, pp. 201-04. Also see "Proposals by the Third Party Group, October 1946," *Ibid.*, pp. 675-76.

by military action, that the National Government had almost run through its financial resources, and that the only solution was to bring the Communists into a coalition without further delay. The Nationalists maintained that the Communists never intended to co-operate with the government and were acting under Soviet influence to disrupt the Chinese state. They insisted that it was necessary to crush their military forces and predicted that this could be done in eight or ten months. Then the Communists would be politically manageable. The Communists, for their part, refused further negotiations except on terms that, in effect, repudiated mediation by the United States.

In December 1946, President Truman restated the American view of what was desired for China. The objective was still a united and democratic country and the policy for reaching this goal was still the original American conception of a political and military coalition. The United States was prepared to extend aid for constructive ends once this basis was provided.[10] The Nationalists interpreted this statement as an endorsement of their position, while the Communists attacked it as an "apology for reactionary policy toward China since March."[11] In January 1947, General Marshall's mission was recalled, and he was appointed Secretary of State. Almost all American personnel, civil and military, were withdrawn from China, and American contacts with events were confined to the ambassadorial level, to a small military mission, and to incidental reporting. The situation was now essentially in Chinese hands, and the deferred test of strength was at hand.

Fighting increased in the north. The Nationalists won victories, but the United States Ambassador reported that these were deceptive. The Nationalists were overextended, and their man-power losses were disproportionate. By June 1947, the Ambassador was warning of potential disaster in Manchuria for the Nationalists. The population was being alienated by Nationalist policy; Nationalist armies were defecting; Nationalist political measures were so inadequate that, in the words of the Ambassador, they would have been "farcical had they not been so tragic."[12]

[10] "Statement by President Truman on United States Policy Toward China, December 18, 1946," *Ibid.*, pp. 689-94.

[11] *Ibid.*, p. 219.

[12] See "Ambassador Stuart's Observations on North China and Manchuria," *Ibid.*, pp. 252-53.

The Wedemeyer Mission

By July 1947 the situation had deteriorated to such an extent that the United States sent a fact-finding mission to China under General Wedemeyer. The mission found the situation to be what has been described here. In its recommendations, however, it proposed a policy of limited objectives. The United States should continue to aid the Nationalists on specific conditions: the aid should be requested through United Nations channels; the United Nations should be asked to act in Manchuria; the National Government should initiate economic, fiscal, political, and military reforms and accept American advisers to assist in making use of aid for the purposes intended. This course was proposed on the grounds that a policy of cutting off all aid would certainly deliver China to control by the Communists, while a policy of conditional aid might force the Nationalists to carry out genuine reforms, which would, in turn, make further aid effective.

The report warned that the Communists had taken the military initiative in Northern China and that their almost certain success would be contrary to the American interest. On the other hand, the report held out no sure hope of a final and complete Nationalist victory. The most that American aid could accomplish would be to maintain a Nationalist regime in part of China. Moreover, even this limited result would depend on reforms that the Nationalists had stubbornly resisted in the past and on the establishment of a United Nations guardianship in Manchuria. Finally, the report considered American military intervention undesirable.[13]

The report was not made public at the time of its presentation to the President, but there is evidence that it created a crisis in official thinking by ruling out the long-standing objective of unification and coalition and recommending instead the choice of a side. The choice of the Communist side was foreclosed by the international situation, by the United States strategic concept, and by the acceptance of that concept by American opinion. The choice of the Nationalist side was unsatisfactory because it was considered that the support required would be ineffectual in the absence of reforms that American pressure had hitherto failed to bring about. On the

---

[13] *Report to the President, Korea op. cit.* General Wedemeyer stated later that the Department of State objected to the possible inclusion of the Soviet Union as one of the guardians. *Military Situation in the Far East,* Hearings, p. 2367.

other hand, the Communists in this view could not be defeated unless the United States were willing and able to engage in an extensive military effort; and in mid-1947 this was considered to be out of the question in view of American unreadiness and of commitments of higher priority elsewhere in the world. Yet, if no action were taken, the National Government would fall and the United States would be confronted by a new and a dangerous situation in the Far East.

The consequent dilemma for United States policy makers was admittedly an almost impossible one to resolve, even in a moderately satisfactory way. Unable to aid the Nationalists effectively because of limitations in available American resources and because of the inability of the Nationalists to use the aid effectively, the United States was nevertheless committed to a continuance of aid. In such circumstances, United States policy was determined more by the extraneous and domestic pressures that were placed on it than by any rational orientation to the objectives of global policy. The problem was made even more intractable because the crisis in policy was not revealed to the American public in its true dimensions. In fact, the proposals that the administration made to the Congress in February 1948, although reflecting an intention to ride along with events and to wait and see, suggested to the public a continuation of familiar policy although on a reduced scale. Actually, the position was misleading in some important respects. It appeared to be simply a variation, adapted to the Chinese situation, of the broad policy of economic assistance that was getting under way in Europe. Furthermore, it could be, and in some quarters was, interpreted as providing a basis for a defensive alliance similar to that being considered for Europe. In reality, it represented neither of these things; instead it meant that the United States no longer sought a reconciliation of the opposing forces in China. As this became apparent, the implication followed that United States policy had chosen to support the Nationalist regime as then constituted. This gave rise to great difficulties at later stages in the Chinese situation.[14]

Meanwhile, the adverse trend in China gathered momentum. The Communists demonstrated superior military and political strength,

[14] For example, in seeking appropriations for economic and military assistance programs, the administration was invariably confronted by demands for an allocation to the National Government of China, demands that became awkward after that government was driven to take refuge on Formosa.

and by the end of 1948 had taken over the whole of Manchuria and Northern China. The official American position was that the United States would continue to support the National Government so long as it remained an important factor in the Chinese situation, but it refused to speculate on the course that would be followed if this ceased to be the case. In January 1949, Chiang Kai-shek retired as President of China, and the Nationalists sent an informal delegation to the Communists to sue for peace.

The Communists were so confident of ultimate success that their terms amounted to unconditional surrender. The United States began to cut its losses, although not publicly. The Department of State opposed a suggested allocation of $1.5 billion for assistance to the National Government on the grounds that it would commit the United States to incalculable future expenditures and prolong the civil war and the suffering of the Chinese people without appreciably changing the final result. In April, Communist forces crossed the Yangtze River and fanned out across Southern China. By the end of the year, the remnants of the Nationalists, regrouped once more around Chiang Kai-shek, had withdrawn to the island of Formosa. American postwar expectations in China had collapsed, and United States policy for China had reached a dead end.

In summing up the actions of the United States in the Far East after the war, what stands out most sharply for the period 1946 through 1948 is the apparent fragmentation of attention and policy. It seems almost as if Japan, Korea, and China were treated as areas of interest widely separated from one another. Although a common focus could be found in the universal goal of a world order, there was much in the Asian picture that made it difficult to relate these three areas on the lower plane of action. Their consolidation as a Far Eastern problem would have required a range of short-term policies at least as broad and as interlocked as those being developed in Western Europe. This condition was not even approached until three distinct courses of action—one for Japan, one for China, and one for Korea—were each exhausted.

There are several possible explanations of this lag. Events moved much more rapidly in Europe, both in terms of Soviet action and American reaction. The strategy of containment had its first application in Europe, and the policies to which it gave rise were initially developed in European terms. Furthermore, the development and execution of policy in the Far East was, by its very nature, the domain of distinct specialist and almost autonomous groups in the United States Government. And, finally, the economic resources that the United States had in surplus could be used effectively in Europe but not in the Far East, while military resources that might have served some purpose in the Far East were scarcely available at all. The only point that is beyond dispute is that, in 1948 and 1949, the United States was forced to re-examine almost completely its purposes in the Far East.

CHAPTER X
Areas of Application: Western Europe

IF THE BROAD lines of United States policy are briefly reviewed, it will be noted that programs of economic, military, and technical assistance, and the formation of a treaty of defensive alliance were all courses of action that were applicable only in regions where the United States and the Soviet Union were not directly and equally involved. The objective of checking Soviet policy was consequently being approached indirectly, and success could be measured only by the extent to which collaborating states were strengthened and the extent to which they could be persuaded to identify their purposes with those of the United States. Consequently, disparate considerations came into significant play as the United States applied its broad lines of policy in what soon came to be known as the free world.

A program of economic assistance—in the American judgment—had two possible ends in view: the rebuilding of the economic activity of a specific state, and the use of this renewed strength to counter the actions of the Soviet Union. In the view of developing American policy, the first of these ends came more and more to be regarded as a necessary preliminary to the second. In the view of associated states, however, the first purpose could be, and sometimes was seen as, an end in itself, capable of being divorced from the operations of Soviet policy. It was partly to check on such a separation of purpose that American policy was extended to include treaties of defense and military assistance programs. The same motive also led the United States officially to encourage the growth of all varieties of association between states that might serve to bind them to collaborate for common economic and security purposes in ways not usually covered by the phrase "national interests and objectives." It is with the intricate problems of developing broad policy proposals under these conditions that this chapter is concerned.

During the years 1946 to 1948, these problems fell into two groups: those involving the countries of Western Europe and the Mediterranean, and those involving countries that can be described in a general way as moving from colonial to sovereign status. The two groups were not sharply distinguishable. Some European states had dependent colonies, certain of which were in process of detaching themselves. The British, French, and Dutch were in this position. Some states, most notably the countries of the Middle East, were not colonies in a strict sense, but were concerned all the same to throw off foreign influence and indirect control. In addition, there was the special case of Great Britain and the Commonwealth. Although involved in various ways in both groups, this association of states, by virtue of its global distribution and the equally wide dispersal of its interests, transcended both Western Europe and former colonial areas. Consequently, the Commonwealth, and particularly the United Kingdom component of the Commonwealth, fell into a special and nearly equal relationship with the United States.

France

By the start of 1946, France was once more occupying the place of a major power in the international system. This was partly the result of British policy that had consistently worked to this end from the start of the war, partly the result of belated American cooperation to this same end, and partly the result of the persistence and skill with which the French conducted their affairs in the closing stages of the war and the early stages of the peace. France had a treaty of alliance and mutual assistance with the Soviet Union. France had a zone of occupation in Germany and Austria, and was a member of the Allied Control Commission. France was a member of the Council of Foreign Ministers. France had a permanent seat in the Security Council of the United Nations. France was a major power in name, and it was French policy to act as such.

France was not, however, a major power in fact. In all respects, except that of artificial status by agreement, its international position had been markedly reduced. The structure of the French economy had become outmoded even before the war. To this deficiency had been added the widespread destruction of capital equipment and transportation systems, and lags in housing and modernization. Furthermore, the French political system had been badly strained by the war, and deep disturbances of the social structure of the country prevented the formation of a clear consensus about what was wanted in the way of a new political system. There was no military power in being of any importance and very little evidence of any real potential. If France were to be able to act effectively as a major power in the postwar world, the means had to be found in the first instance outside France.

By the end of 1945, the significance of France was pretty generally understood and accepted by the United States. France had a geographical position in Europe that was of basic strategic importance both militarily and politically. In both senses, France was a natural channel for the exercise of American and British influence in Western Europe. Unless France were sufficiently stable and strong, however, this position could not be used in any positive way. France could not act for or even with the United States and Great Britain if its weaknesses were open to pressure and exploitation by others. Conversely, and even if it had seemed desirable, France could not be eliminated as a force from the European picture. If left weak and unsupported, it could still act in a negative way on the basis of its geographical position, its recognized place in major power circles, and its nuisance value. Circumstances dictated that because France could not be done without, it had to be maintained.

France was given an Export-Import Bank loan of $550 million before the end of 1945. This was supplemented in May 1946 by a trade and financial agreement that provided $1.37 billion in credits, $1.8 billion in lend-lease cancellations, and a favorable adjustment of $1.4 billion on war surplus sales.[1] But an inflationary trend could not be checked. Outside funds were consumed on a piecemeal basis and could not be applied to constructive purposes. France also received a second Export-Import Bank loan of $650 million in May 1946. It became the first nation to receive a loan from the International Bank for Reconstruction and Development. But further support was needed. By the time it became clear that funds under the Marshall Plan would not be available until 1948, France was dangerously close to economic paralysis. The United States Congress was then persuaded to grant France $308.9 million under an interim aid act late in 1947. This act, unlike those authorizing previous grants, was marked by a significant shift in underlying intention. A precise objective was now visible—resistance to Soviet-Communist expansion. Consequently, the funds were precisely earmarked as limited direct aid, available only to selected liberated

---

[1] U.S. Department of State *Bulletin,* Vol. 14 (June 9, 1946), pp. 994-1000.

countries, and subject to exclusive administration by the United States.

The problem of supporting France, however, was not to be solved merely by grants-in-aid, because the causes of its adverse position were not purely economic and fiscal. In fact, in the course of 1946, the industrial output in France was approaching the prewar figure.[2] But government expenditures mounted rapidly, and corrective measures could not be applied either to fiscal policy or in other areas of economic policy. The reasons for this were basically political rather than economic.

The traditional balance of forces in French political life had been shattered by the war. All that was shown by the first elections after the war was that there was a general demand for a fresh constitutional start, that public opinion was grouped around three political focuses—Communist, Socialist, and Christian Socialist—and that the trend was generally to the left. There was no indication of the relative strengths of these groups, or how the remains of other parties would attach themselves.

The left-of-center trend led to the nationalization of key industries and to an extensive pattern of social legislation. The costs of these programs remained a heavy drain on government finances, a drain that it was politically impracticable to check. The distribution of political power made any but a coalition government impossible, and the requirements of coalition policy making confirmed the maladjustments of the French economy. The extent to which each party was able to act as a check on the operation of the whole was made clear by the effort to draft and to obtain the acceptance of a new constitution. What finally emerged and was accepted with skepticism rather than with conviction by the French electorate was a governmental structure that gave full rein to the unstable balance of political forces. General de Gaulle, who had carried the aura of his wartime career into the office of President, resigned in January 1946 in order to lead a conservative opposition to this development. His convinced pessimism about government by coalition and his reiterated conviction that the French party system would lead in-

[2] Industrial production reached 90 per cent of the 1938 level, and agricultural production was steadily improving. Exports and imports were mounting, although France continued to have a serious balance-of-payments problem.

evitably to national catastrophe furnished a dark background to this testing of political strength.

The national elections of 1946 demonstrated enough Communist strength to lead the French Communist party to claim a number of key ministries in the new coalition—notably foreign affairs, interior, and national defense. The claims were rejected, and for a month the Socialists attempted to govern without either the Communists or the Christian Socialists in the cabinet. They failed, and a new coalition was formed at the end of January 1947. Relations between the Communists and the other members of the coalition became unworkable. The Communists interferred with governmental policy on Indo-China and Madagascar. On domestic issues, they impeded the efforts of the government to deal with the economic problems that were jeopardizing standards of living. In May 1947, the Communists were dismissed from the cabinet.

A return at this point to the chronology of United States policy development makes it clear that these events coincided with the prolonged re-examination of the American position and with the shaping of an attitude of resistance to Soviet-Communist encroachments. The role of the French Communist party in French politics was consequently seen in a new light by the United States. The United States policy of maintaining France as a major power now had to be modified to the extent of defining the kind of major power that France should be—obviously one in which the Communist party exercised no significant influence.

This shift, acceptable as it was to anti-Communist opinion in France, nevertheless made trouble for any French Government of the period. For the Communist party remained strong. It continued to poll about one fourth of the votes in general elections. Its members were in key points of control in many French industries. Any coalition from which they were excluded was bound to have a difficult time. On the other hand, as American policy developed into a program of economic co-operation, it was equally clear to any French Government that the place of France in this European program was certain to be affected by its relations with the Communist party. The other French parties were consequently faced with devising a coalition that, on a very narrow base of popular support, would be able to avoid complete frustration by the forces that were excluded.

The problem was made more difficult by the reappearance of General de Gaulle as the leader of a new party of the right. Opinion could now move two ways from the center, and the number of hostile political combinations that could be made against any government was increased. Nevertheless, from November 1947 on, various coalitions, built around an ill-defined and highly unstable political center, governed France and constituted in international life the major power that the United States had informally committed itself to maintaining.

It can be seen from this record that the policy programs that the United States initiated in 1947, 1948, and 1949 could not be applied effectively to France in their general forms. Modifications were essential in terms of the actual economic and political conditions that existed in that country. So far as conversations for this purpose were carried on with any particular government and were confined to issues of domestic reconstruction, it proved possible for the United States to exercise considerable influence. The flow of American resources had the effect of giving the center coalition an effectiveness that was probably out of proportion to its real political strength.

But the relationship did not work so smoothly in connection with the creation of a North Atlantic Treaty Organization and in the application of the related military assistance program. Here the Government of France was engaged primarily in maintaining the position of France as a major power, and a wholly different set of interests, attitudes, and considerations came into play. A French Government could accede to American advice with respect to the reconstruction of the French economy, and gain strength by doing so. But the same government, if it accepted American advice with respect to French policy for Germany, the role of France in the North Atlantic Treaty Organization, the relations of France with the Soviet Union, or French colonial policy, was immediately exposed to attacks from the excluded right and left and, in addition, became detached from important elements in its own base of public support.

An illustration of how these contending forces worked was given by the fate in June 1948 of the London Agreement on Western Germany. The negotiation of this agreement was the first concrete move toward setting up a Western German Government. It was also an action taken without reference to the Soviet Union or to agreements for a unified control of Germany. The basis of the French position was lost in the process. Not only was German restoration in sight, but the ability of French policy to reverse the process was seriously reduced. France became the weakest member of a Western group of powers instead of continuing in an excellent bargaining position as the middle man of four major powers. Considerable pressure had been brought by the United States during the negotiations, and the French cabinet had accepted the American position with extreme reluctance. When the agreement was presented to the French National Assembly for approval, the government was attacked from all sides: from the right on the ground that French influence as a great power had been given away; from the left on the ground that the Soviet Union might be provoked to take action; and generally on the ground that Germany was now free to displace France in Europe. Although the agreement was finally edged through by a narrow margin, the National Assembly imposed so many detailed restrictions on its execution that French policy was tied, and France could only act as a brake on subsequent negotiations. Furthermore, at the first opportunity, the government was brought down on a domestic issue.

This account, however, cannot be taken to mean that United States policy was without support in France. Many important sectors of French opinion and some very influential centers of action operate in very sympathetic relationship to both the short- and long-term objectives of the United States. The economic and industrial planners maintained continuity of effort in the field of reconstruction and improvement and made use of American economic assistance to help realize their domestic objectives. They also worked to spread and institutionalize the concept of an integrated Europe.[3] In the political field, too, there were equivalent groups, some of which threw their energies into problems of the political integration of Europe, and, in this framework, approached the question of Germany from a point of view consonant with American aims. However, these groups were only elements, and by no means the controlling elements, in the French political scene. They could shape official policy proposals, but they lacked the organized political support that could get these proposals accepted and acted on.

As the requirements of United States policy grew until they amounted to no less than the political, economic, and military or-

---

[3] The most notable fruit of their effort was the formation of a European Coal and Steel Community, on the basis of the Schuman Plan. This was approved in early 1951.

ganization of the free world as a global counterpoise to the Soviet-Communist bloc, the maintenance of so clear and all-embracing a purpose became increasingly difficult in connection with France. The basic and continuing conditions that have been described above did not respond to efforts to change them. The instability of French governments remained. The gaps between any one government and the diverse expectations of the French body politic remained unclosed. French national aspirations and French performance in the international sphere became more and more unrelated. Yet France could neither be ignored, reduced in importance, nor eliminated from the operation of United States policy.

In the execution of the strategy of containment, France was from the start and continued to be a major uncertainty. At the best of times, the governments of France were reluctantly forced to acquiesce in American actions. For the most part, even after a delayed official acceptance of American positions had been won, there was no assurance that a French Government would be able to carry out an agreement. At the best of times, the United States was forced to compromise, to slow down, or to accept unsatisfactory French reservations to its proposals in order to avoid opening the way for the fall of cabinets whose domestic actions were in line with American wishes.

These difficulties grew rather than diminished as United States policies became global in their impact. In Asia, in the Middle East, and in Africa, American efforts to persuade new national states of the importance of adhering to the free world ran into the emotions created by French colonial policy in Indo-China and in North and West Africa. In the North Atlantic Treaty Organization, American efforts to create an integrated military force in Europe ran into French insistence that France had global imperial security commitments similar to those of Great Britain. In respect to the basic objective of creating a counterpoise to the Soviet Union, the American thesis was persistently, if unofficially, questioned by sectors of French opinion.

In spite of all this, the United States could only proceed on the course it had set. There was, for the period under consideration here, no viable alternative. France received the full benefits of economic assistance and shared with the rest of Western Europe in the economic recovery produced by this program. But it was clear to American policy makers and administrators that the expectations of the United States were not being met by France in return, and probably could not be met. No supplementary action by the United States could create political stability, and no amount of American resources could significantly alter the limited positive influence that France could bring to bear on the international situation. Conversely, France could not maneuver freely in the international scene. Although French policy sometimes came close to isolating France, the final step was not taken; for it was pretty generally understood that a France isolated from the United States and Great Britain would instantly lose its status as a major power. In that event, French expectations could never be satisfactorily realized. In terms of the development of United States policy, therefore, there could be no effective solution to the special problem of France.

Italy

In many superficial respects, Italy showed signs of presenting the United States with a problem of policy execution similar to the French problem. The same political groupings—Communist, Socialist, and Christian Democrat—emerged. The same basic leftward trend in political feeling appeared. The same economic dislocations existed.

There were important differences, however. Italy was a defeated state and made no claim to an international position. It was the survival of Italy that was underwritten by the United States and Great Britain, not its status. Italy remained almost a charity patient until July 1947, when the Italian Constituent Assembly ratified the peace treaty. Up to that point Italy was a recipient of vital necessities and guidance, and the question of Italy trying to develop an alternative position for itself scarcely existed. Tests of political strength between Italian parties could not really develop. Finally, when Italy did regain sovereignty, the Christian Democrats proved to be sufficiently strong to govern by themselves. The nature of the political compromises that had to be made were different from those required by the situation in France. By May 1947, both the Communists and the Socialists were excluded from the Italian Government.

The government, although continually pressed from the left—and later from the right—maintained itself and had real authority. No serious difficulties arose between it and the United States. Each had much to gain from the association. Each had much to lose from its interruption. Thus the American programs of economic assistance, military coalition, and military assistance developed smoothly in their Italian climate.

In fact, there were only two problems that fell outside the routine of economic and later of military assistance. These were to maintain the Christian Democrats in power and to ensure the integrity of the Italian state until such time as a defensive alliance was built up in Europe. Both of these problems became active after the American course was set to resist Communist advances. In both cases, the United States, with the full blessing of the Italian Government—but not without misgivings outside the government—intervened unhesitatingly and unilaterally in Italian affairs.

In accordance with the terms of the peace treaty, American troops were to be withdrawn from Italy by the middle of December 1947. Long before this date, however, Greece was being aided to resist Communist forces, and Communist regimes in Yugoslavia and Albania were in an expansive mood. Therefore, the United States, in preparing to withdraw its forces from Italy, expressed itself in terms designed to discourage any notion that Italy might be a worthwhile target for Communist adventures. President Truman stated, in accordance with the intent of the Truman Doctrine:

> If, in the course of events, it becomes apparent that the freedom and independence of Italy upon which the peace settlement is based are being threatened directly or indirectly, the United States, as a signatory of the peace treaty and as a member of the United Nations, will be obliged to consider what measures would be appropriate for the maintenance of peace and security.[4]

When the Communists were forced out of the government, they turned to vigorous opposition. One of their principal sources of strength was organized labor, and, in addition to unremitting political agitation, they initiated a series of strikes and riots. These grew in intensity toward the end of 1947. The government took precautionary measures against a seizure of power, and the United States held up its troop withdrawals to the last permissible moment. All of this built up to the elections of April 1948, in which the Communists sought a real test of strength. The United States did everything possible to influence the result.

[4] U.S. Department of State *Bulletin*, Vol. 17 (Dec. 21, 1947), p. 1221.

In reply to Communist boasts that American economic assistance would be continued even if they were voted into power, the Secretary of State warned that if the Italian elections resulted in a government whose dominant political elements were opposed to the European Recovery Program, the United States would have to conclude that Italy desired to dissociate itself from the program and would thus remove itself from the benefits. The United States sent large shipments of relief supplies, which the American Ambassador called to the attention of the Italian people. Letter writing and broadcasting campaigns were conducted from the United States. Many prominent American citizens of Italian origin urged the Italian people to vote against the Communists. No stone was left unturned, not even that of Trieste. Urged by the United States, Great Britain and France joined in proposing to the Soviet Union that steps be taken to return Trieste to Italy. The propaganda value of this proposal can be judged by the bitterness with which it was denounced by the Italian Communists, Yugoslavia, and the Soviet Union. The elections were a decisive victory for the Christian Democrats, and Italy could look ahead to five years of stable government.

This result confirmed and made secure the resources that the United States had put into Italy prior to the start of the economic assistance program. Italy was prepared to make effective use of the funds and resources that began to flow from the Economic Cooperation Act in the second half of 1948. In fact, the aim of United States policy—that Italy should become a constructive force in a peaceful Europe—met with no basic impediments.

From this flowed other consequences. Italy became an ardent supporter of the proposals for a European military alliance and for the creation of an integrated defense system. Italy made no difficulties and no exaggerated demands with respect to military assistance. Italy was throughout this period consistently willing and able to contribute to the achievement of American objectives. The contribution, in the first instance, was not large. But as the North Atlantic Treaty Organization became operative and military planning advanced, the free use of the geographical position of Italy in the Mediterranean and the value of Italy as a potential base for air and naval operations were definite advantages to the strategic concept of the United States.

The Small States

The place of the small states in the development of United States policy can be treated briefly and as a unit. Although their individual situations and internal problems were not identical, their roles in furthering American objectives and as recipients of American attention were generally similar.

Belgium had been freed of Germans at an early date with a minimum of destruction. The restored Belgian Government, with some American assistance at its disposal, with a relatively stable political atmosphere to return to, and with a plan for reconstruction that ran into no extreme political or economic obstructions, quickly achieved viability. The Belgian colonial system, untouched by either the war or native nationalism, contributed to this result. As carefully formulated programs of the United States were presented, Belgium was willing and able to participate effectively.

The Netherlands, in contrast, had suffered severe war damage, industrial and economic dislocation, and substantial losses of foreign investments. It found its major colonial area, the Netherlands East Indies, no longer available as a source of economic strength. However, the political coherence of Dutch society was unbroken, and the reconstruction plans of the government, austere and demanding as they were, were accepted and acted on with vigor. The requirements for assistance were great, but the Netherlands Government and people were prepared in every important way to make the most effective use of the resources made available to them. Thus the Netherlands was also a ready and co-operative partner in United States policy.

The two Scandinavian countries that required reconstruction, Denmark and Norway, were in reasonably good physical shape, because they had not been areas of more than incidental fighting. Here too, customary political and social cohesion was rapidly restored, and the basic problems of rehabilitation responded to American assistance and to domestic management.

Important as these qualities and conditions were, the essential contribution of the smaller states to forwarding the objectives of the United States lay in their acceptance of the concept of achieving security and renewing national strength by collective effort. This was a proposition that had already been carefully examined; and, so far as Belgium, the Netherlands, and Luxembourg were concerned, had been acted on to form the regional grouping called Benelux. As United States programs were expanded in these terms, the smaller states sympathetically accepted the underlying argument and acted as its most convinced and vigorous European proponents. For in their view, their national interests and their hopes of national survival as sovereign entities could best be realized as part of a larger unity. Thus no insoluble problems of application confronted the United States in these cases. Even the awkward liquidation of the East Indies empire, in the course of which the United States brought considerable pressure on the Netherlands Government, did not seriously impede action in a common interest.

Great Britain

The relationship of Great Britain to the range of United States policies under consideration was unique. The role of Great Britain, the Commonwealth, and Empire was basic to the strategic concept from which these policies developed. The nature of the case was that unless Great Britain could demonstrate that its position in the world was that of a major power, and unless it was disposed to act as a reliable ally of the United States, the cost to the United States of implementing a strategy of containment through a series of interlocking programs would be immeasurably increased.

The fundamental identity of purpose between the United States and Great Britain was generally accepted even before resistance to the Soviet Union became a focus of action by the United States. The original concept of great power harmony that underlay the postwar policy of the United States derived in part from this identity. Consequently, when American objectives became fixed on meeting and checking the Soviet threat to international security and stability, the capacity of Great Britain to act consistently and effectively as a collaborating major power became a matter of intense concern to United States policy makers. If they had been in doubt before, the close relationship between British weakness and a requirement of action by the United States was demonstrated by the British withdrawal from Greece and by the Truman Doctrine. From 1947 on, there seemed to be no alternative to compensating for British weakness except by developing American strength and redeveloping British strength. United States official statements stressed to the American people the importance of British recovery for world recovery and the significance of supporting and being supported by British policy at many key points on the international scene.

It was not always easy, however, for the United States Government to act on this basis. A fundamental identity of long-term objectives did not automatically produce agreement with respect to the means of reaching these goals or imply an identity of short-term objectives in particular situations. Furthermore, in spite of having been seriously weakened by the war, there was still no question that Great Britain was a major power and hence had to be accepted as a co-partner in matters of common interest.[5] British policy did not lie open to American influence as did the policies of some of the other states with which the United States was coming into ever closer relations.

Although the United States heartily supported the British intention of consolidating and maintaining British influence in the world, United States policy makers were often dubious about the strains to which British domestic and economic policy seemed to be subjecting British resources. The widely supported aims of the Labour Government—to achieve an economy of full employment and to create a thorough-going welfare state—seemed to many American observers to be biting off more than Great Britain could possibly chew. It was felt that foreign commitments were likely to be sacrificed to domestic policy, and that more and more of the international burden would fall to the American share.

By the end of 1947, it was becoming clear that the international position of Great Britain was suffering from at least three major causes: (1) the heavy internal demands on British production to meet the requirements of the welfare state and the policy of full

---

[5] The degree of weakness can be judged from the following: (a) By 1945 £1,000 million of foreign investments had been liquidated, and the net income from these sources was half what it had been in 1938; (b) income from shipping, insurance, and foreign banking sources was severely reduced; (c) the overseas debt had increased from £760 million (1938) to £3,355 million (1945); (d) the value of exports had decreased from £471 million (1938) to £258 million (1944), while imports had grown from £858 million (1938) to £1,299 million (1944). When account is taken of the more rapid increase of import as compared to export prices, the true deterioration of the trade position is shown to have been much greater; the volume of imports in 1944 was actually 20 per cent below the volume in 1938, while the volume of exports in that year was less than a third of the volume of 1938. These data were prepared by Williams Adams Brown, Jr. of the Brookings Institution.

employment; (2) the substantial flow of British capital to countries in which Great Britain had a traditionally strong political and economic interest; and (3) the external demands on British production created by overseas debts held in sterling, or to put it in technical terms, the problem of the sterling balances.

To make the problems of the British Government still more difficult, vast expenditures were required to finance British commitments for maintaining peace and security. The British Government endeavored to maintain a balance between these requirements and those of national economic policy. It tried to reduce the armed forces in order to release men and materials for civilian employment. At the same time, it tried to maintain sufficient military forces to meet commitments in Germany and Italy, in the Middle East (particularly in Palestine), in the Indian Ocean, the Far East, and elsewhere. In all these parts of the world, British forces were stationed in order to protect Imperial lines of communication, to carry out obligations assumed under the Charter of the United Nations, and to maintain British prestige. Between 1945 and the spring of 1948, when Great Britain as a signatory to the Brussels Pact assumed additional military obligations, substantial reductions were made in British armaments. The armed forces dropped from 1,427,000 in December 1946 to 940,000 in April 1948. The defense budget was reduced drastically after 1945, and emphasis was placed on long-range research and development rather than on operational strength. Personnel engaged in defense production was reduced from the wartime level of 3.5 millions to 450,000 in 1947-48. However, Great Britain continued to carry a heavy load as compared with other countries. During that period, the United States, with a population three times as large as that of Great Britain, cut its armed forces from about 2.8 millions to 1.34 million.

For reasons to which all of these strains contributed, Great Britain reached a point of fiscal crisis by early 1948. Severe remedial measures were applied by the government, some of which were distasteful to the United States.[6] However, it was clear that American assistance in addition to the loan of 1946 would be necessary. By this time, the Marshall proposal for a European Recovery Program had been made. The British Government did not attempt to

---

[6] Notably, the reduction of foreign military commitments and sharp reductions in imports and overseas expenditures, of which $800 million were to be dollar expenditures.

conceal its reliance on this sort of aid. It stated unequivocally that "the most important uncertainty of all in 1948 is whether United States aid under the European Recovery Plan will be forthcoming."[7] From the start, Great Britain took the lead in the series of conferences of European states that prepared Western Europe for the receipt of American funds by planning the institutions and determining the requirements of a recovery program. In many important though intangible ways, Great Britain was helpful to the United States in these early stages by participating as a European state while acting and arguing like a state to which Europe was only one of many concerns. This approach, although often irritating to European states, was useful to the United States because it tended to lift both planning and requirements above the level of multiple national policies and demands and permitted the United States initially to treat Europe as a regional unit.

This advantage, however, had its political price. It underlined the implicit British claim to a special relationship with the United States, a claim that United States policy accepted in principle, but reserved judgment about in particular instances. Thus so far as the European Recovery Program was concerned, the United States preferred to consider Great Britain as one among many European nations. But, with respect to its policy on Germany, it was prepared to regard Great Britain as a special partner. And, when the whole strategy of containment was set forth policy-wise in the North Atlantic Treaty, the mutual global security interests of the United States and Great Britain had no equivalent in any other phase of American international relations. Finally, when United States policies were applied in the Middle East and to colonial areas, Great Britain and the Commonwealth inevitably played a part that no other state or group of states could aspire to.

In the simplest language, the United States conceded that its security and its ability to achieve its objectives depended on what happened elsewhere in the world. It appreciated that what happened elsewhere in the world still depended to a considerable extent on British policy and on a British capacity to carry out policy. Thus a strong British economy as the foundation for a strong British international position was what the United States found itself committed to, unless—and this was a big order in 1948—the

---

[7] Great Britain, *Economic Survey for 1948*, Cmd. 7344 (1948), Foreword.

United States was prepared to act in many major respects and in many strategically important areas in place of Great Britain.

Western Europe as a Unit

The substance of this presentation has deliberately been set forth in terms of individual states because that is the pattern to which United States policy was obliged to conform as it was developed through the negotiation of supporting agreements and the execution of concrete programs. In addition, this breakdown provides the only device by which the factors of diversified national problems and purposes could be suggested, and the ways in which they forced modifications and compromises on American policy could be indicated. Nevertheless, essential as this approach is, this discussion would be incomplete if it did not also touch on the means that were available to the United States or that were created to counter this tendency toward fragmentation of policy.

It had been firmly insisted, officially and unofficially, that it was the intent of the United States to develop its assistance and security policies for Western Europe in terms of the area as a regional unit, and that the concept of integration was implicit in the policy formulations. Although this represented afterthought to some degree, there is no doubt that the desired end product of a Western Europe acting as a single whole, economically, politically, and militarily, was soon envisaged. There is equally no doubt that the United States expected to withdraw in time from its economic and political commitments to Western Europe and to rest on the military commitments incorporated in the North Atlantic Treaty.

The actual growth of policy, however, did not take this form. The tendency to fragmentation had to be met at all stages by encouraging an opposing tendency to unification. This tendency consisted of two forces: a self-generated European Movement and an American pressure that was partly technical and administrative, and partly a doctrinaire conviction of the advantages of integration.

On the European side, the European Movement culminated early in 1948 in the Congress of Europe, convened at The Hague by the International Committee of the Movements for European Unity. This Congress recommended the establishment of a European assembly, which was subsequently brought into being by the

Statute of the Council of Europe in May 1949. The joint purpose of the Council of Europe was reflected in the setting up of two organs: the Committee of Ministers was an institution of intergovernmental co-operation, in which governments were to reach agreement on common courses of action; and the Consultative Assembly was a deliberative organ for the discussion of questions of common concern. Its one hundred and thirty-two delegates were distributed among the member countries, primarily on the basis of population. They were elected by the national parliaments or appointed according to parliamentary instructions. Most national political parties, except the Communist, were represented. Each delegate served as an individual, and not as a representative of his country.

The United States Government welcomed this development as one that promoted constructive international integration. The functions of the Council, although extensive in principle and covering all fields except defense, were in fact restricted by the creation of other intergovernmental organizations. The United States proposals for economic recovery had led to the Organization for European Economic Cooperation, and the North Atlantic Treaty had resulted in the North Atlantic Treaty Organization. In practice, the principal role of the Council of Europe was to serve as a forum for stimulating action and focusing public opinion on problems of interest to Western Europe. Nevertheless, it exerted a certain amount of influence through its co-operative relationships with other Western European organizations. It furthered the association of Western Germany with the work of European co-operation. It urged the extension of European co-operation through the establishment of specialized agencies, including the European Coal and Steel Community. It supported the establishment of a European Army as "the only possible solution to the defence problems of Europe."[8]

In addition to this informal institution, organizations with more specific functions were established. Starting with the Brussels Pact of March 1948, which set up a Consultative Council, new institutions multiplied rapidly. The Organization for European Economic Co-

[8] See Council of Europe, *Concise Handbook of the Council of Europe*, Directorate of Information (1951), U.S. Department of State Regional Organizations, Publication 4944 (April 1953), pp. 17-19; and Great Britain, *Statute of the Council of Europe*, May 5, 1949, Cmd. 7778 (1949).

operation, charged with preparing and implementing measures of economic co-operation, reviewing action taken by individual countries, and assisting the United States in carrying out the recovery program, followed shortly and developed an elaborate structure of its own, including the European Payments Union and the Commercial Code. The North Atlantic Treaty proliferated organizations: the North Atlantic Council, the Defense Committee, the Standing Group, the Defense Financial and Economic Committee, and the Military Production and Supply Board.

This complex of institutions dealt, in effect, with the widest range of political, economic, and security questions and between them, those questions were handled in ways that led in many instances to an agreed basis of common policies and to co-operative action to carry out these policies. By this means, national interests and purposes were modified by processes of negotiation and persuasion, and pressure by the United States could be tactfully applied to a group of sovereign states rather than clumsily directed to single states.

CHAPTER XI
Areas of Application: The Peripheral World

A LARGE and amorphous area remains to be examined in connection with the early application of the policies and programs that the United States initiated under a strategy of containment. Because there would be little value in trying to make satisfactory geographical-historical distinctions between the regions within this area, it is merely pointed out that the area extends from the Eastern Mediterranean to the outer limits of the East Indian archipelago, and includes the Middle East, South, and Southeast Asia. If the states of this area have any characteristics in common, these can probably be expressed by the current phrase "former colonial and underdeveloped regions." Seen from the point of view of American purposes, as these purposes were understood in 1948, the situations, the needs, and the expectations of these states were so diversified that they did not obviously fall within the range of programs of economic recovery or appear to be suitable candidates for military alliances.

For a variety of reasons, however, these states were continually involved in the development of United States policy. Even if comprehensive programs could not be tailored to fit the countries of the Middle East, the role of these states was undeniably a major one in a strategy of containment. An equivalent role fell to the countries of Southeast Asia when China became a Communist state. In addition, because all of these states had recently been or still were in some sort of semidependent relationship with the states of Western Europe, the political disorders and the economic dislocations attendant on nationalist movements impinged on both the United States recovery program for Europe and on the unrelated but widely held United States position with respect to political self-determination for colonial peoples.

The countries of this area had, of course, been in the American eye when the basic objectives for the postwar world were being shaped. They were obvious candidates for higher standards of living as well as for self-government. It had not, however, been wholly foreseen that they would take the matter of self-government

208

into their own hands and undertake national struggles for independence that would undermine any idea of self-government coming by the slower processes of political maturity and social evolution. Nor was it foreseen that these political revolutions would also tend to become internal social revolutions, marked by harsh words about capitalist imperialism and economic exploitation, and stimulated by a Communist concept of the character and method of social change. While the desire for freedom of colonial peoples and the problems of their social and economic betterment became active, as it was expected they would become, the directing of this important development did not remain in the hands of the United Nations or under the guidance of the advanced Western nations. It became a series of indigenously guided struggles, marked by the inexperience, xenophobia, sensitivity, and self-assertiveness of most of the small nationalist movements of the past one hundred years. It consequently gave rise to situations that could not be easily brought within the scope of the newer pattern of policy that the United States developed.

Nevertheless, growing from the original broad statement in the Truman Doctrine to the effect that "it must be the policy of the United States to support free peoples who are resisting attempted subjugation by armed minorities or by outside pressures," programs of economic and military assistance developed facets that drew these states within their framework. In the same gradual way, the policy that led to the North Atlantic Treaty Organization searched for formulas that might lead to similar defensive alliances in other parts of the world. The Point Four proposal, emerging as the Act for International Development in 1950, was a generalized policy formulation addressed to the states of this area and in part designed to bring them within the elaborate process of organizing the free world to resist pressure, subversion, inroads, or attacks from the Soviet-Communist bloc.

The Mediterranean-Middle East

Although the first application of a strategy of containment was made in the Eastern Mediterranean, in Greece and Turkey, the extensions of this strategy in the two years that followed were not primarily designed for use in this part of the world, nor were they easily adaptable to the situations that prevailed there. Yet, policy makers of both the United States and Great Britain saw this region as one of key strategic importance in relation to the Soviet Union. Consequently, it was tacitly understood that military means were primary and economic means secondary in policies designed specifically for this region.

President Truman, nearly a year before the Truman Doctrine was drafted, stated this point of view:

The Near and Middle East comprise an area which presents grave problems. This area contains vast natural resources of enormous value. It lies across the most convenient routes of land, air, and water communication between the west and east. It is consequently an area of great strategic importance. In this area there are a number of friendly sovereign states, members of the United Nations. They are not strong enough individually or collectively to withstand armed aggression on the part of any great power.

It is easy to see, therefore, how the Near and Middle East might become an arena of intense rivalry between outside powers, and how such rivalry might suddenly erupt in armed conflict.[1]

To this statement can be added the fact that the petroleum reserves of the Middle East, which were estimated in 1948 to be 60 per cent of the proved petroleum reserves of the world, had become a major interest to the United States and Western Europe. Production of petroleum in the Middle East was 13 per cent of the world total. Of this, nearly 80 per cent was consumed in Western Europe and was increasingly essential to its economy.

Furthermore, the Soviet Union, even before the end of the war, had shown an active interest in reviving the role of Imperial Russia in this region. It was exerting diplomatic and propaganda pressures on Turkey and Iran. It was attempting to establish footholds in the region—demanding a trusteeship over former Italian territory, trying to force Turkey to agree to exclusive Soviet-Turkish control of the Straits. It was dabbling with revolution in Iran and Greece. The United States and Great Britain, convinced of the strategic necessities involved, firmly resisted all these efforts. By the end of 1946, the Soviet Union had been checked except at two points: Yugoslavia and Albania were Communist states, and there was a Communist-led civil war going on in Greece. In addition, there was the fact that this was the only region in the world in which the Soviet Union actually bordered an area of long-standing Western

[1] Army Day Address, *Congressional Record*, Vol. 92, Pt. 10, Appendix, p. A-2066 (Apr. 11, 1946).

influence and interest. These considerations were sufficient to keep the political and military strategists of both the United States and Great Britain alert.

Alertness was not enough, however. The region was not amenable to either United States or British policy. In so far as the states of the region were Arab, nationalism tended to resist any continuance of British influence and tutelage. In general, they pressed hard against the political and commercial ties that held them to Great Britain, and that helped to maintain its strategic position. At the same time, the peoples of the region were poor, the countries were economically disorganized, and the governments were politically unstable. If they freed themselves wholly from their ties with the West, they had no means at their disposal for developing into the kind of strong, stable, and secure states that United States and British policy required.

In principle, these conditions should have made this region a suitable one in which to apply programs of economic development, military assistance, and defensive alliance. In fact, however, for various reasons, none of these programs worked. Programs of economic recovery had little meaning in countries whose economies were both agrarian and on a subsistence level. Programs of relief or development found few institutional channels through which they could be effectively carried out, and the social and political structure of the Arab world was resistive to the development of such institutions. Finally, nationalist demands and cultural pride created opposition to all proposals faster than they could be negotiated and applied.

Nevertheless, the United States and Great Britain were committed by their strategic concepts and interests. In particular, the United States was committed by its objective of building an association of free nations. Both countries, therefore, had no valid alternative to continuing to work with this incoherent and resistive material. The joint problem of the United States and Great Britain was made more intractable by the fact that they did not always see eye to eye about the nature of the problem or about ways of meeting it.

Great Britain had treaty ties with Egypt, Greece, Iran, Iraq, Jordan, and Turkey and valued highly the military base rights and other strategic perquisites that these agreements provided. Although British policy was willing to bend to the pressure of Arab nationalism, Great Britain was unwilling to relinquish its advantages unless its strategic requirements were met by something equally satisfactory, such as well trained and equipped local armies and tight military agreements. Anything that could be done additionally to increase economic strength or to provide political stability, although all to the good, was considered a secondary effort. The United States admitted the importance of British rights and shared the strategic advantages they furnished. Nevertheless it tended to place greater relative emphasis on policies of aid and on co-operative efforts to improve the social, economic, and political structure of the Middle East.

In spite of steady agreement between the United States and Great Britain on ultimate objectives, their differences in approach enabled the countries of the region to force the United States and Great Britain into opposing positions on specific issues. Often the United States seemed to act to encourage Arab states to oppose British rights and privileges, or Great Britain appeared to be cool to American proposals for extending financial aid and advice to the Arab world. Conversely, American policy makers often felt that the British were looking too much to their own special interests when they refused to back American insistence that the states of the Middle East should be more conscious of the Soviet menace and more willing to join in meeting it.

Anticipating the troubles in which it would be involved after the war, Great Britain had encouraged the Arab states to develop political unity. This appeared to be the best way of channeling Arab nationalism and of laying the foundations for an Arab world capable of defending itself and hence able to contribute to British security. The Pact of the League of Arab States became operative in May 1945. Its purpose was "the strengthening of relations between the member states; the coordination of their policies in order to achieve cooperation between them and to safeguard their independence and sovereignty; and a general concern with the affairs and interests of the Arab countries."[2] Its establishment was welcomed by the United States and Great Britain, viewed with alarm by France, and denounced by the Soviet Union as an imperialistic device. The League, however, turned out to be an organ of disturbance. It developed none of the corporate strength that its supporters desired. On the contrary, it revealed the dynastic rivalries

<hr/>

[2] *United Nations Treaty Series,* Vol. 30 (1950), p. 248.

and conflicting interests of its members and succeeded in reducing these differences only by directing Arab nationalism against two targets—the Jewish state of Israel and the liberation of the Arab peoples from every last vestige of foreign control.

The problems that have been described here in general terms were naturally presented as concrete and diverse situations, each of which had to be dealt with as it arose. In nearly every case, it was a British position that was called in question. Moreover, a change in the British position involved a question of the security of the region and hence became a matter of concern to the United States. The question of determining what, if any, action the United States should take in these situations was sooner or later raised.

Anglo-Egyptian Treaty

The first attack on a British position came from Egypt, which immediately after the war demanded revision of the 1936 treaty of alliance. The key issues in dispute, aside from a nationalist wish not to be allied at all, were British base rights in the Suez Canal Zone and the disposition of the Anglo-Egyptian Sudan. Negotiations began in April 1946 and dragged inconclusively into 1947 when the Egyptian Government tried to get the matter before the Security Council of the United Nations. The Council, however, was unable to agree on any recommendations. The Egyptians then urged the United States to send a military mission to Egypt to replace British forces. The United States refused. The negotiations lapsed and were not renewed until 1950. In the intervening years, bitterness accumulated, and Egyptian nationalism, fanned by domestic politics, became increasingly vocal. When the negotiations were resumed, they took place in an atmosphere that soon turned them into a test of strength. By this time, United States global policy was being subjected to pressure by the Soviet-Communist bloc, and the United States became involved in a backstage mediating role, concentrating on a search for an alternative arrangement to the presence of British troops that would ensure equally the security of Egypt and the Middle East, and the communications of the free world. At no time, however, could the Egyptian Government be persuaded to see the issues as in any way related to the larger problem of security against the Soviet Union. The protagonists, therefore, argued on wholly distinct levels: the United States on the security of the free world, the British on the security of their own and Western interests in the Middle East, and the Egyptians on the primacy of Egypt among the states of the Middle East.

British Treaty with Iraq

A similar attack on a reduced scale was made by Iraq. On the basis of a prewar treaty, Great Britain maintained two large air bases and garrisons in Iraq. The revision of this treaty was demanded in 1946. In the course of several cabinet changes in the Iraqi Government, each new premier more vigorously asserted a policy of treaty revision. The British Government tried to ameliorate the situation by withdrawing its troops, except for air force detachments. This seemed to make it possible to conclude a new treaty, the Portsmouth Treaty of January 1948. The negotiators, however, had not correctly judged the strength of Iraqi nationalism or the ease with which it could be manipulated by a political opposition. Public opinion reacted so strongly that the Iraqi Government was obliged to refuse ratification. No effort was made to proceed further in the matter until more moderate influences took over in Iraq. The British position remained tacitly unchallenged. However, the incident, linked as it appeared to be with the Egyptian attack on British treaty rights, provided another illustration of the uncertainties that confronted Western policy in the Middle East.

Turkey

The case of Turkey was different. Turkey bordered the Soviet Union. It was sensitive to Soviet pressures. It not only clung to its treaty of mutual assistance with Great Britain and France, but also welcomed agreements with the United States. Without strain on any of the parties concerned, Turkey moved from British military and economic assistance to military and economic assistance from the United States. In many respects, Turkey was an almost ideal subject for United States policy. Its strategic significance was indisputable. American resources, both of money and equipment, could be, and were, directly applied to creating military strength and to establishing an economic base. Turkey was even more intent on containing the Soviet Union than was the United States. Turkey was rewarded with a favored place in United States policy. It was included in the European Recovery Program, thereby becoming a member of the Organization for European Economic Cooperation, and, in due course and at American insistence, a participant in the North Atlantic Treaty Organization. The United States came to believe that in Turkey it had found a possible alternative approach to the strategic problem of the Middle East; for Turkey might replace Egypt as a focal point of strength in the region. The flaws in this view were only gradually revealed. Too much strain was put on an economy that was essentially underdeveloped and that could scarcely support the weight of policy that was erected on it. However, for the period 1947 to 1950, Turkey participated effectively in the development of United States strategy and was regarded as the saving grace in the Near Eastern scene.

Palestine Problem

A saving grace was badly needed because, in addition to inherent difficulties, there was the burning issue of the Jews in Palestine. In May 1946, the report and recommendations of the Anglo-American Committee of Inquiry into Palestine were published and resulted in a split between the United States and Great Britain. The United States called for immediate action on a recommendation to permit extensive Jewish immigration. Great Britain wanted the report as a whole to be implemented because it recommended restraints on the Jews. The British also wanted "to ascertain to what extent the Government of the United States would be prepared to share the resulting military and financial responsibilities."[3] For nine months thereafter, fruitless conversations went on between Great Britain, the United States, and Arab and Jewish leaders. Meanwhile, violence increased in Palestine, and the British, responsible under their mandate for maintaining law and order, were committed to an even more costly police action. President Truman suggested trading the admission of 100,000 Jewish immigrants for a recommendation to the Congress of a plan to assist the economic development of Palestine.

Now American opinion began to divide. On the one hand, there were the humanitarian feelings arising from the treatment of the Jews in Europe. To these were added the strong pressures that Zionist circles in the United States were able to bring to bear on the administration. On the other hand, there were the official views

---

[3] British Information Services, *Britain and Palestine*, ID 716 (1947), p. 11.

of those who linked the security of the United States, Middle East oil, and the general operation of the strategy of containment with the maintenance of good relations with the Arab world. In these views, the claim of the Jews on Palestine did not count for much.

In early 1947, the British Government decided that the only course left was to submit the problem to the United Nations, which set up a Special Committee to investigate all questions and issues relevant to Palestine and to report to the General Assembly. On the basis of this report, the General Assembly, in November 1947, voted to recommend the partitioning of Palestine, the formation of an economic union of the two parts, and the termination of the British mandate. The reaction of the Arab world was that once again foreign influences, principally Western, had imposed a decision on the peoples of the Middle East. The Arab League now had a cause that was more immediate and more significantly localized than British imperialism.

By February, armed detachments of Arabs were entering Palestine, and clashes were frequent. The United States began to back away from the situation and proposed that because the partition plan could not be implemented by peaceful means, a temporary United Nations trusteeship should be established. The proposal was not accepted, and in April the Security Council called for a truce in Arab-Jewish hostilities. By the end of that month, the Truce Commission reported that fighting was steadily increasing in intensity.

In May 1948, Great Britain formally terminated its mandate and withdrew its troops. On the same day, the Jewish state of Israel was proclaimed and was given *de facto* recognition by the United States. Shortly thereafter, Arab armies from Egypt, Iraq, Lebanon, Syria, and Jordan entered Palestine. The Arab League inspired a great deal of Arab feeling, but not much military equipment or skill. Israel ultimately succeeded in defending itself until the United Nations re-established a truce. By the middle of 1949, a series of unstable armistices had been achieved, and the Middle East settled down to a situation composed of uncertainties and unresolved antagonisms.

The peace that was reached was technical rather than actual. The appearance of the new state of Israel and the inconclusive Arab-Jewish war produced some very significant changes in the political and strategic situation in the Middle East. Israel was the victor in the war, partly because of a good deal of assistance from abroad, and partly because of the solidarity of the Jewish people. In contrast, the Arab League showed itself an inadequate instrument of political action. One consequence of the war was to drive almost one million Arabs from their homes. This burdened the surrounding Arab countries and the Arab-occupied parts of Palestine with a considerable refugee problem. The existence of this unabsorbed group helped to keep Arab animosity toward the West alive, especially toward the United States, which the Arabs considered had favored Israel at their expense.

American support undoubtedly played a considerable part in the establishment of Israel. It was largely through the influence of the United States that the resolution calling for partition was adopted by the General Assembly. The United States was the first to grant *de facto* recognition to the new state. Moreover, unofficial economic assistance came in large measure from the United States, and there was promise in 1948 of official United States economic aid. On the other hand, while the British maintained close economic ties with Israel, the over-all interests of Great Britain called for policies and action in support of Arab aims. The divergence between the positions of the United States and Great Britain, slight in reality but large in Arab eyes, increased still more the difficulty of developing a uniform and coherent approach to the Middle East.

It can be concluded, from the story up to this point, that although the policy of the United States had a suitable field for operation in Turkey, the rest of the Middle East was an area in which policy was certain to run into difficulties. The Arab states, taken individually, could not respond effectively to programs of economic assistance and would not respond at all to suggestions for co-ordinated security policies. But they would accept, and even pressed for grants and loans while refusing to negotiate any *quid pro quo* for such aid. Military equipment would have been highly acceptable, as a means of balancing accounts with Israel but not as part of an Anglo-American strategy of containing the Soviet Union. The course of United States policy did not and could not run straight and clear through these obstacles. Yet the requirements of American strategy were such that the United States Government had to continue to search for ways of adapting its policies to the realities of the situation in the Middle East. The nature of these requirements, as well as the problem of satisfying them, is illustrated by the case of Iran.

Iran

Iran, a Mohammedan country but not an Arab state, was the extreme eastern outpost of the Middle East. It also bordered on the Soviet Union, and its recent history had been that of a buffer state between imperial Russian and imperial British interests. Its oil fields were rich producers. Its geographical location was one of the keys to the control of the Middle East, the Indian Peninsula, and the major East-West communication routes. When, at the end of the war, the Soviet Union refused to withdraw its troops from Iran and encouraged a movement to detach the northern province of Azerbaijan, the United States and Great Britain reacted vigorously.[4] When they failed to move the Soviet Union, they supported Iran in bringing the issue before the Security Council of the United Nations in January and again in March 1946. Soviet troops were withdrawn, possibly although not certainly, because of the extremely strong stand that the United States took in public and was reported to have taken even more vigorously in private.

But Soviet pressures were not reduced. There remained in Iran an organized and active party, the Tudeh, which was pro-Soviet. It encouraged labor and civilian disorders, which began to affect the British oil fields and refinery. The Iranian Government began to draw in Great Britain and the United States as a countering force. By October 1947, the United States had agreed to send a military mission to Iran, a move that the Soviet Union protested as incompatible with the Soviet-Iranian Treaty of 1921. Following this, the United States loaned Iran $26 million to purchase military equipment, later brought Iran within the scope of the military assistance program, and still later within a variant of the economic assistance program. However, and this is important, these applications of basic policies to Iran were almost entirely free from the conditions that were attached to the same policies when applied in Western Europe.

While the United States found the Iranian Government willing to participate in the development of United States policies and, at least in principle, not resistive to the strategic implications of these policies, the relationship remained an uncertain one. It rested on

---

[4] The United States, Great Britain, and the Soviet Union had agreed at the Teheran Conference of December 1943 to respect the integrity and independence of Iran during and after the war, and to withdraw their troops within six months after the end of the war.

tacit assumptions, unformulated understandings, and the constant adjustment of Iranian demands and United States proposals. It was always subject to the contingencies of Iranian politics, the rise and fall of Soviet pressures, and the rise and fall of tension in the attitude of the United States toward the Soviet threat.

The Eastern Mediterranean

The relationship of the broad lines of United States policy to the situation in the Middle East must also be looked at from another angle. It will be recalled that the initial move on new broad lines had been the decision to assist Greece and Turkey in resisting Communist subversion and Soviet pressure. If the Middle East was defined as a region of primary strategic importance, then the Eastern Mediterranean had to be rated equally high as a channel of access to the Middle East and as a route by which the Middle East could be outflanked. It was so rated in British policy, and it quickly became so rated in United States policy.

From this point of view, the situation in the Eastern Mediterranean gave rise to considerable uneasiness. In Yugoslavia and Albania, on the northern littoral and separating Greece from Italy, Soviet-Communist forces had access to the Mediterranean. The southern littoral was occupied by Egypt and by the former Italian colony of Libya, whose ultimate status was still unsettled. The eastern littoral contained Syria and Lebanon, engaged in asserting their independence against France, and the sore spot of Israel. The only points at which United States policy could be applied directly were Greece and Turkey. The only additional means of exerting influence was by exhibiting United States naval and naval air power on a continuing basis and by drawing the United Nations into the picture. A United States fleet was maintained in the Mediterranean. The question of Libya was turned over to the United Nations.

The United States commitment was so precise in Greece, and the United States objective was so clearly formulated, that policy was executed with great firmness. By November 1947, it was realized that the original program of economic assistance would have to be subordinated to the demands of the military situation. The change in emphasis was made immediately and was reflected in subsequent congressional appropriations. When the Greek Communists announced the formation of a provisional government in December 1947, the United States declared that any recognition of this government by other states would have "serious implications." In the course of 1948, the strength of Greece was gradually built up, entirely on the basis of American resources and under increasing American guidance and control. In the course of 1949, the civil war was brought to a successful conclusion. By the end of the year, the Greek Government was beginning to talk of a regional Mediterranean defense pact, and the United States was beginning to think of drawing Greece and Turkey into the North Atlantic Treaty Organization.

The winding up of the Greek civil war cannot be dissociated from the course of events in Yugoslavia in 1948. Yugoslavia had, from the start, supported the Greek Communists and had, in effect, enabled them to drain off American and Greek resources by devices that could not be stopped without pulling Yugoslavia into the conflict. Through the whole of 1947, American-Yugoslav relations were as bad as possible, short of a final diplomatic break, which the United States never seriously considered. The situation was changing in favor of the United States although its policy makers were unaware of the change. Yugoslavia was breaking with the Soviet Union. By the middle of 1948, the split was in the open, and the United States, instead of being confronted by a penetration of the Soviet-Communist bloc in the Eastern Mediterranean, was now dealing with a national Communist state that was both willing and anxious to secure itself against reprisals by accommodating itself to the West. Although for some time to come, Yugoslavia was to play a lonely role as an independent Communist state, removed from the shelter of the Soviet sphere but chary of admitting Western influence, the immediate necessities of United States policy were relieved. By mid-1949, Yugoslavia had ceased to support the Greek Communists who were then disposed of in short order. By early 1950, the situation in the Eastern Mediterranean was more or less stabilized, and the Greek Government informed the United Nations that it was settling its differences with Yugoslavia by direct negotiation.

The question of Libya, which never became serious even though it became confused, was resolved by the United Nations. In the fall of 1949, a temporary trusteeship was established, to be administered by Great Britain and France through a United Nations Commissioner, and with specific instructions that Libya was to be constituted an independent and sovereign state not later than the end of 1951. The Soviet Union was frozen out, and the large wartime air base at Tripoli continued firmly in Western hands. It was clear that Libya, as a state without visible means of support, would come wholly within the scope of either United States assistance policy or American-supported British assistance policy.

By the end of 1949, United States action under a strategic concept of containment had scored a measure of success in the Eastern Mediterranean. This success, however, could not be converted into more effective action in the Middle East. It could only serve to keep the problems of the Middle East from becoming more intractable.

Former Colonial Regions

Between the borders of Iran and the reaches of the Pacific Ocean had lain before the war the major colonial territories of the states of Europe. At the end of the war, this extensive colonial region began to fragment into independent and sovereign states. When the victorious European states proved unable quickly to restore the *status quo ante* in the colonial East and the pressure of nationalism mounted, United States policy viewed the process of change with complacency and was only concerned that it should come about slowly and peacefully. In general, the United States urged European states to negotiate new relations with their colonial peoples, arguing that the inevitable should be faced willingly and gracefully.[5]

The possibility that there might be an unfavorable as well as a happy relationship between this process of change and the United States objective of a peaceful and secure international order was not widely examined by United States policy makers in the years immediately following the war. The sole argument was that demands for national self-determination had to be met if a peaceful world was to be achieved.[6] The possibility that the acceptance of such demands might lead to as much disorder and instability as a

[5] United States relations with the Philippine Islands was the often repeated illustration of how this should be done.

[6] The argument ran that the forces of national sentiments released by the war were so strong that, unless the colonial powers acknowledged a responsibility to promote self-government, a continuous source of unrest and instability would exist and be a threat to a peaceful world order. Hence, the trusteeship provisions of the United Nations Charter.

refusal to meet them did not reach the level of serious consideration.

This broad policy position was not significantly modified by the first formulation of a strategy of containment. Consequently, the policies of assistance and alliance that arose from the strategy of containment underwent strange changes as they were applied in regions and to situations in which were operating another range of purposes derived largely from general principles of self-determination.

Before examining the inhibitions on action that followed from this conflict of objectives, the chronology of events should be laid out. Throughout 1946, the major effort of European states went into attempting to restore political control in the colonial belt. Conditions varied widely between the Indian empire, where the British Government was committed to negotiating a new political relationship; the Netherlands East Indies empire, where British forces had taken the Japanese surrender, where a native republican government was well entrenched, and where the Netherlands sought to reassert its authority; and French Indo-China, where a somewhat similar situation prevailed, but in more complicated form. The position of the United States with respect to these efforts was awkward. American military equipment and supplies were available to the European forces involved and were, of course, identified as such by the native regimes. At the same time, the policy of the United States operated to check vigorous police action by European forces. This was equally noted and made use of by native regimes. No clear-cut American policy had emerged by the end of 1946.

By 1947, it will be recalled, the United States had reoriented its policies and focused them on the actions of the Soviet-Communist bloc. And in the course of 1947, the possibility of achieving American objectives in China and Korea was demonstrably being frustrated by both the Soviet Union and indigenous Communist groups. The changes that came about in the colonial belt took place against this background.

In early 1947, the British Government took steps to honor its pledge to the Indian empire. The negotiations proceeded steadily and resulted, in August 1947, in the establishment of three independent and sovereign states: India, Pakistan, and Ceylon. All retained many of their ties with Great Britain and became members of the Commonwealth. A different development took place in the case of Burma. Contrary to its own desires, the British Government was obliged to agree in 1947 to complete Burmese independence and to the severance of all political ties.

Indonesia

The situation in the Netherlands East Indies was brought before the United Nations in January 1946, by the Ukraine, apparently as a Soviet move to embarrass Great Britain, whose troops were policing the region. The Ukranian resolution, calling for a commission to determine the facts, was defeated. In March, the Netherlands landed its own forces in Java, and negotiations began between the Netherlands and the indigenous government of the republic that had emerged from the war. The Netherlands recognized the *de facto* control of the republic over Java, Sumatra, and Madura and agreed to co-operate with it in setting up the states of Borneo and Eastern Indonesia, which, together with the republic, were eventually to form the United States of Indonesia. The two independent states—the Netherlands and Indonesia—were then to join in a union that would handle foreign affairs, defense, and certain matters of finance. The Netherlands was to aid Indonesia in forming or setting up the organs of government. Where required, the approval of the Netherlands parliament was promised. A year later, despite several alarms that the agreement might break down, it was formally signed. The United States and Great Britain soon granted the republic limited *de facto* recognition.

Netherlands armed strength in the islands, however, had steadily increased, and controversy over the political interpretation of the agreement had sharpened. A deadlock was reached, and a possible test of strength appeared likely. The United States Government, now beginning to formulate proposals for restoring the economies, stability, and prestige of the states of Western Europe, intervened in the situation with advice to Indonesia. The effect of this seems to have been the weakening of the Indonesian Government with respect to its own followers. The Netherlands Government, apparently wishing to take advantage of this weakness, began a "police action" in Indonesia to restore order.

The United States and Great Britain attempted mediation to keep the issue from being brought before the United Nations. However, India and Australia got it before the Security Council at the end of July 1947. A cease-fire was ordered and complied with, but the United Nations found it hard to recommend the next step. Soviet-Communist delegates and those of many other states supported Indonesia. Belgium, France, and Great Britain—all colonial powers—supported the Netherlands. The United States tried to find a middle ground from which negotiations between the parties concerned could be reopened. The upshot was a United Nations Committee of Good Offices, of which the United States was a member.

Throughout subsequent developments, the United States found itself officially walking a tight rope between its aims with respect to the Netherlands and the proclaimed principles of the United States with respect to the claims of colonial peoples to govern themselves. United States opinion was itself split. Public feeling and congressional opinion supported the Indonesian position. The executive agencies, particularly the Department of State and the military services, were concerned with strengthening the position and role of the Netherlands in Europe. Some elements of the administration wanted to achieve both results at the same time.

Negotiations under the Committee of Good Offices carried over into 1948. Although paper progress was made, both parties maneuvered for better positions of strength in the islands, and confidence in each other's good faith wore thin. In September 1948, there was an extremist-led revolt against the Indonesian Government. The Netherlands Government claimed that it could not negotiate with a government that did not have effective control of its territory. In December, after an ultimatum, the Netherlands initiated surprise military operations. The report of the Committee of Good Offices to the Security Council on this action was unfavorable to the Netherlands.

The Netherlands military effort was unsuccessful. The Republican armies maintained their cohesion and moved into parts of the country that the Netherlands had previously controlled. By the spring of 1949, the Republican armies had scored many successes in Java and Sumatra. Dutch plantations and industrial establishments suffered heavily from the activities of guerrillas and, from the point of view of the Netherlands, there were unfortunate political repercussions in the separatist states it had previously set up.

Meanwhile, the United States was re-examining its Far Eastern position and policies. The collapse of the Chinese Nationalists was clearly imminent, and the United States Government was becoming concerned about the possible spread of Communist influence in Asia. Because the Indonesian Republic had a clean bill so far as communism went, and because the principle of self-determination was still very much alive, the re-examination led to the conclusion that some degree of freedom from colonialism was the answer. The argument now ran that resistance to the demands of nationalism strengthened extremist elements and played into Communist hands. Furthermore, disorders and strife made it impossible to act to restore economic activity. Thus misery was prolonged, and people became susceptible to Communist agitation. Finally, although it was United States policy to provide economic assistance to prevent this latter development, such a policy could not be applied until a political settlement had been reached. This argument, whether correctly founded or not, was convincing in the climate of 1948-49; for it combined the requirements of a strategy of containment with a widely accepted judgment about the relationship of the process of colonial change to the problem of checking the expansion of Soviet-Communist influence. However, the implication of this line of reasoning was that pressure should be brought on colonial powers to withdraw, after which the United States would be prepared to sustain the new sovereign states that emerged.

Action to this effect was taken in early 1949, much of it in the form of discreet pressure on the Netherlands Government. But the United States Senate was explicit and general. It amended the Economic Cooperation Act to make it mandatory upon the administration to discontinue assistance whenever it determined that such assistance would be inconsistent with the obligations of the United States Government under the Charter of the United Nations.[7]

The Netherlands slowly responded to this pressure, which was supplemented by a critical climate in the United Nations General Assembly. At the end of December 1949, sovereignty was formally transferred to the Republic of Indonesia.

This story has been told at some length because it was the first major test of the position of the United States with respect to the political and strategic implications of the fragmentation of the Asian colonial belt. While it does not illustrate all the factors that

[7] The reference was to Art. 1(2) of the Charter: "To develop friendly relations among nations based on respect for the principle of equal rights and self-determination of peoples."

came to be involved in this kind of situation, it does suggest the pattern of the American reaction that was developed.

United States policy toward Indonesia had originally been to persuade the Netherlands to develop a moderate position. The extreme position of the Netherlands aroused such international antagonism that the principles of the United Nations were shaken, and the Netherlands was placed in an untenable position. However, at this early stage, the United States was careful not to advocate positions that would not be accepted by a large and influential body of Dutch opinion. Any action that weakened the Netherlands economy and the ability of the Netherlands to play a role in Western Europe would have run counter to the United States policy of restoring the prestige, power, and prosperity of that part of the world. In following this course, however, the United States Government was limited by the tolerance of the Congress, domestic opinion, the attitude of other governments—particularly those that had recently achieved sovereignty—and its own commitment to the principles underlying the United Nations Organization. Moreover, it was embarrassed by the fact that Netherlands troops were American trained and were equipped with lend-lease supplies. The official United States policy was consequently to seek a solution through a series of compromises. But the sweep of Communist successes in Asia seemed to make this course untenable from a practical point of view. These successes also made it seem that Indonesia and Southeast Asia generally could be saved from communism only if the colonial powers were strongly pressed to follow a policy of withdrawal. Eventually the United States took a stand that forced the Netherlands to accept a settlement that it would not have made in the absence of the pressures placed upon it.

Indo-China

The case of French Indo-China differed in degree but not in kind and can be briefly described. British and Indian troops took the surrender of the Japanese in the southern part of the region, as did Nationalist Chinese in the northern part. A Government of the Republic of Viet Nam had been set up by a national resistance movement (Viet Minh), made up of Communist and nationalist groups and headed by a veteran Communist, Ho Chi Minh. French forces arrived in January 1946, and took over. Negotiations went on between the French and the Viet Nam Government. These proceeded through a series of accords, breakdowns, limited hostilities, and further accords. Real tests of strength were avoided, and maneuvering went on for positions in anticipation of such tests. Guerrilla and police actions continued unceasingly in the background.

By the end of 1946, a state of virtual war existed between France and the dissident wing of the Viet Nam Government, which now reverted to the name of Viet Minh, for the French were attempting to reconstruct a Viet Nam government that would be more amenable to them. This struggle continued indecisively throughout the period under consideration here. The Indo-Chinese issue was not brought to the United Nations by the Soviet Union. That government, more eager at the time to solidify Franco-Soviet relations than to help the Viet Minh, refused even to introduce a motion for a cease-fire. If a motion had been introduced, France would probably have stood successfully on the ground that the United Nations was interfering, contrary to its Charter, in the domestic affairs of a Member state. Moreover, unlike the Indonesian Government, the Viet Minh was under Communist leadership and received little sympathy, even on nationalist principles, from other Asian states. The United States also declined to intervene. The loss of Indo-China and its probable repercussions in the French North African colonies would weaken the role France could play in Europe. Moreover, the Communist issue was looming larger in American opinion. The official position was confined to expressing the hope that peaceful bases for adjusting the difficulties could be found.

During the years 1948 and 1949, however, American economic assistance to France permitted a greater French military effort in Indo-China than would otherwise have been possible. And at no time did the United States exert on France pressures comparable to those exerted on the Netherlands. The basis of the difference was traceable to the position of France in the over-all scheme of American policy. In addition, France was ostensibly seeking a solution that would lead to self-government. Hostilities were aimed against a dissident group while negotiations were proceeding with a French-sponsored Viet Nam Government. Consequently, the situation was not presented to either a United States or a United Nations judgment in any clear-cut form.

It can be concluded from the preceding account of conditions in the colonial belt that this extended area was of great importance in the strategy of American relations with the Soviet Union, but that nowhere did it lend itself easily to the application of American policies for executing this strategy. The original policy of economic assistance was primarily drawn for countries that were already industrialized. The subsequent policy of technical assistance for underdeveloped countries, as it was finally approved, was not scaled to the costly process of changing from an agricultural and extractive to an industrial economy. It consequently fell far short of the expectations of newly independent states. As for policies of defensive alliance and military assistance, these could not be applied in their intended forms to states that had little to contribute directly to a common strategic cause.

Yet the states of this peripheral world could not be dismissed, or even put into a special category as objects of policy. In the West, they overlapped the regional organization of the North Atlantic alliances. In the East, they were involved in the United States objective of a Far Eastern region stabilized to resist Communist control. And between West and East were the states that had come from the British Empire. Of these, India was relatively strong and in a position possibly to act as a focus for a new basis of cohesion in the newly independent states. Because of this position, India had a certain freedom of action as between the contending objectives and policies of the United States and the Soviet Union. From West to East, with varying degrees of outspokenness and bitterness, the states of the colonial belt resisted overtures from the United States and Western Europe, wary of economic penetration, fearful of granting military footholds, antagonistic to diplomatic advice, and steadily refusing all proposals that remotely suggested the reestablishment of foreign controls.

In these conditions, where United States objectives required that action be taken, if only for the purposes of anticipating possible Soviet action, basic American policies tended to become distorted. In so far as the strategy of containment was a determining influence —and at times it was predominant in guiding policy choices—economic assistance programs were forced into supporting immediate security purposes to the detriment of the presumed long-term values of their developmental intentions. In so far as concepts of social betterment and rising standards were able to assert their claims in policy decisions, they seemed to many in official circles to call for actions and to compete for resources on grounds that had little to do with the short-term urgencies that confronted the United States. In this situation, apparently clashing interpretations of the American interest were argued and officially compromised. The resulting action tended to confuse the states in which those policies were being applied, and to create antagonism, feelings of being subjected to pressure, and a sense of being approached almost entirely in terms of demands for conformity with American needs. Consequently, the linking of economic assistance, defense alliance, and military assistance that furnished a rationale for American-Euroean relations had little meaning when similarly used as a basis for relations with the states of the peripheral world.

CHAPTER XII

Areas of Application: The United Nations

IT WILL BE RECALLED that in 1945 the United States had geared its basic objectives and oriented many of its general policies to the operation and development of the United Nations Organization. Naturally, the character and the role of the United Nations were affected by the dynamic forces that increasingly dominated the relations of the United States and the Soviet Union and hence the world political environment. The United Nations, however, existed as a significant fact in international policies, and it is accordingly given separate treatment as an institutional field in which United States policy had to operate at the same time that it was being applied in other places.

Instrument of National Policies

There are various ways in which a national state might act when participating in the United Nations. It might emphasize the value it places on constructing a framework of universal international law. It might concentrate on carrying out its national policies and strategic objectives. It might emphasize the functioning of the international organization in terms of the principles stated in its Charter. It might try to capture the Organization and use it to advance the interests of a coalition or alliance of which it was a member. Needless to say, no national state has engaged in an unqualified effort to establish international law, international organization, or international policy, although nearly all national states have participated in varying degrees in the qualified pursuit of these ends. So long as national states have effective monopolies of force, they are likely to be the only agencies capable of implementing the policy or protecting the life and institutions of the particular societies for which they act. Furthermore, generally speaking, they are subject to internal pressures to use an international organization for national ends rather than for ends that are important to the organization itself.

Small states have usually championed international organiza-

230

tion. But they often do so to counterbalance their lack of power and to gain influence in the settlement of international questions. Once they succeed in establishing voting rules that over-represent their power, they tend to exercise this voting strength to achieve purposes that are national or regional.

Nevertheless, these tendencies are not necessarily incompatible with the setting up of international law, organization, and policy as desirable long-term goals, even though action to achieve them is customarily given secondary priority in the formulation of national policy. These goals reflect values that operate with considerable force in the political relations of human societies. However, as international tension increases, relative priorities in state behavior increasingly favor those objectives that build national power. While nations originally favoring to a high degree the growth of international law and organization will lower these priorities more cautiously and from a higher base than countries operating on different values, the same process will take place in all states involved directly in an international rivalry. Moreover, the effects of this process will tend to be cumulative and self-reinforcing. If one major state, in moving toward its national objectives, gives low priority to international law and organization, other states, in self-defense, are obliged to act in the same manner.

A certain measure of similar factors of expediency was reflected in the original structure of the United Nations. The juridical equality of states received only modified recognition. The United States, Great Britain, and the Soviet Union agreed that the Organization could operate effectively to maintain peace only if the states that alone possessed the force needed to execute its decisions were given a superior responsibility and status. For this reason, the United States, the Soviet Union, Great Britain, France, and China were given permanent seats on the Security Council of the United Nations. Because no decision could be enforced against one of the great powers without resort to world war, a veto right for the permanent members was written into the Charter. For similar reasons the Security Council was given responsibility for enforcement actions, rather than the General Assembly, in which the juridic equality of nations received recognition. However, these solutions did not mean that in 1944 and 1945, an obstructively high priority was being given to national rather than international objectives. They reflected instead a judgment on the part of major powers that the Organization could not carry out its basic purposes unless the great powers were united in their objectives and able jointly to exercise major responsibilities.

Divisive Influences

Nevertheless from the first meeting of the Security Council and the General Assembly in London in January 1946, the United Nations was subjected to divisive influences. In rapid succession, complaints were brought by Iran against the Soviet Union, by the Soviet Union and the Ukraine against the presence of British troops in Greece, and by Syria and Lebanon against Great Britain and France for maintaining forces in those states. A formula was quickly found for settling this last item, but the proposal was vetoed by the Soviet Union. Then Poland requested an examination of the situation in Spain apparently only to embarrass and divide democratic opinion; and the Ukraine returned to the Greek item. In turn, Greece requested that the question of aid to the Greek Communist guerrillas be looked into. If any further evidence were needed that the United Nations was becoming an instrument of national policies, it was provided by the deadlock that developed in connection with the efforts to negotiate disarmament, the control of atomic energy, and the provision of armed forces for use by the Security Council. Yet the major powers also used the United Nations as a channel for reaching agreement on matters of subordinate interest: the question of Trieste and the disposition of the former Italian colonies.

There were still further signs of its use as an instrument of national policies. At the time of the Syrian-Lebanese complaint, the Arab, Asian, and Latin American states showed that they were capable of joining forces and using their considerable combined voting power to achieve the nationalist aspirations of one of their number at the expense of the Western powers. There were also signs that the Soviet Union was prepared to support this airing of colonial grievances and nationalist aspirations by using the organs and procedures of the United Nations.

New Emphasis on General Assembly

In view of this record, it is understandable that the Truman Doctrine stated that "the United Nations and its related organizations are not in a position to extend help of the kind that is required." With a veto right at the disposal of the Soviet Union, it was clear to United States policy makers that the Security Council of the United Nations was not a channel for effectively countering the Soviet Union. However, other values of the United Nations, as well as the fact that it existed as an operating institution, remained, and there was no serious idea of dismissing it as useless. Attention in official American thinking shifted from the Security Council to the General Assembly.

If the Soviet Union could, in practice, negatively control the Security Council, the United States and other like-minded countries possessed a numerical voting majority in the General Assembly. In this, it was considered, lay a means of effectuating policy by increasing the functions of the General Assembly, by using it for serious policy purposes, and by treating its recommendations as moral authority for action. To serve this purpose, however, it was necessary for the General Assembly to remain in session continuously. As this was not practicable, the United States hit upon the device of an Interim Committee of the General Assembly to be in continuous session. In spite of strong objections from the Soviet Union and its adherents on political and legal grounds, the Interim Committee was established in November 1947.

The use that was immediately made of this committee opened up for the United States new possibilities of using the United Nations Organization as an instrument to counter, at least partially, the use of the veto by the Soviet Union. The General Assembly from this time on became an important factor in disputes and situations in which major interests of the Soviet Union and United States power groupings were involved. Consequently, the Assembly became an object of peculiar interest to the United States in view of the opportunities that were now available for pressing it to participate in a strategy of containment.[1]

---

[1] It should be remembered in this connection that, under the Charter, the Security Council held the exclusive authority to make binding decisions and to order enforcement measures to maintain peace and security, while the General Assembly had only broad recommendatory powers. The Interim Committee furthermore was not empowered to make recommendations directly to Member states, but it was often possible for the General Assembly in advance to delegate to it functions that effectively overcame this limitation. For instance, the United Nations Commission on Korea was ordered to report to the Interim Committee for the interpretation of its instructions. On this basis, elections were held in South Korea when the United Nations Commission was refused access to North Korea.

Through 1947 and 1948 there was a growing tendency on the part of the United States to mobilize the United Nations on behalf of its policies. In quick succession the problems of Indonesia, Korea, and Palestine were approched by the United Nations in ways that were largely guided by American wishes. The United States did not restrict itself to verbal argumentation. Efforts were made to sway the votes of other delegations to the General Assembly by demonstrating the relationship between their votes and decisions of the United States Congress on economic aid. In other cases, normal logrolling proposals were employed to change votes. These devices were employed with greater frequency as the United States began to make greater use of the United Nations as an instrument for the execution of its national policies. There was a growing American desire to enlist the moral values of the United Nations in the Western cause and to put the United Nations on record, particularly on issues in which the United States and the Soviet Union were in conflict.

To a certain extent, it was impossible to avoid some identification of the United Nations with a coalition of free nations. As originally conceived, the Organization depended for its effectiveness on the unity of the great powers. Without that unity the Organization would gradually lose influence through being used as an instrument of cold war. Although it could not carry out its primary purpose—enforcing sanctions against war, for any sanctions would probably now ensure war—it could continue to exercise its other functions.

Limited Coalition

The use of the United Nations as an instrument of policy became more clear in connection with the creation of the North Atlantic Treaty Organization in 1949. A limited coalition, directed defensively against another coalition of states, was legitimized as an international device for ensuring peace and security by being referred to Article 51 of the Charter of the United Nations, providing for the right of individual or collective self-defense, and Article 53, permitting regional organizations to function within the framework of the parent body. This linking of the North Atlantic Treaty Organization with the United Nations perhaps obtained some backing from the proponents of international organization. However, it could not disguise the fact that universal security organizations and limited alliances could frequently be incompatible, and that one of the purposes behind a universal organization was to eliminate rival alliances and the wars to which they were presumed to lead. The formation of extensive alliances during the lifetime of the United Nations implied that the major national states were hedging against a breakdown of the idea of a single comprehensive collective security system. When the unanimity of the great powers did break down, and it consequently became impossible to use the United Nations for the enforcement functions it had been designed to perform, alliances constituted the new line of defense to which national states returned.

Cold War

The free world was being mobilized by United States policies for a struggle with the Soviet bloc of powers. The North Atlantic Treaty Organization and assistance programs were becoming the primary instruments, and the United Nations was becoming a secondary instrument. Utilization of the United Nations, therefore, depended primarily on the presumed cold war advantages to be derived from its use rather than on an analysis of the measures most likely to enable the United Nations to perform effectively those functions specified by its Charter. This did not by any means represent a complete shift in the objectives of the United States and other Members of the United Nations. The major powers, as well as the smaller states, had from the start used the United Nations as an instrument of national policy to some extent. The present difference was primarily one of degree. The change was also indicated by the degree to which the original security purposes of the United Nations came to be regarded as a matter for a more distant and indefinite future.

The growing tendency of the major powers to use the United Nations as an instrument of national policy has been stated here in an unqualified way for purposes of clear exposition. It is important now to state that this tendency did not operate unchecked. There were other elements at work in the United Nations membership. Even though Members, most of them just emerging or only very recently emerged from colonial status, were not averse to using the United Nations as an instrument for national purposes, they did not fall in line behind the efforts of the major powers wholly to absorb the United Nations in their own conflicts. The resistance was not organized or coherent. It fluctuated in terms of the seriousness with which some states viewed the Communist threat and others viewed the threat of renewed Western imperialism. It fluctuated in terms of the extent to which Western culture and values had been accepted by individual states. But generally speaking a loose bloc was formed, composed of Asian, Arab, and occasionally some Latin American countries, that had a common interest in using the United Nations to cushion and restrain the conflict of coalitions and to gain attention and assistance for their own political, economic, and social development. Thus a shifting of the United Nations Organization wholly away from at least the concept of international collective security was not possible so long as the Organization continued to function at all. But the same factors that prevented this did not operate to check the tendency to manipulate the machinery and procedures of the Organization.

The role of the United Nations in international politics and the parts played by the Member states in the operations of the Organization remained largely as described here until June 1950, when hostilities broke out in Korea.[2] Until then, the signatories of the North Atlantic Treaty did not attach much importance to the United Nations as a primary channel for organizing peace and security in Western and Central Europe. They relied on the creation of their own instrument, the North Atlantic Treaty Organization, and on the collective strengthening of their own resources. Certain members of the North Atlantic Treaty Organization, however, particularly the United States and Great Britain, continued to treat the United Nations as a useful restraining influence on the development of Soviet-Communist policy in other areas.

They continued to press the General Assembly to maintain its support of United States policy in Greece and obtained approval of the Assembly for condemning Bulgarian, Hungarian, and Rumanian infringements of the human rights clauses of the peace treaties. In the Far East they maintained, again through the General Assembly, a steady pressure on the Soviet Union to consent to a United Nations solution of the Korean issue. They also began to line up the United Nations to support at least in principle the legal position of the Chinese National Government as the repre-

[2] Developments after that point will be taken up in due course.

sentative of China on the Security Council when this position began to be undermined in fact by the success of the Chinese Communist regime.[3]

In all of these situations, the United States and the Western states were basically concerned to organize world opinion and to draw together the potential strength of the non-Communist states in support of positive actions taken within the framework of the strategy of containment. In contrast, the main lines of Soviet action in the United Nations were negative. The Soviet Union did not and could not look to the United Nations as an instrument that would aid in advancing its policies or would even support existing Soviet positions. The Soviet Union, however, could and did use the procedures of the United Nations to counter and to delay such positive support as the United States sought to enlist. It also used the open forum feature of the General Assembly and other United Nations organs as public platforms from which to conduct propaganda attacks, to maneuver by parliamentary procedure, and to introduce divisionary proposals for disarmament, outlawry of atomic weapons, and reduction of world tensions. The primary design throughout was negative: to embarrass, to confuse, to frustrate the opposition; not to obtain positive and immediate benefits for Soviet policy or for the United Nations Organization.

Armaments

There was a range of general issues—disarmament and the regulation of armaments, the provision by international agreement of armed forces for use by the Security Council of the United Nations to enforce decisions, and the control of atomic energy—that were basic to the establishment of an international security system. Their resolution by agreement seemed a fundamental function of the United Nations. They were, however, issues that were abstract and general when approached by an international organization in terms of the interests of all states, but that were concrete and specific when approached by any two states in terms of their partic-

---

[3] It should be recalled in this connection that China was, under the Charter, one of the permanent members of the Security Council of the United Nations and had a veto right. The existence of two regimes, one claiming legal and the other *de facto* authority, raised the awkward question of which should act in the United Nations as the legal entity called China.

ular pattern of relations. Because the negotiation of these issues was conducted in general terms, while the factors that conditioned the success or failure of the negotiation lay in the actual circumstances of relations between the United States and the Soviet Union, these matters are examined separately.

The Charter of the United Nations did not call for disarmament as something separate from political action to maintain peace and security. Instead, it spoke of the "regulation of armaments," having in mind the need to have enough armaments available to enable Members to maintain peace under the direction of the Security Council. Given the dominating role of the major powers in the Security Council and the overwhelming preponderance of armed force at the disposal of two of these powers, the final determination of issues connected with the control and international use of armaments lay between the United States and the Soviet Union. It is impossible to say what the result might have been if the issues had been discussed on the basis of conventional armaments alone, for this possibility was ruled out once and for all by the advent of atomic weapons. Not all the officials closely concerned with the drafting of the Charter were aware of the work that had been done in this field. The nature of the atomic bomb consequently was a revelation to many of them. In announcing the dropping of the bomb in August 1945, the President of the United States described it as having "more power than 20,000 tons of TNT," and stressed the need to examine "possible methods of protecting us and the rest of the world from the danger of sudden destruction."[4] Furthermore, it soon became known that the United States alone possessed this new weapon.

All that had been thought, planned, and agreed with respect to negotiating the regulation of armaments and the enforcement capacity of the United Nations had now to be evaluated in the light of a fundamental disequilibrium in military power between two major states. The matter was made infinitely more complex by two considerations: first, the disequilibrium could not be easily adjusted because it arose from a confrontation of two types of power that had no common unit of measurement—a superiority of the Soviet Union in conventional forces in a state of readiness and a monopoly by the United States of a new and incalculable weapon; and second, the conflicting objectives and policies of the Soviet Union and the United States.

[4] "Statement by the President," Press release (Aug. 6, 1945).

There is no intention here of following in detail the steps by which negotiations under the United Nations reached the point of deadlock. It will be sufficient to indicate, by a brief analysis of two cases, the way in which issues that were presented for international resolution could not escape being treated in terms of the national objectives and policies of the most powerful states concerned. The two cases were the control of atomic energy and the provision of military forces for use by the United Nations. In both cases, the United States and the Soviet Union steadily professed, and probably were in, agreement in principle. At least, neither rejected the necessity for resolving these issues. But with respect to means, their disagreement soon became final and unshakable. If it is assumed, as many have assumed, that the highest priority purpose should have been the development of an international security system, severe judgment can be and has been passed on one or the other of the major opponents. But because in fact a higher priority was given to the maintenance of relative national positions, the limitations on the alternatives acceptable to the major opponents become clear, and the causes of deadlock stand out sharply.

With respect to the provision of armed forces, the general agreement that such forces should be made available had to be spelled out in terms of their composition, their location, their freedom to operate in a world of national states, and their logistic support. The United States proposed that the permanent members of the Security Council should make available *comparable* contributions of man power and conventional equipment. The Soviet Union proposed that they should make *equal* contributions of all types. Significant implications lay behind this difference. The military strength of the United States rested on air and naval forces; that of the Soviet Union on air and ground forces. It seemed likely, moreover, that enforcement action by the United Nations would take the form of rapid air and naval interdiction and bombardment rather than of slower ground force movements. This would mean, when the requisite base rights and logistic support were taken into account, that the ready military force of the United States could be deployed throughout the world with the complete political support of an international organization, while the ready military force of the Soviet Union would either remain unused or be dispersed in small contingents. In effect, as the Soviet Union saw it, the Soviet Union (one of the five permanent members) would play a secondary role along with China in an evolving pattern of United Nations enforcement authority.

The Soviet proposal was designed to guard against such a development. However, from the United States point of view, this proposal would result in the most tangible and ready form of Soviet power being injected into every situation of conflict, not because of its practical usefulness in settling the situation, but so that the Soviet Union might influence the nature of the settlement. Naval and air forces were useful for enforcing compliance as a preliminary to re-opening negotiations and the processes of peaceful adjustment. Ground forces, however, could not easily be restrained from going beyond the enforcement of compliance to bringing about a predetermined form of adjustment. These opposing estimates of the possibilities that could be seen in the two proposals rested, of course, on mutual suspicions, obviously conflicting national purposes, and a disequilibrium in military power and potential. In view of this, the efforts of other states to find compromise formulas ran into a stone wall. The stone wall became even more solid during the discussion of the control of atomic energy.

The majority of United States policy makers and most segments of American opinion were worried at the end of the war by the atomic weapon. Not only had a force of incalculable consequences been released, but even a layman's knowledge of science and technology led to the conclusion that the American monopoly of the weapon was at best a short-lived advantage. The United States view, co-sponsored by Great Britain and Canada, was that the production of atomic energy should come under international control through arrangements negotiated within the United Nations Organization. This view was almost unanimously supported, but it created a dilemma for the Soviet Union. The Soviet Union could not object to the principle, and yet it did not wish to negotiate the control of atomic energy from a position of weakness; and this was the Soviet position unless it possessed atomic weapons or their use was outlawed and existing stocks were destroyed. The General Assembly, however, established the Atomic Energy Commission in January 1946.

The obvious tactic for the Soviet Union, and the one it employed, was to delay decision—if need be to prevent decision until its position of weakness had been corrected—but to do this without opening itself to a denial of the principle of international control. The United States proposed the creation of an International Atomic Development Authority. This Authority would own all atomic energy activities "potentially dangerous to world security," would have control, inspection, and licensing authority over all other types of atomic activities, and would be responsible for the development of peaceful uses.

In return for the establishment of an adequate control Authority, for a renunciation of atomic weapons, and for agreed penalties for violation, the United States, Great Britain, and Canada would stop making bombs, would dispose of existing bombs, and would by stages turn over to the International Authority full information on the production of atomic energy.[5]

In the United States view, there could be no question of giving away a monopoly position unless the *quid pro quo* was a set of international controls strong enough to ensure that the Soviet Union could not, with the totalitarian techniques at its disposal, construct atomic facilities in secret. The degree of control required for this meant, however, that an international body would exercise supranational authority within national territories to an extent never before advocated by any major power and certainly far beyond that intended by the Charter of the United Nations. The United States maintained that this significant extension of the security system of the United Nations was justified, first, by the fact that the development of atomic energy had not been in consideration when the Charter was negotiated, and, second, by the demonstrably unique character of the atomic weapon.

There is evidence that the United States proposals were sincere and were motivated basically by a hope that an incalculable force might be made to evolve under control and on calculable lines. This hope coincided, of course, with the brief period in United States postwar policy when high priority was being given to the development of the United Nations. However sincerely these proposals were put forward, they contained one implicit uncertainty— the possibility of congressional rejection at some future stage in their execution. They also met with one major immediate obstacle—

[5] The American proposals specified that the veto right could not apply in determining violations or imposing penalties. U.S. Department of State, *International Control of Atomic Energy: Growth of a Policy*, Publication 2702 (1946), p. 53.

the unwillingness of the Soviet Union to deny itself the possible future possession of atomic weapons by giving control and inspection authority to an international agency while the United States had such weapons at its command.

Mutually exclusive positions were immediately developed. The United States would not give up its monopoly without a preceding watertight agreement on the staged development of controls. The Soviet Union would not give up its chance of developing atomic weapons unless the United States renounced its monopoly before negotiating an agreement on controls. Naturally, the unbreakable deadlock that this implied was not made explicit by the Soviet Union. Instead, it advanced counterproposals of an elaborate nature in which the special problems of an unconventional weapon were blended with the well-known problems of conventional weapons and the whole was brought within a framework of disarmament. The fog of discussion thus created led to the desired stalemate while still leaving the Soviet Union relatively free from the condemnation of having sacrificed international security to national interests. Thus Soviet maneuvers led to an American reaction, one part of which was a legislative effort to increase the life of the American monopoly by restricting the exchange of atomic information, and another part the growth of internal security regulations within the United States Government.

When the United States Government began in 1947 to rearrange the priorities of its objectives, the issues of the control of atomic energy, the regulation of armaments, and the provision of military forces for the United Nations were carried as deadlocked items on the agenda of the United Nations. They were brought to life in the General Assembly, most frequently by the Soviet Union, for propaganda purposes or in connection with tactics of national policy. They remained frozen in the substantive committees.

In addition to concrete situations in various geographical areas, the objectives and policies formulated by the United States between 1947 and 1949 led to a shift in American purposes and action within the United Nations. Consequently, the place of the United Nations in the total operation of United States policy was modified. It was seen more consistently as an instrument of policy than as a goal of policy. The original emphasis may have been on the development of a legal international order. The new emphasis was on manipulating an international political institution to support national purposes.

Given the nature of the United Nations, however, the effort to manipulate its organs and procedures from a national point of view could not be either satisfactory or successful. The technique of manipulation was open to all and was increasingly employed by all. So long as the major confrontation was that of the United States and the Soviet Union, the use of these techniques resulted in substantive stalemate. But this was not the whole picture. Other states, especially those whose interests were involved in the satisfaction of the claims of nationalism, could manipulate also. The growth of Asian, Arab, Latin American, and anti-colonial voting blocs gave rise to something like a third force in the United Nations, an amorphous group that could either bargain with the American and Soviet blocs or use its voting strength to embarrass or to force compromises on the major opponents. In this area of manipulation, the United States and the free world were generally at a disadvantage as compared with the Soviet Union. For it was the United States and the free world, and not the Soviet Union, that were engaged with the nationalism of former colonial regions; and it was the small nations, careful of their new independence, eager to assert their claims, and anxious to support states like themselves, that found the United Nations a useful instrument.

CHAPTER XIII

The Pressure of Events: 1949

BY MID-1949 a fairly complete pattern of United States policy had been proposed. It is true that one of these proposals—the technical assistance program—did not get congressional approval until May 1950, and that another—the military assistance program—did not become operational until the start of 1950. Nevertheless the intentions of the United States Government had been pretty thoroughly expounded to the American people and to friendly foreign governments. It can also be assumed that the Soviet Union was in a position to draw its conclusions about the possible effect of these intentions on Soviet objectives and policies.

The situation can be briefly summarized. A policy of economic assistance was proposed in June 1947, was approved by the Congress as a four-year program in the Economic Cooperation Act in June 1948, and was operated by the Economic Cooperation Administration (ECA) through the first two years of its life. It was re-examined annually by the Congress in connection with fresh appropriations. A policy of defensive alliances was initiated in May 1948, and developed as a proposed North Atlantic Treaty in July. Negotiations ran from June 1948 to April 1949. The treaty was ratified by the Senate in July and came into force in August 1949. The executing organization came into being in September, and the North Atlantic Council met three times between then and February 1950. A policy of military assistance was designed in 1948 and presented to the Congress in July 1949. It was approved as the Mutual Defense Assistance Act in October 1949, and the first shipments under the Mutual Defense Assistance Program (MDAP) were made in January 1950. A policy of technical assistance for underdeveloped areas was first proposed in January 1949, in the President's inaugural address, and draft legislation was sent to the Congress about six months later. It was approved as the Act for International Development in May 1950, but it did not become operative within the period under consideration.

The accompanying chart indicates the interlocking in time of these four lines of policy. It also makes clear the exact stage in the

Chronology of Policy Development, 1947-1950

	1947 (Quarters)				1948 (Quarters)				1949 (Quarters)				1950 (Quarters)	
	1st	2nd	3rd	4th	1st	2nd	3rd	4th	1st	2nd	3rd	4th	1st	2nd
Economic Assistance Policy / Economic Cooperation Act / ECA										Reviewed →			Reviewed →	
Defensive Alliance Policy / North Atlantic Treaty / NATO														
Military Assistance Policy / Mutual Defense Assistance Act / MDAP														
Point Four Policy / Act for International Development														

Policy first proposed and presented to the Congress.

First presented to the Congress and approved.

Enacted and initiation of operations under program.

Program operation prior to June 1950.

245

development of each line that had been reached when the Communist attack on Korea subjected the whole pattern of policy to a severe testing.

Inevitably, as these proposals left the shelter of the offices of United States policy planners, they met with obstacles and impediments, and became open to modifying pressures. These were not simply the product of the natural reactions and countermoves of Soviet-Communist policy. In fact, when the reactions and countermoves that were taken by the Soviet Union prior to June 1950 are surveyed, it is clear that there was no important immediate and consistent effort to counter United States policy.

The difficulties and the modifying pressures arose much more from the inherent political, technical, and mechanical problems of operating such comprehensive programs of action in such a variety of concrete circumstances. The problems developed in two different contexts. One was in the field of relations with other governments. Here the problem was one of achieving and maintaining among a number of friendly sovereign states unity of purpose, coherence of effort, and co-ordinated progression toward broadly conceived objectives. The other was in the field of domestic American opinion, policies, and governmental institutions. Here the problem was one of keeping general agreement on purpose from being weakened by arguments about means or distorted by bureaucratic rigidities and conflict between the parties and between the executive and legislative branches of the government.[1]

The term, "program of action," has been used advisedly. Not until the concept of containment, the generalized objectives derived from the concept, and the series of linked policies derived from the objectives were converted into programs by legislation, appropriations, and the creation of administrative agencies was the level of significant action reached. Although it is true that the executive branch tried to forward its policy proposals by diplomatic action, both by direct negotiation with individual states and multilaterally through coalition and United Nations channels, the favored action device was an organized functional program, operated by a specified agency or group of agencies.

[1] Note should be taken of the fact that the designed pattern of policy could only be implemented through programs of action. Programs of action could only proceed on a basis of appropriations, and thus the conduct of foreign policy could not be treated as a prerogative of the executive branch. Both the direction and the operational details of policy were subject to the scrutiny and debate of programs by the Congress.

The programs of action, functionally identified as economic, military, and technical assistance, required large planning and administrative structures staffed by specialists and technical experts. Each program operated within a common framework of national purpose, but each quickly developed its own rationale of goals and methods. Consequently, the national formulations of objectives and policies were divergently interpreted as they were pursued by means of separately organized programs. This situation, with all that it implied in the way of interagency conflict, cannot be ignored in an account of United States action or of the problems encountered.

The problems of execution arose naturally on a month-to-month basis and were dealt with as current operational questions by the agencies concerned. Any attempt to present a full record would result in a flood of intricately related detail. The material presented here is highly selective and aims only at identifying issues so basic that they forced United States policy makers to review the priorities with which they were working, to redirect programs, and even to introduce new policy lines. Furthermore, the issues are treated only in terms of their relation to the underlying United States strategic concept. In this way it will be possible to establish the atmosphere in which decisions were made by the United States Government when Communist aggression took place in Korea.

Economic Assistance

By early 1949, the Economic Cooperation Administration had been at work for more than six months and was beginning to review its activities in preparation for congressional hearings on appropriations for the second year of its program. The original congressional authorization declared the purpose of the program to be to encourage the countries of Europe "through a joint organization to exert sustained common efforts . . . which will speedily achieve that economic cooperation which is essential for lasting peace and security."[2] To this end, countries would be assisted to become independent of outside economic aid. This assistance would have three objectives: to promote industrial and agricultural production, to reach and maintain internal financial stability, and to stimulate international trade within Europe and with the outside world.

[2] 62 Stat. 137.

This concept was one that could be and was spelled out as a technical economic and fiscal operation. It was, however, at the same time involved with political considerations: the position of Spain, relationships between the Western zones of Germany, and trade between Western Europe and Soviet-controlled Eastern Europe. These were all problems on which there were differences of opinion between the United States and the countries of Western Europe, as well as between public bodies in the United States. In an effort to ensure that United States purposes would be maintained, the Congress required a multilateral convention among the recipient countries of Europe as well as bilateral agreements between the United States and each recipient state. The bilateral agreements caused difficulty. Some of the initial conditions imposed by the United States were politically unacceptable: that a recipient state would consult the International Monetary Fund about rates of exchange if the United States so requested; that a recipient state would grant Germany and Japan, occupied by the United States, most-favored-nation treatment in international trade. Although these conditions were either compromised or dropped, they indicated the political differences that immediately arose.

In fact the mandate given to the Economic Cooperation Administration (ECA) by the Congress inevitably raised political issues in the course of the operation of this program. As the ECA interpreted its responsibility, its task was "to promote through the provision of aid . . . the most effective use of the economic resources of the participating countries, looking toward their mutual economic recovery." This meant that "the interest of the Administration . . . [was] focused on the total economic effort of the European nations."[3] But "the most effective use of economic resources" could not be determined by an economist's yardstick alone. An appraisal by an American technician of the recovery efforts of another state might differ widely from an appraisal made by the state in question, for all such appraisals would reflect varying national social aspirations, judgments about national security, and a complex of domestic political circumstances. Even if the United States had, as a basic policy, insisted on the acceptance of its own "judgment," the European countries would probably have been unable to accept the extensive guidance implied, and a major

[3] Economic Cooperation Administration, *First Report to Congress,* For the Quarter Ended June 30, 1948, p. 2.

objective of United States policy—the creation of a defensive alliance—would never have been attained.

Yet some degree of United States control over the programs and some scrutiny of the uses to which American aid was being put were essential if congressional requirements were to be met and further authorizations and appropriations obtained. The exercise of American influence, although usually confined to persuasion, nevertheless contained a slight element of threatening pressure that was kept active by the political questions that lay below the surface of a functionally specialized program. The policy administrators walked a narrow path between the politics of congressional opinion and the politics of recipient European governments.

The Economic Cooperation Administration, in the course of its first year of operation, came to see its task as falling into two phases. The first was the restoration of production and trade to prewar levels. The second was the readjustment and expansion of the European economy so that the countries of Western Europe would be self-sustaining by the time the four-year program approached its end. The first phase, given the fact that it coincided with a crisis situation of which the causes were fairly common to the whole of Western Europe, was completed with a minimum of political difficulties. The second phase, however, proved more troublesome by touching more directly on political issues.

From the point of view of the United States, the program in both phases called for co-ordination, co-operation, and joint planning. Hence it gave rise in the end to a demand for European integration. From the point of view of individual states, excluding the minority elements in each state that pressed for such integration, this demand laid heavy claims on national policy and was accordingly resisted. The Organization for European Economic Cooperation (OEEC), partly from technical conviction and partly in consequence of pressure from the Economic Cooperation Administration, tried to develop an integrated master plan of economic expansion in preparation for the second year of the assistance program. What it achieved was merely a critical comparison and analysis of the national plans.

The sense of the Congress, however, was moving strongly in the direction of integration and was so stated in its authorization for the second year of the program, which declared that the unification of Europe was an objective of United States policy. This trend in American opinion was speeded up by other policy proposals that were before the public and the Congress—the negotiation of a defensive alliance and the provision of military assistance. Both proposals emphasized the basic need for material assistance, co-ordinated effort, and integrated planning. Public discussion of their importance could only generate further pressure on the economic assistance program to make integration the *sine qua non* of its continuation.

North Atlantic Treaty

While the Economic Cooperation Administration and the European states searched for formulas that would reduce this pressure, the new policy proposals themselves created other problems. The OEEC and the countries of Western Europe had worked on the assumption that the recovery programs would require little if any diversion of resources for military purposes. This was in harmony with the American judgment that economic and political stability and improved standards of living would check the spread of the Communist influence. This assumption entered into the negotiations on the North Atlantic Treaty and was responsible for the inclusion in the pact of a provision setting forth as common objectives the promotion of stability, well-being, and economic collaboration. This article, in fact, preceded the one on resistance to armed attack. The treaty was signed in April 1949, and before it was ratified, eight European states requested military equipment from the United States. They pointed out that otherwise they could not fulfill their obligations without endangering their economic recovery, which was the goal of the United States program of economic assistance. The European countries were supported in principle by some ECA technical experts and administrators and by segments of American opinion that objected to the apparent shifting of United States strategy from economic to military means.

At the highest levels in the United States Government, the issues that arose from assumed differences of purpose in separate programs were regarded as irrelevant. At these levels, the point was that the policy programs were different but related ways of moving toward a single set of basic objectives. They made a logical progression: economic recovery needed a basis of security, and the defense treaty that established this basis required the existence of ready military force. No doubt the same logical relationships were accepted in principle by equivalent levels in many European governments. But this acceptance of logical necessity could not be readily transmitted for action to lower political levels in any one country or even to the specialist operators of programs in the United States and Western Europe.

The ·United States could see a program of economic assistance as a device for developing a strategy of containment, while a recipient country could treat it as a means of rebuilding its economic strength, settling its domestic political problems, and re-establishing its international position. It might recognize the American purpose as significant, but this did not necessarily mean that the United States objective was given the highest priority in the determination of its national policies. Consequently, it became a continuing problem for the United States to maintain a balance between the collective effort that seemed essential to its national purposes and the national interests that were the powerful motivations of the states to which United States policy was being addressed.

Similarly, within the United States Government itself, the logic of regarding various programs as related means for reaching a common goal struggled with the inevitable tendency of each program to maintain its own inner logical consistency. This tendency was encouraged by the fact that the programs were presented to the Congress as specialist operations with specified time limits and estimated costs. The Economic Cooperation Act of 1948 established a four-year program with funds to be appropriated annually, the grant for each year to be based on a review of the achievements of the preceding year. As the extent to which the program was producing results in terms of an over-all strategy of containment involved political intangibles and could not be measured, the methods for determining achievement were either the statistical techniques of the economic analysts or judgments about whether the recipients were doing what various sections of public and congressional opinion considered they should be doing.

Day in and day out, the program planners and administrators were guided by specialist considerations, but year by year they found themselves forced to adjust to political considerations. This involved protecting the program as such from political pressures in the recipient states and from domestic political pressures. Consequently, it was a continuing problem for the United States administration to maintain a balance between the requirements of its over-all foreign policy and the requirements of specialist programs as defined by experts and technicians. This problem became more difficult as other programs were initiated and their requirements, as defined by new bodies of technical specialists, began to compete within the administration and before the bar of congressional and public opinion.

While all these difficulties and impediments made themselves felt before the middle of 1950, none of them reached critical proportions prior to that time. On the contrary, they appeared mainly as operational problems, adjustable on a current basis without seriously impeding the development of policy. In fact, the *ad hoc* application of programs to situations that did not fall within their original scope was made without serious controversy.

The United States was able to bring the Western zones of Germany within its concept of Western European recovery without losing control of the process of building up a revitalized defensive alliance. In December 1949, a bilateral ECA agreement made the Western German Republic a full participant in the program of economic assistance, and by March 1950, the Republic was enough of a going concern to engage in bilateral talks with France on such matters as economic union and the status of the Saar. It was also able to raise, in a restrained way, the question of the ultimate reunification of Germany. In these developments, United States policy extended an encouraging and supporting hand.

In May 1950, France proposed a plan for creating a coal and steel community, seeking by this to meet the demand for some degree of economic integration and also to bring a revived German war potential under the control of a supranational European authority. At the same time, the foreign ministers of the United States, Great Britain, and France stated their intention that Germany should progressively re-enter the community of the free peoples of Europe. Later in May, civilian high commissioners replaced military figures in Western Germany. Among their first actions, the commissioners prodded the Soviet Union on German unification. The United States, developing the political implications of economic assistance and defensive alliance, had recreated a West German state and had gone a long way toward including that state in the over-all strategy of its relations with the Soviet Union.

On the domestic side also, the United States Government was handling its policy problems with some success. Administrative difficulties, particularly those of co-ordinating a multiplicity of functions, were being recognized. The National Security Act of 1947 was amended in 1949 and furnished machinery for exercising high-level control over the development and review of policy. The National Security Council, established as a unit in the Executive Office of the President, was given the responsibility of advising the President on the integration of domestic, military, and foreign policies in the interest of maintaining national security. It was backstopped for this purpose by the Central Intelligence Agency. Also, based on the experience of a year's operation of the Economic Cooperation Administration, further steps were taken toward keeping the self-generated objectives of a functional agency within the scope of the purposes and direction of national policy. The machinery of co-ordinating the work of ECA, the Department of State, and later the Department of Defense by means of committees was expanded. This machinery worked reasonably well until the outbreak of the war in Korea. The external pressures on policy were not too severe, and the policies themselves were not being debated politically in the Congress in terms of their relative exclusive merits.

Assessment of Soviet Policy

Generally speaking, the administration presented its pattern of policies as related aspects of a strategy for meeting the threat of Soviet expansion and Communist subversion. In doing this, the analyses of Soviet action that had been made in 1946 and 1947 were heavily relied upon. The actual Soviet-Communist reactions and countermoves to United States policies and actions were not extreme and did not pose basic questions in 1949 and early 1950. The Communist *coup d'état* in Czechoslovakia, the Berlin blockade, and the efforts of French and Italian Communists to interfere with programs of economic recovery during 1948 were dramatic. They could be regarded as evidence that the strategy of containment was necessary to the security of the United States and as indications that American action was having an impact.

But for the most part, the Soviet Union appears to have confined itself to consolidating its position in Central and Eastern Europe, and adjusting itself to meet the implications of United

States policies as and when these began to develop concrete results. Early in 1949, the Soviet Union and the satellite states established a Council for Mutual Economic Assistance. In March, a draft constitution for a Democratic Republic of all Germany was approved by a People's Council of Eastern Germany. In May, elections for a People's Congress were held in the Soviet zone. In October, after protesting the establishment of the West German state, the German Democratic Republic was established and a Soviet Control Commission replaced the Military Administration. Concurrently, the Communist governments of Eastern Europe were strengthened, and their links with the Soviet Union were tightened.

While the Western European Communist parties continued to conduct political and economic warfare against programs of economic and military assistance and against the creation of a defensive alliance, the Soviet Union contented itself with denouncing the North Atlantic Treaty as indicative of the aggressive intentions of the United States and Great Britain. In April 1949, it protested formally to seven of the smaller governments participating in the North Atlantic Treaty Organization (NATO). Throughout this period of initial build-up, it attributed the delay in negotiating an Austrian treaty to the aggressive plans of the United States.

But Soviet policy was not entirely free to act with greater vigor. The break with Yugoslavia was in the making. When it became open and final, it presented the Soviet Union with a dilemma. Unless strong measures were taken, other Eastern European states might move in the same direction. Yet if strong measures were taken, Yugoslavia would be pushed toward the West in self-defense. The latter course was chosen and, by the end of 1949, Yugoslavia, although not a participant in the European Recovery Program, was a beneficiary of economic assistance from the United States and Great Britain. By the spring of 1950, the question of Trieste was being re-examined by Yugoslavia and Italy, with the blessing of the United States and Great Britain, and without reference to Soviet interests.

The Soviet Union, however, was not inactive. The center of gravity of Soviet action began to shift to the Far East, and a diversionary pressure began to be felt by the United States. It will be recalled that it had not proved possible readily to apply the pattern of United States policy in the Far East. This difficulty of execution was now probed.

Early in 1949, it was clear that the National Government of China was on the way out. The United States let it be known that no further aid to the Nationalists was contemplated. However, the Republic of Korea, later joined by Chiang Kai-shek, pressed for the creation of a Pacific security pact and a union of Far Eastern states against communism. In October, a People's Republic of China was proclaimed and was recognized immediately by the Soviet Union and the states of the Soviet bloc. In December, the Nationalists withdrew to Formosa.

Segments of congressional opinion insisted on treating the strategy of containment at its face value and called for action, military action if necessary, to defend Formosa. The administration rejected these demands, but at the same time advised against premature recognition of the Chinese Communist regime. From this point on, the programs by which the pattern of United States policy was being implemented were exposed to domestic political demands for extension, shifts of emphasis, or basic diversion. In each congressional review of these programs, the administration was confronted by a renewal of such demands and obliged in some respects to compromise the progressive achievement of its aims in Western Europe to meet the well-organized critics of its actions in the Far East.[4]

In February 1950, a treaty of friendship, alliance, and mutual assistance was signed by the Soviet Union and the People's Republic of China, and China was promised the equivalent of a $300 million credit. The previous month the Soviet representative on the Security Council of the United Nations had walked out of the Council, stating that he would not return until the representative of the National Government of China was unseated.

These developments, taken together, confronted the United States with a basic policy issue. A comprehensive strategic concept had been defined, but the actual programs of action were more precisely and much less comprehensively designed. In the Far East an older policy line was brought to a dead end, an alternative policy line did not exist, and the pressures of circumstances as well as of opinion were combining to force programs that were already in operation to act as stopgaps in a situation for which

[4] The problem was made more difficult because Great Britain, although closely tied in with American programs in Europe, parted company with the United States in the Far East in January 1950 by breaking with the National Government and recognizing the Chinese Communist Government.

they were not designed. The Economic Cooperation Administration found itself conducting relief and developmental programs in the Far East, and the Government became involved in providing military assistance under conditions that were technically unsound for purposes that were almost entirely political. Funds were appropriated beyond the possibility of effective use. By May 1950, piecemeal extensions of existing programs had forced United States policies into more diversified channels of action than had been originally envisaged.

These pressures in the Far East had a consequence other than the ones just described. They focused anew the attention of United States policy makers on the military security aspects of the strategy of containment. Consequently, many advisers began to press for a higher priority of action to rebuild military strength in the United States and in the members of the North Atlantic Treaty Organization and for a diversion of resources from programs of economic assistance. A sense of emergency began to be communicated by the United States to the NATO planners and to the proposed military assistance program. By the end of 1949 the Defense Committee of NATO announced unanimous agreement on a strategic concept, on an arms production program, and on the machinery for co-ordinated defense planning. In January 1950 the President approved the recommendations of the North Atlantic Council and the bilateral agreements that had been negotiated, and the military aid program became operational. In April the NATO Defense Committee produced plans for "an integrated defense of the entire North Atlantic area," and in May the Council agreed to the establishment of "balanced collective forces."

International Communism

There is still one other theme to be treated as an essential part of this examination of the actions and problems of United States policy in the period preceding the Korean War. It is the use by Soviet policy of the world Communist movement and the disciplined apparatus of that movement. The mere existence of this instrument confronted the states of the West with an unusual obstacle to the development of policies directed toward restraining the Soviet Union.

It was clear that members of national Communist parties rejected the social obligation to defend the state when those who controlled its institutions, whether installed by majority vote or otherwise, operated those institutions to pursue values in conflict with Communist goals. This naturally constituted a threat to existing governments. If the Communists were not willing to confine their activities to legal measures and were unwilling to defend the state against external enemies, then the defense of Western democratic institutions had to be pursued on two fronts: an external front, against the Soviet Union, and an internal front, against domestic Communist parties.

The defense of the internal front raised a number of difficult questions of state relations. One country could have a reasonable concern with the internal fronts of other countries. For instance, the United States had a real interest in preventing the French and Italian Communists from gaining political power either by legal or revolutionary means. In colonial areas, the Communists might lead national rebellions or encourage them, if only for their disruptive effect on the strategic, economic, and political goals of the Western powers. The United States would thus be concerned either with defeating nationalist colonial revolutions or with ensuring democratic leadership of those revolutions. In all these cases the Communist threat would be internal with reference to an area external to the United States, and the United States would find itself involved in the domestic affairs of other nations.

The Communist apparatus could also constitute an internal threat by sabotage, by encouraging industrial slow-downs, and by undermining public confidence in the policies followed by the government of the country. Finally, the Communists could engage in espionage. This last activity opened up the entire question of internal security.

In consequence of all these possibilities, United States policies developed in unanticipated ways and were exposed to unexpected pressures. On the fringes of the assistance programs, areas of frank subsidy appeared: military supplies to the Philippines to deal with a Communist-led revolt, diplomatic support for Iran, special assistance to dissuade the Italian electorate from voting Communist, the provision of funds to help in undermining Communist influence in the French and Italian labor unions, and the assignment of resources to Southeast Asia to maintain resistance to Communist guerrilla forces. The sensitivity of United States policy to these dispersed impediments made it possible for the recipients of American aid to play on American fears. The firmest demands by the United States for acceptance of its recommendations could be softened by suggesting that the political authority of a government would thus be weakened, and that the Communists might be able to step into the resulting political vacuum. In the disturbed and unstable colonial belt, United States policy was in constant danger of becoming committed to unpopular political groups in its search for some authority that might be built up to resist Communist subversion.

The last and in many ways the most confusing and potentially inhibiting result of the internal Communist threat was the emphasis it caused to be placed on the protection of governments from internal subversion and espionage. Starting with the uncovering of the Soviet spy ring in Canada at the end of 1945, a considerable bill of particulars was pieced together of the extent to which democratic institutions and governments had been penetrated by professional agents operating through subverted nationals. From late 1948 on, a series of much publicized loyalty cases combined to create a widespread belief among the public and the members of the Congress that the internal security of the United States had been compromised. By 1950 the general feeling of uneasiness had become a specific charge that United States policy in the Far East had failed because of the subversive advice of Communist sympathizers in the Department of State. By the time the administration was confronted with making basic decisions in connection with Communist aggression in Korea, it was simultaneously under serious political pressure to take vigorous action at home against a hidden—and hence overemphasized—menace.

CHAPTER XIV

A Key Test: Korea

BY THE END OF 1949, the difficulties that were inherent in the development of the United States policy lines had been rather fully experienced and reasonably well taken in hand. The obstacles that the Soviet-Communist bloc could create and exploit had also been experienced and if not overcome, at least kept from seriously diverting American action from its objectives. The general conclusion was that the selected courses were the correct ones. They might well call for a long pull and might well require more consistency of effort and greater assignment of resources than had been originally thought, but the desired result of increased strength and co-ordinated resistance to Soviet policy seemed ultimately attainable. It was officially understood that the big question mark was China and the Far East. This situation was under constant analysis and full-dress re-examination at all relevant policy-making levels.[1]

Therefore by the start of 1950, the Far East was not so much an area of policy decision as it was an area of policy revision. In the complex of Far Eastern problems, Korea occupied a peripheral position. It was being reported that the North Koreans were able and willing to attack. The South Korean Government was believed to be willing to attack the North Koreans when it felt able to do so. It is a matter of record that the United States had eliminated Korea as a region of vital importance to its security. It is equally a matter of record that the United States proposed a program of economic assistance for the Republic of Korea. Furthermore, administration spokesmen had testified that the object of the proposed aid was to strengthen the republic to enable it to withstand the threat of the Communist North Korean regime and to create the foundation for the peaceful unification of Korea.

---

[1] It should be remembered, however, that this review of the Far East, motivated as it was by a wish to adjust realistically to circumstances that were beyond control by the United States, was confined to the executive policy-making branch of the United States Government. Considerable bodies of American opinion and powerful segments of the Congress, motivated by other purposes, moved in an opposite direction and called for vigorous action to restore the situation to some undefined previous form.

Finally, it is a matter of significance that the Korean case had been in the hands of the United Nations for some time, and that the United Nations was generally committed to the maintenance of peace and specifically committed to a particular solution of the problem.

The Development of the Korean War

When the North Korean regime began full-scale military operations against the Republic of Korea early in the morning of June 25, 1950, a key test of United States objectives and policies was precipitated. This consequence may or may not have been anticipated; there is no certain evidence one way or the other. But in the event, that is what happened.

The United States, standing on the objectives and policies of the three preceding years, defined the situation as one of fundamental importance and then acted accordingly. Action involved choosing a position from a range of possible ones, relating this position to the immediate past, and modifying past policies as required. Furthermore, action involved balancing diverse considerations: the estimated threat of Soviet actions, the demands of policies for building up a coalition of free nations, the political problems of operating through the United Nations, and the day-to-day requirements of the military situation. The course of events will not be recounted here except as needed for analytical purposes. What is important is the reciprocal effect of current decisions on the broader ranges of policy and of longer-term objectives on current decisions.

Within the very general framework of a strategic concept, decisions with respect to Korea were apparently made informally as the situation developed. An integrated master plan did not exist, nor was one worked out by the United States Government. As a consequence of day-by-day developments, the alternatives open to the United States changed. The range of possibilities narrowed. The specific available alternatives became clearer as the costs became more definite and the drain on existing resources easier to estimate. If estimates of the strategy and motivation behind the Communist attack did not necessarily become more accurate, they did gain in consistency. From an initial phase of bewilderment and doubt, an official American image of the place of the Korean campaign in

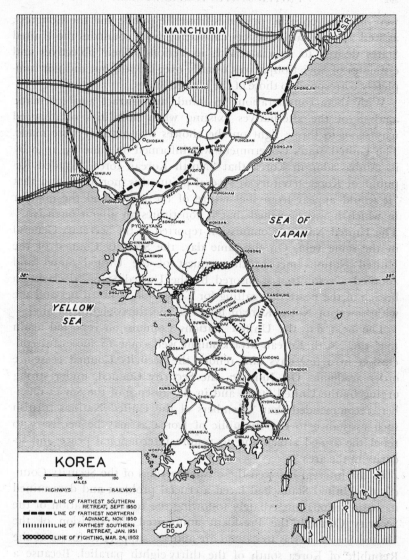

Communist world strategy began to crystallize. This image formed the basis for official judgments of possible Soviet responses to United States moves. A congeries of untested—and often untestable—assumptions formed the framework within which the consequences of alternative policies were estimated and courses of action officially decided on. Influencing this framework of decision-making were internal political pressures from the public and the Congress, as well as external influences emanating from countries the United States desired to associate with its actions. Their objectives and estimates of Soviet objectives usually over-lapped, but did not completely correspond to those of the United States.

With these considerations in mind, an abstract and schematic analysis of the alternatives existing when hostilities commenced may serve to throw light on the choices that actually were made. The United States Government was informed on June 25, 1950 by its Ambassador in Korea that "North Korean forces invaded Republic of Korea territory at several points this morning," and that "it would appear from the nature of the attack and the manner in which it was launched that it constitutes an all-out offensive."[2] The United Nations Commission reported to the Secretary-General in the same vein. On the same day, the Security Council of the United Nations met at the request of the United States and adopted a resolution sponsored by the United States, declaring a breach of the peace and calling for a cessation of hostilities and the withdrawal of North Korean forces to the thirty-eighth parallel.

The next day the United Nations Commission reported again that the North Korean attack might well come to successful conclusion in a few days and render the Security Council cease-fire order academic. On June 27, the Security Council, under strong urging by the United States and in the absence of the Soviet member, recommended that "Members of the United Nations furnish such assistance to the Republic of Korea as may be necessary to repel the armed attack and to restore international peace and security in the area."[3]

In the interval between these two meetings of the Security Council, the United States had faced a crucial problem and determined its basic action. Immediately following the recommendation of the Security Council, the President announced the decision of the United States. It was to extend air and sea support to forces of the Republic of Korea south of the thirty-eighth parallel. Because a Chinese Communist assault against Formosa was feared, and it was considered that such an assault would prejudice United States security interests in the Pacific and interfere with United States

---

[2] U.S. Department of State, *United States Policy in the Korean Crisis*, Publication 3922 (July 1950), p. 11.

[3] U.N. Security Council, Fifth Year, *Official Records*, No. 16, 474th Meeting (June 27, 1950), p. 4.

support of Korea, the Seventh Fleet was ordered to prevent any attack on Formosa. As a corollary, the President called upon the Chinese National Government in Formosa to cease all air and sea operations against the mainland of China. It was also decided to step up aid to the French forces in Indo-China.

The crucial problem was whether to intervene; whether the United States should engage its limited military forces in an area of admittedly limited strategic importance in order to prevent a Communist regime from successfully completing a flagrant act of aggression against a friendly state to whose existence both the United States and the United Nations were committed. There were strong reasons available to those who argued against American intervention in Korea. Korea was not within the recently defined American defense perimeter in the Far East. The highest military authorities saw small strategic importance in Korea and had recommended against committing military resources there. The United States had no formal obligation to defend Korea against attack. The decision had been made to withdraw United States forces from Korea under circumstances that did not cause a loss of prestige.

Although South Korea was friendly to the United States, it could not be convincingly described as a democratic country. The South Korean Government did not conceal its wish to bring North Korea under its control by force. The struggle could be viewed as a civil war—and thus as a purely internal affair—between two belligerent political groups. Therefore, it was possible to maintain that no great principles were involved.

The United States was in reduced military circumstances, both in man power and supplies. Only a skeleton Eighth Army, on occupation duty in Japan, was available for combat duty. It was doubtful whether it could be deployed quickly enough to influence events. Reserve forces were relatively nonexistent.

If the Korean aggression were a "soft-spot" operation—as many assumed—the argument could be developed that the action was initiated because the Communists had been given reason to believe, by official American pronouncements, that the United States would not intervene. Therefore, there was no certain danger of further aggression if this one isolated action were permitted to succeed. On the other hand, if the United States were to intervene in these circumstances, the Soviet Union might view the action as provocative and enter the fray directly, thus initiating a world war. Since no one challenged the thesis that the North Koreans had attacked on orders from the Soviet Union, it could be maintained that the Soviet Union was committed to the success of the intervention. Intervention thus might involve the United States in an infantry war against China or the Soviet Union on the continent of Asia. The United States did not have the man power or resources to conduct this type of operation and, therefore, should not assume such great military risks.

Furthermore, North Korea was only part of the Soviet third or fourth team. To send an American first team against such opposition would be an error in political strategy. This was particularly true because the logistics of the situation were advantageous for the North Koreans. They were prepared, and their offensive was rolling. The war might be over before sufficient American power could be deployed to influence events decisively. Defeat by the North Koreans would be extremely damaging to United States prestige.

It was also argued with vigor that the operation in Korea might be a diversionary move, designed to commit limited United States power in a relatively unimportant spot so that vital strategic regions would be left unprotected. These vital regions were variously identified. Some believed that the main Communist effort would be directed against Iran or Formosa. Others were concerned that Western Europe would be open to Soviet attack while the West was tied down in Asia.

In contrast, arguments for intervention were forcefully presented. They were developed mainly by applying existing objectives and policies unreservedly to the immediate situation. If the Soviet Union were not opposed this time, it would be encouraged to strike again. A successful aggression could only whet the appetite of the aggressor. Moreover, the next act of aggression might be difficult to localize, and the strategic position of the Western powers would be worse. This was the time to act: before the situation got out of hand. Furthermore, given the Oriental respect for visible power, failure to react to the aggression could lead only to the view that communism was an irresistible force. Asian nations would bow to external Communist threats, and would prove weaker in the case of internal Communist uprisings. Formosa would fall, then Indo-China, Malaya, Burma, and eventually Indonesia and India. Vast natural resources and man-power reserves would be brought within the Communist camp. Logistic problems would become more difficult for the West, and even Europe would prove more difficult to defend. More specifically, if a Communist power were to control Korea, it would threaten Japan. Given the accepted strategic importance of Japan to the American defense perimeter in the Far East, it was important to keep at least the southern part of the Korean peninsula in neutral or friendly hands.

It was admitted, in the pro-intervention view, that the European powers would be concerned if United States strength were committed in Asia. But it was maintained that they would be even more concerned if the United States did not oppose Soviet aggression. If the United States accepted defeat in Asia, Communist propagandists would proclaim that the United States was powerless and that it would retreat before the might of the Red army. Given the superior military strength of the Soviet Union in Europe, this argument would appear plausible. Therefore many Europeans would attempt to find a neutralist solution to international political problems. The coalition that the United States had painstakingly constructed would collapse. Eventually, European industry and man power would be brought within the Communist orbit, and the United States would end up isolated in the Western Hemisphere.

The Soviet Union, the argument went on, whatever its basic objectives and policies, had not publicly committed itself to a North Korean success. Although United States intervention would naturally involve the risk of Soviet or Chinese reaction, it was still possible for the Soviet Union to pull back without suffering a serious blow to its prestige. Thus if a pattern of aggressive Soviet probing were in the making, this was the proper time to discourage it by demonstrating the willingness of the United States to use armed force to resist a planned policy of aggression.

Finally, this pattern of argument concluded by noting that an act of aggression was being committed in defiance of an order of the Security Council and against a state for which the United Nations was responsible. If the aggression went unopposed, the United Nations and the principle of collective security would suffer a blow from which it would be difficult to recover. If it were a long-term goal of the United States foreign policy to help build a strong world security organization, a clear-cut act of aggression could not be allowed to go unchallenged.

This survey of considerations has been given in full in order to indicate the raw material of fact, judgment, opinion, and relative values out of which the decision of the United States to intervene was quickly shaped. It is not known how these considerations were weighed or the final balance that underlay the ultimate choice. One point is certain, however: the decision to intervene did not require action through the United Nations. A supplementary range of alternatives existed, and a supporting secondary decision was needed about how to channel action. The considerations involved here justify a full exposition also.

On the negative side the arguments ran largely as follows. The Security Council had no forces at its disposal and in the absence of a Military Staff Committee, no means of directing any national forces that were put into action. Consequently, there was no co-ordinated system of enforcement existing in the United Nations. To submit a problem of military action to the United Nations would throw military operations into confusion and impede effective resistance to the North Korean aggressors. The result would be that the United Nations would have the responsibility for policy, but would not be able to control the military steps needed to carry it out. The United Nations would not be in a position to make continuing decisions. The Member nations would have different objectives, different conceptions of the situation, and would make different estimates of the consequences of alternative patterns of action. Even though there might be initial agreement on opposing aggression, the differences on how to oppose it and on what to do as the situation changed would produce indecision and paralysis when action was necessary.

In the most practical sense, given the Soviet veto right in the Security Council, and accepting the thesis that the North Korean aggression was an act of Soviet policy, it was inconceivable that the Soviet Union would not use its position in the United Nations to frustrate action, muddy the issues, and at the end participate in a settlement. From this, the argument rightly moved to a consideration of the national objectives of the United States, and asked how these could be realized through an international body of which the Soviet Union would be a member.

Even if the United States enlisted from Member states enough United Nations support to block the Soviet Union, this could only be achieved by submitting the objectives and policies of the United

States to international direction. As it was, the decision to intervene was a United States decision. All that the United Nations did and could do was to approve the decision, and thus bring it within the framework of law and order associated with the United Nations Charter. While this had an undeniable value in terms of the United States purpose of creating a free world opposition to Soviet-Communist policies, it would in the long run open the way for divergent influences to operate. In particular, it would expose both military operations and ultimate settlement to a minimum composite judgment of members of an international organization, or to a diversity of judgments expressed in an international forum. Especially in view of the influence of public opinion on policy in this modern age of communication, it would introduce an undesirable and an unnecessary note of rigidity into a difficult situation.

The considerations that favored action through the United Nations fell into two groups. One set derived from the assumption that it was still a valid operational goal of United States policy to maintain and to advance the prestige and effectiveness of the United Nations. On this ground alone, it was held essential to associate the United Nations with the decision to intervene. This was necessary because the United Nations was *the* world security organization, and had, as one of its primary objectives, the eliminaton of the resort to force to obtain political objectives. United Nations participation was particularly necessary now, because of the intimate manner in which the organization had been associated with the Republic of Korea. Furthermore, in spite of the difficulties that would certainly follow, to enlist the United Nations in the Korean venture would give its enforcement agencies a chance to grow.

The positive set of considerations derived from the assumption that, although the interests of the United Nations had a low priority in the operations of United States policy, it was an instrument that the United States could not overlook in trying to construct an anti-Soviet coalition and in seeking organized support from free nations for its policies. From this point of view, if United States intervention took the form of a United Nations action to enforce international peace and security, it would arouse the enthusiasm and support of the peoples of the world in a manner otherwise impossible to gain. In addition, it would ensure the support and perhaps even the co-operation of nations that would otherwise remain indifferent. In the forums of the United Nations, other states would find it difficult to evade their international responsibilities, and these responsibilities could now almost certainly be defined as calling for support of the United States position. Because this was the admitted goal of existing United States policies, and because these policies had seemed to be negating the importance and role of the United Nations, now if ever was the time to combine national and international action in one coherent pattern of resistance to aggressive Soviet-Communism.

The long-run benefits of this combination, it was argued, would be well worth the price of the short-run difficulties. Even these difficulties could be in great part avoided. It should be possible to have military responsibility delegated to the United States, while the United Nations merely sanctioned the actions taken. Thus the United States would gain the legal and moral support of the United Nations for the pursuit of its basic strategic and diplomatic objectives.

Here again it is impossible to say with authority what balancing of these considerations actually led to the decision to intervene under the authority of the United Nations. The fact is that it was decided to bring in the United Nations, and that when the Security Council recommended that assistance be given to the Republic of Korea, the United States issued the relevant orders to its forces in the Far East.

The initial public reaction of the free world to both decisions was highly favorable. Officially, twenty-eight Member states of the United Nations offered assistance within their capacities in execution of the resolution of the Security Council. On June 29, the purposes of the United States and of the United Nations were completely identified. The Secretary of State said: "This action pursuant to the Security Council Resolutions is solely for the purpose of restoring the Republic of Korea to its status prior to the invasion from the north and of reestablishing the peace broken by that aggression."[4] A political position was thus staked out with little or no reference to the possible requirements of the situation in which it would have to be maintained.

These requirements rapidly became clear, however, and step by step, led to further important decisions. By the end of June, after United States air and naval forces had been in action, it was reported that United States ground forces would also be needed if even a

[4] U.S. Department of State *Bulletin,* Vol. 23 (July 10, 1950), p. 46.

beachhead were to be held in Korea. Their use was authorized, and the area of operation of the air and naval forces, hitherto held south of the thirty-eighth parallel, was extended to North Korea. Early in July, the United States was requested by the Security Council to assume command responsibility and to report on the course of action taken.

In August, the Soviet Union ended its boycott of the Security Council and the Soviet representative took his turn as president. Although the position of the United Nations could not be reversed by his authority, the development of the position could be made very difficult. Political action was consequently blocked, and political attitudes were confused by the bringing up of irrelevant issues. At the same time the military situation became steadily worse. The conjunction of military reverses and Soviet manipulations of United Nations procedures had the effect of focusing American attention on the Soviet Union as the controlling agent. The United States commander in Korea spoke of bringing in Nationalist Chinese forces from Formosa. Some American officials began to hint at preventive war. It recalled that as early as July, the Prime Minister of India had said that in order to "bring the Korean conflict to a prompt and peaceful conclusion," the presence of both the Soviet Union and the Chinese Communist Government in the United Nations was necessary.[5] How, it was asked, could their presence be reconciled with the objectives of the United States and the United Nations?[6]

In September, following a brilliant amphibious operation by United Nations forces, the military situation was reversed. By the end of the month the North Korean forces were in full retreat and were no longer an organized army. The United Nations "police action" was reaching its originally designated end: the restoration of the status and integrity of the Republic of Korea and the reestablishment of peace. Consequently, the basic politico-military objective was achieved, and a new point of decision arose. The problem was what should be done when the thirty-eighth parallel was reached.

This question was debated at several levels—within the United Nations, within the United States Government, and by American public opinion. The crosscurrents are hard to identify, as the policy makers were involved at all levels. Within the United Nations,

[5] *New York Times* (July 30, 1950).
[6] *Ibid.* (July 8, 1950).

those who argued against crossing the parallel pointed out that the objective had been achieved. Aggression had been repelled so effectively that the North Korean forces were no longer even a potential threat to the peace and security of the area. Further action would threaten the security interests of Communist China and the Soviet Union. China had announced both publicly and through diplomatic channels that it would be obligated to act if other than South Korean forces crossed the parallel.

Both within the United Nations and the United States Government, it was maintained that the collective enforcement had proceeded thus far with surprising unanimity among the participants. Any further action, especially if it ran into difficulties, would jeopardize this achievement and make it hard to obtain equal cooperation in the future. Moreover, the conduct of an extended operation would itself be affected adversely by the increased doubts of Member states. For example, while all supported the right of the United Nations to deal with threats to the peace and while most had supported action for this purpose, it was by no means equally agreed that the Charter gave the United Nations the right to impose a political solution by force.

On the other hand, it was argued that the United Nations was committed to the unification of Korea by its own previous decisions. There would probably never be a better time than the present for honoring this commitment. The means were available for sweeping away a purely artificial barrier and for holding free elections throughout the whole of Korea. Claims that the United Nations did not have sufficient authority were legalistic hair-splitting. The difference between restoring the peace and imposing a political solution was at best indeterminate.

From the point of view of the United States as leader of a military coalition, the argument maintained that it would not be possible to restore internationl peace and security without eliminating the Communist redoubt in North Korea. The resources of the United States that were needed to guard Soviet expansion in other parts of the world, particularly in Europe, could not otherwise be made available. In this connection, the lack of support given the North Koreans by the Communist powers indicated that they would not risk intervention. Therefore to complete the operation by destroying the North Korean forces would entail little risk while promising great gains. If the operation succeeded, the Communist bloc would suffer a loss of prestige so disastrous that recovery would be difficult. The final and purely American addition to the argument was that if United Nations forces halted at the thirty-eighth parallel, a growing domestic opposition in the United States would accuse the administration of appeasing a beaten Communist foe. If these accusations gained public credence, the conduct of United States foreign relations would be gravely handicapped.

At this point the United Nations commander informed the United States Joint Chiefs of Staff that he could protect his forces only by occupying North Korea. He was authorized to do so on September 29. On the same day, a resolution was introduced in the General Assembly of the United Nations recommending that (1) all appropriate steps be taken to ensure conditions of stability throughout Korea; (2) all constituent measures be taken, including the holding of elections under the auspices of the United Nations, for the establishment of a unified, independent, and democratic government in the sovereign state of Korea; (3) United Nations forces should not remain in Korea any longer than necessary to achieve the first two objectives; and (4) all necessary measures be taken to accomplish the economic rehabilitation of Korea.[7] Although the resolution did not specifically authorize the crossing of the thirty-eighth parallel by the United Nations forces, it seems to have been regarded as permissive.

The General Assembly approved the resolution on October 7, by a vote of 47 to 5, with 8 abstentions, and established a United Nations Commission for the Unification and Rehabilitation of Korea.[8] By the end of October, United Nations forces were approaching the Yalu River border between Korea and Manchuria.

There is no certain knowledge by what weighing of conditions the decision was reached to extend the police action to the whole of Korea. It cannot be stated positively whether United States national policy or some momentary crystallization of international policy by the United Nations was the prime mover; or whether both influences were moving together in the same direction. With hindsight, however, there is little doubt that the circumstances surrounding this decision, the new factors that had to be taken into account, and the gravity of the possible consequences combined to give the decision an importance comparable to the origi-

[7] The resolution was sponsored by Australia, Brazil, Great Britain, the Netherlands, Norway, Pakistan, and the Philippines.
[8] Res. 376(V), Oct. 7, 1950.

nal decision to support the Republic of Korea against the aggressor. It constituted a "turning point" in the diplomatic history of the period and profoundly influenced subsequent events.

Chinese Intervention and Stalemate

Early in November, the United Nations Commander reported that Chinese Communist forces were entering Korea. Later in the month, the United States Joint Chiefs of Staff made public the joint concern of Members of the United Nations. They suggested that United Nations forces should go no further and do no more than was necessary to permit Korean unification without stirring the Chinese to wholesale intervention. The suggestion was rejected by the United Nations Commander on grounds that combined both military arguments and political judgments. On November 25 the Chinese attacked in force, and the United Nations armies were pressed back until by the end of December, the battle front was again south of the thirty-eighth parallel. The Joint Chiefs advised the United Nations Commander that no more troops could be spared for Korea and directed him to defend successive positions, to inflict as much damage as possible on hostile forces, and to make advance arrangements for an orderly evacuation if necessary. The United Nations Commander countered the directive by advocating a blockade of China, the bombing of the Chinese industrial capacity, and the use of Nationalist Chinese troops as reinforcements in Korea and for diversionary attacks from Formosa. The Joint Chiefs informed him in early January 1951 that his suggestions were not practicable.[9] They received in reply a report that, in view of these political restrictions on military action, the military position in Korea was untenable.

It now becomes useful to go back to early November 1950, and follow the political developments that ran concurrently with these military reverses. The United Nations began consideration of the

[9] The underlying reasoning was: the danger of general war made it unjustifiable to increase the armed forces in Korea; the concurrence of the United Nations would be necessary and probably could not be obtained; a blockade would require negotiations with Great Britain; and the use of Chinese Nationalists would complicate United States Far Eastern policy and American relations with friendly states. *Military Situation in the Far East,* Hearings before the Senate Committee on Armed Services and Committee on Foreign Relations, 82 Cong. 1 sess, Pt. 5, pp. 3541-42.

problem of Chinese intervention on November 5. The intervention posed a number of issues, each difficult in itself, and all so complexly interlocked as to make agreement and clear decision almost impossible. Was the permissible role of the United Nations as clear or as certain as it had originally appeared to be? At the start, the United Nations had acted collectively to check a threat to international peace and security made by one small group against another. Subsequently, the United Nations had collectively decided to enforce a political solution on one of these groups. Now it was confronted by a direct denial of its authority and by an attack on its own designated forces. There were certain to be widely divergent attitudes. The legal status would be determined by the judgments of the Member states, not by legalistic interpretations of the Charter. All Member states, except possibly the United States, might well think that the circumstances had changed out of all recognition and that a modification of the position was in order. This would mean that proposals to extend hostilities would be resisted. Yet an extension of hostilities was the only way of enforcing compliance on the Chinese Communist regime if it refused to acknowledge the authority of the United Nations.

On the other hand, there was evidence that the United States, now confronted by a major Communist aggression and partially committed to maintain the Nationalist Chinese regime, which represented China in the United Nations, would have less regard for the legal arguments about the role of the United Nations than for keeping the United Nations tied to the strategy of containment. Consequently, the United States might call for the United Nations to stand firm on its prestige, and thus lead to a requirement to extend hostilities. There was no evading the fact that the United States by increasingly bearing the brunt of the fighting in Korea, had succeeded in identifying United States and United Nations policies, and was increasingly the dominating force. The United States could force the issue, if it so decided. If the American decision were to extend the war, the other Members of the United Nations had one of two courses before them. They could follow the American lead and end up as a coalition guided by the United States. They could reject the American line and end up either under the domination of the Soviet Union, on the sidelines of international politics, or, as groups of smaller states hopefully argued, exercising a restraining influence on both the Soviet Union and the United

States. These questions were not settled by the United Nations as an institution to enforce peace. They were determined by the interplay of American hesitations and the mounting uncertainties and reservations of the Member states of the United Nations. In short, they were settled by a general understanding not to extend the war, but to try to negotiate a solution.

The United States apart from the United Nations was confronted by a situation that was, if possible, more serious than that brought about by the North Korean aggression. The quick conclusion that had seemed possible after the defeat of the North Koreans had plainly gone by the board. Yet the basis on which action had originally been decided—the necessity of meeting Communist aggression —was as valid as ever. However, the original choice of means—to act with and through the United Nations—showed signs of losing its value. It had provided moral and political support, but only token material support. If the haul now became hard and long, it was very possible for both the political and moral support to fall off, leaving United States policy the prisoner of United Nations decisions at the very time when the United States might most need freedom of action. The situation threatened complications of the most alarming kind.

The problem from the point of view of the United States was a three-pronged one: what action to take with respect to Communist China; what concurrent adjustments to make in general policy for the Far East; and, what the situation required in terms of reorienting the basic policies of economic, military, and technical assistance and defensive alliances. Account must be taken of the fact that, although the administration had started the Korean "police action" with a pretty firm grip on a policy line and with its action quite solidly based on a consensus of public opinion, the grip had weakened and the foundation had become shaky by early 1951. Divergencies that had been submerged by the critical decisions of June 1950 had reappeared, and opposition pressure groups were becoming effective. The administration, as it approached the new complex of problems, was almost certain to be pushed by segments of domestic opinion toward more extreme solutions than it desired, while at the same time, it was being nudged toward weaker compromise solutions than it wished by other segments of American and United Nations judgment.

The most pressing issue was of course the line to be taken toward the Chinese Communists. At the decision-making level, this issue was not a simple matter whether to put in enough United States force to settle with the Chinese Communist regime. Nevertheless, many debated it in this form. Even if the argument were accepted that the United States could outbid Communist China in force, and that the Soviet Union would not intervene to bail out its Chinese allies, there were still many uncertainties left for the policy makers, particularly in connection with the United Nations.

A group of Asian-Arab states was expressing collective reservations about enlarging the scale of operations in Korea. American control of operations was also being more openly criticized within the United Nations. On November 16, 1950, the President had felt called upon to say: "Speaking for the United States Government and people, I can give assurance that we support and are acting within the limits of United Nations policy in Korea and that we have never at any time entertained any intention to carry hostilities into China."[10] The Soviet Union was active in exploiting the hesitations of Member states and in using procedural devices to impede decisions.

Although the Western European states supported the United States in the United Nations, they were frankly worried by the possibility that United States resources might be committed to a war in Asia, that programs of economic and military assistance might be curtailed, and that the North Atlantic Treaty might become a mere paper treaty. The possible use of the atomic bomb inadvertently became part of the undercurrent of the debate, adding an indefinable supplementary tension. At the end of November, Churchill urged the Western powers to avoid falling into the strategic trap of a war of attrition with China. A hastily arranged consultation with the British Labour Prime Minister specified the differences of judgment between the United States and Great Britain, and led to a joint statement on the importance of the role of the United Nations.

On the other hand, domestic opinion was hardening. The Republican opposition was beginning to talk of appeasement and "a Far Eastern Munich in the making." One of the alternatives to extending the war by United Nations action—that of standing on the defensive and then negotiating—was in danger of being foreclosed by internal political conflicts. The other alternative—that of

[10] U.S. Department of State *Bulletin,* Vol. 23 (Nov. 27, 1950), p. 552.

extending the war by unilateral action, or, as it came to be called "going it alone"—was brought to the fore as part of the argument in favor of dealing forcefully with China. This line, although it had its attraction so far as the problem of Korea and the Far East was concerned, did not accord with an over-all strategy that called for the organization and strengthening of a free world coalition. It was never seriously considered by the administration, which maintained that the economic and social costs of creating a military establishment for this purpose would weaken the stability of the United States, destroy the coalition, and lay the world open to Soviet domination.

The United States did not reach a clear-cut decision. Instead, by a process of restraining extremist domestic proposals and of pressing for moral support and minor action from the United Nations, it moved toward a defensive position from which negotiations could be developed at a suitable time. But this movement was more in the nature of a drift before the winds of circumstance than of a deliberate policy choice.

At the start of January after the United Nations had failed to extract satisfaction from the Chinese Communists, the United States representative pointed out to a committee of the General Assembly that the Chinese Communist regime, by its large-scale offensive across the thirty-eighth parallel, had defied the United Nations and aggravated the situation in Korea. He emphasized that the objective in Korea continued to be what it was before the Chinese Communist aggression: the repulsion of aggression and the establishment of a unified, independent, and democratic Korea. The United Nations should, he said, demonstrate to the Communist aggressors that the free world was united in its opinion that they were aggressors and would be resisted. However, the United States was ready to engage in discussions with the Chinese Communist regime at an appropriate time.[11]

At the same time, it was revealed that the United States had communicated to thirty countries its views concerning possible United Nations action to meet the situation created by China. Alternative courses were suggested, including an economic blockade, economic sanctions and embargo, severance of diplomatic relations, and other collective measures. It was pointed out that no

[11] U.N. General Assembly, Fifth Session, First Committee, *Official Records*, 419th Meeting (Jan. 3, 1951), p. 461.

specific course of action was being recommended because the decision should properly be made by the United Nations. It was indicated by other means, however, that American opinion would be influenced by the decision taken and that the question of United States support for the United Nations was at stake. Nevertheless, the United Nations made a further cease-fire proposal, which was characterized by one United States senator as signifying that the United Nations has sacrificed moral principle for expediency. The proposal was rejected by the Chinese Communists, who said that a peaceful settlement might be achieved if United States forces were withdrawn from Formosa and if Communist China were admitted to the United Nations.

The United States then submitted a resolution to the General Assembly, finding that Communist China had engaged in aggression in Korea and calling on it to cease hostilities and to withdraw its forces. The resolution also affirmed the determination of the United Nations to continue its actions in meeting aggression and called on other states to lend assistance to the United Nations activities in Korea and to refrain from giving assistance to the aggressors. The General Assembly, however, gave prior attention to an Asian-Arab group resolution calling, in effect, for an examination of the Communist proposals. Furthermore, the British Prime Minister declared that it was too soon to give up hope of a peaceful settlement.

These weakenings, as American opinion considered them, of the United Nations position appeared in the worst possible light when seen in conjunction with the military reverses that American troops were experiencing in Korea. The United States Senate voiced this feeling in two resolutions passed at the end of January.[12] The first stated that "it is the sense of the Senate that the United Nations should immediately declare Communist China an aggressor in Korea." The second stated that "it is the sense of the Senate that the Communist China Government should not be admitted to membership in the United Nations as the representative of China. A third resolution, calling on the United Nations to take all necessary measures including full-scale military action to halt Chinese aggression was referred to committee for further study. The administration was left with no choice but to exert full pressure in the United Nations. The pressure worked in the

[12] *Congressional Record*, Vol. 97, Pt. 1, 82 Cong. 1 sess., p. 346.

sense that the United States resolution condemning Communist China was passed. But it was passed at some cost to American prestige in the United Nations and to United Nations prestige in the United States.

The effect was to foreclose on all but two courses of action for the United States: to participate in a negotiated settlement as a member of the United Nations, or to resist the Chinese aggression unilaterally. Negotiation would endanger some of the most specifically defined features of the strategy of containment and could well open the door to their being ruled out by United Nations decisions. On the other hand, a refusal to negotiate, and a taking-off on a unilateral course, would undermine the build-up of the free world resistance to Soviet-Communist expansion and leave the United States cut off from its natural allies.

The tide of events had already caused dissent among the nations represented in the United Nations Command. To refuse to negotiate would only increase dissension. Until this alternative had at least been explored, many nations would not be satisfied. It was at the least possible that the Communists would be unyielding and so would facilitate the reunification of views at present divergent among the Members of the United Nations. Furthermore, even if it was becoming clear that the United Nations lacked the means and the corporate will to complete the task it had been assigned, both the United Nations and the United States were prisoners of the original decision to accept the task. Some form of responsibility for Korean affairs had to be confirmed if the Organization were not to be wholly discredited. These considerations all pointed to an ultimate acceptance of negotiations by the United States.

This line of argument, however, ignored the thesis in favor of unilateral action—"going it alone"—that had developed. This thesis proceeded by three stages: (1) the United States interest and the strategy of containment, which was also the real interest of the free world, required an extension of the conflict; (2) negotiation would conflict with effective military action; and (3) the nations associated with the United States, by pressing it to negotiate, were preventing it from taking the steps necessary to complete the Korean police action, punish the aggressors, and prevent further adventures of a similar kind. The United Nations Commander in Korea transformed himself at this point, first into a purely American field commander, and then into an American political figure. He summed up the views of all those who supported this position in a letter to the leader of the opposition in the House of Representatives.

It seems strangely difficult for some to realize that here in Asia is where the Communist conspirators have elected to make their play for global conquest, and that we have joined the issue thus raised on the battlefield; that here we fight Europe's war with arms while the diplomats there still fight it with words; that if we lose the war to communism in Asia the fall of Europe is inevitable; win it and Europe most probably would avoid war and yet preserve freedom. As you pointed out, we must win. There is no substitute for victory.[13]

It is not certain at what point in this flow of argument and counterargument a choice was made by the administration. It is certain, however, that the decision was to move with the United Nations, toward negotiation if need be, while trying to keep the United Nations as close to an American line as possible. Consequently, the United Nations Commander was relieved of his duties on April 11, 1951. The policy of the United States now explicitly became one of limiting the Korean conflict, of exacting a heavy price from the Chinese Communists and thus discouraging other aggressions, and of inducing negotiations on reasonable terms at some unspecified future date.

This position was officially justified by the fact that by the end of February the United Nations forces had checked the Communist advance and had stabilized a defense line from which they were able to take a disproportionate toll of Communist strength. It was apparent by April that the situation was under control, but that it could not be finally resolved militarily without additional troops and material. A military policy of attrition was continued instead with considerable success. In early July 1951, negotiations for an armistice were begun between the North Korean commander and the United Nations Commander. The negotiations dragged until October 1952, when they were recessed, although without a renewal of large-scale fighting.

[13] *Ibid.*, Pt. 3, 82 Cong. 1 sess., p. 3831.

CHAPTER XV

Shifts in Priorities: 1950-1951

WHEN IN KOREA Soviet-Communist policy appeared to take the form of expanding Soviet influence by armed force, the United States regarded the situation as a critical test of American objectives and responded by a series of significant decisions. The effect that the war in Korea and the actions taken by the United States in that war had on the total pattern of United States policy can be summarily stated as follows: a general strategy of containment designed to operate over a long period of time was converted into a specific strategy for meeting a Soviet threat that could become war within a defined period of time. This shift in the time scheme affected the purposes of the existing programs of action and rearranged their priorities in fundamental ways. The goals of economic recovery programs were gradually displaced by the more pressing claims of programs to rebuild the military strength of free nations, and a policy of military aid and defensive alliances was expanded to include precise commitments of American forces. These two areas of modification led to the assignment of a high priority to such hitherto subordinate purposes as the extensive rebuilding of American military power and the rearming of Western Germany.

These adjustments had their effects on the general conduct of United States foreign relations. The whole complex of American relations with the free nations of Europe did not remain static under these changes of purpose and pace; nor did the relations of the United States continue unaltered with the states that were anti-Communist but not committed to being exclusively associated with American purposes. It was no minor matter, either, that the coherent support that American opinion had given to the general build-up of policy from 1947 to 1950 began to lose its cohesiveness under the dramatic impact of the Korean War and the unexpected demands of a specific strategy of resistance to a sharply posed threat to national security. The administration had to thread a difficult way between those who wanted it to go further and faster

280

than it wished and those who wanted it to pull back and go slower than it intended.[1]

As a basis for examining this range of policy developments, it will be useful to recapitulate briefly United States objectives in Korea. The initial purpose was to demonstrate the firmness of the strategy of containment, and it seems to have been felt that action under the United Nations, by demonstrating the validity of collective security as a method of containing, would serve this end. While the course of military events was adverse, this purpose stood unchanged.

But as military prospects improved, the objective was widened. On the assumption that neither the Soviet Union nor Communist China would intervene, the purpose now became to unify Korea and hence to eliminate what had long been an area of United States-Soviet conflict. In effect, this expanded the purpose from halting aggression to defeating the aggressor and imposing a desired political solution. Simultaneously, in the interest of a possible future need, the United States obtained the passage by the General Assembly of the United Nations of a resolution establishing a Collective Measures Committee, the main purpose of which was to enable the General Assembly to act when the use of the veto prevented the Security Council from acting to oppose aggression.[2] However, Chinese intervention opened the possibility of an extension of hostilities for which the United States was not prepared. The objective now became one of limiting the war in order to conserve American resources for more important uses elsewhere, particularly in Europe.

While Asian and Arab members of the United Nations were trying to find a political compromise solution for this new situation, the Communists were apparently sure of military victory and indifferent to these efforts. The United States, having just passed

[1] In the course of a long struggle with a fragmented public opinion, a struggle that reached its crisis in a concerted attack on the integrity of high government officials, the administration won the battles but was stalemated in the struggle. In general, as it made adjustments to a varied opposition, it lost its previous power to lead opinion and its freedom to develop real policy alternatives. The gradual narrowing, under domestic political pressures, of the possibility of making rational choices among courses of action became in itself a major problem of United States foreign policy.

[2] This was embodied in the "Uniting for Peace" resolution, presented by the United States in September 1950, and adopted in November by a vote of 52 to 5 (the Soviet bloc), with Argentina and India abstaining.

through its period of optimism and insistence on total victory, was by the end of December considering the possibility of a forced evacuation of Korea and did not see much chance for a negotiated solution. Instead, it sought ways of keeping the conflict alive but confined, and worked to get United Nations support for measures that it thought might be necessary. In respect to these measures, the administration was pressed by minority congressional groups that treated anything short of drastic military action as appeasement of the Chinese Communists.

From the time when a battle line was stabilized in the spring of 1951 and through the first abortive period of armistice talks, the aims of the United States did not change. American action, however, under changing conditions of opinion and events made these aims at times seem contradictory and self-defeating. The government condemned Communist China and hence made a negotiated solution more difficult to achieve. At the same time, it was determined to confine hostilities to Korea, thus making a negotiated solution almost essential. The government attempted to find a basis for negotiation on terms acceptable to the Congress, and hence came around again to condemning China. These somewhat conflicting actions represented the adjustments deemed necessary to satisfy opposing political elements in the United States, the fears of associated and neutral states, and the requirements of limiting hostilities; and also to use the limited resources of the United States to maintain its purposes in Korea and to be prepared for contingencies in other parts of the world.

The reference to contingencies in other parts of the world leads to the heart of this discussion—the wide range of adjustments in general policy that accompanied the development of specific objectives and action in the Korean situation. The major contingency that soon became explicit in the minds of the policy makers was that aggression in Korea might be a diversionary tactic of Soviet policy; at best, designed to occupy American resources while the Soviet Union scored points elsewhere; at worst, designed to get the United States off balance as the opening move in a general war. This possibility assumed alarming proportions as the unreadiness of the United States was demonstrated in the early stages of the Korean War.

United States policy, based on estimates that were generally shared by its European associates, had been developing on a time scheme of five to ten years. Korea, however, suggested that the timetable of the Soviet action was shorter than had been anticipated and that consequently the danger of an attack in force in Europe was not a remote theoretical consideration. The strategy of containment called for a reaction in force in Korea in order to demonstrate the reality of this strategy as a foundation for the programs of economic and military assistance and the defensive alliance to which the states of Western Europe had been persuaded to adhere. These programs, however, had not yet produced the end results of economic strength, political stability, and military power that would be needed to confront effectively a speeded-up Soviet timetable.

Korean hostilities placed tremendous strains on the North Atlantic Treaty Organization (NATO). The defense of Korea was not deemed as important an objective of policy by the European NATO countries as it was by some vocal and influential elements in the United States. In Europe there was a fear of general war in the Far East with the consequent diversion of American strength. This fear increased after the Chinese entry into the Korean War; for an American war with China would have left the Soviet Union disengaged and capable of acting in Europe.

Conversely, the United States, although sensitive to these hesitations of European governments, was powerfully impressed by the military weaknesses of itself and its allies, and increasingly concerned that the defensive alliance it was building might be called on to perform at short notice. The only ready answer, in the American view, was to shift priorities from economic recovery to military build-up on a crash basis, and simultaneously to keep associated states politically committed to the principle of collective action under the United Nations.

These concepts influenced and limited the development of United Nations action in Korea. As the United States preferred to act under the aegis of the United Nations, it was limited by the need to obtain support within that organization. This limitation was in practice minimized, however. The United States provided the bulk of military forces and equipment, and command of the operation was a strictly American function operating from the Supreme Commander through the Joint Chiefs to the President of the United States. Nevertheless, the United States wanted formal approval for the actions it took in the name of the United Nations.

At nearly every stage, the opinions and pressures of its allies played a role in influencing the conception of the problem held by the American high command. There is no substantial evidence, however, that the United States was forced by allied pressure to revise a major military decision. Nevertheless, the general impression of an American willingness to accommodate its actions to the judgment of its associates was an essential ingredient in the efforts of the United States to focus its policies more sharply on rearmament and readiness for war. The efforts, in the course of time, affected the general pattern of United States policy. Their tendency will be adequately shown if a few key areas of action are examined, such as the North Atlantic Treaty Organization, the rearmament of Germany, domestic opinion, and relations with the free world.

NATO and Assistance Programs

United States objectives with respect to the structure of NATO, the rearmament of its members, and the use of German man power were all matters that had to be negotiated. American action within NATO was specifically limited by the policies of its allies. European rearmament involved domestic constitutional decisions by European states; German rearmament and participation in NATO involved the renegotiation of existing contractual relationships. The influence of the United States on the outcome of these negotiations stemmed from its continued willingness to maintain its assistance programs, from its great potential military strength, and from the desire of the European states and especially France to commit the United States to a land defense of Europe.

It was Europe that wanted a unified command for NATO, with an American at the helm, with all that this would imply for the commitment of American man power to the Continent. Europe had nowhere else to go for its economic, political, and military support against possible Soviet encroachment. Recognizing this fact, the governments of Europe were forced to follow the lead of the United States with respect to decisions they might otherwise have opposed.

On the other hand, the attempt of Western European countries to commit the United States to the defense of Europe did not find the United States entirely reluctant to assume the burden. The construction of a Western alliance was a major objective of United States policy. It was based on American security requirements and could not easily have been revised even if Western Europe had proven very reluctant to arm and to put teeth in NATO. Therefore, some subsidiary objectives of the United States had to be modified. For instance, if the United States had refused to compromise on the use of German man power, any French government that accepted the American position would have been defeated in the National Assembly. To get any German rearmament, the United States was obliged reluctantly to accept French reservations on the form of the German contribution.

The NATO military committees began work in October 1949, and by December reported agreement on a general plan for defending member states against possible Soviet aggression. Although not confirmed officially, it was believed that the general strategic plan adopted rested on four propositions: (1) the United States would assume responsibility, in case of hostilities, to use the atomic bomb in an air offensive against the aggressor and would possibly have an obligation to aid the ground campaign; (2) Continental Europe, France in particular, would be obliged to supply the ground forces to blunt the enemy offensive; (3) the United States, British, and French fleets would secure control of the seas; and (4) Western Europe would supply the aircraft for short-range tactical bombardment and for air defense. Again, according to reports, although the military planners took account of the possibility of aggression at any time, they did not feel that there was a definite time by which their plans would have to be completed. They were also influenced by the consideration that American atomic superiority would become less decisive as a Soviet atomic stockpile grew and that it would be necessary to equalize the existing superiority of Soviet ground forces.

On the basis of this plan, military assistance agreements were negotiated, and the United States announced that equipment and supplies would begin to move in March 1950. By that time, the military committees had developed detailed plans from the approved general plan. These were considered to indicate that the proposed defense system would require heavier financial outlays and greater allocations of resources by the European participants than would be possible if the pace of economic recovery was to be maintained. The United States was the only alternative source.

During mid-April the Brussels Pact countries—also members of NATO—held meetings and agreed on tentative steps for pooling their resources. They had difficulty, however, in finding a formula for the joint financing of defense. They presented a list of their deficiencies to the head of the United States mission for the co-ordination of military aid to Europe. It was understood that they hoped American aid would eliminate the difficulties of joint finance. Meanwhile, the United States showed coolness to a French plan for unifying the defense, the economic, and the political actions of the North Atlantic Treaty nations. In May, the North Atlantic Council of foreign ministers met. It established a permanent council of deputies to translate decisions into detailed plans for action; agreed on the functions of the organization; issued directives for future committee work; agreed on mutual assistance for integrated defense activities; made plans for the economic utilization of available forces and materials; and established an ocean shipping planning board. It was also understood that the Council had agreed to the principle of building balanced collective forces rather than balanced national forces.[3]

In May 1950, the NATO powers had on the continent of Europe fourteen divisions and about 1,000 planes of various categories, while the Soviet Union had twenty-five divisions on occupied or satellite territory backed up by more than 6,000 aircraft based in the Soviet Union. It is, therefore, worth noting that in early June it was reported that the NATO defense plans were then based on two assumptions: (1) Western superiority in atomic weapons would deter the Soviet Union from engaging in acts of aggression for several years; and (2) by the time the Soviet stockpile of atomic weapons was sufficient for a major war, the West would have developed defensive weapons of such scope that the Soviet Union would not dare to attack. It need occasion no surprise that, at this time, the Senate Committees on Foreign Relations and on Armed Services issued a joint report declaring that the day of neutrality, anywhere in the world, had passed, and that "the Mutual Defense Assistance Program must be carried to a successful conclusion if the world is to maintain peace under conditions which will permit men to live free";[4] nor that the Executive requested well over $1 billion for the second year of the military assistance program.

[3] This meant that air, naval, and ground forces, as well as the development and control of unconventional weapons, would be balanced in terms of the total NATO force and not in terms of the forces of the individual member states.

[4] *Military Assistance Program,* Hearings before the Senate Committee on Armed Services and Committee on Foreign Relations, 81 Cong. 1 sess., pp. 3-4.

Then at the end of June, the Korean aggression completely altered the situation and the assumptions of these plans and programs. Funds for military assistance were not only approved, but were criticized by opponents of the program as inadequate. The Secretary of State announced that the other members of the North Atlantic Treaty Organization would be asked to increase the size and pace of their rearmament programs. There was an emotional acceptance of the need for a prompt shift in the policies of the Atlantic community from recovery to defense. The NATO deputies met to map an intensive armament effort, starting from the assumption that all previous time schemes had been invalidated by the aggression in Korea. American officials stated that some way would have to be found to fuse the funds of the Economic Cooperation Administration (ECA) and machinery with the American military aid program. The Executive entered a request to the Congress for $4 billion in military assistance funds, of which $3.5 billion would be for the North Atlantic area. The Congress called for a Pacific pact similar in design and purpose to NATO.[5] Turkey and Greece began to press for inclusion in NATO.

Gradually two points began to stand out of this confusion of strong reactions. The European members of NATO were thinking of military assistance on a scale and in a form similar to wartime lend-lease. The United States Congress and a growing number of officials were dissatisfied with the scale on which European states were planning their own efforts to rearm. The latter attitude was strengthened as the demands laid on the United States by the Korean War steadily increased while the conversations of the NATO deputies revealed the discrepancy between what the military thought necessary for defense and what the member governments were prepared to pledge. The key issues that emerged were: What commitments of armed forces to Europe was the United States prepared to make? What diversion of resources from economic to military uses were the countries of Western Europe individually prepared to make?

In circling around these questions, United States policy makers began to consider such related matters as American rearmament and its effects on the American economy and on domestic political alignments, and the relative value to the American interest of

---

[5] A proposal that was repeated in September 1950 by the Australian Government.

conducting policy through alliances or of acting unilaterally. The question of the unused man power and industrial potential of Western Germany began to take on merit as a means for stirring the states of Europe and as an alternative source of power in its own right.

German Rearmament

When the North Atlantic Treaty Organization began to operate, the Western German Government asked the Western Allied High Commissioners to inform it officially what, if any, plans were being made to defend Germany in the event of war with the Soviet Union. The fear was expressed that only a holding operation on the Elbe was intended, and that no serious Western defense effort would be made east of the Rhine. The Bonn Government, however, did not indicate that it desired to rearm in order to defend its territory. The importance of Western Germany was appreciated by the NATO planners. Without that area, the strategic planners would lack sufficient depth for defensive maneuver. The first NATO plans called for the use of German territory, but not for the existence of German armed forces. The concept of a rearmed Germany became an immediate objective, however, of the United States in direct consequence of the implications of the war in Korea.

The issue had never been entirely absent from American thinking after the punitive policy for Germany was officially reversed. However, it had always been reserved for discussion in the remote future, and the primary American effort had been confined to linking Germany with its economic and political aims in Europe. France was explicit in stating that, even though the German Federal Republic was gradually incorporated into the integrated recovery of Western Europe, it could not come within the military framework of NATO. This limiting factor was recognized by the United States until the aggression in Korea.

In late July 1950, just prior to the first meeting of the North Atlantic Council deputies, a French spokesman, referring to reports that the United States would like to discuss the subject of German rearmament, stated that he did not see how the subject could be placed on the agenda. He declared the French position was unchanged both on the impossibility of establishing any kind of German army and on the need for international control of the Ruhr as well as limitations on German heavy industry.

The assumptions underlying American strategic reasoning were outlined during the preparatory conference for the formal meetings of the North Atlantic Council. It was stated that when the Atlantic Foreign Ministers had met in May, it had been assumed that the Western nations would have at least five years to organize their defenses against a Communist assault, and that the Soviet Union and its satellites would not attack until they thought themselves fully prepared to gain an assured victory. That assumption had been negated by the North Korean attack. Korea had convinced Western strategists that aggression could be expected at any time and that, therefore, the Western powers must revise their strategic timetable.

During the Council meetings, the United States representative pointed out that the real job was to raise thirty-six divisions by 1952, or 1953 at the latest, to defend Western Europe. The Korean fighting had emphasized the importance of ground troops; European defense could no longer be viewed as merely a question of American dollars, atomic deterrence, and increased arms production in Europe. Man power was the crucial item. The critical defense area was Western Germany. The forty million people in Western Germany might some day provide about twenty-five divisions for European defense. France proposed to raise and equip, with American aid, fifteen divisions, contingent on the United States and Great Britain each agreeing to station five divisions in Continental Europe. With this statement, the question was out in the open, and the pattern of discussion was set.

The United States, fully concerned to develop the military means of continuing the strategy of containment, moved steadily toward a militarily ready NATO that would include Western Germany. France steadily resisted the last item, but pressed for precise American commitments. The United States, although short of troops and equipment for Korea, felt that it had to commit ground forces to Europe on practical grounds as well as to bolster European morale. However, it had also reached the conclusion that the ground defense of Europe required a German man-power contribution and began to hint that an American commitment to European defense was contingent upon a European acceptance of a German contribution. But this *quid pro quo* had not been arranged by September 1950, when a substantial increase in American forces in Europe was approved.

The matter of the principle and the form of a German contribution now became the point on which United States, British, and French policy for Germany turned. Foreign ministers, the NATO Council, NATO deputies, economic and military assistance administrators, and national parliaments, assemblies, and congresses found it at the heart of their deliberations.

The country that benefited most was the Federal Republic of Germany. United States and British policy had set it on the road toward sovereignty. As the Republic grew economically more viable, its dependence on the Western powers became less absolute. When the United States decided that German man power was essential to the defense of the European continent and began to press this view on Great Britain and France, Germany was able to play a reluctant role that placed it in a very strong bargaining position. Moreover, because a German man-power commitment was impossible except as a free contribution of the German people, the rearmament of Germany could not take place without a new contractual relationship with the Republic that would restore its internal political autonomy.

These contractual arrangements, however, required French assent, and consequently France, in addition to resisting German rearmament in NATO councils, had a second area of negotiation in which it could hold a checkrein on the United States. When the United States put the role of Western Germany on the agenda of the September 1950 meetings of NATO, the item caused intense disagreement. Not even agreement in principle on the future creation of German divisions could be obtained. The United States was held to be risking Western European unity by pressing its case. France argued that the American pressure conflicted with earlier assurances that France should take the lead on matters concerned with the continent of Europe. It maintained that only on the basis of French leadership and Franco-German understanding could the issue be settled in a manner consistent with European unity.[6] France proposed the formation of an integrated European army into which German man power would be absorbed.

The United States began to stiffen in its position. It was pointed out that American defense expenditures had increased 500 per

[6] In particular, it was asserted that the German Republic had been given strong cards to play at just the moment when the negotiation of an agreement to establish a European Coal and Steel Community of Western Europe was proceeding in a way favorable to bringing Germany safely into the Western European community.

cent since the start of the Korean War and that the American contributions to NATO had gone up by 400 per cent in the same period. Furthermore, the administration was being pressed from all sides by its domestic opponents. Some of these were urging cessation of aid until Europe demonstrated a genuine will to oppose communism. Others were arguing the recklessness of sending American divisions to defend people who would not make an effort to defend themselves. Still others questioned the legal power of the President to send troops to Europe without the consent of the Congress.

Under great pressure France pledged itself to furnish twenty divisions to NATO, and early in December 1950, decided to compromise with American demands. The French feared that the United States might neglect Europe for the Pacific, and therefore felt that they would have to modify their opposition sufficiently to permit organization of the Atlantic pact forces. They could do this only by meeting some of the conditions of the United States with respect to German rearmament. It was tentatively agreed to permit German combat teams the size of a third of a division, without the equipment of a heavy division or a divisional staff. France would be permitted to go ahead with the organization of a European army provided it could get the other states concerned to agree. German strength was not to exceed 20 per cent of the total, or about twenty combat teams in an army of thirty-five divisions. There was to be no German ministry of war or armaments. German recruiting was to be handled by civilian agencies. Priority in matters of equipment would be given to non-German nations. A civilian high commissioner would supervise continental military affairs. These provisions were to be subject to West German agreement.

On the basis of this compromise, the North Atlantic Council asked the United States to appoint an American as supreme NATO commander. The request was acceded to. Furthermore, it was announced that more United States forces would be sent to Europe. The Chancellor of the German Republic, however, had previously stated that Western Germany would contribute to the defense of Western Europe only if it enjoyed equal rights and was part of a coalition sufficiently strong to deter Soviet aggression. He thus warned against proposals that put limits on Germany but not on the NATO powers, and at the same time indicated an unwillingness to provoke the Soviet Union by arming Germany until the West was strong enough to discourage Soviet aggression. Accord-

ingly, the German Government found the Franco-American compromise plan unacceptable. It demanded units of divisional strength
and a defense ministry.[7] The three allied occupying powers informed the German Republic of their readiness to place relations
on a contractual basis. The High Commissioners informed the
Chancellor that the form of the German contribution to Western
defense was still a matter for negotiation and that the Germans
were not being confronted with a *fait accompli.*

By the end of 1950 and six months after the start of the war in
Korea, the pattern of United States policy as it had been developed
in Europe was in a process of rapid change. With respect to Germany, the appearance was one of startling reversal; yet the major
change was primarily one of pace. The basic assumption that Germany was a threat to be controlled had been abandoned at a much
earlier date and been replaced. The role of a major threat had been
assigned to the Soviet Union in American thinking. However, the
same shift had not taken place in the thinking of the states of
Western Europe, and it had been considered politically unwise to
press the new American view to its logical conclusion except by
easy stages. This restraint seemed unreasonable in the face of the
pressure of time created by armed Communist aggression. Given
the sense of urgency, political difficulties were regarded as secondary. The United States Government took the unequivocal position
that if Soviet ground strength in Europe were to be counterbalanced, German military man power was the key.

From the American point of view, this was eminently reasonable. The United States was deeply and actively committed in
Korea on behalf of the United Nations. The United States was
deeply committed in principle and by active policy in Europe.
An expansion of American contributions would have meant, in
effect, a partial mobilization of American man power and industrial resources, and this would have meant such a comprehensive
domestic reorganization as to be politically dangerous. To the extent that Europe was the key or vital area that had to be safeguarded from Soviet aggression, to the extent that the primary
means of defense was infantry man power, and to the extent that

[7] The Soviet Union contributed to the turmoil at this point by informing
Great Britain and France that the rearming of Western Germany would be
regarded as a violation of their treaties of alliance with the Soviet Union.
While this had little practical significance, it introduced some tensions into
French and British domestic policies.

American military man power had to be employed in the Far East, the man power of Western Germany appeared an inescapable need: so inescapable, in fact, as to be insisted upon in the face of all other considerations.[8]

Primary attention was consequently given to the goal of German rearmament. It was assumed that speed of decision was vital. And it was finally assumed that American economic and military predominance could be used to obtain acceptance of the demands being made on the associated NATO states. Superficially, these assumptions were justified. Agreement was obtained on the principle of German rearmament. This agreement was linked with a commitment of American forces to Europe, with an expansion of the military assistance program, with larger European budgets for defense purposes, and with the American acceptance of a strategy of continental defense as the basic NATO plan.

These interlocking adjustments imperceptibly limited the alternatives that were open to the United States with respect to its future courses of action in Europe. The full extent of these limitations was not to become apparent for some time. At the moment the desire of the Western European nations to commit the United States to a ground defense of the Continent gave the United States a bargaining position sufficient to impose seeming agreement on the other NATO powers, particularly France. After American ground troops had been pledged, after an American had been appointed supreme commander, and specific strategic commitments had reduced the bargaining power of the United States, the long struggle to implement the agreement revealed the difficulties involved in organizing the free nations of Europe around a common program of action.

Domestic Reactions

The same considerations that led to adjustments in the substance and pace of foreign policy programs also had their effects on do-

[8] There was considerable congressional opposition to committing American troops to Europe—especially in view of the gravity of the situation and American man-power sacrifices in Korea—unless it was demonstrated that European man power was being used to the fullest extent. Ideological, historical, or foreign policy reasons for not using German man power did not count for much when congressional mail was heavily laden with the complaints of American parents. Nor did the electoral problems of French legislators strike the Congress as a reason for going slow in the matter.

mestic policy and on the political discussion of foreign policy. The main result was to force an apparent sharp distinction between an American interest in the Far East and an American interest in Europe, and to develop an argument that a choice could and should be made between these areas of interest. Consequently, despite the virtually unanimous support given to the underlying principle of a vigorous defense policy, bitter partisan debate attended the specific measures proposed. A hemisphere defense policy was pressed by some because of the "unwillingness" of European countries to take adequate measures for their own defense. The President was accused of usurping authority in sending troops to Korea and Western Europe without congressional approval, and it was claimed that plans for a unified Western army would only provoke the Soviet Union. Vigorous objections were entered to a commitment to fight a land war in Europe, for which the United States did not have sufficient man-power resources, while the Navy and the Air Force were available to deter the Soviet Union. Other groups saw the Far East as the region in which the United States had suffered a fundamental set-back and maintained that the validity of the strategy of containment could only be demonstrated by effective action in this theater. The Soviet Union, it was argued, through the agency of the Chinese Communists, would launch a drive to eliminate the Western powers from their remaining footholds on the continent of Asia. Therefore, every present foothold —Japan, Formosa, Indo-China, Malaya, Indonesia, Korea—had to be retained and strengthened.

While these opposition views could not force the major lines of foreign policy to take wholly new directions, they could force adjustments in the execution of policy. The result judged from hindsight was to expand the operation of existing programs to cover the specific demands of the opposition. Military and economic assistance were given to the Chinese National Government on Formosa. Over $300 million in ECA aid was earmarked for Indo-China. United States activity was stepped up throughout the Southeast Asian area in 1950 and 1951. By April 1951, the administration had become persuaded of the need for a Pacific defense pact and proved receptive to overtures from Australia and New Zealand to this end. The desirability of a Japanese peace treaty began to come to the fore. This active extension of policy programs in the Far East soon led back to the European scene. Quite apart from the fears that arose about a possible neglect of United States commitments in Europe, American short-term objectives in the Far East raised awkward questions with respect to the authority and policy of France in Indo-China, to the attitudes of Great Britain and the Commonwealth about Japan, and to the general European rejection of the rigid United States position on the Chinese Nationalist and Communist regimes. This latter difference of opinion carried over into the United Nations in due course.

Finally, the pressures of opposition views had to be responded to for another important reason. Although American opinion generally accepted the necessity for United States rearmament and was ready to assume the financial costs, agreement on the course rested on three factors: a continued awareness of an immediate threat to national security; a demonstration that the associated states were making equal sacrifices; and a conviction on the part of the more vocal and organized sections of public opinion that resources were being applied for purposes and in ways that were acceptable to them. The first gave little trouble. The second could never be demonstrated to the satisfaction of everybody. The third was met by expanding policies and programs until every proposal that could not be rejected was covered to some extent. This last form of compromise had the effect of increasing the costs of foreign policy while introducing conflict and contradiction into its execution.[9]

The Free World

The shifts of emphasis in United States policy with respect to NATO, rearmament, military aid to friendly governments, and the expansion of American commitments to Formosa and other Asian areas can be viewed as merely changes of pace in a pattern of action that predated the outbreak of war in Korea. The evidence is that they were so regarded by United States policy makers. Nevertheless, they reflected profound changes with respect to American concepts of the urgency of the Soviet threat, the risks involved in measures being taken to meet that threat, the

[9] The proposed United States budget for the fiscal year 1951-52 was $71.6 billion, 78 per cent above that for the fiscal year 1950-51. Of this, $39 billion was to go to the Department of Defense for expanding and equipping the American armed forces.

scope of the defensive measures required, and the diversion of resources necessitated. The significance of these underlying modifications of estimate and judgment are best seen in connection with the concept of a free world organized and strengthened to confront a Soviet-Communist world.

The concept of an organized free world was a political abstraction. In reality, at the start of 1950 the free world consisted of states in formal alliance with the United States, of isolated entities like Spain and Yugoslavia, Iran and Thailand, of newly emerged entities like India, Pakistan, Ceylon, Burma, and Indonesia that were intent on demonstrating their independent exercise of state power, of xenophobic entities like the Arab states of the Middle East, and of still subsidized entities like the German Federal Republic, Japan, the Republic of Korea, the Philippines, and Libya. Obviously this congeries could not be made to respond to any principle of organization or to any planned and scheduled development of collective strength. And initially, except in the case of the states of Western Europe, the process of developing a collective strength was regarded as inevitably slow and evolutionary, without time scheme and without specific design.

This reasonable approach was somewhat modified by the development of the cold war and the view that the world was bipolar. It seemed increasingly both right and advantageous to the United States to call on the recipients of its assistance for support and co-operation in the general strategy of containment. With the start of the Korean War, and under the compulsion of urgency and emergency, the demand for an organized free world alignment became precise and positive. When long-term policy became pressure for immediate results, the states of the free world proved less unresponsive.

The reaction of India, although relatively restrained, can be taken as roughly characteristic of the attitudes of the states of the so-called colonial belt. India argued that the positions of the two blocs would become inflexible unless moderated by some external force. The more the two blocs came into direct territorial contact, the more friction would increase and the greater the chances that world conflict would break out. Therefore India was convinced that an important role existed for a nation uncommitted to either bloc. This did not necessarily mean that India was neutral in the sense of being indifferent to the outcome. It did signify that India would use its uncommitted position to attempt to moderate and to compromise differences between the blocs of powers. India believed that only if a number of important states essayed such a role, could enough flexibility be maintained in the international system to prevent an atomic world war. Furthermore, as other states in a similar position appreciated, this permitted them to concentrate on and to further their own interests and policies in ways and to a degree that would not be possible if they became the agents of an anti-Communist alliance in which they would be junior members.

The United States was consequently in a dilemma. To the extent that it desired to enlist the support of these nations for reasons of military security or feared that their attitudes would interfere with United States policies and objectives—for instance, in the conduct of the Korean hostilities—it naturally took an unfavorable view of their activities in the United Nations and elsewhere. At the same time, any drastic action by the United States, or even a failure to extend some degree of economic support, might result in opening these states to Communist influences. As this would have been undesirable from the standpoint of longer-term American objectives, the range of policy alternatives open to the American leadership was extremely limited, and a final choice something to be avoided. Thus while the United States frowned on uncommitted states and frowned more fiercely as its feeling of urgency mounted, it was obliged to recognize that it was not always possible to persuade other states of the justness of its position. Yet, if it applied too much pressure, it ran the danger of antagonizing such states irrevocably and possibly also of injuring the reputation of the United States among the states already allied with it. No straight path could be cut through this wilderness of conflicting considerations, and in the course of trying to move at all, the United States accepted still further limitations on the alternatives open to it and accepted still further restraints on its freedom of action.

By the end of 1950, a number of factors had combined to increase the complexity of the process of executing United States policy. Confronted by an increased and easily identifiable threat, the United States altered the character but not the direction of the basic pattern of policies that it had established. Acceptance of these alterations by other states was obtained by concessions whose full significance was not revealed until a later date. In the emergency that prevailed in late 1950 and early 1951, the fundamental nature of the issues that were being released and of the differences that were being patched over remained under the surface. However, they did not stay hidden for long, and the major problems of United States foreign policy after 1950 can be largely traced to their subsequent growth and influence.

PART THREE

POLICY LINES ENTANGLED: 1950-1955

CHAPTER XVI
Changing Structure of the International System

AT THE END of the Second World War, the structure of the international system could not be clearly defined. The components of the system were national states, and the open question seemed merely to be what basic pattern of relations between these components did the major victorious powers wish to establish. The answer to that question was given, so far as the United States was concerned, by the wartime agreements with Great Britain, the Soviet Union, and China, modified and confirmed as these were by the negotiation of the Charter of the United Nations.[1] Essentially, the United States view rested on three concepts: the sovereign equality of the component nation-states of the system; a hierarchy of power within the system; and the harmonization of sovereign power within and through a freely negotiated international organization. But the events of the five years from 1945 to 1950 gave the international system a structure that differed considerably from that implied by these concepts. The presumed agreement of the wartime allies did not stand. In the upper hierarchy of power, relations became competitive, largely, the evidence suggests, because the Soviet Union refused to act on the self-denying agreements it had entered into.

Even if this had not been the case, it could still be argued that the United States had misjudged the capacity of the other forces operating in the international system to develop a structure other than the one desired. The vacuums that total victory left in Central Europe and in the Far East were vacuums of political authority that subjected the relations of the members of the successful coalition to immense strains. The loosening of colonial authority was a trend of much greater impetus than had been conceived, and the co-ordinate multiplication of national sovereignties conse-

---

[1] The substance of the United States view has been given in Chap. II above.

301

quently proceeded at a greater rate than had been anticipated. The re-establishment of a functioning international economy was underestimated as a problem. Finally, the capacity of France and China to act as effective members of the upper hierarchy of power was overestimated. Consequently, except for such support as could be given by a weakened Great Britain and a loosely organized Commonwealth, the United States found itself alone confronting the Soviet Union competitively in the highest bracket of power in the international system, while the states that it had anticipated as being associated with it at this level were in fact more or less confined to a lower place on the scale. It is understandable that a picture of a so-called bipolar structure was soon drawn.

Although this bipolar picture provided the basis for a strategic concept of containment and became a guide line for United States policy, it did not replace in American thinking the concept of a more desirable structure for the international system. It merely shifted priorities—and successful operation in a bipolar structure became a condition precedent to the achievement of the structure sketched by the United Nations Charter and by the original post-war pattern of United States objectives and policies.

For five years, therefore, United States policies and programs of action were developed on a contingent basis. They sought to strengthen and to organize a free world coalition for action in a theoretical bipolar world structure without destroying the possibility of achieving a structure of multilaterally harmonized sovereign interests. They further sought to keep alive the principle of collective international action in an open system of relations without foreclosing on an organization for action in a closed bipolar structure. The year 1950, during which Communist armed force appeared to indicate with finality the necessity for acting almost wholly on the bipolar assumption, was a period in which United States policies and programs were vigorously reoriented to a drastically shortened time scheme and to a single-minded judgment of the nature of the international system. The framework of United States action consequently became more rigid. Policies and programs became increasingly inflexible after 1950, and remained so for nearly five years. For this reason, this part of the study drops the chronological presentation of material and instead analyzes broadly the major problems of policy decision during these five years.

The Communist Bloc

From the standpoint of the structure of the international system, the Communist movement introduced a new element into international relations. The operational principle of obtaining unity of action by requiring that policy once decided would be executed without further debate at various echelons, resulted in an organization that could be adjusted to changed conditions with a minimum of effort by orders issued from a central executive. When the Communist party succeeded in capturing the Russian state apparatus, it adapted this principle of organization and operation to the requirements of an international revolutionary movement operating in an international system that was structured in terms of nation states. The Third International, known as the Communist International, or Comintern, was the product of this adaptation. Although the Comintern theoretically represented a higher level of authority, it soon became clear that it was a subordinate instrument of the Communist party of the Soviet Union.[2]

Nevertheless the Comintern introduced a new element into the international political picture. A world-wide apparatus, responsive to a single center of control, emerged. It cut across the normal political divisions of the nation-state structure. National states were now confronted, within their own borders, by groups at war with existing social systems and prepared to use legal or illegal methods to disrupt them. These groups, moreover, co-ordinated their political moves with those of a powerful national state, the Soviet Union. Only the relative weakness of the Soviet Union and of the world Communist movement in the period between the two world wars prevented the full consequences of this new kind of organizational strength from being felt and reacted to by other national states.

Even then, the Comintern was a constant irritant to the nation-states of the West, where the principles of comity among nations forbade states at peace with one another to direct organized conspiracies against each other's internal social systems. In the critical year 1943, the Soviet Union agreed to dissolve the Comintern in

[2] The decreasing importance of the Comintern is emphasized by the fact that, although the sixth Congress was held in 1928, the seventh and last Congress was not held until 1935. The Comintern eventually became a mere administrative apparatus subordinate to the Politburo of the Soviet Communist party.

order to improve relations with the United States and Great Britain. There was, of course, no way of determining whether the organization had been completely dismantled. In any event, the war disrupted communication between the Soviet Communist party and other European Communist parties so that even if the Comintern had formally existed, co-ordination between them would have deteriorated, and a certain degree of autonomy in the national parties would have re-emerged.

In fact, in each of the Eastern European countries, there were factional differences between the Communist leaders who had directed guerrilla activities and those who had remained in the Soviet Union during the war and had returned with the Red army. Yugoslavia was an exception. But, in this case, virtually the entire leadership began to display nationalistic tendencies.[3]

Evidently the lack of organizational cohesion proved undesirable in the postwar era. Certain disturbing evidences of initiative in the satellite governments were noticed by the Soviet Union. Moreover, the Truman Doctrine, the Marshall Plan, and developments in Germany made the continuation of relatively loose relations between various Communist groups appear threatening to Soviet objectives and policies. In all probability these factors were connected with the decision to organize a Communist Information Bureau, the Cominform, in September 1947. The Cominform had the function of permitting the member parties to exchange views, to publicize their positions, and to co-ordinate their activities. Whether the organization was intended to perform more important but unannounced functions is not known.

At the same time, an interlocking network of treaties was developed to bind the Soviet satellites to each other and to the Soviet Union.[4] During 1947 and 1948, the satellite regimes were reor-

---

[3] It should be noted that, in this case, it proved impossible for Russian policy to split Yugoslav leadership in any significant sense, and control by the Russian Communist party eventually broke down.

[4] Poland and Czechoslovakia concluded treaties with Yugoslavia during 1946, but political differences between Poland and Czechoslovakia prevented the conclusion of a treaty of friendship, co-operation, and mutual assistance until March 1947. Hungary concluded treaties of mutual assistance with Poland, Rumania, Yugoslavia, and Bulgaria in 1947 and 1948, but was unable to reach agreement with Czechoslovakia until later. Yugoslavia allied itself with Albania in 1946 and concluded treaties with Bulgaria and Rumania in 1947. Bulgaria concluded treaties with Albania in December 1947 and Rumania early in 1948. In 1948 and early 1949, Rumania and Bulgaria each concluded treaties with Poland, Czechoslovakia, and Hungary.

ganized, and firmer Communist control was established. This was the case particularly in Hungary where the regime was taken over by the Communists and in Czechoslovakia where a Communist *coup d'état* was engineered in February 1948. Purges were organized in 1948 in Bulgaria and Poland. Some informed observers believe that one of the principal purposes of the Cominform was to tighten organizational control over the Yugoslav Communist party.

New industrial plans were projected for Czechoslovakia and Poland, the satellites with the most developed economies. In January 1949, representatives of Bulgaria, Czechoslovakia, Hungary, Poland, Rumania, and the Soviet Union formed the Council for Mutual Economic Assistance as a counterweight to the Marshall Plan. Thus economic co-ordination was one of the reasons for developing a tighter structure. Similarly, during 1949 the armies of the satellites were rebuilt and armed with automatic weapons, tanks, artillery, planes, and large supplies of modern offensive equipment. Bulgaria, Hungary, and Rumania equipped armies several times the size permitted by peace treaty limitations. In 1950, Soviet military regulations were introduced into the satellite armies, and an attempt was made to standardize equipment. In 1951, heavy arms were given to police groups in Eastern Germany.

Other organizations were used by the Communists to increase co-ordination within the world Communist movement. The World Federation of Trade Unions was utilized to infiltrate the world labor movement, to interfere with Western rearmament efforts, to sabotage military shipments, to interfere with the economic programs of the West, and to propagandize the workers.[5] These organizational, political, economic, and military modes of activity all had the purpose of increasing the monolithic unity of the Communist bloc of powers in Europe. But the organizational means by which non-European Communist policy was co-ordinated with European Communist policy are obscure.

In the course of 1950, the Communist party of China, which had consolidated its control of the mainland of China, began to assume responsibility for Asian Communist affairs. The Asian Peace Con-

[5] Other channels of action, such as the World Congress of the Partisans of Peace, the World Peace Council, the International Economic Conference, the World Federation of Democratic Youth, and the International Union of Students, are noted in order to indicate the range of peripheral supporting functions that were developed and co-ordinated.

ference, which took place in Peking in 1952, served to emphasize Chinese leadership in the Asian movement. Consequently, relations between China and the Soviet Union, with respect to directing the Communist world movement, became the subject of interested speculation. The Soviet Union evidently learned from its experience with Yugoslavia not to issue orders that might alienate the Chinese leadership. The Chinese revolution had been won with at most limited support from the Soviet Union, and the national leadership had loyal and powerful armed forces at its command. Flushed by victory and convinced of the soundness of its theoretical position, the Chinese party was not likely unquestioningly to accept Soviet Communist guidance. By 1952, the Soviet Union had agreed to withdraw from Port Arthur and Dairen and to give up its economic privileges in Manchuria, North China, Sinkiang, and Turkestan. There is no conclusive evidence that instructions can be given by the Communist party of the Soviet Union to the Communist party of China. Nevertheless, their objectives can be regarded as parallel, if not necessarily always identical.

Thus with regard to the control of the world Communist movement and its role in the execution of Soviet policy, the principle of centralism was limited by the rise of a parallel and co-ordinated, but independent center of direction. By 1955, the Secretary of State of the United States was reliably reported to think that the Soviet Union was concerned lest the expansionist tendencies of China force the Soviet Union into a war for which it was not prepared. Still others believed that changes in the hierarchy of authority within the Soviet Union were related indirectly to the requirements of its relations with China, and that the Soviet Union was not eager to have China develop into a state strong enough to challenge Soviet predominance.

If, however, the centralized control of the world Communist system was loosening in consequence of the rise of Chinese power, the control of the European wing was being tightened in the light of the United States participation in the organization of Western Europe and in the proposals for German rearmament. Soviet policy led to an announcement by the Soviet Foreign Minister in February 1955 that foreshadowed a unified army command for the Soviet Union and the satellites, and a treaty of friendship, assistance, and mutual aid that would link Albania, Bulgaria, Czechoslovakia, Eastern Germany, Hungary, Poland, Rumania, and the Soviet

Union in a confrontation of the North Atlantic Treaty Organization (NATO). This development was significant, not only in linking the European Communist powers in an internationally presented treaty, but in formally extending Soviet guarantees to Albania and Eastern Germany.

Among the European satellites, Czechoslovakia, Eastern Germany, Hungary, and Poland contributed important industrial strength. The others provided a substantial reservoir of man power, food supplies, and raw materials. Within each of them, totalitarian political agencies permitted the imposition of domestic and foreign policies in a manner not possible in the democracies. Ability to ignore domestic resistance permitted a unity of policy among the Communist countries that could not be achieved by the countries of the free world.

If equivalent co-ordination of Soviet and Chinese policy could not be so easily arranged, at least common principles, objectives, and dangers bound them together. China needed Soviet help in industrializing and in carrying out its economic plans. For the Soviet Union, defeat of communism within China would check the dynamic of Communist expansion and threaten its control over the European satellites. Whatever fear of future Chinese power the leaders of the Soviet Union might have, their current objectives apparently permitted them no alternative to that of supporting, although possibly trying to moderate, Chinese policy.

By these processes the Soviet Union succeeded in giving a definable structure to the postwar international system by developing a bloc of states that could simultaneously seem to function as sovereign nation-states while being, in effect, centrally directed in terms of the objectives and policies of the dominating component. The Soviet Union no longer functioned in the international system as an isolated pariah among nations, but as a state whose actions could determine to its own advantage the reactions of other states. In 1949, China added its vast man power and resources to this bloc, although at the cost of some weakening in the central direction of the whole. It thus emphasized the basic international structure that Soviet policy had shaped. Yet by virtue of its own potential as a major power, China might make it more difficult in the long run for the Soviet Union to manipulate this structure exclusively for its own purposes. For the period 1950 to 1955, however, the Communist bloc was bound by theory, linked by treaty, and interlocked organizationally. In this form it acted vigorously in the world scene.

The Free World Coalition

The free world organized itself slowly and painfully in opposition to, or in fear of, the challenge presented by the Communist bloc. No coherent philosophies, political doctrines, or organizational methods united the nations of the free world. No international monolithic party served to unify their actions or to impose uniform policies. Initiative had to develop within individual countries that found a common ground mainly in the common danger. Wedded to the concept of the national state, these nations found that organized combined action in time of peace required a break with tradition and habitual practice. Alliances were a familiar framework, but unified commands, economic co-operation, and supranational production schedules were not.

The most significant device of free world organization, and the one that was most clearly dictated by the need to counter Soviet policies and methods, was embodied in the North Atlantic Treaty. Its significance lay not in a joint guarantee to take immediate action to meet armed attack, but in the creation of an organization designed to reduce the possibility of armed attack. Originally a North Atlantic Council of foreign ministers was established for general policy purposes, and a Defense Committee of defense ministers was established to draw up unified defense plans for the North Atlantic area. A Military Committee for policy purposes and a Standing Group for executive purposes were established. Finally, a Financial and Economic Committee was assigned the tasks of developing over-all financial and economic programs and of considering plans for the mobilization of economic and financial resources in time of emergency.

In December 1950, the responsibilities of the Standing Group were increased, and a body permanently in session was authorized to make important policy decisions with respect to military matters. To compensate for this organizational concentration of control, a permanent Committee of Military Representatives composed of representatives from each member country was established in Washington. Its task was largely consultative. The principle of concentration was further extended by the decision to establish an integrated command rather than to co-ordinate the national commands of the member countries. It was agreed that an American would be appointed Supreme Commander, and that he would establish his headquarters in Europe with "authority to train the national units assigned to his command and to organize them into an effective integrated force." He would be assisted by "an international staff drawn from the nations contributing to the force."[6] Integration to this degree had previously been achieved by the free nations only under wartime conditions. Supplementary centralizing devices were developed in the course of 1951 and 1952, by naming permanent officials, and by establishing a Secretary-General with an international secretariat.

The steady tightening of organizational forms went on in direct relation to a growing sense of the opposing and threatening organization of the Communist bloc by the Soviet Union. The process became most rapid after the outbreak of the Korean War. In 1951 and 1952, planning became more and more detailed and laid heavier claims on member governments for implementing action. Ten military commands were established.[7] These commands had common airfields, communication systems, fuel tanks and pipelines, radar warning systems, navigational aid stations, and port installations. This integrated physical plant was known as the NATO infrastructure. Its costs were shared, and its construction and control were supervised by the NATO staff.

The Production Division of NATO engaged in long-term logistical planning, facilitated the exchange of information among member states, guided technical studies, participated in the analysis of equipment requirements and resources, and co-operated with the national defense production counsellors. This activity, as it impinged on the economic planning of member governments, kept NATO in close working contact with the Organization for Euro-

---

[6] Lord Ismay, *NATO, The First Five Years, 1949-1954* (1954), p. 186.

[7] Command functions under the Standing Committee were the Supreme Allied Commander in Europe (Paris); the Supreme Allied Commander Atlantic (Norfolk); the Canada-United States Regional Planning Group (Washington); and the Channel Committee, under which were the Allied Commander-in-Chief (Portsmouth, United Kingdom) and the Allied Maritime Air Commander-in-Chief Channel (Northwood, United Kingdom). Under the Supreme Headquarters Allied Powers Europe were the Allied Forces Northern Europe (Oslo); the Allied Forces Central Europe (Fontainebleau); the Allied Forces Southern Europe (Naples); the Allied Forces Mediterranean (Malta); and the Allied Land Forces Southeastern Europe (Izmir, Turkey).

pean Economic Cooperation, the European Coal and Steel Community, the administrators of American economic and military assistance programs, and with the Council of Europe and groups that worked for the full integration of the European states.

The North Atlantic Treaty Organization, between 1949 and 1953, became the prototype for organizing the policies and power of non-Communist nation-states. As a structure, and in terms of its impact on the international system, it can be theoretically compared with the structure of the Communist bloc, in spite of obvious differences of purpose and method. However, from the point of view of the United States, preoccupied as United States policy was with security after 1950, NATO was regarded as an incomplete answer to the Communist bloc. The greater the development of NATO as an institution of collective defense, complete with strategy, plans, and institutional machinery, the more necessary it seemed for the United States to undertake the supporting actions needed to keep NATO from being suspended in a strategic vacuum. These actions were determined to be of two kinds. The first was to ensure that the flanks of the North Atlantic Treaty area were secured. The other was to strengthen the politico-military posture of the United States along the rest of the periphery of the Communist bloc in order to ensure that the full range of American interests would be protected, and that the United States could continue to act as the major support of and influence in NATO.

In the first respect the United States, generally supported by Great Britain whose global interests called for much the same type of supplementary action, sought to bring Greece and Turkey within NATO, to establish working relations with Yugoslavia, and to patch up relations between Yugoslavia and Italy and between Yugoslavia and Greece. This course of action was showing results by the end of 1952.[8] Simultaneously, the United States, Great Britain, and France attempted to create a Middle East defense arrangement as a still further supplement to NATO strategy. This effort ran into Arab indifference to the Soviet threat and Arab distaste for association with France, Great Britain, and the United States. After 1952 the United States and Great Britain tried again, now confining

[8] Greece and Turkey became members of NATO in March 1952. By September Yugoslavia, Greece, and Turkey were holding conversations about Balkan defense arrangements. These culminated in a treaty of friendship and collaboration in February 1953. Trieste, however, proved the stumbling block to any quick and easy adjustment of Yugoslav-Italian relations.

policy to creating a coalition of states bordering the Soviet-Union—Turkey, Iraq, Iran, and Pakistan. A pact to this effect was completed in March 1955, to which Great Britain acceded. The United States did not accede to it, although American support and co-operation were clearly expressed. Acting unilaterally, the United States completed its defensive pattern in Europe by negotiating base rights in Spain. In spite of the fact that this action ran counter to the views of its NATO associates, the negotiations were completed late in 1953. The agreement was definitely dissociated from NATO and from United States commitments under the North Atlantic Treaty.

The pattern of expansion, largely the result of American initiative, can very properly be seen as a series of actions designed to supplement the commitment that the United States had made in Western Europe. As a pattern, it was not directly applicable to the national security interests of the states of Western Europe. In fact, they tended to regard it as an unsatisfactory and indirect extension of their commitments and as possibly converting a collective defensive alliance into a support for a unilaterally offensive American strategy. To the United States, however, the structure created in NATO was valid only if American power could be deployed at the same time through other similar structures. In its most theoretical and comprehensive form, United States policy envisaged a free world coalition, built up by repeating the NATO structure in regions other than Europe.

The development of comparable structures in the Pacific and Asian areas was slow, hesitating, and inadequate. Initially, the United States resisted pressures to commit itself: insisting that the time was not ripe for such efforts, that internal differences within the area would have to be settled first, and that for the moment more selective methods would be needed because there was no community of interest in the Pacific-Asian region similar to that existing in the North Atlantic area. Nevertheless, the Chinese Nationalist regime, the Republic of Korea, and the Philippines continued to call for the formation of a Pacific pact. Not until February 1951 did the United States Government make any serious effort to explore the possibility of a defensive arrangement in the Pacific area. Even so, no real progress took place until negotiations for the Japanese peace treaty were well under way. Then as a supplement to a treaty of peace, the United States negotiated a security treaty that bilaterally linked the United States and Japan and provided for

American bases in Japan to be used for the defense of that country. Also, in order to ensure acceptance of the Japanese Peace Treaty by other Pacific states, a bilateral treaty of mutual defense was concluded with the Philippines, and a similar pact (ANZUS) was completed with Australia and New Zealand.[9]

By 1954, when Communist China had come to loom large as a security threat, the final step was taken. At the Manila Conference of September 1954, a Southeast Asia Collective Defense Treaty was initiated. The Southeast Asia Treaty Organization (SEATO) reflected the NATO model, but with variations and reservations. It provided for joint action to meet aggression. An unusual feature was a provision recognizing the danger of subversion and indirect aggression and providing that if any party to the treaty believed the treaty area to be menaced by other than armed attack, the parties should consult immediately and agree on common measures to meet the danger. The United States entered a stipulation that only Communist armed attack would constitute a danger that would automatically invoke American action. If danger threatened from other quarters, however, the United States would consult with its treaty partners concerning the measures to be taken.

SEATO had no joint forces or commands. Military action would have to rely on individual contributions from countries willing to send armed units in case of attack or danger. The only states able to provide equipped forces were not Southeast Asian states, but the United States, Great Britain, Australia, and New Zealand. India, Indonesia, Burma, and National China were conspicuous by their absence, the first three because they did not want to participate in the pact, and the last because its inclusion was opposed by other participants who feared to provoke Communist China. In short, SEATO lacked definiteness, cohesiveness, organization, and committed power.

Various proposals were made within the United States administration to remedy these defects—to expand programs of economic and military assistance and to tie them in with SEATO. But the highest policy levels stood firm on a decision that the United States could not divide its strength and irrevocably commit the parts

[9] These pacts were originally designed as guarantees against future Japanese aggression. The preamble to the ANZUS pact, however, stated that it was an interim arrangement to be superseded by a general Pacific pact. It could, therefore, be converted into an anti-Soviet instrumentality.

separately to widely dispersed areas of danger. The United States did not know where a Communist attack might be launched, and it had to maintain a substantial mobile reserve that could be moved quickly to an attacked area. In other words, the structuring of the free world that had been set in motion by NATO and that had developed certain clear specifications for political, economic, and military co-ordination was not to be pushed to completion as a counterpoise to the Communist bloc. It is debatable whether this was more a consequence of sober second thought on the part of the United States Government about the growth of its commitments, or of the intractability of large sections of the international system.

This account of an American intent to draw the free world together needs for its completion a brief reference to the Western Hemisphere and the Organization of American States (OAS). In 1951, acting within the framework of the Rio Treaty of 1947, the foreign ministers of the members of the Organization adopted measures for military and political defense against the dangers emanating from the world Communist movement. In 1954, at the Caracas meeting, a "Declaration of Solidarity for the Preservation of the Political Integrity of the American States Against International Communist Intervention" was adopted. This resolution specified that the control of the government of an American state by participants in the international Communist movement would constitute a threat to the hemisphere. But although the states of the Western Hemisphere were allied in a sense, their organization did not provide for integrated military units, joint staffs, common bases, or common policies; and their economic co-operation was severely limited.

When the structure of the free world is examined, it is clear that the European, Asian, and Western Hemisphere organizations were not directly linked, except for the fact that the United States was a party to NATO, SEATO, OAS, and ANZUS, and that the viability and effectiveness of each grouping directly depended on United States policy and American resources. The degree of organization, integration, and independence differed considerably for each regional defense setup. Only in NATO had a special organizational relationship been developed. Given common commands, bases, equipment, and facilities, the NATO powers, with respect to the areas subject to NATO guarantees, were linked organically.

The integration of their forces on the continent of Europe was considered to have reached the point at which individual action by most of the member states was no longer feasible. In fact, given the problems of warfare in the age of the hydrogen bomb, it was felt that action by the NATO command could be automatic and independent of the directives of the individual states constituting NATO. Structurally, NATO was the only element in the organization of the free world that was equivalent in any significant way to the Communist bloc.

There has been a tendency among theoretical analysts of the international system—a tendency that has not been discouraged by United States Government spokesmen—to equate the structure of NATO with the free world and to treat the whole as an organizational counterpoise to the Soviet Communist bloc. On this basis, the bipolar concept of the international system was given continuing emphasis and the United States strategy of containment continuing validity. Apparently, therefore, Soviet action and United States reaction had forced the international system into the simple form of antagonistic groupings of power. But only apparently, for these were actions and reactions that created resistances in other states. After 1950, when the pressures of the Communist bloc were more sharply felt and when the reactions of the United States were more emphatically developed, these resistances multiplied and began to play a part in the operation of the international system.

Uncommitted States

The dispersed groupings of the free world and the more integrated Communist bloc do not, in fact, confront one another directly except in limited ways. Between them, both geographically and ideologically, are uncommitted nations—states that for some purposes appear to act with one or the other of the power groupings, but that for other purposes act independently. Organizations of uncommitted states, although frequently planned, have remained loose, amorphous, and of uncertain duration. Only the Arab League pretends to an external façade of integration, unity, and permanence. Many lines of sentiment and cultural community criss-cross these uncommitted regions. Religion creates ties of interest between the Arab League members, Libya, the French colonial peoples in Tunisia and Morocco, Pakistan, and Indonesia. Common resentment against the colonial nations and against the white peoples produces limited unity of action between a number of Asian and African nations. Yet attempts to formulate positive courses of common action have usually revealed the absence of a community of positive objectives.

The most prominent uncommitted state—India—is a member of the British Commonwealth of Nations and, for many purposes, cooperates closely with that entity. In the Arab League, Iraq and Jordan are linked by treaty to Great Britain, as was Egypt, although Egypt, unlike the other two states, chafed at the bonds. For religious reasons, the other Arab states, although technically neutral or uncommitted in a political sense, are strongly anti-Communist in ideology. Ceylon is vigorously anti-Communist. Only Burma and Indonesia seem uncommitted in any sense. In so far as Burma is concerned, the presence of Communist China on its border and the passive philosophy of Buddhism contribute to the lack of commitment.

So long as United States pressure on the international system remained negligible or was confined to Western Europe, American policy did not produce very significant reactions among the uncommitted states. But following the initial impulses of the war in Korea, the situation changed. Not only did individual uncommitted states, such as Egypt, seize the opportunity to realize national aspirations, but also groupings of uncommitted states began to act effectively as blocs within the United Nations. Early in 1952 the Asian-Arab bloc in the United Nations very actively began to fight French colonial policy in Africa.[10] In December of the same year, the bloc with the substitution of Iran for the Philippines, met in Cairo to plan a campaign against French North African policy. The same bloc, guided by India, also acted steadily to force American action in Korea toward conformity with the wish of the United Nations for a negotiated solution in the Far East.

In late April and early May 1954, a Southeast Asian conference of prime ministers was held in Colombo, Ceylon. The prime ministers of Burma, Ceylon, India, Indonesia, and Pakistan attended.

---

[10] It consisted of Afghanistan, Burma, Egypt, India, Indonesia, Iraq, Pakistan, the Philippines, Saudi Arabia, Syria, and Yemen. Lebanon, Ethiopia, and Liberia supported the activities of the bloc.

The conference was widely split by the efforts of Pakistan and Ceylon to obtain the adoption of an anti-Communist resolution and by the equally determined opposition of India and Indonesia to any such move. The five powers agreed on the need for a compromise settlement in Indo-China; favored the banning of hydrogen bomb tests; advocated the entrance of the People's Government of China into the United Nations; and favored self-determination for the peoples of Morocco and Tunisia.

Early in 1955, Marshal Tito of Yugoslavia traveled to India, Burma, and Egypt to confer with other state leaders who were taking an independent political line. The leaders of the four countries reached agreement, in separate discussions, that the formation of a neutral bloc was not desirable, but that it was important for the four states to take an independent position in world affairs.

In April 1955, an Afro-Asian conference was held at Bandung in Java. This was distinctly a gathering of colored and former colonial peoples. Israel was conspicuously absent because of the opposition of the Arab powers. South Korea and North Korea were equally marked by their absence. Nationalist China and the Soviet Union were not invited, although Communist China was the showpiece of the gathering. Twenty-nine African and Asian states, some committed to one of the power blocs by formal alliance, some to the other, some associated with one of the blocs in an informal status, and others uncommitted, proclaimed a set of common objectives and interests arising from geography, culture, or economics that were independent of the objectives of the two blocs of opposed world powers. A protest was clearly registered at the effort of the major opposing states to force the international system to conform to a bipolar concept. The object of this resistance movement was not to create still another regional organization, or to develop a common policy for the uncommitted states. It was rather to explore the role of these states in the international system, to see if their composite influence could be used to increase their freedom of action, to moderate the impacts of two power structures, and to reverse the apparent trend toward bipolarism.

Except for periodic conferences and *ad hoc* groupings, no formal organization of the uncommitted states existed or was, in fact, possible. The situation was one in which the major elements in two power structures exerted constant pressure on these states, and occasionally succeeded in committing some of them for specific purposes or for limited forms of co-operation.[11] However, the uncommitted states did not constitute a vacuum. Nor were they merely suspended between two equally powerful magnets. Instead, they had a composite as well as an individual force of their own and were able to use their positions to resist, moderate, and even divert the organizational activities of the major powers. Not only did India have the means to maintain its uncommitted status, but it also had the means and the will to support the uncommitted status of a large area.

Thus the bipolar concept was neither realistic nor adequate as a description of the structure of the international system as it began to be revealed after 1950. It is correct to note that the two major powers in the international hierarchy continued, by their actions and reactions to each other's policies and security objectives, to press the world of nation-states to act according to this formula. But it is also important to note that a latent capacity to resist and to modify this trend was lodged in a large number of smaller states, and that various circumstances contributed to the release of this capacity after 1950. The uncommitted states developed skill in using the instrumentality of the United Nations for political maneuvering on the basis of this capacity, and consequently increased its value to them. The development of equivalent atomic armaments by the United States and the Soviet Union had a limiting effect on the actions of these two states and consequently increased still further the capacity of the uncommitted states to resist alignment.

While this influence was slow to develop, there are plenty of indications that between 1950 and 1955 the uncommitted states achieved a more positive role in the international system by becoming the necessary objects of major power attention rather than remaining merely the weak recipients of major power decisions. In small but identifiable ways, this counter trend affected the structure of the major power blocs by making it possible for some of the junior members of these blocs to regain some slight freedom of action. The gradual effect was to make it increasingly necessary for

[11] For instance, Yugoslavia was organizationally a part of the Western military structure, because of the intimate links between the other two Balkan pact members and NATO, but it was uncommitted politically and followed independent policies. And, again, Egypt bought arms from the Soviet bloc and by so doing indirectly served Soviet purposes, but without any known loss of freedom of action in Egyptian interests.

the Soviet Union and the United States to operate their policies respecting one another in terms of the requirements of the bloc and coalition structures they sought to maintain and in terms of the impact of their policies on their relations with the uncommitted states. In short the international system did not consist solely of two organizations, organically held together by political, military, economic, and cultural institutions. These organizations were admittedly present in incomplete forms. But between them and cushioning their current impacts, were expanding circles of inescapable relationships with more or less neutral areas.

CHAPTER XVII

The Framework of American Decision

IF THE INTERNATIONAL system of 1950 could have been looked at objectively and an attempt made to define the probable way in which its components would act in relation to one another, it is unlikely that a single, clear definition would have emerged. More likely a range of possibilities would have been set up, and the analyst would have felt obliged to say that any point on this range had a potential validity.[1] Obviously, a great deal depended on which of the possibilities seemed to a given state to provide the most realistic working picture of the international system; for once a judgment was made on this matter, it tended to establish a frame of reference for policy choices. Certainly the framework within which the United States pursued its objectives was a product of an American judgment about which of these potential patterns was the most valid basis for action.

In 1950, this judgment seemed almost predetermined. The fluid situation following the close of the Second World War had apparently congealed. Rigid barriers outlined the limits of the rival blocs, and efforts to overstep these limits would—with few exceptions—seem to require military measures likely to call forth equivalent and undesired military countermeasures. In this sense, the Korean War put the Communist bloc on notice that the United States was ready to take military countermeasures whenever the national armies of a Communist power overstepped national or other *de facto* boundaries. From this time both the United States and the Soviet Union appeared to direct their policies toward the

---

[1] The range would probably have been somewhat as follows:

(1) *Bipolar:* two blocs dominated by the United States and the Soviet Union.

(2) *Partial bipolarity tending toward complete organization:* two blocs, maintained and partially controlled by the United States and the Soviet Union, and an amorphous in-between group of states.

(3) *Partial bipolarity tending toward dispersal of power:* the United States and the Soviet Union, a loose free world grouping, a tighter Communist world grouping, and uncommitted states.

(4) *Power dispersed among an increasing number of states:* the United States and the Soviet Union, loose free world and Communist groupings capable of pressing for adjustments, and fluctuating groupings of uncommitted states capable of exercising a mediating influence.

further organization of their respective areas of influence or control and toward the build-up of their military strength and military potential. Neither seemed prepared to challenge the other directly within its own orbit.

The Soviet Union, in effect, accepted a period of leveling off and consolidation. The United States, in effect, recognized the apparent solidity of the Soviet-Communist bloc and turned to building up American strength. Yet Communist China kept United States policies off-balance in the Far East by its evident challenge to the bipolar *status quo*. In turn the United States kept Soviet policy off-balance in Europe by its evident intention of rebuilding Germany as a major component of the North Atlantic Treaty Organization (NATO). There consequently appeared to be a situation in which two major powers were vigorously organizing and strengthening coalitions of force and were doing this in the ever-present shadow of a possible all-out war between themselves. In these conditions the United States judgment was that the world was a partially bipolar system tending toward complete bipolarity and that the immediate end of United States policy should be to press the process on. This judgment, in addition to being supported by the evidence of 1950-51, had also the advantage of seeming to call for no more than intensified action along existing policy lines.

The situation, however, was not as simple as this, nor was it a mere extension of the one that had prevailed up to 1950. The basic difference was that the Soviet Union had previously appeared as a general future threat to American security. Now it appeared as a specific and present threat. Furthermore, in the years between 1945 and 1950, there had seemed to be areas of maneuver for the United States and the Soviet Union. Consequently, efforts—no matter how abortive—to maintain diplomatic contacts and to go through the motions of negotiation had continued. By the end of 1950, however, in the United States view, the areas of maneuver and significant negotiation had been closed off, one by one.

Thus the United States decision to press on rapidly with the establishment of a security organization, tightly and organically held together, envisaged this action as a consequence of the need to establish a position of military readiness in respect to the Soviet Union and its possible courses of action. This was a tighter and a more restrictive framework for United States policy than had been the case before 1950. Existing policies—economic assistance, military assistance, technical assistance, the extension of alliances and commitments—were subjected to greater strains, to more rapid shifts in priorities, to more comprehensive modifications than had been anticipated. In addition, the increased demand for measurable results in terms of security and military effectiveness that accompanied this stepped-up execution led to resistances in the states to which these policies were being addressed.

But these difficulties were not the heart of the matter; that lay in the problem of the basic strategy of United States relations with the Soviet Union. The more extensively a rigid framework was accepted as a valid basis for determining United States action, the more two key issues came to the fore. What sort of power position relative to the Soviet Union would satisfy the requirements of American security? Was negotiation, adjustment, or accommodation with the Soviet Union foreclosed? Obviously, these were not questions to which wholly acceptable answers could ever be found, but they were bound to be asked so long as United States policy operated within the framework that had been defined.

The Desired Power Position

The strategy of containment prior to June 1950 had worked in terms of developing "situations of strength." The thesis ran as follows: the war had created areas of weakness in the world—in Asia, in Europe; wherever they existed, they were an invitation to the Soviet Union to engage in probing.

However, the official exposition continued, as the United States built up economic and defensive military strength, it would be made clear to the Soviet Union that the non-Soviet world would not collapse and that it could not be taken apart bit by bit. At this point, it was possible that the aggressive policies of the Soviet Union might be modified and that the Soviet Union would recognize that its own best interests would be served by co-operating in international political life. The American hope, therefore, was that a strong collective security system would make a return to genuine negotiation feasible, and that genuine negotiation would result in peace and co-operation. The meaning here is that "situations of strength" were not regarded as ends in themselves, but as techniques for creating the conditions in which negotiations with the Soviet Union would become possible on terms acceptable to the United States. Where basic objectives were clearly irreconcilable, agreement could be reached only on secondary objectives. But this would not be possible unless the opportunity of achieving the primary objectives was first blocked off for the Soviet Union. Only by building situations of strength and by pushing into the indefinite future the possibility of communizing the world could the immediate points of conflict with the Soviet Union be negotiated and adjusted.[2]

This concept of "situations of strength" and of an equilibrium of power did not go unchallenged. On the one hand, it was argued that the inherent nature of the cold war and the fact of competitive rearmament would make it impossible to reach a point of accommodation, and that, instead, suspicions would multiply and positions harden. On the other hand, it was argued that an equilibrium of power was not enough, but that what was wanted was a position of superior strength. The United States and the states of Western Europe, given their democratic political structures, would find it difficult to maintain an equilibrium over a long period of time. Public weariness with continued tension and open-ended armament costs would continually work against policies that aimed only at equilibrium.

The give and take of this still unsettled discussion cannot be followed here.[3] Three points should, however, be noted. The first is that the discussion became immediately tangled with the question of atomic weapons—their value as deterrents, the life expectancy of the American monopoly, and the measurement of this form of military power against other and conventional forms. The second is that the rises and falls and the twists and turns in this discussion were very closely related to changing estimates of Soviet capabilities and intentions and to varied judgments about possible Soviet interpretations of United States actions. Agreement about Soviet objectives was possible and hence permitted acceptance of a defined framework for decision. Yet disagreement regarding Soviet capabilities or Soviet interpretations of United States policy quickly led to different policy conclusions. The third is that the discussion

---

[2] What the elements of a "situation of strength" were was neither clearly specified in official statements nor clearly determined in public feeling. The combination of military power, economic power, and social cohesiveness that might be required to constitute a "situation of strength" remained basically unsettled. After 1950 the general tendency, however, was to lay increasing emphasis on the military component backed by economic power.

[3] See below, Chap. XVIII.

was not a purely domestic American debate. It involved nearly all of the states with which the United States was associated or which it sought to bring into association with itself.

The Desired Political Relationship

The immediate conclusion drawn from the events of 1950 was that there was very little likelihood of reaching an accommodation with the Soviet Union. The accepted framework for action practically ruled out negotiation as an end to be pursued. The effort to achieve an equilibrium of power was guided by a search for security and not by a search for political adjustment. Consequently, the implied end product of a successful security policy would be either an equilibrium indistinguishable from a stalemate or a readiness for full-scale hostilities.

From 1950 onward, therefore, the United States and the Soviet Union focused their efforts inwardly, more concerned to improve and stabilize their areas of influence and their domestic policies than to explore the possibilities of negotiating differences. Heroic solutions to existing problems were eschewed. Instead, a slow and protracted feeling out process went on, while policy concentrated on strengthening and perfecting parallel politico-military organizations. In fact, the outstanding feature of United States-Soviet relations, following the outbreak of the Korean War, was an unwillingness to adjust existing relations and a *de facto* acceptance of the existing pattern of relations. For a few years after 1950, appearances suggested that two world powers faced each other belligerently from the battlements of partially constructed security organizations, unprepared to negotiate, and equally unprepared to unleash a major effort to topple the other from its position.

The situation could not remain in this form indefinitely, at least so far as the United States was concerned. The American action-framework might reduce an intent to negotiate to a low place in the range of practicable objectives; but, so long as the logic of this framework led in the end to a choice between accommodation or war, a willingness to negotiate could not be officially abandoned. If this was the case with respect to American public feeling, it was an even more important consideration with respect to the relations of the United States and other free nations. The over-all operation of United States policies tended accordingly to be ambivalent. The possibility of accommodation was in practice rejected in order to complete the organization of the free world and to maintain the impetus necessary to rearm the United States. A willingness to negotiate was in principle retained in order to keep the motivations of the United States and the free world in consonance. Beyond these considerations was the judgment that the United States, with or without a free world organization at its disposal, might at any time be forced by a Soviet decision to engage in war. Consequently, United States action after 1950 continued to be described in terms similar to those used in connection with the earlier thesis of "situations of strength."

The Implications

A great deal depended on the accuracy of the judgment that the international system was polarized. If the judgment corresponded with existing reality and with future developments, United States policies could reasonably be expected to produce the desired results. If it did not, one of three situations would result: United States action would have to be intensified in an effort to make the future conform to an American preconception, or the immediate goals of United States policy would become stranded in an unreal world, or a dangerous misconception would have to be corrected. These were possibilities about which it could never be easy to achieve certainty. However, the evidence appears to indicate that the international system has tended toward a form different from that postulated by the United States in 1950. Specifically, it is considered that the trend has been toward greater diversification and away from polarization. It is further considered that this has taken place in spite of the efforts of both United States and Soviet policy to produce a contrary effect.

The fact was, however, that by 1950 a polarized system could be postulated. Even before 1950, the strategy of containment had assumed that polarization was at least a tendency. But this tendency had not been given a rapid time schedule, and policy was in the first instance aimed more perhaps at ultimately reversing the trend than at conforming to it. The judgment of 1950, however, altered the meaning of the strategy of containment by accepting polarization as a fact and by envisaging a not too remote future time when the process would be complete. The primary aim of policy accordingly was to adjust to this fact as rapidly as possible. This specifically meant completing an existing pattern of alliances so that an organized free world bloc would confront the Soviet bloc at every point on its periphery. A bipolar world and a strongly felt need to perfect an organization around the American pole made a particularly demanding framework for action.

In this light, the problems of executing United States policy became significantly interlocked, and a consideration of the reciprocal effects of actions taken in different areas became essential to success. Then each policy choice, each allocation of resources, affected the capacity of the United States to reach its predetermined object. Each United States decision—and in the defined context, each Soviet decision—had the quality of seeming to alter the relative position of the United States vis-à-vis the Soviet Union. It became only too easy to convert these relationships into a picture on a map. In this light if the United States could maintain pressure on the Soviet periphery, the Soviet Union would be forced to allocate its resources to meet the strains placed upon it. To the extent, however, that Soviet policy reversed the process and pressed outward from its boundaries, the United States would have to shift its forces to meet threats posed at times and places of Soviet choosing.

The strategy of containment, hitherto a loose blend of political and economic operations, backed by a reserve of military potential, now took on more and more the characteristics of a military operation supported by diplomatic and economic means. This meant a tendency to shift the values by which policy was operated. A military strategy justifiably called for an extension of alliances in terms of air bases, naval bases, and strategically disposed real estate. The degree to which such alliances were politically viable and could duplicate the organic structure of NATO became secondary considerations in view of the definite short-time scheme to which the strategy was operationally geared. On the same basis, a strategy primarily military could justify an increase in, and a wide dispersal of, United States commitments in a way that could not be justified by a strategy primarily political. This goes a long way toward explaining the speed and the willingness with which United States policy expanded the area of American responsibility after 1950, multiplying commitments and opening new channels of action with the minimum of hesitation.

This redefinition of the strategy of containment in more exclusively military terms left blank spots at some crucial points. The bipolar framework to which is was addressed was clear enough, but the nature of the end to which it might lead was much less clear. It postulated that general war might come at any time. It simultaneously postulated that the purpose of the strategy was to deter the Soviet Union from initiating a general war. It noted, however, that there was a range of lesser alternatives, scaling down to hostilities that were pinpointed and limited as in Korea. To what point on this scale was planning to be directed? Or did plans have to cover the full range? The choice would determine the nature of the United States military establishment, initiate production schedules for military equipment, allocate resources for different kinds of military use, allocate man power, and above all establish the balance between the short-term and the long-term values to be sought in a system of alliances.

The number of contingent situations that could be identified was so large, and the consequences of wrongly settling for any one as the most probable were so obvious, that it became almost impossible to make a choice that could stand as a basis for a military strategy of containment. Consequently, even though United States objectives were sharply focused between 1950 and 1954, American action—both with respect to domestic formulations of policy and with respect to the external implementation of policy—appeared to be marked by confusingly abrupt changes of pace and direction.

One more factor—that of atomic weapons—must be examined if this stage of the analysis is to be complete. From 1945 on, the existence of the atomic bomb introduced a fundamentally new factor into the calculation of both military and political strategy.[4] The significance of this factor underwent changes between 1945 and 1950. Initially, the United States had an effective monopoly of the atomic weapon. However, the knowledge of theoretical physics needed to produce the bomb was already in the possession of the Soviet Union. So the monopoly could have only a short life at

[4] The essential consideration can be briefly stated. A single atomic bomb in 1945 was the equivalent of 20,000 tons of TNT explosive. It could be carried by a single bomber in 1945 over a nonreturn distance of 6,000 miles. Any single industrial-urban complex in the world could be destroyed by ten such bombs. These magnitudes have been greatly increased since 1945, and limited defensive measures against the air carriers have been developed. On the other hand, the atomic weapon has been adapted for tactical use in connection with ground forces.

best. According to well-informed estimates, the Soviet Union would be able to solve the problems of production and would be able to marshal the economic resources to begin quantity production of the bomb within five to ten years from 1945. When that time came, the American view was that it would no longer be possible to negate the man-power and logistic advantages of the Soviet Union by the monopolistic possession of the atomic bomb. Therefore, the United States had to consider the measures that it could take to maximize its present advantages and to minimize the future dangers arising from the multilateral possession of the bomb. At the same time, it had to attempt to relate its possession of the bomb to the measures that it was taking to contain the Soviet Union.

Two extreme alternatives were available. One was to use the brief period of superiority to wage a preventive war against the Soviet Union. The argument was that if the Soviet Union were as dangerous a threat as the evidence suggested and as the strategy of containment implied, then the risks involved in permitting the Soviet Union to break the United States monopoly were too great to be acceptable. Although this course was advocated in some quarters, there is no evidence that it was considered seriously by responsible policy makers. The other alternative was the international control of atomic power. This was seriously advocated by the United States Government, but the effort to negotiate an agreement to this effect in the United Nations soon revealed that the plans for control proposed by the United States and the Soviet Union could not meet the security needs of the other party sufficiently to permit their adoption. The United States could not be coerced by a state that did not possess the atomic bomb. The Soviet Union would not accept a control by graduated stages that would interfere with Soviet efforts to produce the atomic bomb. International control, therefore, became a long-range objective of the United Nations, and United States policy operated instead on a contingent basis.

The actual policy line developed was to treat the atomic monopoly as deterring the Soviet Union from acting on its superiority in ground forces and conventional weapons, while the United States organized the means of confronting this Soviet superiority by comparable forces. This thesis of deterrence was shaken when the Soviet Union exploded its first atomic bomb in 1949. The thesis was then shifted to the deterrent effect of the superior United States stockpile of atomic weapons. The argument then ran that the United States stockpile had reached the point at which a crippling attack against the Soviet Union was feasible. The bases and air striking power to carry out the attack were being brought into being. Sufficient strength on the continent of Europe was being built to delay and make more costly Soviet attack and occupation. The Soviet Union, as yet, had no stockpile of atomic weapons and, therefore, lacked the ability to retaliate decisively against the United States. In this view, therefore, an equilibrium of military force was achieved, and the Soviet Union was deterred from waging war.

This was approximately the position in 1950, when the Communist aggression in Korea took place. Quite apart from the other considerations involved, this action indicated that, although the Soviet Union might be deterred from general war by the atomic superiority of the United States, Soviet-Communist policy was not deterred from beginning local wars even if the risk of general war were involved. In other words, American intentions with respect to the use of a deterrent weapon were capable of being probed. The upshot was to make it clear that the United States had not included the possibility of atomic retaliation as a logical component of the thesis of deterrence. Allied opinion now came vigorously into play to restrain United States policy from exploring this related possible course. For its part, Soviet policy began to exploit the fears of international public feeling by the double technique of peace movements and atomic blackmail. The significance of the factor of atomic weapons shifted once more.

The position now became one in which it was assumed that the United States and the Soviet Union would quickly achieve equivalent atomic capabilities. This was the form in which the atomic factor became an integral part of the framework of American action after 1950. But the nature of its role and the weight that should be given it as a factor became less rather than more certain. It has remained uncertain from 1950 to the present time.

Whatever deterrent effect the United States monopoly had was in process of becoming a reciprocal limitation on both the United States and the Soviet Union. Whether this meant that there could be no war except an atomic war, or whether it meant that conflict might increase because it might be limited to the use of conventional weapons and techniques, became open and unsettled questions. Yet some sort of working judgment with respect to these questions was essential to the development of a security policy by the United States. The nature of the judgment reached would plainly condition the United States approach to the future handling of its political, economic, and military relations with the free world.

The Balance of Power Concept

The account of the framework of American decision cannot end without reference to a long-standing feature of international policies—the technique of balancing power. The phrase "balance of power" was frequently used in connection with relations between the United States and the Soviet Union. As a technique, it is still thought of as operative by some policy-making groups. Its validity, in terms of the existing world structure, however, needs examination.

The balance-of-power technique is best exemplified by shifting coalitions of states designed to keep any single state or group of states from obtaining a decisive preponderance of power within a given geographic area. The use of this technique has generally been associated with an international system in which individual national states have been the effective operating units. A moment's reflection suggests that this condition did not, and scarcely could, prevail in any significant respect in the period immediately following the Second World War. Communist methods of organization subjected the national state to the party and the national party to a world movement more or less directed by Soviet policy. States allied with the Soviet Union, if they were under Communist regimes, were no longer free to shift rapidly to an opposite coalition in order to halt Soviet expansion, even if they had the desire to do so. The basic conditions for the use of the balance-of-power technique no longer existed. The most that the non-Communist states could aspire to was to seek a massive global equilibrium of power.

The requisite structure for this purpose, however, could not be created overnight by an act of will. It involved composing internal differences and integrating military, social, political, and economic policies in order to gain the fullest value from otherwise dispersed resources. And, although many of the non-Communist states had democratic doctrines in common, their objectives were oriented toward the nation rather than toward some organic association.

Nevertheless, between 1947 and 1952, the economic and security dilemmas of the European states and the ability and eagerness of the United States to help resolve these dilemmas provided the means to overcome this orientation in some small degree.

By 1951 it looked very much as if the structure that was being developed under the North Atlantic Treaty was leading to a situation in which each European state was so dependent on the whole, and the whole so dependent on the United States, that national policy divergencies could no longer be pressed to the point at which NATO would be destroyed. It furthermore looked, at least to the United States, as if this association would have a compelling attraction for the free nation-states not originally associated with it, and that it could consequently be expanded until it embraced the free world. At this point, two organically constituted blocs could be conceived as confronting each other in an equilibrium of power.

But the traditional balance-of-power technique had no meaning in an international system brought to this point of bipolarity. Only a few small states would still retain the freedom to shift from one bloc to another, and their capacity seriously to disturb the equilibrium would be limited. However, this picture represented only the presumed intent of two major powers—although both moved to make it real. The Communist *coup d'état* in Czechoslovakia brought that country within the Soviet structure. Considerable Soviet pressure was exerted on Iran and Finland to harmonize the policies of those countries with the policies of the Soviet Union. On the other side, the United States extended NATO to include Greece and Turkey, facilitated agreements between Iran, Iraq, Pakistan, and Turkey, entered into military arrangements with Spain, and sought to form a Southeast Asian security organization. And both major powers were held to rigid and constricting policies in Germany in order to prevent any change in a still unstable equilibrium.

Until about 1950 it seemed almost impossible that these pressures on small states could be resisted. But then, as has been noted, a latent capacity to resist became effective in these states. In a sense, the uncommitted nations mounted a conscious struggle against being organized. Their technique, not clearly developed, appears to be to operate on the lines of strain that exist within each bloc and hence to influence the objectives and policies of the dominating power of the bloc.

India apparently seeks to exploit differences between China and the Soviet Union; between Iraq, Pakistan, and the West; to protect the independence of Laos and Cambodia; and to exploit the grievances of all ex-colonial and colored peoples against the European powers. The purpose seems to be to blur, or even to erase, existing organizational lines and to attempt to compromise existing disputes. On the other hand, although each major power resists this process, neither apparently is willing to risk actions that might drive uncommitted states into the arms of the other.

In the new international system of action, the uncommitted states fill an essentially mediatory role. Although it is possible for them to praise resistance to aggression, as in the case of Korea, and even to supply field ambulance forces to the resisting side, their major functions are conciliation, mediation, and the mobilization of world opinion for compromise. But this part cannot be played, as it occasionally was in the days of the concert of Europe, by threatening to intervene if the role of honest broker is not accepted. The uncommitted states do not possess sufficient power to act in this way. Nevertheless, unless the major blocs—or, more precisely, unless the United States and the Soviet Union are intent on a "show down" decision, these umpires are beginning to exercise influence in spite of the hard words addressed to them.

This development since 1950 has produced a temporary degree of stability in the international system. However, it is an open question at the present time whether this stability will achieve a longer life or will be overthrown. The potential exists for either development. On the one hand, the major powers continue to seek an equilibrium as between their respective blocs, and the uncommitted states may find long-run difficulties in maintaining the minimum freedom of action necessary to the role they now play. On the other hand, the major powers may be approaching the outer margins of their capacity to maintain the structures they have built up, and the uncommitted states may find that they have fallen heir to the balance-of-power technique even though at present no one of them and no group of them is powerful enough to employ it consistently in order to force adjustments on the major states.

CHAPTER XVIII
National Security

As the United States interpreted the international situation in the closing months of 1950, problems of national security took precedence over all others. The highest priority was given to security objectives, and established policy lines were vigorously reviewed and adapted to fit security needs. As the general policy lines had been developed in relation to a strategic concept of containing the expanding influence of the Soviet Union, programs of action could in principle be redirected quickly for this purpose.

The problem of security can be discussed on various levels. There is a level of abstraction in which the relation between United States and Soviet power and potential is examined in broad terms. It is the normal responsibility of military establishments to conduct such examinations in all conceivable contexts. This kind of analysis had been going on continually from 1945, and the outlines of the problem were generally known.

The problem, however, is usually presented on a concrete level. In current discussions, there is always a question of the extent to which the abstract analysis of requirements is understood and has entered into the formulation of concrete proposals for action. Theoretical mobilization and production plans can always be drawn up. However, the question how much of them should be converted into an action-plan remains open until a consensus has been reached about the nature of the situation in which a state is being called upon to act. Until this point comes, the theoretical analysis must remain adjustable to a large number of contingencies. A state with objectives that call for definite changes in the international system, and with policies designed to bring about these changes in finite time, is at an advantage because it is able to narrow the range of contingencies by acting to foreclose some of the possibilities. In the view of the United States in 1950, the Soviet-Communist bloc had acted in this way by initiating armed aggression. Consequently, the United States considered that the contingencies it had to keep in mind had been reduced in number, and

332

that more sharply focused action was both required and possible. But in determining how to act on the security problem that had now been presented in concrete form, the existing theoretical analyses played a considerable part.

The Scope of the Problem

The relative military strength of a modern state is a product of its technology, resources, productive capacity, and organizational skills. The influence of the United States in world politics during and after the war was directly related to its possession of an industrial system incomparably more productive than that of any other national economy. Unlike Soviet victories in the Second World War, which rested upon the sheer weight of virtually inexhaustible man power, those of the United States were the result of superior technology, production, and organizational skills. Similarly, mobilization of the free world for the purpose of resisting Communist expansion would not have been possible except for the expansion of the American economy in the postwar era.[1] By any method of reckoning, therefore, the relative position and hence the security of the United States could be said to depend on retaining this economic preponderance. Only that preponderance, it was argued, enabled the United States to compensate for its man-power limitations. Furthermore, the problem of security could not be restricted simply to the organization and equipping of armed forces. Its scope involved resources, man power and productive capacity, transportation, organization, research, military establishments, bases and facilities, and a ready and cohesive society.

Starting from premises such as these, the considerations that entered into a theoretical solution of the problem of security became extensive. Despite the fact that the exploration of these multiple facets of the problem led in all directions, resources remained basic. The United States contained only 10 per cent of the total population of the non-Communist world, but the American economy consumed almost 50 per cent of the raw materials available

---

[1] The gross national product of the American economy was $264.7 billion in 1950, as compared with $233.8 billion in 1946 and $145.9 billion in 1938. The gross national product per capita (in 1947 prices) was $1,745 in 1950, as compared with $1,654 in 1946 and $1,123 in 1938, although the population had grown by nearly 25 millions. See Appendix C.

to the free world. Study after study, and report after report, underlined the extent to which the United States was dependent on resources that lay outside the territorial limits of the country. Some of the requirements of the United States could be satisfied from reasonably secure sources in the Western Hemisphere. Other sources in Europe, Asia, and Africa were, however, potentially vulnerable to the operations of Soviet-Communist expansion. Although it was true that substitutes might be developed in an emergency, this was not the whole story. Security not only required United States access to resources, but because strength was relative, it also called for the denial of resources to the Soviet Union. The stockpiling of critical materials provided a hedge, but in the larger view, American security was considered to be related to the maintenance of large areas of freedom in Europe, Africa, Asia, and the Western Hemisphere.

Almost as important as resources were productive capacity, man power, and transportation—the logistic planning factors. Although American productive capacity was demonstrably superior and was likely to remain so for a considerable time in spite of an alarming annual rate of increase in Soviet capacity, conversion of productive capacity into competitive strength was more difficult for United States than for Soviet policy. The patterns of civilian consumption in the United States were not as readily susceptible to governmental direction as they were in the Soviet system. The channeling of production into instruments of power required only a high-level Soviet policy decision regarding which of two ends—security or civilian consumption—came first. An equivalent choice by the United States could be made only after prolonged public discussion through political channels, and the choice would usually represent a compromise between conflicting views and mutually limiting considerations. Modification of the normal pattern took place only in an atmosphere of emergency and crisis.

The use of man power was subject to similar limitations, complicated in this instance, by quantitative and qualitative differences in the man-power structures of the United States and the Soviet Union, and by the fact that, in the United States, the military establishment and the productive system directly competed for the use of the available man-power resources.[2] The allocation of re-

---

[2] Although the population of the Soviet Union, at approximately 200 millions, is only 20 per cent greater than the United States population of 165 millions,

sources is not an arbitrary matter in which a pool of man power and goods can be viewed as available for any purpose decided on. Only selective changes can be made without disrupting the system within which production is carried on. A shift of man-power resources from industry and agriculture to the military establishment has its effects on the industrial base of the armed forces unless civilian consumption can be curtailed. In a democracy in peacetime, it is no easier to curtail civilian consumption than it is to provide for the large-scale drafting of man power.

There still remained, however, a further consideration—transportation: the movement of strength in time and space, or logistical capability. If the internal transportation facilities alone were compared, there was no doubt that the capabilities of the United States were immeasurably beyond those of the Soviet Union. But this was not the root of the matter. The real question was the relative capacity to deploy strength competitively in the areas of significant contact. These, in the view of the United States, lay on the periphery of the Soviet-Communist bloc—in Europe, in the Middle East, in South and Southeast Asia, and in the Far East. This situation was held to give the Soviet Union the advantages of interior lines of communication. The compensations sought by United States security planners were overseas bases, both air and naval, and defensive alliances. Air bases would literally ring the Soviet Union and would force the Soviet bloc to take such comprehensive defensive measures as would strain its resources and logistic facilities. Alliances would give access to the naval bases of the free nations. The bases would enable the United States to maintain surface control of the oceans and ease the logistic problem of transporting man power and weapons.[3]

Alliances would do more, however. They would provide space for

the Soviet Union found it possible to mobilize an army of over 4 millions, whereas the United States had constantly to review and to reduce the man-power demands of its armed services. The more primitive structure of the Soviet productive system, less sensitive to strains than the highly developed, complex, and integrated American system, made the system easier to maintain when man-power calls were made on it.

[3] Any analysis of the difficulties of the Normandy landing during the Second World War or of the island-by-island campaign against the Japanese power, reveals the tremendous logistic and strategic advantages accruing to possessors of forward bases. Without them, it is almost impossible to build up and to maintain an attacking force more rapidly than the defense can concentrate and counterattack in overwhelming strength.

stationing ground forces, as well as for the essential paraphernalia of modern war—repair shops, supply dumps, transportation and communication facilities, and fuel supply systems. If the system of alliances were adequately developed, still more benefits could be expected. Allies also meant man power, productive capacity, and resources: in Europe, skilled man power, existing productive capacity, and access to colonial raw materials; in the Middle East, oil and control of vital transportation routes; and in Asia, mass man power and access to raw materials. The system of alliances, taken as a whole, meant that the United States could deploy its strength in the most flexible way possible. Asiatic bases prevented the Soviet bloc from concentrating its offensive forces exclusively on Europe. The North Atlantic Treaty Organization (NATO) prevented a similar exclusive concentration on Asia. Both combined to prevent a concentration on the Middle East. And these advantages were in addition to the obvious political desirability of an organized and integrated free world.

There was one final item on the list of considerations envisaged by the analysts of the theoretical security problem. The United States was the heart and brain center of the free world system. On its defensibility and on its maintenance as a "going concern," the whole depended. The adequate physical defense of the United States was the *sine qua non*. For if the United States were put out of commission, even if only temporarily, nations associated with it would become indefensible when confronted by massed Soviet man power. The existence of nuclear and thermonuclear weapons and the development of the means of using them directly against the United States made this more than a mere matter of internal security forces to cope with sabotage and to prevent landings in force on American soil. The physical defense of the United States meant radar-warning systems, interceptor and radar-warning planes, anti-aircraft, and coastal defense units. In some strongly held views, it also meant an offensive air arm and a superiority in atomic weapons, first, in order to act as a deterrent against pressure on weaker allies, and second, as a retaliatory means of destroying the bases from which an attack on the United States might be mounted. It also meant reducing the industrial plant needed to support such an attack.

The examination of this set of considerations opened up some relevant questions that bore on the patterns and values of American society. Even though the analysts of the security problem could not agree on the nature of, or on the best way to fight, a future war, there was general agreement that both factors were in progress of being revolutionized by scientific advances and technological change. Consequently, security implied an immense expansion of governmental subsidized scientific research, co-ordinated by governmental agencies for ends useful to the needs of the state. The problem of the relationships between science and government in a free society became crucial as the influence of science on the course of international politics and the relative power positions of states became more marked, and as the border line between technical and political advice became difficult to define. For this, as well as for other reasons, personal loyalty to the state became a matter of serious moment. The cohesiveness of the American society became an aspect of the national security problem. The destructiveness of the new weapons and the complexity of modern society considerably increased the vulnerability of society to espionage and sabotage. Security now seemed to involve a justifiable governmental concern with the private lives of its citizens.

This analysis of the problem of national security, although it was always in the background of the thinking of policy makers, must be scaled down to practical size. Until 1950 the problem was treated as a theoretical one that could be kept under control by a range of limited selective actions. In 1950 it became, in the official view, a concrete and pressing problem calling for immediate action on a wide front. Specifically, in this view, the Soviet-Communist bloc had precipitated a situation that could lead to full-scale war with the United States and the associated free nations. As the United States examined its policies and its position in relation to this possibility, the conclusion was drawn that the position was weak and the policies not sharply focused. The choices at this moment were: to concentrate all effort and resources primarily on putting the United States in a position of military readiness; to concentrate all effort and resources primarily on pushing policies of assistance and alliance to quick completion in terms of military readiness; or to try to combine these two courses by pressing associated states to make their maximum military contribution while the United States simultaneously reconstructed its military establishment and geared its productive capacity to the military needs of the free world.

The first choice, although it always had supporters after 1950, was ruled out in effect by a firm official conviction that the United States, even if rearmed, could not deploy its power effectively except in company with allies, nor could it afford to leave large areas in Europe and Asia open to Soviet-Communist absorption and risk finding itself confined defensively to the Western Hemisphere. The second choice was ruled out in practice by the fact that the United States was actually committed to military action in Korea and was engaged in taking the steps necessary to maintain this action. The third, and in some respects the compromise, choice emerged almost inevitably.

A common feature of all these choices was the measurement of United States action by estimates of Soviet objectives, capabilities, and short-term intentions. The theoretical security problem was now converted into a concrete security problem with a specified time limit and a definable basis for selecting and concentrating on the management of some rather than all of its elements. The evidence that this did take place is found in the distinct change in the order of priorities in the formulation and development of United States policy and the allocation of American resources after June 1950.

The security problem, after this date, appears to have been seen in much the following form: how to resist specific Communist aggressions while completing the organizations and providing the means to meet the possibility of a war with the Soviet Union in the near future; and how to carry out both of these purposes in such a way as to deter the Soviet Union from initiating a war. Certainly the greater part of United States action came to be comprehended within this formulation: the operation of programs of assistance, the expansion of systems of alliances, the tightening up of existing alliances, the reconstruction and reorganization of the American military establishment, the adaptation of domestic and foreign economic policies, the focusing of research programs, and the development of psychological readiness in American and foreign opinion.

The Key Issues

There arose from this formulation of United States action the key issues that were discussed and rediscussed within the United States, between the United States and its allies, and between the

United States and countries that it sought to associate with its purposes.

Nature of the Threat

The essence of this issue lay in the reinterpretation of the strategy of containment that was initiated by the war in Korea. Previously, the concept had remained generalized, and action could be taken on a broad front. The problem was now pinpointed in Korea, and action involved making choices and determining priorities. This issue developed controversial aspects. Was the strategy of containment to be understood as a short-term or a long-term pattern of action? If the former, it involved relatively few contingencies. The United States should work to be strong enough to deter the Soviet Union from going to war; or if this were impossible, to be strong enough to fight a war successfully. If the latter, then the United States should maintain its existing pattern of policies, but should focus action on achieving more adequate and more thoroughly organized means of containing at an earlier date. The scale on which the strategy had to be implemented would have to be increased, but the intent and the basic character of the strategy would be the same. These alternative interpretations were both vigorously advanced.

In the course of the argument, however, two other questions arose. Was the problem of containing Soviet-Communism actually still the same? Korea could be taken as solid evidence that the strategy of containment was being tested by military force. It was therefore argued that the strategy of containment had to be basically revised to operate at a higher level of tension. The same evidence was taken to mean that the Soviet Union, blocked in Europe by the policies of the United States and its NATO associates, had shifted the center of gravity to the Far East. The question involved the extent to which the United States should allow its attention, its resources, and its policies to be drawn into conformity with a Soviet intention. Was the major area of threat and hence the major effort at containment the Far East, was it still Western Europe, or was it now irreversibly global?

The initial position of the administration, which was cautiously sketched out, rejected final answers to any of these questions. The defense budget for 1950-51, as it was approved after the outbreak of Korean hostilities, was $44.1 billion. An armed man-power target of 3.5 million men was set. This was described as the basis for a military establishment adequate to contain the Soviet Union and to resist localized Communist aggressions. The national budget for 1950-51, however, allocated $4.7 billion for an item described as "International Security and Foreign Relations."[4] In short, although calling for stepped up action, the United States was holding its policy lines across the board and seeking to keep its options open.

This careful approach, however, came under pressure from all sides. The mounting claims of military operations in Korea were quickly translated into demands for a review and a possible redirection of policy. The efforts of the administration to speed up the implementation of existing policy were similarly translated into problems that militated against caution and restraint. A single illustration will suffice to show the complexity of the argument that developed and the extreme difficulty of choosing a coherent line of action and maintaining it consistently.

Action in Korea was defined as a police action under the United Nations and was consequently viewed by American planners as a limited effort. But in terms of the security problems of the United States, the presumed Soviet intention that underlay the Korean aggression required compensatory action in Europe. The United States, therefore, agreed to a substantial increase in the forces it would station in Europe, and pressed for an integrated NATO force under a centralized command. This man power and strategic commitment was resisted by sectors within the government, as well as by some elements of public opinion, on the ground that it might interfere with man-power and equipment needs in Korea. It was accordingly decided to press for a German man-power contribution to the defense of Western Europe and to call on NATO members for increased military budgets and greater efforts to produce military equipment from their own resources. Although this pressure from United States policy was accepted in principle, in fact it created political resistances in many of the NATO countries and tended to divorce NATO planning from public feeling.

---

[4] This was broken down as $4.5 billion for military and economic assistance programs of all sorts, with four fifths of the whole allocated to the European members of NATO. The remaining $230 million went for information and education programs and for participation in the work of various international organizations.

This led to a questioning in the United States of the strategic commitment that had been made in Europe and permitted those who considered that the center of gravity had shifted to Asia to argue more convincingly for a realignment of United States policy. In particular, it gave rise to the view that a limited effort in Korea no longer met the security needs of the United States. What was required now, it was maintained, was a maximum effort that would eliminate the possibility of any further development of Soviet-Communist policy in Asia; in short, not to rest on containment in this area, but to throw the Asian Communists back on their heels for a long time to come. The United States could then return without undue strain to its general strategy of containment.

The administration rejected this position, arguing that until the military strength of the United States was rebuilt, the area of actual hostilities had to be kept limited. It was further held that actions that might be justified in terms of the conduct of the Korean war were not justified if they risked involving Japan and Western Europe in large-scale hostilities.[5] But in view of the widespread public debate about these choices, the United States Government found itself on the defensive with respect to public opinion. It could no longer continue to operate its established policy lines in accordance with the unrestricted judgment of the Executive and Executive advisers. While the policy lines were generally held, they were open to critical attack; alternatives were widely publicized; policy operations underwent adjustment to these public pressures.

The nature of these adjustments complicated the security problem further. Action taken to meet the pro-Far Eastern school of thought alarmed the uncommitted and neutralist states in the United Nations and made United States policy appear more and more unilateral. Demands for greater exertions in Europe gave rise to counter pressures in NATO and elsewhere that frustrated official purposes and increased domestic American pressures on the administration to bring allies into line with the security needs of the United States.

[5] This, of course, was the basis of the controversy between the proponents of conclusive action in Asia and the administration that was fully reviewed in the hearings of the Senate Committees on Armed Services and Foreign Relations in May and June 1951, and issued under the title *Military Situation in the Far East*, 82 Cong. 1 sess.

Nature of United
States Action

It was erroneously presumed that a choice between collective and unilateral action was freely open to the United States. It was assumed that the security policy of the United States had since 1945 been based primarily on developing and committing the United States to organizations for collective action. By 1951 it was argued by some Americans that this policy had failed to get its intended results: in Korea, and in responding to the Soviet threat generally, action was collective in form only. Because the United States was doing the work and at the same time was being restrained by the views of its associates from doing it effectively, the alternative of unilateral action should be accepted.

Although this had always been a theoretically possible choice, it was now presented and discussed as if it were a practically available one. While it is true that, from 1945 on, the United States Government had pursued its foreign policy objectives collectively or unilaterally as particular situations had seemed to require, it had never seriously considered "going it alone" as a general basis for policy. By 1950, however, the United States was committed to a range of organizations that both met some of its security requirements and limited its freedom of action. It was in a position in which its policies, to be effective, required the broad support and sympathy of other states. It was not in a position to act unilaterally simply because it disagreed with its associates on the most desirable course of action in a given situation. Once joint organizational forms for policy development and action had evolved, certain types of unilateral action were no longer possible even when they did not require the co-operation of other states.[6]

The issue was not generally debated with these limiting con-

[6] It is worth noting, in this connection, that policies resulting from joint consultation are normally compromise policies. One of the political difficulties involved is the need to keep confidence with respect to the reasons for compromise. This often produces public impatience—and, in the United States, congressional impatience—for the process of reaching compromise agreement among nations cannot be easily employed in company with a public debate. Policies designed to obtain international agreement often are incapable of obtaining support from the public and the Congress, whereas policies geared to the expectations of the Congress and the public are incapable of providing a basis for international agreement. National policy makers have the task of steering a course that obtains sufficient international support to be effective and yet receives enough public support to be backed by the nation.

siderations in mind. The arguments went straight to their most extreme forms. If the United States could not satisfy its security requirements through a system of alliances, it should withdraw from these hampering commitments and apply its resources to looking out for itself. This extreme conclusion also tended to force the alternative argument to extremes, and the case for collective action was overstated. The debater's overstatement was perhaps less significant than the actions taken to justify the policy of organizing the free world. On the one hand, these actions served to increase official pressures on existing alliances. On the other, they worked to proliferate organizations and agreements on the assumption that the security problem could best be met by completing the structure of collective action until it encircled the Soviet bloc.

On the whole, until this argument began to affect the direction of policy, the United States had tended to emphasize collective action in Europe where the assistance of strong allies was an important device for achieving United States objectives. In Asia, however, where the free nations were weak and the European allies of the United States were either unwilling or could not afford to commit themselves for purposes that the United States considered important, the United States found it advisable to retain a freer hand. Now the situation began to be reversed. The supporters of an active Asian policy pressed the United States into agreements that reduced American freedom of action. The American effort to get quick results out of its European agreements created resistances that reduced the willingness of these allies to support policy objectives as unilaterally redefined by the United States.

In addition to the general form of the issue that has been examined, mention must be made of some of its specific aspects. A constitutional angle was developed: the authority of the President to commit American forces abroad without the approval of the Congress. This question, once raised, was capable of being applied to a much larger range of commitments than that of troops. Another aspect was concerned with the character of the American military establishment: Should American resources be primarily allocated to the Army, the Navy, or the Air Force? If action were collective, it could be argued that the contribution of the United States should be air and naval, and that American man power should go into the production of equipment. On the other hand, if action were unilateral, a two-way domestic argument followed. One school maintained that a larger army, supported by balanced air and naval forces, was implied. Another school maintained that security, in these circumstances, could be achieved only in terms of air power and atomic weapons because these alone compensated for an unfavorable man-power differential.

But the most touchy aspect of all in the issue of collective versus unilateral action came in connection with United States possession of atomic weapons. Other nations were legitimately concerned because the United States was in a position to use such weapons at its own discretion, while they would be the ones most directly exposed to atomic retaliation. The American position, backed by congressional demand and public opinion, was that the United States could not afford to give even its closest associates a veto on the use of the highest card in the American security hand. For example, if NATO forces should prove unable to prevent a Soviet conquest of Europe, it might be necessary to employ these weapons in order to protect the security of the United States. Furthermore, ambiguity was essential in this matter in order to protect friendly states from the atomic blackmail to which they would be exposed if it were known that they were able to exercise a restraint on American action. On this point, the official position was also the generally accepted position. It was that the United States reserved judgment on whether to act unilaterally or collectively with respect to the use of atomic weapons. This position, although it settled the question so far as the domestic American debate went, had the effect of increasing the uneasiness that public opinion elsewhere in the free world was beginning to feel about the policies and actions of the United States.

The Military Establishment

The considerations that entered into the discussion of the nature of the military establishment were, of course, directly related to the positions taken or reached on the preceding issues. Generally speaking, it was discussed in two forms. It was approached in terms of the establishment needed to maintain the security of the United States under the most adverse conditions and without reference to the possible benefits of collective arrangements and alliances. It was also approached in terms of these collective arrangements and alliances.

The first approach involved adjusting the claims of the three armed services and determining a basic military strategy for meeting the most extreme form of threat. The second approach involved modifying the somewhat theoretical answers produced by the first approach to fit the strategic concept of collective action, the political problems of collective action, and the requirements of maintaining a free world coalition. The two approaches were linked in that the second was valid only to the extent that the United States was capable of maintaining itself against direct attack and continuing to function as the main support of collective action.

Considering the number of points of departure that could be found in the interplay of these two approaches, it is understandable that this issue remained unsettled throughout the five-year period covered. Not only could too many contingencies be envisaged, but the security problem itself presented different aspects at different times. Nor did the evidence ever become convincing for making a final choice among so wide a range of alternative proposals, especially because a decision to have one kind of military establishment rather than another would, by being translated into the production of equipment and the setting up of tasks and organizations, inhibit adjustment and changes of direction if the decision later turned out to be wrong.

The official position in this babel of voices and confusion of advice was to multiply everything as much as possible in relation to as many contingencies as possible. This was to be done within a framework of collective action and a strategy of containment that sought only to restrain and not to roll back aggression. The picture that emerged was one of opposing aggression while avoiding general conflict. The position rested on more than the existing inability of the United States to engage effectively in a general war. It was based instead on two explicit assumptions. The first was that given a bipolar international system and given modern technology, the costs of global war were so great that it was not a course that could be deliberately chosen. It was a course into which the United States might be forced, but only in self-preservation. The second assumption was that the strength of the free world could be built up to a point sufficient—even after the Soviet bloc acquired a stockpile of nuclear weapons—to discourage Soviet policy from pursuing its global objectives by means of armed conflict.

This position, however, implied certain supporting actions: building up ground, air, and naval forces sufficient to fight local, limited engagements with some hope of success, while having sufficient strength in reserve to be able to defend Western Europe successfully. It also implied a state of armed readiness sufficient to discourage, if not absolutely to inhibit, the deliberate precipitation of a global conflict. As Western man power could not balance Communist infantry strength, this program of preparedness included the maintenance of a superior degree of technology and productivity, access to greater physical resources, larger stockpiles, and a greater variety of nuclear and thermonuclear weapons.

Although this was the position that was developed and was—except for one or two brief excursions in other directions—adhered to, it did not develop easily or clearly, and it was maintained only with difficulty. Opinion and judgment, both domestic and foreign, were so unsettled and pressed so heavily against the position from all sides that it appeared constantly unstable. It was difficult to locate the dividing line between building up and equipping a military establishment that would be adequate for a not clearly determined purpose without slipping over into preparations for a major war. Technological advances blurred the distinction as fast as it was made. The concept of a ready mobile reserve of ground forces undermined it because no real agreement was possible on the size or composition required for such a force. Furthermore, agreement was not possible on the relation of such a reserve to the contributions of the allies of the United States.

On the other hand, the requirements of collective action also worked to confuse the position. After 1952, the North Atlantic Council began to force modifications on the United States. The acquisition of German man-power reserves was still in the future. European member states were more effectively resisting demands on their resources, and the politics of NATO were being made especially difficult by the attitude of France toward Germany. By December 1952, the United States had agreed that "more emphasis should be given to increasing the effectiveness of the forces of the Alliance and the units necessary for their support rather than to the provision of greater numbers, to the extent that resources were not available for both tasks."[7]

---

[7] Lord Ismay, *NATO: The First Five Years, 1949-1954* (1954), p. 193.

In January 1953, with the inauguration of a new administration in the United States, accompanied as it was by promises of disengagement in Korea and of governmental economy, the position underwent further reinterpretation. So far as domestic security policy was concerned, defense expenditures were reduced about 20 per cent, and the emphasis was shifted from greater size to greater efficiency, with the intention of leaning more heavily on technical superiority and of achieving economies in the use of man power. The administration argued that the change was justified by the need to maintain economic stability and by the fact that the security problem had been recast as a long-term proposition. It had to be approached, therefore, in terms of reducing defense expenditures while maintaining an adequate posture of defense. The same line of argument operated in the North Atlantic Council. Here it led to the concept of "balanced" security, or a middle course between military demands and economic recovery and stability. By April 1953, the security problem was redefined as no longer calling for rearmament by a specific date of peak danger, but as requiring a gradual build up and steady maintenance over an indeterminate period.

This shift was resisted by the Department of the Army in the United States and by the NATO Supreme Command with the argument that ground forces were being weakened without any corresponding reduction of their mission and responsibilities. The opposition was joined by others, on the ground that the proposed reliance of the United States on technology would reduce an adaptable strategy of containment to a rigid strategy of a single weapons system—the atomic. Some credence was given to this contention, by an official reformulation of the strategy of containment as a capacity for "instant and massive retaliation." The official statement ran:

So long as our basic policy concepts were unclear, our military leaders could not be selective in building our military power. If an enemy could pick his time and place and method of warfare—and if our policy was to remain the traditional one of meeting aggression by direct and local opposition—then we needed to be ready to fight in the Arctic and in the Tropics; in Asia, the Near East, and in Europe; by sea, by land, and by air; with old weapons and with new weapons. . . . This could not be continued for long without grave budgetary, economic, and social consequences.

But before military planning could be changed, the President and his advisers, as represented by the National Security Council, had to take some basic policy decisions. This has been done. The basic decision was to depend primarily upon a great capacity to retaliate, instantly, by means and at places of our own choosing. . . . That permits of a selection of military means instead of a multiplication of means. As a result, it is now possible to get, and share, more basic security at less cost.[8]

It was pointed out, however, that this formula could not be easily reconciled with the fact that the Soviet Union now also possessed nuclear capabilities.[9] The official answer was that the United States had developed a wide variety of what were known as tactical weapons, and had, in fact, a well-rounded nuclear weapons system at its disposal. It was therefore prepared, as the Soviet Union was not, for massive retaliation in localized situations. But this was not the whole answer, as the events of the following year showed. The new formulation of the strategy of containment might have been applicable to a genuinely bipolar situation. However, it ran into trouble in an international system in which numerous smaller states were acquiring, and certain of the larger allied states were seeking to regain, some freedom of action.

Uncommitted nations, seeing conflict between major powers as immediately leading to atomic warfare, began to put impediments in the way of major power policy. Even states associated with the United States began to resist being held to an unconditional support of American purposes. Consequently, the security problem for the United States gradually moved out of the military orbit, in which it had for some time been considered, and into a political orbit. The political conditions at the start of 1955 were very different from those of five years earlier under which a North Atlantic Treaty Organization had been created and programs of economic and military assistance developed.

Claims on Resources

If the Soviet Union were able and willing to go to war in the immediate future, then without question, restrictions could not be put on the United States defense budget. However, if this estimate of Soviet intentions were wrong, and if the United States Government were to miscalculate in this way over a number of years, the

---

[8] U. S. Department of State *Bulletin,* Vol. 30 (Jan. 25, 1954), p. 108.
[9] It was confirmed, in October 1953, that the Soviet Union had exploded a thermonuclear (hydrogen) bomb.

costs of defense might exhaust the nation economically, make it impossible for the United States to support its foreign policies, and hand the world over to Soviet-Communism by default.

Yet both military security and the maintenance of a "healthy economy"—to use a commonly employed term—were agreed objectives; so the risks of economic distortion had to be weighed against the risks of military insufficiency. The issue was not one of absolute choice, but of balancing relative claims on existing resources. The action form of the issue was the allocation of money, man power, and materials. If other issues, such as the form of the American military establishment, the basic nature of the threat, and the effective pattern for United States action could have been settled, no doubt a workable solution of the issue of costs versus economic health could have been reached by statistical analysis.

But in the absence of working agreements on these matters of interpretation and judgment, it was difficult to adjust satisfactorily to the competing claims of the military services, the designers and operators of foreign assistance programs, and the American producer and consumer. These claims were pressed in political forms. Because the interpretation of Soviet capabilities and intentions on which they rested could neither be proved nor disproved, and because their value as a basis for decision fluctuated with current small changes in the international situation, this issue remained permanently open.[10]

The initial official position was that the current security threat was great enough to justify accepting a short-term danger of economic distortion. This position, however, could be maintained only by the assumption that an emergency existed. The more firmly this assumption was maintained and accepted as valid, the more it opened up for examination the other issues of the national security problem. What kind of military establishment did the United States need? What was an effective pattern of action for the United States? What was the real nature of the threat that had created the emergency? In other words, the more concretely the security problem was presented, the more it was revealed that the problem was unfocused for purposes of coherent action, and the more it was

[10] For example, military insufficiency was heavily weighted in late 1950 and early 1951. When armistice negotiations in Korea began, the possibility of dislocating the United States economy was more heavily weighted. Yet in fact the aspects of American-Soviet relations that had been emphasized to justify the earlier weighting remained unchanged.

felt necessary to establish a focus even at the cost of doing violence to previous objectives and policies.

The situation from late 1950 to 1955 with respect to the problem of national security can be summarized as follows. The United States was in a position to apply atomic retaliatory power to local Communist aggressions. However, its ability to fight containing police actions with conventional weapons was decreasing. The United States was in a position to engage in an intercontinental war with atomic weapons. But the deterrent value of these weapons no longer rested on a monopoly. It rested instead on technological and quantitative superiority. Therefore, while the effective firepower of the United States forces was increasing, the consequence of the use of this firepower had radically changed. A strategy of action for these circumstances remained undetermined. Theoretically, an effective strategy would have to be unilaterally determined in order to keep the initiative in choosing times and places for its execution. Practically, however, this freedom of choice could only be had at the cost of ignoring the interests and judgments of states with which highly integrated relations had been evolved, or of losing to the Soviet Union the support of a growing body of uncommitted states. Thus the security problem continued to be a complex of unresolved issues, with the choices under each issue contining to be vigorously debated, and the consequences of settling for any one choice remaining as unacceptable as ever.

CHAPTER XIX
Foreign Political Relations

UNTIL 1950 the major foreign policy lines of the United States were developed with relatively little friction in the field of the political relations of the United States and the free nations of the world. Even though from the American point of view these lines of action were seen as relevant to the strategy of containing Soviet-Communist expansion, other nations were not specifically required directly to commit themselves to this purpose. They were primarily the recipients of benefits, and consequently, the common objectives that they worked for along with the United States were economic reconstruction and political stabilization. Within this framework, political relations involved little more than working out agreements and making adjustments for joint action to these ends.

When, however, in the course of 1950, security considerations began to predominate in United States policy and action, the center of gravity of the foreign political relations of the United States was shifted. The same policy lines continued to be followed, but now the states with which the United States was associated were called on to take joint action against a specified threat: a Soviet policy of aggressive expansion in a specified form—armed aggression in Korea. The end of action now lay outside the free world. Therefore, basic questions of national interest and national policy were raised for each of the free nations. The effort to reach the common basis for action that the security aims of the United States required altered the character of political relations and gave rise to a range of problems in conducting them.

Development of American Positions

The primary external political problem of the United States at the end of the Second World War was held to be the restoration of political stability in the areas in which hostilities had taken place. With this as the immediate aim, United States policies were not anti-Soviet or anti-Soviet-Communism. The United States hoped for concerted action with the Soviet Union to prevent a basically regional organization of the world political structure. An important element in this picture was the aim of converting colonial areas to stable, functioning, and independent political units in the international community. Even the occupation policies of the United States had the clear subsidiary purpose of restoring the defeated enemy states to the international community in a reconstructed form. The part to be played by the United Nations Organization in realizing this broad concept need not be restated here.

The objectives of reconstruction, stabilization, and co-operation for peace and security never ceased to occupy a place in United States policy. However, in 1947 the priorities of action began to change. In a sense the Marshall Plan can be taken to mark the shift. Although its primary purpose was the reconstruction and stabilization of Western Europe, it soon proved an important tool in building a defensive alliance against the Soviet Union. Thereafter, programs of reconstruction and stabilization became increasingly the instrumentalities of a policy of coalition.

It is probably fair to say that the expansion of Soviet power checked the growth of American plans for the postwar world, and that the gravitational pull of Soviet power required some corresponding organization under American influence as the only possible way of halting the attrition of democratic strength. There seems to have been no intent at the time of uniting the entire non-Soviet world in a gigantic counter-Communist alliance. Even though the over-all problem was seen as one of containing Soviet expansion, it was considered that the problem called for different solutions in different areas. The conditions varied so much that United States policy sought maximum flexibility, the scale of which ranged from the high degree of integrated commitments of the North Atlantic Treaty Organization (NATO) to almost complete American freedom of action in the Middle and Far East.[1]

Simultaneously with the policy of developing defensive alliances, and in a sense as a complement to that policy, the United States

[1] The advantages of flexibility were felt more strongly as the Korean War developed into a prolonged armistice negotiation. In the absence of formal commitments, the United States was better placed to adjust policy to the exigencies of a rapidly changing situation. While the resulting shifts were severely criticized by segments of opinion that were without action responsibility, there is little doubt that a relative freedom to adjust was appreciated by responsible policy makers. This comment, of course, does not involve a judgment of the value of the actual choices made at any given time.

formulated another objective: the mobilization of the free world. This meant in essence that the United States sought to obtain support for its objectives, not only from its formal allies but also from states that were unwilling to enter into formal commitments, or that were even reluctant to become involved in an American-Soviet conflict of interest. Generally, the United Nations Organization served as a forum for this purpose; its outstanding use as an instrumentality of United States policy came at the time of Communist aggression in Korea. But unilateral techniques were employed as well: diplomatic advices and good offices, and economic programs with generalized aims. These instruments did not lead to the type of organic relationship developed in NATO or to the establishment of continuous common policy with other states. Their values were primarily supplementary; and as instruments they were most effective when used for specific and limited ends.

In addition to these basic positions, the United States formulated some broad long-range policies. Proposals for disarmament, for the regulation and control of armaments, for the collective enforcement of security by the United Nations, and for the international control and use of atomic energy belong to a category of policies not necessarily intended for immediate execution. They were, however, kept alive on the ground that if positions were prepared in advance on these questions, favorable opportunities for action would not be lost if and when they opened. Nor was the value ignored of building a body of international opinion that was aware of the ultimate aims of the United States.

These positions and policies, all of which were operative by 1950, were gradually brought within the context of judgments about the capabilities and intentions of the Soviet Union. They were, consequently, subject to review and adjustment, to changes in priority and emphasis, as official and public opinion saw these intentions and capabilities as immediately threatening, or as short-term, the middle-term, or the long-term threats. Thus it is necessary to add one more basic position to this list, although it was not specifically formulated until the end of the period now being discussed. This was the position of the "long haul."

Official American opinion, after a number of years of cold war, had gradually settled down to the conclusion that the Soviet regime was stable, was unlikely to have its controls over neighboring Communist regimes weakened, and was unwilling to make more than slight and momentary relaxations of its expansionist pressures on the free world. Consequently, while continuing to prepare for immediate contingencies in its relations with the Soviet Union, and while continuing to stand on all of its previous positions, United States policy makers also began to orient policy and action to the possibility that American-Soviet tensions might be indefinitely prolonged without rising by stages to a predetermined point of concrete threat. In other words, the United States Government came more and more to plan and to operate, not in terms of broad objectives to be reached by defined steps, and not in terms of *ad hoc* emergency programs designed to meet specific needs, but in terms of continuous policies adaptable to changes over long periods of time. Previous positions and general objectives, it was found, could be reformulated to fit this concept of the "long haul."

There was a strong argument in favor of operating policy by this guide line. If a situation were regarded as unique and as not likely to recur, resources could be allocated in a wholly different way from what would be possible if the situation was recurring. The initial approach to the Soviet threat had been to treat it as unique and nonrecurrent, in the sense that it would probably rise to a critical point in the near future. This had led from one emergency action to another. At last, however, the threat was defined as indefinitely persistent. Therefore less costly and less rigid policy alternatives had to be sought.

The Political Problem: 1950-1955

All these positions were present in men's minds during the critical years 1950 and 1951. They were some of the elements determining the choices of the United States policy makers. They were significant factors in the reactions of the free nations to United States policy. It should also be remembered that the political relationships between the United States and the free nations were fundamentally changed by the events of those critical years. Before 1950, United States policy sought to develop co-operative support among the free nations for mutually shared, generalized objectives. After 1950, United States policy called for co-operative action from the free nations for the specific purpose of countering Soviet-Communist expansion wherever and in whatever form it occurred.

This, it must be noted, was a more precise specification. It introduced a new range of implication into political relations. Several new and unpredictable variables entered in at every stage in the conduct of relations: the rise and fall of Soviet-Communist pressures; the particular respects in which United States and individual free nations would differ in their interpretations of the significance of these pressures; the intensity and the continuity of American reactions; and the intensity, continuity, and focus of the pressures that the United States put on its allies and associates and on the free world generally.

From the point of view of the United States, the essential political problem in 1950-51 was to get broad support and coherent progressive action for a sharply envisaged security purpose. As the action requirements of this problem impinged on the separate foreign and domestic policies of all the states of the free world, the American problem was one of achieving uniformity out of great diversity.

From the point of view of the states of the free world that were the objects of American action, the essential political problem was to maintain national purposes to the maximum extent possible without divorcing themselves wholly and finally from such American purposes as were relevant to their interests or from such purposes as they had in common with the United States and with one another. Because American resources were frequently an important factor in the pursuit of national objectives, and because in the showdown their security depended on the strength the United States was willing to deploy on their behalf, the problem was an extremely delicate one.[2]

Furthermore, it was difficult to reach stable levels of compromise between these two approaches to the problem of political relations. In each state involved, including the United States, there were differences between the level at which government officials were prepared to seek adjustments and the level at which public feeling was prepared to accept compromise. Generally speaking, governments were content with a level of common action that would avoid

---

[2] Note should be taken, however, of the fact that this did not inevitably prevent choices being made that, in advance, seemed likely to be destructive of both the national interest of the state concerned and of the future relations with the United States. Reference is made to the action of Iran with respect to the Anglo-Iranian Oil Company in 1952; to the refusal of the French Assembly to ratify the European Defense Community Treaty in August 1954; and to the position taken by the Greek Government with respect to Cyprus at the end of 1954.

disruption. Peoples, on the other hand, demanded either more or less than that. For example, it was the political opposition and the vocal sectors of American opinion that asked for clear alignments and vigorous action from the recipients of American aid. Similarly, it was the political opposition and the vocal sectors of British, French, German, or Japanese opinion that demanded release from restrictive or, as they saw it, dangerous United States policies. In either case, governments were inhibited from arriving quickly at satisfactory working compromises.

The problems of political relations that confronted the United States Government between 1950 and 1955 and the solutions that were available were confused by external events and domestic debate. The global political problem, from the point of view of the United States, consisted of four intimately connected parts, any one of which, however, could be acted upon separately. The first was the relations of the United States with the Soviet Union and its European satellites. The second was the relations of the United States with Communist China. The third was the relations of the United States with allied, associated, and uncommitted free nations. The fourth was the relations of the free world as a whole with the Soviet-Communist bloc as a whole. A specific problem usually arose and was, at least initially, handled within the context of one of these categories. It was only a matter of time, however, before the attempted solution began to generate equally specific problems in the other categories. Soon the whole political problem field would be active. The increasing speed with which movement in one area became motion throughout the whole is one of the features of international relations in the preceding five years.

Because relations between the United States and the Soviet Union were not of a kind that permitted much direct action, both states tended to act indirectly and in terms of their influence on third parties and in intermediate regions. To the United States, this had for some years meant acting through coalitions, alliances, and amorphous groupings of non-Communist states. Political relations with the free nations were consequently the center of gravity of the American foreign political problem.

Several terms, indicative of underlying attitudes, were employed whenever the desirable pattern of relationships between the United States and the free nations was discussed. They were: dominator, leader, guide, and partner. Since there was no ignoring the fact that the elements of national power were combined in a way that put the United States beyond competition for first place so far as the free world was concerned, the question was always one of the terms on which this superiority was to be exercised: as a dominator, a leader, a guide, or a partner?

There was a tendency in policy debate to talk as if these terms stood for distinct patterns of action that could be chosen and exclusively followed. This way of thinking about the conduct of United States foreign policy introduced much that was misleading and unrealistic into argument about the way in which the United States was or should be acting. Naturally, the repeated choice of any one mode by a state creates the impression that it has a policy of acting in this manner. And it is correct to observe that, in any given historical period, some states will seem to stand out as acting consistently on a policy of domination. It can be observed in this connection that such states are momentarily motivated by purposes that cannot be achieved except by comprehensively altering the structure of the international system in which they operate. At the present time, a policy of domination would be in fundamental conflict with the American concept of satisfactory world order; but Soviet objectives, at least as these are understood by the United States and many free nations, seem to be such as to imply the existence of a deliberately chosen policy of domination.

This is an important distinction to keep in mind, because the position of the United States in the international system is such that by the mere fact of its existence, it is bound to have a determining influence if it acts at all. Or, as will be noted below, even its refusal to act can be a prime determinant in the decisions of others. Once the United States decides to play a part in a given situation, its influence is very likely to be predominant. Thus without necessarily planning to dominate, the United States cannot escape the consequences of its power. No matter what restraint is exercised to avoid imposing solutions for other states, United States policy can scarcely avoid setting the limits within which solutions can be found.[3] On the other hand, and in particular situations, it may well be both necessary and desirable for the United

---

[3] Of course, less powerful states produce the same effect—as France did in Indo-China in 1954—but usually only as a single action. It is inherent in the position of the major powers consistently to establish the limits of action for other states.

States to impose solutions. Such a situation existed during the war in Korea, where decisions had to be made in accordance with a timetable imposed by the course of military events. Consequently, although preserving the appearance of collective solutions, the United States had no hesitation in imposing its choices.

Such a method, however, gives rise to difficulties that often outweigh the advantages of this mode of action, particularly for the United States, which cannot count upon a doctrinal or party unity among the free nations to mitigate the irritations that tend to accumulate in these circumstances. Even the Soviet Union, with doctrinal unity and the Communist party organization at its command, was confronted by the secession of Yugoslavia and is presumably unable to carry out a policy of domination in Communist China with any assurance.

The mode of leader is more congenial to the American temperament as well as better suited to the pattern of relations that the United States has sought to develop since the Second World War. Moreover, leadership in the free world is a role that the United States, in many phases of its foreign policy, is unable to escape. Action on the part of individual free nations, and collective action by the free world, were on the whole confined to the range of alternative policies that was acceptable to the United States. This was the case both with respect to national policies and with respect to collective counter-Soviet policies. An immediate consequence of this relationship was that, until the United States indicated the direction in which it was prepared to go, other free nations were unwilling, and often unable, to commit themselves to specific courses of action. Thus in a pattern of relations that calls for leadership, and in which other states are actually forced by circumstances to look to the United States for the lead, a failure on the American part to meet the needs of the relationship is as likely to result in political problems as if the United States had consistently and as a matter of policy attempted to dominate.

There is a variant of this that is worth looking at. Failure to provide a lead is one thing. Unpredictable vacillation between several possible leads is another thing. Both exacerbate political relations when states are willy-nilly closely held together. But the problem of relations becomes most difficult when a lead is given and is resisted, and no acceptable alternative lead has been prepared.

The United States ran into this difficulty in Western Europe when it gave the lead on German rearmament. It ran into the same difficulty again by providing no solution to the Soviet threat except a military solution. In these circumstances, even though a policy of imposing a solution was not intended, the lack of an alternative forced the United States to press so vigorously for its particular solution that it was felt to be trying to dominate. If, as at times was felt necessary, the United States did officially formulate a preferred mode of action in policy terms, it was the mode of partnership that was emphasized. Its use as a basic pattern did not exclude other modes, especially not that of leader. In the case of the Marshall Plan and NATO, the United States did give the lead, but, within the framework of the agreed general policy, acted as a partner with other states in implementing policy and in developing alternative solutions to current problems.

In some areas of action, the United States has followed this mode in the formulation of joint general policies. From time to time, it has worked as a partner with Great Britain in the Middle East, with France in Indo-China, and with Great Britain and France in Central Europe. But it should be noted that in situations where third parties are involved and where one of the partners has prior interests, partnership is not an easy pattern to follow. In the cases last mentioned, superior American resources have made partnership precarious and have subjected joint action to frequent review.

Finally, partnership, when applied to the relations of a number of sovereign states, is often taken to mean that the good faith of the stronger state is to be measured by the extent to which it supports the purposes of the weaker. From the point of view of the United States, any effort to produce unity in the free world by backing the divergent objectives of its component states, could only lead to a dispersal of influence and a dissipation of resources. Yet this very closely resembles what the free nations individually seek as a satisfactory pattern of political relations with the United States. This is especially true of the states that have only recently achieved a sovereign status. But as has been remarked from time to time, it is equally characteristic of even the states most closely associated with the United States. In their cases, however, it is based on a desire to regain some freedom of action and not on a need to prove that they are at last free to determine their courses.

These observations have been very general, but they have a background relevance to the examination of the political problem as this problem was seen and dealt with by the United States between 1950 and 1955. Obviously, it is not possible to examine the problem in connection with individual situations. It is discussed instead in terms of the broad key questions inherent in every individual case. The essential point of these questions was: What pattern of relations with the free world best contributed to the immediate objective of countering Soviet-Communist policy at the least cost to the long-range objective of creating a peaceful and secure international community? In this sense, the key issues were: how to weigh the advantages and disadvantages of unilateral action against those of collective action; how to rate the value of working through regional alliances with the value of operating through a universal international organization; and how to estimate whether the secure international community derived would be better or worse if it consisted of a large number of small sovereign units or of groupings around a strong state in which some attributes of sovereignty would be foregone. Finally, because each of these issues had as one of its points of reference American-Soviet relations, a separate question existed concerning the nature of this relationship.

In the climate of the years 1950 to 1955, particular facets of these issues came uppermost, and it is in these terms that they are presented here. Given the fact that for at least two and a half of these five years, the United States was very conscious of a Soviet threat, fighting a war against Communist aggression in an Asian colonial area, expanding its alliances and commitments, and pressing for more co-ordinated action on the part of the free nations, the form in which these issues came up for discussion was inevitably particularized. Were United States aims best pursued through regional alliances or through the United Nations? Were United States purposes best served by accepting the nationally assertive tendencies of the free nations, or should the United States continue to press for an integrated coalition? How, within the free world, should the United States adapt its actions to the often contradictory claims of its closest allies and of the uncommitted states in former colonial areas?

It need scarcely be said that the United States Government did not make exclusive and final choices in any of these matters. In the course of five years, policy operations shifted back and forth on the range of possible choices, but never came to rest at any one position. Nevertheless, the range of possible alternatives was more than adequately explored both within and outside the government. The tensions of these years required that policy be constantly reviewed within the government and made it inevitable that policy would be criticized in the light of the frustrations and dissatisfactions of the public. In this atmosphere, even the always present question of the value of unilateral over collective action as a basis for United States policy was vigorously reopened.[4]

The Key Issues

In this exploration of possible alternatives, five possible issues arise as key ones.

Regional Alliances and World-wide Organization

The core of the first issue—regional alliances versus world-wide organization—opens up the choice between building an international community on an American concept of desirable state relations or standing on a type of group relations geared to short-term policy needs. This choice, however, was rarely identified except by the proponents of extremes. The extreme positions were stated by those who called for unilateral action only and those who called for universal collective action only. It was certainly not in the nature of the American political system, and it was probably not feasible in international politics, ever to adopt a basic course of action so exclusive as to ignore important and obvious alternative considerations.

The actual position developed by the United States was that a policy of operating only to further the principles of the United Nations could not be made to jibe with a strategy of confronting the Soviet Union in the present; for if present needs were ignored in favor of future hopes, the chances were that the future would be shaped by Soviet policy and not by United States policy. Present needs

[4] One form of this debate was the controversy about the conduct of the Korean War as recorded in *Military Situation in the Far East,* Hearings before the Senate Committees on Armed Services and Foreign Relations, 82 Cong. 1 sess. It is also reflected in the concept of "massive retaliation" at times and places of American choosing.

called for a less universal type of collective action: the coalition and the alliance. But in the official view, this did not mean the abandonment of the long-term objective of a peaceful and secure international community. It only meant a change in the relative priority to be given to short-term and long-term purposes. The practical result was that when a concrete problem was considered vital, its immediate needs had priority. If, however, the problem was not felt to be pressing, a case could be made for favoring longer-term purposes.

Although the United States gave priority to constructing alliances, it interpreted this course of action as in harmony with the Charter of the United Nations. However, alliances such as NATO developed in ways that were not wholly compatible with the intent of the United Nations. The planning and command structure of NATO was set up to conduct defensive military operations and not to prepare the way for the United Nations to take over and restore peace. Nor was NATO organized to settle disputes within the region on which it was based. It was organized to defend a region against an external threat to the security of its members.[5] Thus the seeds of theoretical incompatibility did exist and were nourished, at least to the extent that action in international affairs was channeled away from the United Nations.

But this incompatibility can be overemphasized. Certainly, any view that maintains that the short-run purpose should always be secondary to the long-run goal, denies a principle of operation that is basic for virtually all social organizations. The most that can ever be asked is that action-decisions should try to serve both objectives simultaneously to the greatest extent possible. With many shiftings and several contradictions, this was the pattern of official United States choice.

In 1950, the United States brought its Korean operation within the framework of the United Nations. Not only was a long-run interest in collective security action thus asserted, but the United States was able to mobilize an *ad hoc* coalition for the Korean War. However, as the war continued, the collective security aspect of the initial decision was gradually felt both within and outside the

[5] NATO, for example, did not deal directly with the dispute between Greece, Turkey, and Great Britain over Cyprus. In this respect NATO differed from the Organization of American States, which was prepared to handle intra-regional disputes.

government to be an impediment to effective action. The international organization and its purposes became subsidiary to the influence of a selected few of its Members intent on achieving their particular aims. In the case of the United States, so low a priority was given at one point to its long-term interest in the United Nations that the possibility of choosing between this interest and the presumed needs of present policy was seriously presented. The administration, however, backed away from this choice in spite of strong domestic pressures. Generally, however, the United States moved ambivalently on this issue. In instance after instance, the considerations on which action was based were so complexly balanced between the present requirements of policy and the future hopes of policy that it is literally impossible to conclude that a "guiding principle" was present. It was officially maintained, however, that the purposes originally expressed by the formation of the United Nations were a guiding principle in United States policy, and there was considerable evidence in American action to support the statement.

The United States did not oppose a discussion of the claims of the Tunisian nationalists by the General Assembly in 1952, although it opposed United Nations action on the issue. It chose to support the jurisdiction of the international organization against the position of a NATO associate, France. But, at the same time, it did not choose to antagonize influential Arab opinion needlessly.[6] To take another example, in 1954 the American atoms-for-peace proposal rested on a blend of short-run and long-run considerations. Its unreserved emphasis on the authority of the United Nations suggested continued support of the concept of a universal international organization. The context and the timing of the proposal indicated an intent to influence world opinion favorably along this line.

On the other hand, whenever the Soviet Union or any of the uncommitted free nations, such as India, raised the question of the incompatibility of regional alliances with the purposes of the United Nations, the United States "dug in its heels." Nor did the United States accept the thesis—frequently advanced by some Mem-

---

[6] It is important to note, however, that the same set of choices was not available in 1955 when an effort was made to bring Algerian claims before the United Nations. France foreclosed the question by withdrawing temporarily from the General Assembly.

bers of the United Nations—that the points at issue between itself and the Soviet Union were negotiable within the framework of the Organization.

Examples could be extensively multiplied in both respects. But no more are needed in order to make the point that, so far as this issue was concerned, the United States Government was at no time prepared to make the choices that were pressed upon it from all sides; by segments of domestic opinion, by segments of world opinion, and even, in some instances, by the seeming demands of United States relations with the Soviet Union.

*The Free World: Loose Association or
Close Alliance*

In light of the estimated Soviet-Communist capabilities and intentions, would the United States be better advised to accept a loose association of free and sovereign states as the probable maximum obtainable and work to strengthen them as separate entities; or should it hold to a policy of providing strength only to integrated politico-military alliances? Both possibilities had been defined, and relevant operative policies were in being by 1950. Prior to the outbreak of the Korean War, the choice was occasionally debated almost as an abstract issue. After 1950, however, as the demands of policy on resources increased at an alarming rate, the issue became specific, and a choice seemed both necessary and possible.

Whether the build up of dispersed strength in the free world excluded the development of a tight system of alliances, and if so, how to weigh the alternative advantages of the two courses were difficult questions when put in concrete terms. There were many facets to the concept of strength and stability. From the economic point of view, the two courses were not incompatible. Assistance to develop an alliance could, with a little adjustment, also contribute to strengthening the individual members of the alliance. Equally, assistance to individual free nations to develop their economies made each better able both to contribute effectively to joint action at a later date and in the meantime to resist the pressures of Soviet policy.

At the political level, however, the choice depended more on the nature of particular situations than on a general policy decision. Entry into an alliance might increase the political stability of a

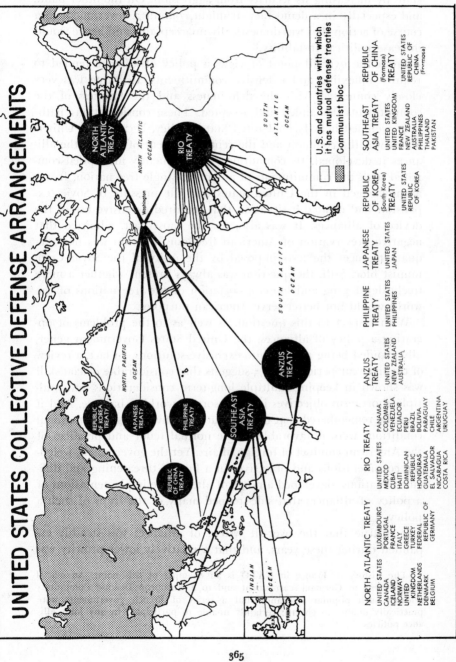

UNITED STATES COLLECTIVE DEFENSE ARRANGEMENTS

Legend: U.S. and countries with which it has mutual defense treaties / Communist bloc

NORTH ATLANTIC TREATY

UNITED STATES
CANADA
ICELAND
NORWAY
UNITED KINGDOM
NETHERLANDS
BELGIUM
LUXEMBOURG
PORTUGAL
FRANCE
ITALY
GREECE
TURKEY
FEDERAL REPUBLIC OF GERMANY

RIO TREATY

UNITED STATES
MEXICO
CUBA
HAITI
DOMINICAN REPUBLIC
HONDURAS
GUATEMALA
EL SALVADOR
NICARAGUA
COSTA RICA
PANAMA
COLOMBIA
VENEZUELA
ECUADOR
PERU
BRAZIL
BOLIVIA
PARAGUAY
CHILE
ARGENTINA
URUGUAY

ANZUS TREATY

UNITED STATES
NEW ZEALAND
AUSTRALIA

PHILIPPINE TREATY

UNITED STATES
PHILIPPINES

JAPANESE TREATY

UNITED STATES
JAPAN

REPUBLIC OF KOREA (South Korea) TREATY

UNITED STATES
REPUBLIC OF KOREA

SOUTHEAST ASIA TREATY

UNITED STATES
UNITED KINGDOM
FRANCE
NEW ZEALAND
AUSTRALIA
PHILIPPINES
THAILAND
PAKISTAN

REPUBLIC OF CHINA (Formosa) TREATY

UNITED STATES
REPUBLIC OF CHINA (Formosa)

Source: Robert L. Bostick, U. S. Library of Congress Legislative Reference Service.

365

state by increasing its security from aggression. On the other hand, and especially in a democracy, it might commit a government to a course of action that was domestically unacceptable and hence would increase political instability.[7]

From the over-all point of view, a policy of alliance tended to require inflexible and extensive commitments. Its value was very closely connected with the definiteness and the firmness of the commitments demanded and accepted. These considerations naturally weighed heavily on United States policy, because the United States was the common and the central element of each of the alliances it developed. Its commitments consequently multiplied compared with the commitments of any other single free nation. It was acknowledged in the United States that the pressure of Soviet expansion had created a situation that required extensive use of the device of alliances. It was also, for the most part, admitted that negative preservation of American freedom of action was not adequate to meet the tests imposed by the unity of the Soviet-Communist bloc. Still, the question was always present whether a more freely developing and looser association of the free nations of the world would not better serve American purposes.

With respect to this question, as well as to the problems of operating a policy of alliances, the United States Government generally avoided being pressed into exclusive solutions. In fact, a review of the five-year period 1950-55 suggests that considerable official skill was shown in keeping multiple long-term considerations and multiple short-term objectives in some sort of working balance. And it must be remembered that throughout these five years, international conditions were unfavorable to the normal tenor and practices of the American conduct of foreign affairs. Yet the government, weighing considerations and objectives in a flux of threatening and difficult situations, developed a range of alternative implementations of a policy of alliances that side-stepped many of the traps of such a policy.

It is true that the over-all system of alliances was steadily expanded during these years, and that a relatively lower priority was

[7] The history of France in NATO is an example of this point. An official commitment to German rearmament and to a European Defense Community released such popular resistance that a series of French governments were practically unable to govern; certainly unable to participate in any joint alliance policies.

assigned to policies of assistance designed to strengthen the recipients generally, but this is not the significant point. The point is that varying types of alliances were developed for various concrete sets of circumstances. In Western Europe, where the stake was held to warrant firm long-term commitments and where American power could be effectively applied in concert with the power of other states, the policy of alliances was unreservedly and vigorously pushed.

In other instances, where the stakes were not considered so high, where the goals were political rather than military, or where the use of American power would be less effective, less exacting formulas of relationship were developed. In these cases, American purpose tended to be more precisely defined and short-term. In Southeast Asia, for example, the commitments were limited, and the nature of the United States objective was made unusually explicit. In spite of the Southeast Asia Treaty Organization (SEATO) being an alliance in form, the United States reserved considerable freedom of judgment and action. In SEATO, unlike NATO, the United States remained free to take military actions at times and in ways of its own choosing and even, if it wished, to act only against Communist aggression. In the Middle East, still another type was developed. The Baghdad Pact, initiated, encouraged, and supported by the United States, did not include it as a participant. Great Britain, whose security interests were intimately linked with those of the United States in this region, acted as the hard core of the alliance. On the other hand, the record is not perfect. The United States entered into a binding bilateral agreement with Nationalist China that met only a few of the criteria of high stakes, feasibility, and effective deployment of power.

So long as the objective was to meet possible military aggression with military defenses, the policy of alliances retained a higher priority. But this was not the only form of Soviet-Communist expansion. Guerrilla actions, internal subversion, and economic and political pressures were also used by Soviet policy. In such instances, a policy of economic assistance seemed applicable and tended to get equal or higher priority. In many such cases, United States policy restricted its goal to a primary and short-term one of political stability. A great deal of American action in the Far East after 1950 was predicated on an objective of stabilization.

In the over-all operation of United States policy from 1950 to

1955, however, decisions were shaded between a policy of alliance, a policy of general strengthening, and a retention in American hands of ultimate freedom to act with reference to the Soviet Union. Economic assistance merged with military assistance, and both merged with a system of alliances. A principle of stabilization for its own sake merged with stabilization to check communism, and both merged with a policy of organizing a free world coalition. And increasingly after 1950, the United States, with an eye on the development of Soviet nuclear and thermonuclear capabilities, maintained its freedom to confront the Soviet Union on this ground without reference to either its policies of alliance or its policies of stabilization.[8] Thus so far as this issue was concerned, the current answer was that the choices were not exclusive and that the alternative courses presented by the issue could be simultaneously developed. The significant choices were choices of applicability to particular situations.

Integrated Alliances and National Self-Determination

The conflict within the free world between the Western European colonial powers and the states that were newly formed or were pressing to be formed from their colonial holdings was a real one. It presented the most concrete of the issues that have been examined. It impinged on American objectives and policies in a wide variety of ways and forced on the United States choices that were certain to be unsatisfactory. The issue lay in these choices. Its essence was how to balance American concepts of international order against the immediate requirements of a strategy of containment that was accepted as necessary. The issue was present in a general form in the discussions and negotiations that resulted in the United Nations. It was present in the initial policies for a postwar settlement. As an issue, it became increasingly specific, and was continually presented by one situation after another. It became peculiarly acute after war broke out in Korea, and the United States began to develop an extremely active security policy.

With respect to this issue, the United States seemed to stand historically and irrevocably on a principle of self-determination.

[8] This last reservation began to create difficulties in relations with the free nations by 1955. An examination of this fairly new problem is made in Part Four below.

Some of the free nations, and of these most were important allies of the United States, were not so committed. The position of the United States as a world power did not rest on a colonial system. This was not the case with some of its allies. For France, in particular, the colonial empire was a mark of greatness; its loss would be a clear manifestation of the declining international status of that country. A sizable percentage of the prewar national income of the Netherlands came from investments in the Netherlands East Indies. Yet no old colonial power possessed the means to resist the disintegration of its empire by force unless the United States was prepared to support such action. On practical grounds as well as on principle, the United States could not whole-heartedly underwrite such courses. United States policy consequently had to pick its way carefully and painfully through conflicting considerations.

Economic assistance for Western Europe was initially directed toward reconstruction and the development of stable, expanding economies. Simultaneous action to encourage nationalism in the colonies and former colonies of these states would have caused economic and political disturbances and conflicted with high priority American purposes. At the same time, flat opposition to nationalistic claims would have antagonized new states, exhausted American influence on their policies, and also have been resisted by popular sympathies in the United States. No pat solution was possible for the varied problems that confronted the United States policy maker in this area of decision.

So far as existing colonial territories were concerned, the United States tried to balance its position so as to avoid threatening the stability of Western Europe on the one hand, or, on the other hand, foreclosing on the hope of self-determination. It advocated evolutionary solutions. It sought to keep demands, expectations, and changes within the range of the possible. Its objective was to smooth an inevitable transition and, by so doing, to avoid economic instability in Europe and political instability in colonial areas. Beyond this objective lay the more encompassing one of not exposing its allies or their colonies to Soviet-Communist pressures. This delicately balanced policy was subject to easy upset by unsympathetic established interests and to sabotage by local extremists. The Soviet Union and its party instrument lurked in the background, ready to exploit mistakes in judgment.

After 1950, the American position was further exposed to the organized and combined attacks of the states that had recently emerged from colonialism. These states increasingly found ways of co-ordinating their pressures on the colonial powers and increasingly used the forum of the United Nations to pursue their particular objectives. Their opportunities multiplied in connection with United Nations collective action in Korea and with United Nations responsibilities in the Israeli-Arab conflict. Their positive support of one another's national policies became very adroit. Egypt confronted Great Britain with demands to be released from the restrictions of the Anglo-Egyptian Treaty. The Arab League confronted the United Nations with the demands of French North and West Africa for freedom. India confused the Korean situation. The more these efforts multiplied, the more the European colonial powers tended to resort ineffectively to the use of force. The only result was a retreat into unsatisfactory solutions through a series of actions that militated against the American goal of integrated strength for the free world. From the point of view of the United States, what had hitherto been a policy wilderness now became a jungle. The process of carefully balancing considerations no longer worked under these intensified conflicting pressures. By 1954 the United States seemed no longer able to develop action on this issue; at least no action that furthered its major objectives.[9] The issue consequently carried over into 1955.

The Nature of United States-Soviet Relations

At every stage in the discussion of the preceding issues, the conclusive factor in determining the decision reached was American-Soviet relations. The question always was: What would be the effect on these relations of acting on any one of the courses available for choice?

Any judgment about the nature and requirements of these relations was, of course, bound to be an American judgment. It was an American judgment about Soviet intentions that denied the negotiability of differences with the Soviet Union. In these respects, this issue was primarily a self-contained American problem.

[9] This development was revealed at the Geneva Conference on Indo-China in April 1954. There, in the absence of a clear United States position, the initiative fell to others. It was further revealed by the American inability to influence French action or to restrain Moroccan demands in 1954 and 1955, although a compromise solution was obviously of direct importance to NATO.

The position taken, however, by the United States Government on this issue had so determining an effect on all questions concerning the relations of the United States with the free world that it is essential to include it in this examination of the political problem. As has already been noted, the American position became increasingly rigid after 1950, and many important consequences flowed from this rigidity. Policies of alliance were strained. Policies of general assistance were distorted. Long-term objectives were severely reduced in priority. The further successful development of the strategy of containment came to depend very significantly on the extent to which the free world accepted and would continue to accept the American judgment on this all-important matter.

In the early stages of the Korean War, the American judgment was accepted and acted upon. Some Asian states were reserved, but generally the American lead was followed. In 1951 a shift began, initiated perhaps by the new factor of Chinese intervention. The position of the United States, however, did not change, even though more and more of the free nations moved away from the American position and sought alternatives. It was at this point that the problem of political relations with the free world grew difficult for the United States.

The United States Government found no grounds for altering its views, but the inescapable fact was that it was no longer able to make these views prevail as a basis for concerted action. The previous leverages of assistance programs worked less effectively. The governments with which it had earlier done business were increasingly sensitive to their own public opinions, and these public opinions were increasingly sensitive to the demands and the pressures of United States policy. And in any case, where was the global war that Soviet policy had been judged to threaten?

In view of this situation, the administration that took office in 1953 initiated a review of United States policies. Its initial reaction to what it found was first, to reaffirm the previous judgment of Soviet intentions and capabilities; second, to insist that the main lines of American action were still valid, but that a greater return on them must be obtained and made applicable to resistance to Soviet-Communist policies; and third, to bring heavier pressures on its alliances to perform. The reactions of the free world to these spartan demands were immediate and critical.

New factors operating on both free world and American opinion began to be felt. An atomic equilibrium, publicly interpreted as a stalemate that could be broken only by a willingness to destroy and to be destroyed, seemed to be reached. The Soviet Union, following the death of Stalin, appeared to be in a state of self-examining quiescence. While the Chinese Communists continued to make trouble, this was coming to be regarded more and more as a problem for the United States to handle, with the advice and the restraining influence of free world opinion. Finally, in several test cases, the free nations demonstrated that they were prepared to resist United States policy decisions while continuing to share American long-run objectives.

The United States Government, although still refusing to modify its opinion of Soviet intentions, gradually found itself obliged to act as if some modification had taken place. It was being irresistibly pressed by the need to maintain its partially integrated system of alliances to negotiate matters that it still regarded as unnegotiable. By the time the period 1950-55 came to an end, a new judgment of Soviet intentions had actually been made: and this judgment reflected the somewhat differing views of the associates of the United States. The Soviet threat was still a primary concern, and to meet it was still the highest priority objective of policy. But, and the point deserves special emphasis, *the threat was now defined as persistent and long-term. It was no longer immediate.* Policies and relations could be reviewed in this new situation; pressures and demands could be relaxed; and conversations, even if not negotiations, could be safely entered into with the Soviet Union.

The Unresolved Elements

This examination of the political problem of United States foreign policy makes it clear that many of its elements will continue to remain unsettled. The degree to which the United States can safely use its political and economic strength to impose its decisions on the free world will vary considerably and will continue to be debatable. The relative value of immediate agreement under pressure measured against possible future needs for co-operation will continue to be a source of controversy. The question of extending the network of defensive alliances remains open. For every decision to extend, other questions immediately come up concerning the structure of the alliance, the degree of American strength to be committed, and the extent to which the commitment to act shall be automatic.

Questions of the form and substance of relations within the United Nations have become more complex and difficult. It is awkward, but still possible, for the United States to advance and then retreat policy-wise, or to shift the order of its policy priorities in the relative privacy of bilateral agreements and in its alliances. This freedom is severely reduced by participation in a general international organization. To operate any major part of national policy through an institutional structure designed for universal collective action and openly debated adjustments of differences by nations that have agreed to co-operate is patently impossible in the world of today. Yet many aspects of policy must still be preserved within the United Nations framework. The effort calls for a combination of caution and co-ordination that is extremely difficult for the United States policy maker to achieve.

Each of these general questions returns again and again in connection with every need to make policy choices and is argued and reargued with every shift in the context of international relations. This discussion has followed those shifts into 1955, and has indicated the modifications of judgment and policy that emerged from a constant flow of debate. The basic questions were still undetermined when the year 1955 drew toward an end.

CHAPTER XX

The Economic Aspect

THREE AREAS of purpose, policy, and action must be distinguished if confusion is to be avoided in examining the economic aspect of the problems under consideration. At the end of the war, the United States had a well-developed *foreign economic policy*, in the sense of planned action to move toward a preconceived pattern of international economic relations.[1] The United States also had, at the end of the war, a *domestic economic policy;* that is, an intention to take government action to maintain the maximum levels of production and employment consistent with competitive enterprise.

In addition to these two areas of interest, a new area was opened and a new direction indicated after 1947, when national security considerations began to play an emphatic part in reshaping the patterns of United States policy. This was not an area of economic policy as such. It was an area in which *economic resources could be used as instruments to pursue political and security ends.* Action in this area would, by levying claims on economic resources, both compete with and tend to distort the operation of domestic and foreign economic policy. It would not, however, necessarily raise any questions about the basic values of the objectives of either domestic or foreign economic policies.

Nevertheless, an element of stress was inherent in these competing claims and when, after 1950, security goals were given the highest priority, these stresses led to considerable public and official discussion.

The 1945 Base

The United States formulated a broadly aimed foreign economic policy for the postwar world. Its basis was the restoration and maintenance of the convertibility of national currencies, nonrestrictive and nondiscriminatory commercial and payments policies, and the elimination of prewar "beggar-my-neighbor" economic policies. It was believed that action along these lines would gradually re-

[1] See above, Chap. II.

374

sult in the best possible use of resources and in a steady and widespread improvement in standards of living throughout the world. The American actions required by these purposes were to negotiate the international agreements, set up the international institutions, and to obtain the necessary support for the working of these institutions.

These objectives and these actions were consonant with the aims of domestic economic policy, namely, to convert the American economy from wartime to peacetime activity without an intervening period of instability; and after that, to maintain a steady growth of economic activity and a rise in individual living standards. This latter goal was obviously linked with a similar goal for the international system.[2]

Furthermore, the United States recognized that its foreign economic policy could not be immediately executed in its entirety. A transition period was envisaged. This period began with the facts of the economic devastations and dislocations of the war and would end when the countries of the world were economically rehabilitated and could be expected to participate in maintaining a system of international economic liberalism. Direct action was designed for this period. In addition, general agreements on economic policy were modified so that states—under specified safeguards —might take the restrictive measures believed necessary to protect full employment, to guard their balance-of-payments positions, and to develop new industries. It was considered, however, that this necessary transition period would be short, and that by 1950 or 1951 a world-wide multilateral system of trade and payments could be functioning as intended.

Departures from the Base

The period of transition showed no signs of coming promptly to an end. Instead, confronted by an economic-political crisis in

---

[2] It is important to appreciate that the general international goals comprehended such subordinate objectives as (1) the reconstruction of war-damaged countries, (2) full employment and the avoidance of economic depression, (3) the development of less developed areas, and (4) the long-run improvement in the use of resources. The purposes, of course, were given different priorities and different emphasis in the policies of different countries, even though all might agree on the broadly stated goals. And in United States policy, the emphasis shifted from time to time in the face of external circumstances and domestic pressures.

Great Britain and Western Europe and with non-co-operative and expansionist Soviet policies, the United States began to move toward using its economic resources for foreign policy objectives that were more politico-security in character than strictly economic. The Marshall Plan was a middle-range program of predetermined duration, designed to create conditions of economic stability as a basis for strengthening the political forces of democracy.

The underlying assumptions of the Economic Cooperation Act of 1948 were that:

1. The recovery of Europe as a whole was vital to world recovery and was a prerequisite for achieving the general aims of United States commercial and financial policy.

2. In the interests of American security, strong measures had to be taken to check the advance of communism in Europe.

3. The Communist threat took the form of exploiting low standards of living and economic stagnation, rather than overt military aggression.

4. The most suitable way to counteract this form of threat was to use economic and financial resources.[3]

It was further thought in some official quarters that the revival of economic activity in Europe would enable states to increase their military strength and to contribute to their own defense if Soviet policy became openly aggressive.

Consequently, there was a variety of motives inherent in this programed use of economic means. There was a general foreign policy goal—the success of the strategy of containment—to be supported. There were incompleted transitional needs to be met. And there were general foreign economic policy aims to be advanced. The programs, therefore, meant different things to different people. They were given variable emphases as the international situation changed, or as different counsels prevailed at the high policy-making levels of the United States Government. But through it all, the goals of United States foreign economic policy remained unaltered. Foreign aid operations were presented and administered as transitional actions that simultaneously safeguarded the security of the United States and promoted the objectives of foreign economic policy. By 1950 accumulated actions on these grounds had reached the point at which the United States was allocating, or planning to

[3] Paraphrased from *Staff Papers Presented to the Commission on Foreign Economic Policy* (February 1954), p. 27.

allocate, some proportion of its economic resources, in some form or other, to nearly every non-Communist state in the world.[4]

By 1950 and for a period following, events gave increasing priority to the security purpose. The Mutual Security Act of 1952 authorized about $4.2 billion for military assistance and about $1.8 billion for economic and technical assistance, but these figures were not the whole story. The sharpening of the focus of United States foreign policy on security goals had the effect of postponing the objectives of foreign economic policy to so remote a future that they ceased to have an important influence on either foreign or domestic policy decisions. Instead, middle-term and short-term purposes intervened: middle-range, so far as purely economic and technical programs were concerned; short-range, so far as the establishment of a defense organization for the free world was concerned.

In fact, some of the operations that seemed essential to the success of programs of economic and military assistance militated against the long-term goals of foreign economic policy. Once the purely reconstructive aspects of the assistance program were completed, the pressure to create a stronger Europe raised the specter of regional trade and payments arrangements that would be more favorable to countries within than to those outside the region.

The demands of rearmament programs, although adding to the economic resources of underdeveloped countries, awakened fears of economic colonialism by stressing the role of these states as producers of raw materials. Immediate American security goals began to play a more decisive role in the selection of recipients for economic aid and technical assistance programs. Finally, in the interests of national security, the United States restricted trade with the Soviet bloc and generated conflicts within the free world that impeded the pursuit of its economic goal. The justification in each instance—and there was no gainsaying its validity in the circumstances—was that while the objectives of United States foreign economic policy still stood unchanged, the action priorities had to be modified for the short term.

This development, however, was less significant in giving rise to problems than the gradual influence of political pressures and public attitudes on domestic economic policy that began to be felt. The expanding allocation of American resources to the demands of foreign policy seemed without end in view of increasingly critical

[4] The chief exceptions were Argentina, Canada, Sweden, and Switzerland.

relations between the United States and the Soviet Union. This fact imposed severe psychological and political strains in that indefinable area where American economic activity and American public opinion met. Steadily mounting commitments for economic assistance, military assistance, and American rearmament raised a barrage of questions about taxes, relative values of domestic and foreign obligations, and the size of the load that the national economy should be asked to carry. The last point, in particular, was treated by many people as a basic issue, on the ground that the continued growth of the American economy was essential if the United States were to maintain the superior productive capacity that was essential to its security and to its influence in the world.

The evidence that was marshaled around these questions was not convincing. The strains that were felt were strains on aspirations. They implied sacrificing improvements in the American standard of living and not actual decreases. Still less did they refer to the minimum standard that could be borne in an emergency.[5] Nevertheless, they were real enough in terms of domestic policies and the willingness of the American people to support the demands of United States foreign policy. It is enough to say that as the Korean War settled down into a limited test of strength, proposals with respect to domestic economic policy began to reflect a deep concern with these strains. This was especially the case when a new administration took over in the United States in 1953.

In the context of these unfocused stresses, certain key questions concerning the economic aspect of United States foreign policy came up for vigorous discussion. The essence of the issues was not new. The necessity for meeting Soviet capabilities and intentions was still the omnipresent backdrop against which the discussion ranged. There was a new emphasis, however. The validity of the objectives of foreign economic policy as a distinctive set of goals was more vigorously questioned, and the assumptions by which the use of economic resources to carry out foreign policy had originally been justified began to be attacked.

[5] The following table shows the estimated value, measured in 1947 prices, of total production of goods and services and of goods and services used for national defense, for foreign aid, and for all other purposes from 1946 to 1955. It indicates that the increase in total production was great enough to permit expansion of the combined total of defense and foreign aid between 1950 and 1953 without reducing the volume of goods and services used for other purposes in any year. It also shows that the total volume of goods and services available

The Key Issues

The points of view that were most often pressed on the government and to which the government became most sensitive in respect of its plans and actions can be regarded as centering on the question of the drain on resources, particularly the drain of military costs. Behind all the arguments that could be advanced on this question, lay a real and persistent problem for the United States, the problem of adjusting its economic policies in general, both foreign and domestic, to the mounting requirements of its national security policies. Although it was not consistently discussed as such, this was an operational problem of maintaining long-term objectives and of not foreclosing on long-range goals, while meeting the pressing needs of immediate purposes.

Military Costs

For the period 1950 to 1955, the issue of military costs appeared

---

for these other purposes decreased in only one year of the postwar period, that it increased 38 per cent over the whole period, and that this increase was sufficiently rapid to permit an increase of 18 per cent per capita, despite the increase in population.

GROSS NATIONAL PRODUCT AND ITS DISTRIBUTION AMONG NATIONAL DEFENSE, FOREIGN AID, AND ALL OTHER USES, IN 1947 PRICES, 1946–55
(In billions of dollars)

Year	Gross National Product	National Defense (Excluding military grants to foreign countries)	Foreign Aid (Including military grants to foreign countries)	All Other Uses	
				Total	Per Capita (In dollars)
	(1)	(2)	(3)	(4)	(5)
1946	233.8	21.2	6.0	206.6	1461
1947	232.2	12.2	6.6	213.4	1481
1948	243.9	11.2	4.9	227.8	1554
1949	241.5	12.8	5.9	222.8	1493
1950	264.7	12.7	4.3	247.7	1633
1951	282.9	27.0	4.1	251.8	1631
1952	293.3	36.8	4.4	252.1	1606
1953	306.5	38.9	5.5	262.1	1642
1954	300.5	32.4	4.0	264.1	1626
1955	318.8	29.8	3.7	285.3	1726

The above table and explanatory note were prepared by Walter S. Salant of the Brookings Institution. See Appendix C, "Distribution of United States Production Among National Defense, Foreign Aid, and All Other Purposes, 1946-55," for sources of above figures.

as a central one. There were good reasons for this. Actual military operations were in progress. A major military alliance, the North Atlantic Treaty Organization (NATO), was being built up to a climax of readiness. The military establishment of the United States was being rebuilt, expanded, and modernized. Major foreign policy efforts were being redirected and multiplied on a global scale to meet what was regarded as an immediate and critical threat to the security of the United States. When it is remembered that the combined expenditures for defense and assistance of all kinds, measured in 1947 prices, jumped from $17.0 billion in 1950 to $44.4 billion in 1953, it can be understood that fears of straining the economy might outweigh the fact that the gross national product had also increased between 1950 and 1953 from $264.7 billion to $306.5 billion.

At any rate, the possibility that the combined claims of security policy might seriously impinge on domestic standards was so widely felt that the United States Government was confronted by the necessity of making choices in public policy. The essence of the issue, as it was discussed during the presidential campaign of 1952 and during the first two years of a new administration, was to determine the basis on which security costs were to be balanced against the presumed requirements—economic, social, and political —of domestic public policy. It is important to note in this connection that the extent to which the maintenance of the habitual standards and the satisfaction of the expectations of a society are treated as secondary to the military readiness of the society fluctuates in relation to the degree to which a dangerous threat is realized or believed in. It is this that tends to establish the politically acceptable level of military readiness.

If the threat is realized as clearly defined, immediate, and nonrecurring, a calculated level of readiness is likely to be accepted that would be questioned and resisted if it had to be achieved and maintained for a long period of time. If, on the other hand, the threat is felt to be diffused and of indefinite duration, a different level of readiness is likely to be pressed for—one at which resources are husbanded and risks spread out in time—even though this may involve greater degrees of risk at any given moment. In the first case, other demands on the economy are adjusted to the requirements of the level of readiness selected. Even long-run consequences are not heavily weighed. The argument that there will be no future to consider if the present is not saved is likely to seem convincing. In the second case, competing claims on the economy quickly become debatable and are balanced and compromised. A consideration of the long-run effects of allocating resources between military readiness and other needs of the economic, social, and political institutions of society exercises great influence on decision.

Neither government officials nor the public have, however, a clear basis in fact for determining into which category of threat a given situation falls. Both the officials and the public changed during the period after 1950. Between 1950 and 1952, there was a tendency to define the threat as immediate. After 1953, there was a tendency to see the threat as long term. Generally, however, the key variables in determining what level of costs will be supported are: judgment of the degree of danger; judgment of the duration and character of the threat; judgment of the level and type of readiness required; and estimates of the state of the national economy.

With the possible exception of estimates of the condition of the economy, these are not matters that are ever likely to be settled to the complete satisfaction of all segments of either expert or public opinion. The issue is consequently one that is continually reassessed in the light of changing world conditions and changing domestic economic and political conditions. In a sense, it is never settled except by temporary compromises and tentative choices made on the basis of the contingencies most explicitly envisaged at a given moment. But this is unstable ground for initiating courses of action that take time for their development and that cannot be readily modified once they have been set in motion. This is particularly so when to reach a predetermined level of military readiness requires the operation of complexly integrated industrial processes.

Between 1950 and 1955, all combinations of these variables were quite thoroughly explored by professional analysts and in public discussion. At the start of the Korean War, the threat was widely accepted as clearly defined and immediate. It was also considered to be localized, and if rapidly and effectively met, to be probably nonrecurring. The level of readiness needed was seen as little more than a partial rebuilding of the military establishment from the low estate to which it had fallen after the Second World War. The economy was considered able to absorb this demand without strain. However, with the entry of the Chinese Communists into the war, the judgment changed, but without leading to a generally accepted revision of the level of readiness that might be required. Some, both inside and outside the government, would have scaled it upward to a full mobilization of resources. This conclusion was not, however, accepted by the administration in spite of the serious view that it took of the threat. Although the American economy was still regarded as able to absorb increased demands, the possible long-run consequences of making such demands began to be given some weight. By late 1952, as the threat did not materialize, even though all of its elements remained, both the degree of danger and the timing of the threat were judged to be spreading out in time and space. Although it was maintained that security demands on the economy could not be quantitatively reduced, it was considered that they, too, could be spread out in time. Long-run considerations now began to exercise greater influence. The center of gravity of the discussion shifted from quantitative questions of level to qualitative questions of the type of military readiness required.

From this point on the issue was scarcely debatable as a problem of economic policy. It became chiefly a many-sided argument among the supporters of various security policies. However, there was one very important difference from the more tense days of the Korean War. Then security policy had been debated in terms of alternative courses within the strategy of containment. The debate was now expanded to include alternative types of military readiness and establishments, and relative costs became a factor in the argument. Furthermore, the debate took place within new and different considerations set by the administration with respect to domestic economic policy. The administration now assessed the requirements for maintaining the growth of the national economy in a different way and gave a higher priority to the reduction of governmental expenditures and to balancing the budget. The variables of judgment involved in the issue of military costs and domestic economic policy had now combined to develop a course of action known as the "long haul."

The Resources Drain— Competing Claims

So long as United States foreign policy was being primarily carried on by economic means, the general question of competing claims on American resources was not a lively one, except to those who rejected the basic idea of foreign assistance programs. These were a small minority of the American people, and because the domestic economy was functioning at a high level, their numbers did not increase. The additional burden of military assistance programs on the economy led to no significant increase in this minority. But when to the claims of the economic and the military programs were added the costs of a rapid and large-scale rearmament program, the issue did come to life in a very simple and direct way. What, in short, was the meaning of all this for the American economy and the "American way of life"? Although very few voices were prepared to challenge the assumptions of national security policy, the general question persisted. Because there was considerable room for controversy about specific short-term decisions under security policy, the question tended to be argued piecemeal. What, for example, was the desirable distribution between aid and domestic defense programs?

An extreme form of argument concentrated on a single contingency and made it the basis for opposing any foreign allocation of resources except as emergency grants for relief, or for limited political ends. It pointed out that after recipient countries were strengthened economically and militarily, there was no assurance against shifts in popular sentiment or against Communist subversions that could throw these countries over into the Soviet bloc. Consequently, the first claim on American resources should be to build and to maintain the armed strength of the United States. The next allocation should go to increasing the productive capacity of the American economy, and after that, to raising standards of living. A realistic security policy, it was maintained, could not be separated from a realistic domestic economic policy; for in the last analysis, security was a function of a healthy economy, a satisfied society, and military power.

The official rebuttal asserted that the United States could not stand alone. Economically, its strength could not be developed in isolation from the raw material resources and the man power and skills of the free nations; nor could its well-being be maintained by shutting itself up in a hemispheric isolation ward while other states sickened. Politically, the only kind of world in which the United States could look forward to continuing its way of life was one whose economy was expanding, in which severe depressions were avoided, and in which the exchange of goods and services was relatively unimpeded. Programs of assistance, whether for reconstruction or development, were both economically and politically justified as a means of maintaining progress toward this larger end.

Two sets of facts justified these programs in terms of security policy. The first was that while a modern and adequate United States military establishment was being constructed, the composite man-power and material resources of the United States system of alliances were essential. The second was that the existing economic superiority of the United States could not be brought to bear on the international situation except in conjunction with other states. There was the positive advantage of access to strategically located areas and resources and the negative advantage of denying such areas and resources to the Soviet-Communist bloc.

Even if there were no security problem, this argument continued, the United States would not be able to operate in economic isolation. The maintenance of its productive capacity and of a satisfactory rate of economic growth were already geared to a regular access to raw materials and would increasingly depend on a relatively unimpeded movement of goods in an expanding international economy. In general, both administrations stood on this argument between 1950 and 1955 and resisted all frontal attacks upon it.[6] However, this was only general ground. The position was less easy to maintain in specific instances than as a guiding principle. In practice, the relative claims of foreign aid, American rearmament, and the domestic economy were compromised in an *ad hoc* way in terms of changes in the international situation and in response to domestic political pressures.

[6] The following list of the governmental commissions and government-sponsored analyses that reported on this issue in terms comparable to the position sketched above indicates the persistency with which the position was theoretically maintained and also suggests the equal persistency of the counter-arguments:

1. Gordon Gray, *Report to the President on Foreign Economic Policies* (Nov. 10, 1950).

2. *Partners in Progress,* Report of the International Development Advisory Board under the chairmanship of Nelson Rockefeller (March 1951).

3. President's Materials Policy Commission, *Resources for Freedom* (The Paley Report), (June 1952).

4. *A Trade and Tariff Policy in the National Interest,* submitted by the Public Advisory Board for Mutual Security (The Bell Report), (February 1953).

5. *The Dollar-Sterling Relationship and Its Effect on U.S. Foreign Policy,* Report to the President by the Douglas Mission (August 1953).

6. Commission on Foreign Economic Policy, *Report to the President and the Congress* (The Randall Commission), (January 1954).

A variety of pressures from both within and outside the government can be identified as recurring in one concrete instance after another. There were those who argued that a particular allocation was either more than adequate to or was inadequate for the situation. There were those who argued that the desired result would be better achieved if the same resources were employed in a different way. And there were those who argued that the resources were being applied to the wrong situation. The governmental position, always subject to slight modification by the political strength of the preceding arguments, tended to be that within the framework of its general foreign economic and security objectives, and subject to the needs of domestic economic policy, its allocations should be tentative and contingent so that it would remain free to shift the emphasis as circumstances dictated. Above all, the government wished to avoid irreversible decisions and fundamental changes in basic policy.

It is correct to note that until 1952 fundamental changes were not called for by American public opinion. It is equally correct to note that in terms of priorities, allocations in support of foreign economic policy as such were outpaced by those for military assistance, and both were outdistanced by rearmament.[7] The most active opponents of this trend were those who had been supporters from the start of the principles underlying United States foreign economic policy, and the strongest advocates of using economic means to reach the political goals of foreign policy. The basic argument was that too exclusive concentration on short-range security problems would foreclose on the longer-range interest of the United States in developing a peaceful and secure international community. The need to expand world economy and to improve standards of living generally was, if anything, greater because of the Soviet-Communist threat. Consequently, economic policy judgments and security requirements came together. What was needed was to pursue both courses of action in ways that would be mutually supporting. In fact, a vigorous development of general foreign economic policy toward its own objectives was held to

[7] In the course of this downgrading, the Economic Cooperation Administration, for a period in 1950-51, became a guardian of economic assistance against the claims of military assistance and hence a firm exponent of the thesis that economic strength was the essential foundation of military strength. The second half of this argument was equally used by those who sought to guard the American economy against the encroachment of foreign assistance programs.

be an essential part of a strategy of containment, or, to use a term that was coming into vogue, a strategy of "competitive co-existence."

Although a good deal of statistical evidence was developed on both sides of this issue, the arguments were essentially political rather than economic. The actual course pursued was broadly that advocated by the argument above. The concrete differences of opinion came with respect to the point at which a balance should be struck between competing claims on resources, and no real consensus developed in American opinion on this point. Although some important groups were prepared to accept the possibility of a slower rate of increase in American standards in order to make resources available for generally improving international standards, and other less organized groups would have rejected practically all foreign policy claims on the American economy, there is no evidence that these were influential views. Official judgment did not recommend, and therefore no large body of public opinion had an opportunity to demonstrate either willingness or unwillingness to accept sacrifices for a long-term purpose, as distinguished from sacrifices to achieve definite military-security goals.

In addition to the give and take of argument at the level of action, note should be taken of a pattern of rather fundamental questioning of some of the bases of United States foreign economic policy as well as of some of the economic aspects of short-term security policy. The position of the specialists who took a gloomy view of the rising pressures of human populations on limited resources can be left to one side, although some of their opinions entered into the critical judgments of other professionals. More specifically, the question was raised whether the structure of the international economy had not been altered to such an extent that the concepts and objectives of United States foreign economic policy were historically outdated. At least three developments were noted that were held to challenge a policy of economic liberalism. The Soviet Union had created a self-contained economic bloc with which commercial relations could not be conducted on the principles of economic liberalism. Smaller and newer states—mainly the so-called underdeveloped countries—were giving economic expression to their sturdy nationalism by policies involving economic planning and protective controls. The older industrialized nations were using the powers of government to pursue the twin objectives of high employment and a balance-of-payments equilibrium. Finally, it was pointed out that the United States Government itself, in many aspects of its domestic economic policy, was also engaged in restrictive and protective practices that ran counter to the aims of its foreign economic policy.[8] The more obvious of these had developed in connection with the agricultural sector of the economy and were reflected in protective and price-support legislation and in proposals for dealing with agricultural surpluses. These and similar developments were interpreted as evidence of the need for an adjustment of earlier policies to the realities of the world economic system.

Another target of specialist criticism was the assumption that subsidized economic improvement, particularly in underdeveloped regions, was both good in itself and an essential part of the strategy of containing Communist expansion. The critical view did not deny that slow evolutionary change, with plenty of time available for compensatory adjustments, was all right. However, it did suggest that vigorous, forced draft efforts to bring about economic change were more likely to create revolutionary situations than to prevent them. Given the complexities of the processes of economic growth, promises of improvement were likely to release mass expectations of higher standards faster than economic growth could produce satisfactions. This gap could easily become a major source of social and political instability, the atmosphere in which Communist promises were presumed to find their prime opportunity.

Other specialists, as well as established official opinion, countered this view by maintaining that the process of change was already under way and that the pressure of mass expectations, particularly in underdeveloped areas, was a primary political fact of the mid-century. American action in this field, it was held, need no longer be justified primarily in terms of general foreign economic policy for an international community, but could stand on the additional premise that the United States was obliged to compete

---

[8] The commissions listed in the footnote on page 384 above also noted these restrictive practices, but in these cases in order to point out that proper purposes were being frustrated. The *Staff Papers* of the Randall Commission, for example, noted that "domestic programs which result in attempts to insulate them against imports, bring into use practices which the United States has been urging other nations to abandon in the interest of an expanding multilateral trade of mutual benefit to all participants." *Staff Papers Presented to the Commission on Foreign Economic Policy*, p. 160.

with the Soviet Union if the peoples of the underdeveloped countries were to remain within the free world.

It is pretty clear that, while the basic economic grounds on which the United States acted between 1950 and 1955 were not changed by any fundamental decision, the broad conceptual bases were subjected to closer scrutiny and that a considerable shift in emphasis had taken place. Action on programs of economic assistance was increasingly divorced from the service of economic objectives and more and more attached to the service of national security policy. Action on United States rearmament and on the claims of the domestic economy was given ever higher priority. But these shifts in emphasis were plainly not considered to mean the decisive abandonment of any long-term economic goals, even though the short-term decisions seemed to point accumulatively in this direction.

Nor can these shifts be attributed primarily to the change in administrations that took place in 1953. The economic problems of the postwar years and the security problems of the late 1940's and early 1950's initiated the essential modifications. However, the new administration, by placing great emphasis on reducing governmental expenditures, judged the economic aspects of foreign policy operations—particularly in the political and security fields—more strictly.

Actually, throughout the period under consideration here, it was probably more to the point to think in terms of the allocation of American resources in relation to political and security choices. There is little evidence to indicate that vital economic choices were necessary. The American economy was at no time in so tight a bind that absolute choices between fundamentally conflicting claims were necessary. There was, in fact, no automatically operating conflict between standards of living and military expenditures. This could come only if the economy were at full stretch. If resources, man power, and plant capacity were not being fully utilized, increased military expenditures were more likely to stimulate production.

It will, consequently, be appreciated that the differences of opinion and judgment that were argued during these years arose much more from deeply ingrained economic and social attitudes and from widely varying estimates of the nature, degree, and permanence of the threat to American security than from any evidence provided by current economic conditions. The differences that showed in policy formulation, or in the execution of policies, reflected differences in the analysis of major facets of the problem as well as in manner and tone, instead of shifts in basic direction. For, in the last analysis, the issues examined here involved questions that could not be settled with finality by any official act of decision. From their very nature, they were bound to be recurring and to be continually reassessed. The guide line of security and the guide line of guarding the domestic economy undoubtedly made for easier choices in some fields of action, but with equal certainty created fresh problems in other fields.

The process, however, left United States foreign economic policy hanging in the balance, and economic assistance programs, even when their goals were clearly political and security, had become so hedged about with restrictions and so inflexible that they created uncertainty and gave rise to a good deal of restiveness among allied and associated states. American pressure to restrict East-West trade began to lead to considerable bickering. Relations were further embittered as fears were generated in different parts of the free world by various domestic proposals for the disposal of American agricultural surpluses and for the protection of American industries. While the Soviet Union did not, as it was to do early in 1956, move into this unstable situation, lines of cleavage within the free world were revealed and opened to exploitation. In a very general way, the contradictions and the unresolved issues that had accumulated in the economic relations of the United States with its associates began by the end of 1955 to play a serious part in opening up a new range of basic foreign policy problems.

CHAPTER XXI

Events in Retrospect

THE STARTING POINT for this discussion is the Communist aggression in Korea in June 1950. The international response to this event was largely dominated by the American reaction, which was composite: a unilateral reaction to what was regarded as an indirect but provocative Soviet move; an effort to create a joint reaction along with allies; and an effort to achieve a collective reaction on the part of the United Nations. For approximately the next six months, this complex course succeeded.

It was accompanied by supporting actions in Western Europe. Assistance programs were redirected to increase the military strength of the European allies, and the North Atlantic Treaty Organization (NATO) was pressed to become a cohesive defense force with a unified defense plan. In addition, the United States, impressed by its estimates of Soviet capabilities and intentions, proposed to include Western Germany in the defense plans of Western Europe.[1] Although the full consequences of this last action were not anticipated, the actual choices available to the United States at the time were limited. Soviet aggressive policy appeared to be on the move. American man power was being increasingly committed in Korea. A concurrent threat to Western Europe was generally held to exist. The man-power resources of the European members of NATO were tightly stretched. Western Germany was a politico-strategic liability unless some way could be found to make use of the German economic and military potential.

The Soviet Union reacted in diplomatic notes, reminding the

[1] This proposal was made in September 1950, at a meeting of the United States, British, and French foreign ministers in New York. Its shock effect, particularly on the French minister, produced the explanation that the United States was not considering a re-created German national army, but the participation of the German Federal Republic in an integrated force. It was made clear, however, that the United States wanted German man power and productive potential to be available to the West. The communiqué of this meeting stated that the three governments would "increase and reinforce their forces in Germany" and would "treat any attack against the Federal Republic or Berlin from any quarter as an attack upon themselves." U. S. Department of State Bulletin, Vol. 23 (Oct. 2, 1950) p. 531.

West of Soviet views on the German threat and German rearmament. The Chinese Communists began to send volunteer forces and war matériel into Korea. By the end of the year, the United Nations was fighting an army of Chinese and North Korean Communists and was suffering military reverses.

1951

No moment could have been more favorable for the Soviet Union to act on the American estimate of Soviet intentions than early 1951. The Soviet Union did not so act, and the United States, while stabilizing the military position in Korea, stepped up its diplomatic and economic efforts to prepare itself and the free world for an ultimate contingency. Action was speeded along two established lines: United States rearmament and the putting of real teeth into NATO. At the same time a new line was opened up. Earlier resistance to proposals to expand the system of defensive alliances gave way, and urgent attention was given to the strategic and political extension of this system. In April the United States increased military aid to National China and signed an agreement with Denmark for the defense of Greenland. It landed forces in Iceland in May, and in June, in company with France and Great Britain, announced substantial economic aid to Yugoslavia, and signed an agreement with Saudi Arabia for an air base.

An agreement was signed in July with France for five air bases in Morocco, the draft of a proposed peace treaty with Japan was released, and negotiations were begun with Spain for naval and air bases. In August a mutual defense treaty was signed with the Philippine Republic. In September an agreement was reached with Portugal for bases in the Azores. Greece and Turkey were proposed for membership in NATO; a peace conference on Japan was held and the resulting treaty was immediately followed by a United States-Japanese security pact; and increased aid for use in Indo-China was promised. In October, France, Great Britain, Turkey, and the United States proposed to establish a Middle East Command with Egypt as an equal partner; and in November a military aid agreement was signed with Yugoslavia.

These efforts met considerable opposition from all sides. Soviet warnings were expected and were given. European opposition was less expected, but it also developed. Some countries objected to

United States actions in the Far East; some objected to the extension of their commitments under NATO to Greece and Turkey; some objected to the implications of the United States entering into closer relations with Spain. The most significant resistance developed, however, among the new states of the Middle East and Asia. Proposals for a Middle East Command were flatly turned down. Egypt and the Arab world professed to be content with the protection of the collective security arrangements of the Arab League. In Asia, India showed the greatest reluctance to having the states of that region drawn into an anti-Communist bloc dominated by United States policy. In this attitude, India was supported by Burma, Ceylon, and Indonesia. Consequently, a split developed between a small group of states—South Korea, National China, and although for different reasons, the Philippine Republic—whose existences depended almost wholly on the United States, and a larger group of states, headed by India, that sought to free their positions and policies from entanglement with the United States.

But the most immediately serious obstacle arose within the United States. American opinion, stimulated by news from the battle front and by the political party in opposition, reacted to the inconclusiveness of the Korean War and to the restraints that the United Nations put on dealing with the Communist Chinese intervention. The pouring of resources into Europe was questioned, alliances were deprecated, and unilateral action was called for. The administration held to its course in spite of all these difficulties.

To make matters worse, the states of the Middle East seized the opportunity to press their claims for complete economic and political independence from the West. In April 1951, Mohammed Mossadegh became premier of Iran and promptly nationalized the British-owned oil resources of the country. In September, the Iranians occupied the great refinery at Abadan. When an allied Middle East Command was proposed in October, Egypt rejected the proposal replying that it must first regulate its relations with Great Britain and denounced the Anglo-Egyptian Treaty. The United States, although driving hard toward a system of global security and conscious that the Middle Eastern states overstated their ability to protect themselves, found no way of checking and reversing this development beyond trying to be an honest broker between an ally, Great Britain, and the countries with which it sought to be allied. Unfortunately, the reputation of the United States was spotted in Arab opinion by its Palestine policy.[2]

When in June 1951 the door was suddenly opened by the Soviet Union for the discussion of a cease-fire in Korea, these difficulties led the United States and the United Nations into the prolonged Korean armistice negotiations. Extremely diverse pressures now operated on United States policy: the growing frustrations of American opinion; the European feeling of having been taken close to the edge of real war by the United States; and the increasing success with which an Asian-Arab bloc operated within the United Nations in favor of compromise. The United States Government was concerned to limit hostilities in the interest of developing its security policy for the larger threat of the Soviet Union. Consequently, it entered into the armistice talks without any real conviction of their desirability.

1952-1953

The lull in the Korean War, accompanied as it was by a Japanese peace treaty and the beginnings of a security arrangement for the Pacific region, gave rise to a more favorable impression of the situation than was justified by the facts. Asian Communists, geared to the militant policy of the Communist Chinese regime, increased their pressures in Indo-China, Malaya, Thailand, and Tibet. In the course of the year, they achieved a position from which, at any time of their choosing, they could have precipitated another crisis for United States policy. In this situation, the United States was unable to take affirmative action, except for negotiating separate security agreements with Japan, the Philippines, and Australia and New Zealand, and making commitments to National China in Formosa and to Korea. The security pacts themselves were not applicable to the movements of events on the Asian mainland. These events could only be affected by direct American action

[2] It should be noted in this connection that United States policies were virtually hamstrung. Expert opinion doubted the capacity of the Middle East to absorb more economic aid than was already being given. Military assistance was out of the question for fear of upsetting the precarious balance of force between the Arab League and Israel. The United States could not bring effective pressure without being conclusively identified by the Arab world as an exploiting power along with Great Britain; nor could it press Great Britain to accept solutions that would weaken an essential ally and compromise American security.

against Communist China. But such action, although demanded by minority American opinion, was inhibited by other and more powerful considerations. The Asian bloc in the United Nations was pressing for a settlement in Korea; the European allies, although they could find no alternative to following the lead of the United States in the Far East, were becoming dissatisfied with many aspects of United States policy; and finally, there was no real evidence that American opinion was really prepared to bear the costs of direct action. In this last respect, the hands of the administration were tied by the fact that 1952 was an election year, and that it could easily be placed on the defensive in foreign policy.

A tendency toward improvisation very naturally resulted. This was strengthened by dispersed small and adverse developments. Indonesia refused to sign a bilateral aid agreement in February, on the ground that the military assistance features would commit it to unacceptable courses.[3] The position of the French in Indo-China steadily worsened, and appeals for American aid became more pressing. However, no commitment was possible beyond a promise to increase assistance under the Mutual Security Act.

Furthermore, the restiveness of the uncommitted states of the Arab world steadily mounted. The British-Iranian conflict over oil holdings dragged on until Iran broke off diplomatic relations in October. There was a bloodless revolution in Egypt in July that removed the King, but did not lower the nationalist fever. The new Egypt sought to strengthen its position in the Arab world by activating the Arab League—an Arab security pact came into force in August—and by stimulating nationalist movements in French North Africa.[4]

The major United States effort was gradually shifted to Europe and, on the European scene, NATO and Germany were the focuses. Interlocking negotiations were carried out within NATO: between Great Britain, France, and the United States with respect to Germany and with respect to their common position toward the Soviet Union on the German question; with European states on the subject of a European Defense Community; and with Great

[3] In January 1953 the United States agreed to separate economic assistance grants to Indonesia from military aid.

[4] There were disorders in Tunisia throughout the whole of 1952. Morocco requested a revision of its protectorate status, and rioting also had broken out there by the end of the year.

Britain and France separately on policy and action elsewhere in the world.

The effect of each of these negotiations on all the others was constant and marked, because they all bore on a set of related questions. These were the steps to be taken to carry out the NATO rearmament programs that had been agreed in 1950 and to incorporate Western Germany in the North Atlantic security system.

The first of these issues was taken up at the Lisbon meeting of the North Atlantic Council in February 1952. Here two conflicting positions were identified, explored, and compromised. The European states, especially the smaller ones, insisted that they could not meet their obligations to rearm without further American assistance. The United States refused to increase its aid beyond what was specified in existing programs. The compromise that emerged was the result of two changes in American thinking: a partial acceptance of the political inhibitions and economic restraints that operated in Europe to prevent action on rearmament proposals that cut into domestic standards of living; and an implicit acceptance of a European thesis to the effect that the Soviet threat was more remote and more generalized than the United States had been insisting. The effect of the compromise was to reduce the goals for military readiness and to lengthen the period of time in which those goals were to be reached.

In an effort to compensate for these modifications, the United States pressed for a greater military integration of national forces under NATO and for quick action on Germany. Negotiations respecting Germany had gone on through 1951, and a considerable measure of agreement had been reached on the political and economic position of Germany in Western Europe. Negotiations on German rearmament, however, were deadlocked.[5] The United States and Great Britain sought a way out by supporting French proposals for a European Defense Community (EDC). This brought political, economic, and military issues together.

The key problems stood out sharply by this time. They were:

[5] France rejected a German national army and proposed instead a European army in which German units would be absorbed. France also opposed any move toward any kind of German military establishment until a European army existed at least in skeletal form. Germany had no expressed interest in creating an army unless its sovereign equality in the councils of Western Europe was also established. Consequently, further action even on political and economic agreements was also halted.

(1) the degree of sovereignty to be restored to Germany; (2) the place of Germany in the political system of Western Europe; (3) the place of Germany in the North Atlantic security system; and (4) the guarantees that the United States and Great Britain were prepared to give against both possible German aggression and German predominance in Europe.

The North Atlantic Council faced these issues at Lisbon and came up with a formula. Germany would enter a European Defense Community. The European Defense Community would act as a unit within the North Atlantic Treaty Organization. Guarantees would be developed to meet both the French and the German reservations. This formula was approved. However, it merely set in motion a fresh series of implementing negotiations, the end of which was not reached until 1954. In hard fact, the execution of this formula required the negotiation and ratification of a European Defense Community Treaty, the negotiation and ratification of a protocol to the North Atlantic Treaty defining relations between EDC and NATO, and the development of guarantees to France, to Germany, and between France and Germany.

The European Defense Community Treaty was negotiated but was not ratified by the end of May 1952. The European Coal and Steel Community Treaty, a measure of economic integration with political and military implications, was ratified and came into force in July. The United States ratified the protocol to the North Atlantic Treaty in July. But the EDC Treaty bogged down in the German Bundestag, as it did in France because the various governments that came to power hesitated to present it to the National Assembly for ratification.

Meanwhile, another component in the situation—the Soviet Union—became more active, possibly because it regarded the Lisbon meeting of NATO as a real step toward a *rapprochement* between Western Europe and Western Germany. At any rate, Soviet policy began to explore ways of impeding, interrupting, and finally checking such a development. Pressure was exerted, both through the Eastern German regime and in notes to the occupying powers, for the formation of a government for the whole of Germany. In March 1952, the Soviet Union proposed a four-power meeting to consider a German peace treaty. This was countered by a Western statement that a freely elected government for the whole of Germany was a precondition. In April the Soviet Union proposed a four-power investigation of electoral conditions in Germany. This proposal was rejected in May, and was immediately followed by a new note requesting a four-power meeting on the German question. This was answered in July by a Western restatement of free elections as a precondition. In August the Soviet Union rejected proposals for free elections, and in September the Western powers rejected proposals for a meeting without a previous agreement about elections.

Throughout these interchanges, the Western powers had to move cautiously. The Soviet proposals could not be flatly turned down, for they were stirring German opinion by appearing to make the possibility of German unification depend on a German refusal to enter the European Defense Community. The more German feeling was stirred up, the more alarmed French opinion became. The more rigid the French position became, the more Great Britain and the United States were pushed toward extensive guarantees in favor of the French.

The result, from the American point of view, was that further programs along the existing lines of United States policy were slowed down even in Europe. There appeared to be no way of stimulating action except by further commitments and additional assistance, neither of which was feasible as the year drew on to the presidential election. The marking time that resulted was not, however, the whole story. What was happening under the surface of governmental relations was that in Europe public feeling was beginning to take forms contrary to official policy and to official commitments. In a very precise sense, United States policy, formulated in conjunction with specific European governments, had to run a race against time. It was trying to bring about the incorporation of Western Germany into Europe and to develop NATO into a "situation of strength" before Soviet policy and public feeling in Europe created an irresistible pressure to seek an adjustment with the Soviet Union. An important consideration in American decisions at this time was that a negotiation with the Soviet Union could not be entered into until the relationship of Western Germany with Western Europe and NATO was satisfactorily signed, sealed, and delivered.

The impression of drift that some critical observers began to find in United States action was strengthened as the presidential campaign of 1952 took shape. Certain key points stood out. A solution was wanted and would be sought in Korea. The costs of foreign policy were being questioned in some quarters, either because of the presumably bad effect on the national economy or because policy was not producing decisive results. The political exposition of these points suggested to the allies and associates of the United States that important changes affecting their interests might be in store for them: increasing political and economic strains if the United States were to go all out for quick results, a thoroughgoing shift of American interest to the Far East, and a dynamic United States policy that might lead to a crisis with the Soviet Union. Friendly governments, consequently, took to putting off awkward decisions, and foreign public opinion became suspicious of joint policies with the United States. This suggested to unfriendly governments the possibility of widening and exploiting these growing strains on the relations of the United States with its associates.

1953-1954

The new administration stated that "the free world would not remain indefinitely in a posture of paralyzed tension." Accordingly, "a new positive foreign policy" would be devised. It would be "a coherent, global policy."[6] As detailed statements and actions accumulated, the impression was given that vigorous action would be taken in the Far East, that trouble would be made for the Soviet Union in Eastern Europe by liberating captive peoples, that Western Europe would be pressed to make a return on the benefits it had received, and that the initiative would be snatched from Soviet policy all around the globe. The new Secretary of State and the Director of the Mutual Security Agency visited Europe in January 1953 to speed up action on the European Defense Community and visited the Middle East in May to reassess policy. Official statements linked aggression in Korea with war in Indo-China as a single Soviet-Communist policy action. National China was released from the neutralizing bonds in which it had presumably been held from the start of the Korean War. But at the same time that foreign policy seemed to be taking an active turn, the new administration was initiating domestic policies that suggested retrenchment. In April it was announced that cuts in defense spending would be recommended and that the military budget would be geared to long-term

[6] U.S. Department of State *Bulletin*, Vol. 28 (Feb. 9, 1953), p. 207.

strategic planning. Further details on this subject suggested that new weapons systems were being considered that would reduce the demands for military man power.[7]

Those two courses appeared contradictory in the view of much foreign opinion. On the one hand, the United States seemed to be stepping up the pace of resistance to Soviet policy and might cross the line that separated defensive from offensive action. On the other hand, it appeared to be economizing not only on its own rearmament, but on assisting other states to rearm.

There were many signs during 1953 that the free nations were trying to find alternatives to being pulled along in the wake of American policy. The death of Stalin in March and a lull in Soviet action that followed gave encouragement to this search. The European Defense Community Treaty was submitted in January to the French Assembly, but no effort was made to bring it to a vote. France negotiated in May a convention with the Government of the Saar that gave the territory nominal political autonomy while affirming its economic dependence on France, and then insisted that this status had to be recognized before the EDC Treaty could be ratified. Burma discontinued its acceptance of American aid in March. Disorders increased in Tunisia and Morocco, and the Sultan of Morocco was deposed in August. In June, Egypt became a republic and continued to press Great Britain to withdraw from the Suez Canal Zone; and the Iranian oil controversy continued unsettled, but here the United States brought pressure by withholding further economic aid.

In April armistice negotiations began again in Korea and were concluded at the end of July. One of the armistice articles ambiguously called for a political conference on Korea within three months. The Republic of Korea objected. The states of Asia led by India demanded a voice in the discussions. The General Assembly of the United Nations felt that the Soviet Union should participate. The United States, with no wish to submit its general purposes in the Far East to international criticism, wanted to restrict the participants as much as possible. But the heat was on, and the United States retreated step by step from an extreme posi-

---

[7] This was "the new look" and "more bangs for a buck." To public opinion in the free world, it indicated nuclear and thermonuclear war as the basic American concept, an idea that was given further credence by the subsequent formulation by the United States of the concept of "massive retaliation" for future acts of aggression.

tion. It did, however, conclude a mutual defense treaty with the Korean Republic in August, initiated a similar agreement with Japan in July, expressed a clear interest in Formosa, made gestures to India about participation in the conference, earmarked $385 million in additional aid for use by the French in Indo-China in September, and declared a general intention of moving toward a Pacific security pact. Procedural discussions looking to a political conference were begun in October, just under the deadline of three months, but they came to nothing and were broken off by the United States in December.

Long before this point was reached, however, the Korean question was lost among larger items. What was happening was that the United States was being pulled, pushed, cajoled, and pressured toward some sort of conference with the Soviet Union. After a long period of apparent rigidity in the international situation, the United States seemed to be losing control. A sense of relief was felt by many states, and some showed an inclination to maneuver more freely for position. In April the Soviet Union suggested a "Big Five" peace pact, bringing in Communist China. In May the British Prime Minister proposed a meeting with Soviet representatives "at the highest level." In July the United States, along with the governments of Great Britain and France, proposed instead a conference on Germany and Austria. In August the Soviet Union replied that the conference should also consider ways of reducing international tension generally, and that Communist China should take part. A few weeks later a second Soviet note suggested a German peace conference. The Western powers repeated in September their suggestion of a conference on Germany. Finally, at the end of November, the Soviet Union agreed to meet in Berlin in January 1954 without prior conditions. In anticipation, the three allied powers met in Bermuda in December 1953 to prepare a common position, only to find that they had little to consult about.

These professional exchanges at the governmental level were good enough for the United States. They avoided action and put off the moment of confrontation. They did not, however, reduce the public demand for such a confrontation. This had grown through 1953 in Europe, in the uncommitted states of Asia, and even in the United States. The official United States position was buffeted on the one side by demands for a general conference, ostensibly about Korea, but inevitably about broader Far Eastern problems, and on the other side for a conference about Germany that might open out to cover the world. The fact that the Soviet Union had exploded a thermonuclear device in August 1953 did not increase American enthusiasm for a meeting.

In a very important sense, other United States actions blew hot and cold on this pressure to negotiate. Early in 1953 the American search for a "new look" in rearmament had met the European search for ways of reducing the costs of their defense obligations under NATO, and the North Atlantic Council approved a "long haul" schedule of defense planning in April. But in the American view, the new concept did not permit a relaxation of effort. On the contrary, it required a firmer, continuous commitment of resources and a fairer distribution of effort throughout the alliance.

The United States accordingly continued to press its NATO associates to this end, although with decreasing success. At the December 1953 meeting of the North Atlantic Council, the Secretary of State spoke of a possible "agonizing reappraisal" of United States policy toward Europe.[8] He was referring specifically to the continued unwillingness of French governments to proceed to the ratification of the European Defense Community Treaty. At the same time, partly to compensate for this resistance from NATO members, the United States proceeded to extend its security arrangements elsewhere. An agreement for base rights was signed in September with Spain. An agreement was signed in October with Greece for the development and joint use of airfields and naval facilities. In September emergency aid to Iran in the amount of $45 million was announced;[9] and conversations were opened with Pakistan on military and economic assistance, producing a violent and antagonistic reaction in India.

The United States became increasingly sensitive to the awkwardness of the position into which it was being edged. It was being pressed toward a conference with the Soviet Union, yet signs were accumulating that it might be dangerously isolated at such a conference. It had disagreed with its European allies about the desirability of having the meeting, and alternatively about the substance of the meeting if one had to be held. The major uncom-

---

[8] U. S. Department of State *Bulletin,* Vol. 30 (Jan. 4, 1954), p. 5.

[9] Mossadegh had fallen from power in August. Iran and Great Britain resumed diplomatic relations in December.

mitted states of Asia were in open opposition to its Far Eastern policies. Above all, there was a perceptible tone in free world opinion that regarded United States policy as preoccupied with military security and the development of a strategic air-atomic capability, and as indifferent to the larger interest of mankind in peace and plenty.

With these considerations in mind, the President interrupted the Bermuda meeting to propose to the General Assembly of the United Nations an "Atoms-for-Peace" program. He said in effect that the United States was prepared, in accordance with a specific plan to be agreed by interested states including the Soviet Union, to make atomic energy available for the peaceful development of the international community. Such a plan was, of course, to go hand in hand with the control of atomic weapons. The public reaction to this proposal was all that a public relations expert could have desired. Its practical result, however, was to add to, not to diminish, the pressures for an international conference.

Significant tendencies in the international situation were clearly indicated as the year 1954 opened. The United States no longer had manifestly concentrated in its hands, as it did in 1950, the power of decision with respect to the courses of action of its European allies. Similarly, the capacity of the United States, Great Britain, and France to set a direction for the entire free world had been reduced. Even in these three major states, public feeling had moved somewhat away from official policy, and the freedom of action of the governments of these states tended to be more circumscribed. These were, at the start of 1954, tendencies only, but they were not reversed during the year.

The foreign ministers of the four major powers met in Berlin at the end of January 1954 for the first time since 1949. The Western foreign ministers concentrated on German unification, carefully guarding their proposals to ensure that the resulting Germany would not be a Soviet satellite. The Soviet foreign minister rejected these proposals and offered instead a plan designed to prevent a unified Germany from entering the defense system of Western Europe. There was nothing in these positions that was open for negotiation, and the final communiqué reported only inability to reach agreement on the German and Austrian questions and on the problem of European security. The four powers did, however, agree to meet in April, adding Communist China to their number, to consider the issues of Korea and Indo-China.

The United States had neither expected nor sought at this conference any solution so far as Germany was concerned. It considered that a necessary gesture had been made, and that the onus of failure had more or less been put on the Soviet Union. The United States was, accordingly, free to continue its policy of integrating Western Germany with the security arrangements of Western Europe. Some fears were felt, however, about the approaching conference in April on the Far East.

Between the end of January 1954 and the opening of this conference, the international situation became more fluid still. The Communist forces in Indo-China, equipped by Communist China, attacked the strong point of Dienbienphu, which France had defined as a symbol of a new Indo-Chinese strategy. The Republic of Korea acted recalcitrantly, announcing that the Berlin agreement to negotiate a settlement was "an audacious deception," that the Korean armistice had been "killed," and that the South Koreans would be "justified" in marching north against the Communists.[10] India formally and loudly protested any mutual defense agreement between the United States and Pakistan. The United States went on, however, with its conversations, and in addition, encouraged Pakistan and Turkey to negotiate a treaty of mutual defense. This was signed early in April.

Bearing more closely on the American concern with NATO, a local movement to free Cyprus from Great Britain became active in March, and in March and April a new government in Egypt brought increased pressure on Great Britain to pull out of the Suez Canal Zone, and nationalist terrorism in Tunisia and Morocco mounted.[11] By April also the French were engaged in a losing battle at Dienbienphu and their political controls in Indo-China were rapidly dwindling. The United States, although con-

[10] *New York Times* (Feb. 11, 1954).

[11] Cyprus was being developed as an alternative Middle East base to the Suez Canal Zone. One or the other, or both, were to be part of the Mediterranean defense structure of NATO. Trouble in North and West Africa not only affected NATO air and naval bases in that area, but also resulted in France transferring three divisions from the NATO command to Africa to control the situation. France reached a settlement with Tunisia at the end of July. Great Britain and Egypt reached an agreement about the Canal Zone in August. The troubles in Cyprus and Morocco were still serious at the end of 1954.

sidering the idea for a moment, found it impossible to intervene in force in the absence of supporting domestic opinion and in the face of the resistance of its associates.

The Geneva conference on Korea and Indo-China opened in this atmosphere on April 26, 1954. France was determined to get out of the Indo-Chinese struggle. The United States refused to be party to any agreement that involved recognition of Communist China. Great Britain took the initiative in handling a very complex series of negotiations between France and Communist China; among France, the Indo-Chinese states, and representatives of the successful Indo-Chinese Communist forces; and between France and the United States. The United States had almost nothing to bargain with, and it had no alternative policy to act on except the unacceptable one of separating itself from its NATO associates in order to follow a unilateral course in the Far East. While the talks were proceeding, the French forces capitulated at Dienbienphu. The end result was a cease-fire and partitioning of Indo-China. The United States neither approved the agreement nor associated itself with the implementing declaration. The conference did not succeed in addressing itself to a Korean settlement.[12]

The United States then began to repair its weakened position in the Far East. In company with Great Britain and France it initiated conversations that in September resulted in the Southeast Asia Collective Defense Treaty.[13] It affirmed, jointly with South Korea, an intention to move forward in accordance with the United Nations Charter and with the resolutions of the General Assembly to "a unified, democratic, and independent Korea"; an affirmation that was somewhat blotted when, the next day, the President of the Korean Republic called United States policy "short-sighted" and remarked that it had "not got common guts enough to face the problem."[14] Later in October it was reported that the United States would no longer follow a "soft policy" toward the Republic of Korea. Nevertheless, a mutual security treaty with Korea came into effect in November. These actions tended to separate the United States from the general drift of

---

[12] The significant feature of the conference was the fact that the West, in default of a willingness to redress the situation militarily, was actually negotiating an armistice in a struggle that it was losing.

[13] The signatories were Australia, France, Great Britain, New Zealand, Pakistan, the Philippines, Thailand, and the United States.

[14] New York Times (Aug. 1, 1954).

Asian opinion and to identify it with an Asian minority rather than to re-establish an American influence in the Far East.

But the major United States diplomatic effort was made in Europe. The United States sought concrete results on the issue of German rearmament. It had, however, by this time so committed itself to the concept of a European Defense Community that it had no alternative prepared when the French National Assembly in August 1954 finally refused to ratify the treaty. The only positively suggested alternative—a complete re-examination of the United States position and commitments in Europe—had been more in the nature of a threat to France than a feasible course of action.[15] Other alternatives—agreement with the Soviet Union to keep Germany disarmed and neutralized, or the basing of American security policy on Germany rather than on France—never left the realm of the theoretical.

The initiative again fell to Great Britain, this time with American approval, for the United States had now concluded that the European states themselves were the only possible source of a workable solution. A nine-nation meeting, guided largely by Great Britain, was held in London at the end of September. An alternative was developed, largely because Great Britain committed four divisions and a tactical air force permanently to the defense of Western Europe, and the United States reaffirmed its commitments to NATO. This alternative was to restore full sovereignty to the Western German state, to amend the Brussels Pact so that Germany and Italy could accede to it, and to convert the dead European Defense Community into a Western European Union with a Council to control armed forces, munitions, and military equipment.[16]

The necessarily complicated approval—nine-power, NATO, and national parliaments—of these linked proposals was completed by the end of 1954. France attempted to obtain a final verdict on the disposition of the Saar as part of the arrangement, but in effect failed. The Soviet Union, after having at first assumed that

---

[15] This threat had, however, been pushed to the extent that the United States Congress insisted that no American military supplies should be delivered to countries that refused to ratify the treaty.

[16] France agreed to go along with the inclusion of Western Germany in NATO and in the Western European Union. The German Federal Republic agreed to accept limitations on its military forces, not to manufacture atomic, chemical, and biological weapons, and not to use force to unify Germany or to modify its present boundaries.

the defeat of the European Defense Community Treaty was a victory for its policy of obstruction, returned vigorously to the attack. It threatened Germany with permanent partition. It informed the British and French governments that it would annul its nonaggression treaties with them, and did so in May of the following year. It flooded France with information about the dangers of German unification. And it proposed a four-power conference on German unification, warning that it would take up the matter directly with the Federal Republic if such a conference were not held before the new defense proposals were ratified. The Western allies replied that it would be useful to consider an Austrian treaty, but that the Soviet proposal contained nothing new and was "openly and explicitly aimed at delaying or preventing the ratification of the [new] agreements."[17]

Although a big hurdle in Europe was thus jumped, other obstacles appeared elsewhere before the end of 1954. Some of the more important uncommitted states began talking about a joint policy line. Yugoslavia and India stated an informal policy of nonalignment, insisting that no bloc action was anticipated, but merely a positive, constructive effort to achieve peace collectively. The Asian prime ministers, who had conferred in April 1954, were preparing a conference of Afro-Asian states for early 1955. India, after defining the SEATO defense arrangement as running counter to a "trend of peaceful thinking in south-east Asia,"[18] accepted a Soviet offer to erect a steel mill and admitted Soviet technicians. Japan had become restless under its dependence on the United States and cast about for alternative courses of action, of which the most attractive was the revival of commercial relations with the Chinese mainland. The conflict in Cyprus became more ominous. Turkey joined in on the side of Great Britain. The Greek Government tried unsuccessfully to get the question before the United Nations. The United States, having voted against the request, was heartily abused by the Greek press. When at British and American prompting, Iraq showed an interest in joining the Turkish-Pakistani defense pact, Egypt took counter steps to maintain the authority and influence of the Arab League. It repeated that its defense policy rested on the collective security pact of the Arab League and that this pact excluded alliance with nonmember

[17] U.S. Department of State *Bulletin*, Vol. 31 (Dec. 13, 1954), p. 901.
[18] *New York Times* (Aug. 27, 1954).

states. It refused to accept arms from the United States because the offer involved signing a mutual defense agreement. It called a meeting of the Arab League Council for January 1955, and announced that it would demand the expulsion of Iraq.

It was reasonably certain that these developments—indicating as they did the success with which the smaller uncommitted states of the free world could maneuver—would continue in 1955 unchanged and unresolved. Increasing strain between the governments of the major allies, increasing wariness on the part of the United States and the Soviet Union as they moved closer to a "summit meeting" and tried to prepare positions in anticipation of the next stage in their relations, increasing restraints on the American administration following the congressional election of 1954 that put the opposition party in control—all combined to reduce the checks that might otherwise have been attempted. But perhaps most significant of all, the fact that these developments could take place indicated that the international system had undergone some important alterations in the course of ten years, and that the position and possible role of the United States might need reassessment. There was even some evidence that Soviet policy makers found themselves confronted by the same general question.

1955

In January the Soviet Union and Yugoslavia signed a trade agreement. Iraq and Turkey negotiated a defensive alliance that was promptly denounced by Egypt, which called a meeting of the Arab League to expel Iraq. Nevertheless, in February the Turkish-Iraqi agreement became the basis of the Baghdad Pact.[19] The original American initiative, taken in 1953 when United States policy in the Middle East was comprehensively reviewed, thus resulted in one more regional security arrangement.

In March, however, Greece actively entered the conflict in Cyprus and raised what had been a localized issue to the level of a NATO problem. In March also the Soviet Union took the electrifying step of inviting the Austrian Government to discuss a state treaty.

---

[19] Pakistan, on the basis of an earlier treaty with Turkey, joined the pact in September. Iran, in spite of Soviet warnings, joined shortly afterward. Great Britain also adhered and became the major power core of strength. The United States withheld formal commitment, but set up informal contacts.

The negotiations were completed in April, and the United States, Great Britain, and France were invited to join with the Soviet Union to wind up the business. With what can be called timorous satisfaction, the invitation was accepted, and a treaty was signed in May. Meanwhile, in April, Egypt, after failing to make its point in the Arab League about Iraq, announced that it had entered into barter trade agreements with the Soviet Union and Rumania.

In April also the states of Africa, the Middle East, and Asia met at Bandung in Indonesia, and collectively asserted their independence of action in the international system. The tone of the conference slightly confused both Soviet-Communist and United States policy, because neither could find much ground for either comfort or despair in the proceedings. Each could, however, find evidence of a composite resistance to its objectives.

May was a month of great international activity. The German Federal Republic became, with the signing of the Paris agreements, a sovereign state and a member of NATO. The Austrian state treaty was signed in Vienna. The two highest Soviet officials paid a visit to Yugoslavia to restore relations and returned with a declaration of friendship and collaboration.

But the important event of May was the decision of the United States to accede to the pressure for a meeting with the Soviet Union "at the summit." The Secretary of State had gone to the North Atlantic Council early in the month with instructions to work out an invitation to such a meeting. His instructions were guarded: "The invitation itself should make clear that the meeting was not for the purpose of solving specific problems, but was rather to inaugurate new efforts for solution and, if possible, to infuse these efforts with a new and hopeful spirit." The decision was later explained as follows:

The success of Western policies coupled with consequent apparent change of attitude on the part of the Soviet Union indicated that the time had come when a meeting at the level of Heads of Government might usefully be held. Sentiment for this had found increasing expression in France during the debate of the Paris Accords by the French Senate. It was also manifest in Great Britain during the general election campaign. In the United States . . . [the] Chairman of the Foreign Relations Committee . . . publicly expressed himself as favorable to such a meeting.[20]

[20] U.S. Department of State, *The Geneva Conference of Heads of Government* (October 1955), p. 2.

On the fringes of the approaches of the major states but relevant to the context in which they would meet, Turkey announced a vital interest in the Cyprus dispute, Great Britain called a tripartite British-Greek-Turkish conference for a later date, and France and Tunisia reached a basis for settling the future of the Tunisian state—an agreement, however, that stimulated more vigorous nationalist efforts in Morocco and Algeria. But the focal point in June was preparations for the summit meeting. The Soviet Union invited the Chancellor of the German Federal Republic to come to Moscow for talks. Before accepting, the Chancellor went to Washington where it was agreed that neither party would deal with the Soviet Union on matters involving the rights of the other without prior consultation. It was also agreed that the visit to Moscow should take place only if it did not imply recognition of the Eastern German Government. Finally, it was understood that the Western powers, at the summit conference, would try to pave the way for the unification of Germany, would reject proposals to neutralize Germany, and would maintain the right of Germany to enter into collective security arrangements. Later in the month, the foreign ministers of Great Britain, France, and the United States met in New York City to prepare a common position. Still further conversations were held at San Francisco during the United Nations commemorative celebration, including some with the Soviet foreign minister.

These labors carried over into July. An advance working party (American, British, and French, with Western Germans on the side lines) was set up in Paris. A special meeting of the North Atlantic Council was held to review the situation and the Western positions. And on July 18 the Geneva Conference of the Heads of Government began. It ended on July 23 with a formal directive to the foreign ministers of the four powers to meet later in the year to consider three questions: (1) European Security and Germany, (2) Disarmament, and (3) Development of Contacts between East and West.

The record of the conference, as it has been made available, indicates a close adherence to the agreed purpose and predetermined tone of the meeting. The United States was intent on doing away with the judgment that its policy was provocative and intransigent and with recovering its influence over free world opinion. The Soviet Union was intent on establishing the opinion that it was seeking a reasonable accommodation with the West, with several possible ends in view—to strengthen the tendency that existed in the West to relax its defensive efforts, to give itself a breathing space in which to estimate the international situation and decide its next line of attack, and perhaps to test the chances of favorable accommodation. Great Britain and France, in contrast, presented fairly concrete proposals as a basis for future negotiation. The former proposed a European security pact between the four major powers and a united Germany, and a reciprocal joint inspection system for the armed forces confronting each other in Europe. France proposed reduction of armaments under national budgetary controls and the allocation of the resources thus saved to an international fund for use in underdeveloped regions.

The United States brought a surprise proposal to the fifth plenary session. It was that the United States and the Soviet Union should exchange "blueprints" of their military establishments and arrange for aerial inspection of each other's territory, in order "to convince the world that we are providing as between ourselves against the possibility of great surprise attack," and to "make more easily attainable a comprehensive system of inspection and disarmament."[21] The Soviet Union, less surprisingly, proposed a General European Treaty on Collective Security in Europe, in order "to achieve concerted efforts by all European states . . . instead of the formation of groupings," and to "facilitate the earliest possible settlement of the German problem through the unification of Germany." Less surprisingly still, the Soviet Union proposed a joint declaration of the four powers in which each would undertake "not to be the first to use atomic and hydrogen weapons against any country."[22]

All of these proposals were referred to the foreign ministers for consideration, and the meeting "at the summit" was adjourned. The character of the meeting was described by the United States Secretary of State.

The Conference did not press national viewpoints to a point where there would have been a breakdown, which would have dimmed the hopes of future peace. On the other hand, the Conference avoided the equal danger of creating an illusion that all was now so well that we could safely relax our efforts to build individual and collective self-defense.[23]

[21] *Ibid.*, p. 58.
[22] *Ibid.*, pp. 48, 56.
[23] *Ibid.*, p. 88.

The reaction of world opinion to the conference—a reaction that was in general encouraged rather than checked by the participants—is well expressed by the journalists' phrase, "the Geneva spirit." This phrase expressed the illusions that the United States feared and that the Soviet Union encouraged, the grounds for relaxing effort that the United States and NATO feared and that the Soviet Union wished to inculcate, the exposure to the pressures for accommodation that both the United States and the Soviet Union sought to avoid until they had reviewed its significance for their relations and policies, and lastly, the encouragement that the smaller states took in the effectiveness of their policies of noncommitment.

Between July 1955 and the convening of the conference of foreign ministers at Geneva at the end of October, the international situation became much more confused by action on all of these cross purposes. In July the Japanese Diet refused to vote on the National Defense Bill. South Korea demanded the removal of the Neutral Supervisory Armistice Commission of the United Nations. In August the United States and Communist China began talks at the ambassadorial level. Japanese officials visited Washington and left with the understanding that the existing security agreement would be replaced as soon as possible by a mutual defense agreement, that United States forces would be progressively withdrawn from Japan, and that the United States was aware of the Japanese need to trade with Asia. France and Morocco began talks that led in September to a considerable change in French policy toward the national claims of its protectorate. The German Federal Republic reported to NATO that its rearmament plans called for the creation of twelve divisions in three years.

In September the pace increased. Burma rejected the concept of a Southeast Asian pact and refused all economic aid through SEATO channels. The British-Greek-Turkish conference on Cyprus opened, but was suspended after violent anti-Greek riots in Turkey. The Greek Government withdrew its forces from NATO exercises that were being conducted in the Mediterranean, and a NATO commander was sent to mediate the awkward situation. France walked out of the United Nations General Assembly when it voted to put the issue of Algerian nationalism on its agenda.[24]

[24] A resolution to this effect, which had been introduced by fourteen Afro-Asian delegations, had been rejected by the General Committee. The decision

In the same month, the Chancellor of the German Federal Republic went to Moscow. There emerged from this conference an agreement to establish diplomatic relations, provided that German prisoners of war still in the Soviet Union were released. The long-term significance of the agreement was unclear. It was only certain that the Soviet Union was the sole former occupying power that now had official direct relations with both German governments. The Chancellor stated that it would be regarded as an unfriendly act if governments in diplomatic relations with the Federal Republic were to establish similar relations with the East German regime. The member states of NATO approved this interpretation, but the ability of the Federal Republic to maintain the position still remained to be tested. Before September was past, the Soviet Union and Eastern Germany signed a treaty that was accompanied by an exchange of letters putting the control of Berlin traffic in East German hands. These agreements seemed designed to force the Federal Republic to deal with the Eastern regime. East German officials asserted that unrestricted sovereignty had been granted, including the right to negotiate directly the reunification of Germany. The Western powers formally rejected the suggestion that there was a state in the Soviet zone, reaffirmed that the Federal Republic alone spoke for Germany internationally, and stated that this would be their position at the approaching Geneva conference of foreign ministers.

These events had a familiar quality. Not so the Egyptian announcement at the end of September that it had arranged to obtain armaments from Czechoslovakia in exchange for cotton and rice. This was followed early in October by a Soviet announcement that it was prepared to give Egypt, or any other Arab state, assistance in carrying out major economic development projects. The United States, Great Britain, and France officially expressed grave concern. The British Prime Minister, commenting later on these

---

of the General Committee had been reversed by the Assembly, by a vote of 28 to 27, with 5 absentions. U.N. General Assembly, Tenth Session, Plenary, *Official Records*, 530th Meeting (Sept. 30, 1955) , p. 196.

In October the Afro-Asian bloc, concerned by the implications of its earlier success, devised a formula under which the decision was undone, and France returned to the General Assembly. The Indian delegate was careful to explain, however, that this action was merely procedural: it implied no change in political, juridical, or moral judgments about the case. U. N. General Assembly, Tenth Session, Plenary, *Official Records*, 548th Meeting (Nov. 25, 1955), pp. 380-81.

actions, spoke for the United States as well when he said: "It is fantastic to pretend that this deliberate act of policy was an innocent commercial transaction. . . . It is a move to gain popularity at the expense of the restraint shown by the West, and by this means . . . to make it easier for communism to penetrate the Arab world."[25]

In October with the Geneva conference approaching, the European Statute of the Saar, on which so much Franco-German negotiating effort had been spent, was rejected when put to popular vote. India praised Egyptian co-operation in developing a fruitful policy of nonalignment with either bloc, and later asserted that the way to end international tension was to dissolve all military alliances. Iran chose this moment to join the Baghdad Pact and close the defensive "northern tier" alliance on the southern border of the Soviet Union. The Soviet Union promptly charged a violation of treaty obligations.

By the end of October this stream of events, with their implications interpreted in a thousand different ways, converged on Geneva and the foreign ministers' conference. Chief among these interpretations, on the Western side, was that "the Geneva spirit" was breaking down and that the free nations had to be on their guard. A reading of the available accounts of the meeting suggests strongly that neither of the parties was prepared actually to negotiate the key issue of Germany. The Western position, in spite of being presented in a package of European security, was tied up with a proposal for German unification that could only lead to the complete consolidation of German strength in the Western security structure. The Soviet position, without reservation, brushed this aside as a pretense and offered suggestions that could only have resulted in a unified but Communist Germany. The United States, less bluntly but no less certainly, dismissed these proposals as requiring a dissolution of NATO with no concurrent agreement to dissolve the Soviet military bloc in the East. The other two items on the agenda—disarmament and East-West contacts—fell quickly by the wayside. The conference ended without any attempt being made to gloss over its failure.

The reaction—not throughout the world, but in the Western official view—was that the Geneva "honeymoon" was over and that

[25] Great Britain, British Information Service, "Official Text of Speech by . . . the Prime Minister, at the Lord Mayor's Banquet, November 9, 1955," T. 48 (Nov. 10, 1955).

both the Western allies and the Soviet Union could now return to the serious business of rigidly confronting each other. Other observers, however, noted that certain fundamental changes had taken place in the relations between the United States and the Soviet Union as well as in the relationship of each of these major powers to the international system. A more gloomy judgment was that the Soviet Union, by removing the fear that it would embark on military aggression, had acquired diplomatic freedom to exploit the lines of cleavage in the non-Communist world. The most optimistic judgment would not go beyond calling for a review of United States policies in order to make them more adaptable to a world that was freeing itself from American influence. The most objective judgment, perhaps, was to the effect that the two Geneva conferences had resulted in a clear although tacit understanding that the atomic weapon systems of the major powers had reached a point of stalemate and that these powers would not, because in the existing equilibrium of power they could not, regard atomic war as an instrument of policy. In general, this last view corresponded with the less precisely formulated reaction of world public opinion.

The total range of judgments and opinions had a common implication: either the major powers had recognized a *status quo* and would now go about their business in their own areas of control and influence; or they would develop new policies of confrontation from which the threat of general war had for the time being disappeared. Either development seemed to favor the smaller states by opening up for them greater freedom of maneuver and greater opportunities for influencing the actions of the major powers. But the precise form that subsequent developments would take was, of course, still undetermined at the end of the year.

Meanwhile, in the weeks that remained, evidence was produced that supported all of these judgments. The heads of the Soviet state made a spectacular tour of Southeast Asia. In the course of a journey that covered India, Burma, and Afghanistan, they made it clear that Soviet policy was being effectively directed to the uncommitted states of the former colonial areas. Nationalist neutralist policies were praised. Nationalist economic policies were encouraged. Trade and technical assistance were freely promised, and negotiations to these ends were quickly set in motion. Anticolonial feelings were exploited in every possible way. Public speaking was on an unlimited scale and unrestrained in content. The Soviet Premier set the general tone.

Attempts are still being made to push . . . [the people of Asia] off the path of peaceful development and on to the path of militarisation and preparations for a new war. It is this purpose, incidentally that lies behind all kinds of military pacts and blocs knocked together in South-East Asia, in the Near East, and also in other areas of the world. They arouse the justified suspicion of the peoples of Asia, because sponsoring them are the forces which at one time implanted and defended the colonial order.[26]

At the end of November, the signatories of the Baghdad Pact met in Iraq and set up a permanent defense organization. The United States, although it resisted suggestions that it adhere to the pact, implied that American economic and military assistance, formerly provided under bilateral agreements to members of the pact, might now be channeled to them through the new organization. In December the North Atlantic Council held its regular meeting, and noted that Soviet tactics and increased military capabilities had "created new problems and a new challenge to the free world." It also recommended that NATO forces be equipped with "the most modern weapons," that a common air defense and warning system be constructed in Europe, and that Article 2 of the treaty—specifying economic co-operation—be more effectively acted upon.[27] On the other hand, some NATO members acted in terms of relaxation rather than increased effort at collective security. Great Britain announced a reduction in its armed forces of 100,000 men over a period of thirty months. Norway reaffirmed that bases on its territory would not be available except in case of war or threat of war. France continued to transfer units out of the NATO command to North Africa. Other members reduced the length of the period of national military service.

In December there were some stirrings of Soviet policy in Germany. The control of the zonal boundary was transferred to the East German regime. That government was also made responsible for traffic into West Berlin. The Soviet Union was apparently setting up a situation by which it hoped to force the German Federal Republic to negotiate with the East German regime as with a

[26] N. A. Bulganin and N. S. Krushchev, "Full Texts of Speeches and Statements in India, Burma and Afghanistan," *Soviet News* (London, 1955), p. 20.
[27] U.S. Department of State *Bulletin,* Vol. 32 (Jan. 3, 1955), pp. 10-12.

sovereign state. The West German Government reaffirmed its refusal to admit the existence of a legal government in the East. Considerable political pressure developed for bilateral negotiations with the Soviet Union on unification although it was clear enough that the Soviet Union could convert such an effort into a negotiation between Eastern and Western Germany.

The General Assembly of the United Nations also showed a high-spirited appreciation of new possibilities. The smaller states, the uncommitted states, and the determined neutralists showed increasing independence of action as the Soviet-Communist bloc encouraged their expectations and supported their actions. The tangible evidence came in December when Canada proposed a resolution to break the ancient deadlock on new members. Both the United States and the Soviet Union accepted the idea of a "package" deal.[28] The long procedural wrangling that developed is not significant here. When the matter was settled, sixteen states had been admitted and the Soviet Union had traded the exclusion of Outer Mongolia, a dubious claimant, for the exclusion of Japan, a state that had been vigorously supported by the United States, but whose exclusion for the time being gave no serious offense to members of the Afro-Asian group.

Finally, in the period following the second Geneva conference, the United States began to review its position and its policies, starting with an effort to reappraise Soviet capabilities and intentions. This process was still in its initial stages when the year ended, but certain points had begun to stand out. It was officially concluded, for example, that the phase "violence and threats of violence" in major state relations had fallen off. This was not seen as a change in Soviet purposes, but as a shift in tactics. It was officially maintained that this shift had been induced by United States and free world policies of collective security and by American programs of assistance.[29] The United States did not want a

[28] Eighteen applications were under consideration. Twelve of them had United States support, but had been vetoed by the Soviet Union. Five were Communist states and had never received the necessary majority backing in the Security Council. One—Spain—had never been voted on.

[29] These policies and programs were specified by the United States Secretary of State as "political warnings" against aggression—as in NATO and other security organizations—and as readiness to implement "political warning with deterrent power." See U.S. Department of State Bulletin, Vol. 33 (Dec. 19, 1955), pp. 1003-07.

violent phase to be re-opened. Therefore, those policies and programs had to be kept alive and flexibly used. In effect, the American system of alliances would be maintained and nourished, and the American capacity to wage nuclear and thermonuclear war would be maintained.

Other sectors of official judgment went further and concluded the Soviet Union as well did not seem to want to reopen the violent phase. Instead, it was developing new patterns of policy and was flexibly using diplomatic, propaganda, and economic techniques as instruments of action. It was showing signs of having adapted its policies to changes in the influence and role of the uncommitted states in the international system. This interpretation of Soviet intentions and capabilities quickly led some United States policy makers back to the theses of the Marshall Plan and the Point Four program. Proposals began to be put out for a revived, enlarged, and redesigned policy of economic and technical assistance.

These proposals ran counter to the domestic economic policies of the administration and to its budget plans for 1956, as well as to the understanding of the Congress that all assistance programs, as distinguished from security programs, were to be progressively reduced. The result was that a discussion was re-opened on alternative ways of using American resources for foreign policy ends. When the year 1955 ended, this discussion was still confined to administration circles although some indications had been given that a tentative reversal of certain basic positions was in the making.

PART FOUR

THE POSITION OF THE UNITED STATES: 1956

CHAPTER XXII

Changes of a Decade

THE UNITED STATES and the Soviet Union were still, at the end of 1955, the two major powers in the international system. Their views of a desirable structure for this system, their interest in shaping events to create the desired structure, and their short-term objectives with respect to specific areas, countries, and situations seem to be as diametrically opposed as at any time in the past ten years. If the free world alone is considered, the United States is still the dominating influence. Even if the United States were to disengage itself from its system of alliances and to reverse its policies of assistance and support, its decisions and actions would continue to have a powerful determining effect on the policy choices available to other non-Communist and Communist states. At first glance, therefore, the position of the United States, either with respect to the Soviet Union, or with respect to the free world, does not seem to have undergone basic alteration. But this view overlooks the influences to which United States policies have become increasingly exposed. These are essentially the influences exerted by states that could not be coerced except at the expense of the objectives that United States policies are designed to reach. In a different sense, and with somewhat different implications, Soviet policy has also become exposed to similar influences.[1]

In trying to identify the major problems of foreign policy that confront the United States Government as the second postwar decade opens, various questions arise from these considerations. Is the focus of American action still the direct confrontation of Soviet power and policy? Has there been any significant change in the position of the United States in the international system? Was United States policy addressed to the same kind of world at the end of

[1] It should be understood, however, that this statement is valid only so long as neither the United States nor the Soviet Union determines that war between themselves at a reasonably certain future date is inevitable. Such a determination would commit both states to enforcing bipolarity by all the means at their disposal; that is, forcing other states to make final choices. Much of the behavior of other states in recent years becomes explicable if it is seen as an avoidance of precisely such choices.

1955 as during the greater part of the preceding decade? These are not questions that can be answered categorically. They can only be explored.

In 1945, the problems of United States foreign policy were generally conceived in political and institutional terms. Political adjustments, following from conferences and negotiations, were considered the main form of policy implementations. Two years later, a different conception had crystallized. Soviet policy was held to have ruled out a steady course of political adjustment and to have made negotiation abortive. Negotiated adjustments were then considered possible only after the United States had developed situations of strength by actions that were not necessarily designed to prepare the way for negotiation. Economic programs were the preferred form of implementation. After June 1950, American attention was focused on the possibility of overt armed aggression, and policy, although continuing to be conceived defensively, was with increasing thoroughness carried out by military assistance programs and by military action. By 1953, the defensive conception became equated with a negative failure to act, and an effort was made to restate policy positively. Of these efforts, the concept of massive retaliation created the greatest stir.[2]

The concept as it was originally stated and understood had a relatively short life. It was simply taken to mean that another adventure on the Korean model would result in a global war. Because such an adventure was conceivably in the making in Indo-China, opinion and national policies in the free world reacted strongly against the idea of massive retaliation as a basic instrument of United States policy. When, in addition to this immediate reaction, the Soviet Union exploded a thermonuclear device and appeared to be in a position to develop an equal capacity to retaliate massively, not only did the United States have to reconsider the concept, but it found itself under great international pressure to

---

[2] Massive retaliation—at times and places of American choosing—rested on the assumption that the Soviet Union and the other Communist powers could, by choosing peripheral points for local acts of aggression, overload the American power to react and strain American resources by dispersal and attrition. It was considered necessary to find a mode of action that by increasing the probable costs of such actions, would deter the Soviet Union and its Communist allies from further adventures. The implication of the concept of massive retaliation was, however, an American military establishment geared to engage in atomic rather than in conventional warfare.

return to political adjustment as a basis for the planning and execution of its foreign policies.

Throughout 1955, the official explanation of the American reaction to these influences was that the United States had reached a position of strength from which it could afford to negotiate with the Soviet Union. The promise of German rearmament was defined as a diplomatic defeat for the Soviet Union. It was held that recent accommodating moves by the Soviet Union were a consequence of its deteriorating political position, worsened economic conditions, and confrontation by American strength. Regardless of the correctness of this explanation, it was clear that political negotiations with the Soviet Union were rising in priority as a means of executing United States foreign policy, although they were still subordinate to military measures and to the utilization of the system of alliances.

The considerations affecting action in foreign policy had, however, shifted slightly. The problem was becoming one of maintaining sufficient public alertness at home and abroad so that the process of negotiation would not result in a reduction of the strength without which negotiations could not succeed. From 1948 to 1953, public fear and suspicion in the United States had prevented any latitude in relations with the Communist powers. However, in 1955 feeling in both the United States and the free world seemed to be placing so much emphasis on negotiation that it threatened to force the administration into compromises it desired to avoid. These pressures were given added weight by the increasing capacity of the uncommitted states to influence the direction of international developments.

Indeed, once a compromise armistice was reached in Korea, the American public, free world opinion, and the national policies of many free nations and of the uncommitted states combined to press for further progress toward adjustment. Official American proposals to intervene in Indo-China came to naught. Efforts to enunciate a vigorous policy in the Formosa Strait collapsed when Chinese threats gave the impression that war might indeed develop. By mid-1955, substantial bodies of public opinion were demanding that the administration negotiate its differences with both the Soviet Union and China. Whereas in 1952 one of the problems of the United States foreign policy operation had been to find sufficient public support to negotiate issues where accommodation seemed possible, the problem in 1955 was to avoid being involved in the negotiation of issues that the administration felt were not negotiable.

This situation was widely interpreted as a consequence of short-term changes in the equilibrium of relations between the free and the Communist worlds. There are grounds, however, for seeing it as a stage in the longer-term evolution of the postwar international system. United States objectives and policies were not unexpectedly confronted by wholly new factors. These objectives and policies had been adjusted to changes in the international system over a ten-year period.

Some former enemy states had become associates of the United States. Some former allies—China and the Soviet Union—had become antagonists. Specific American objectives were correspondingly modified. Action on the new lines led to changes in more general objectives. After June 1950, the United States sought to prevent the further spread of communism in the peripheral areas of Asia, and made for this purpose a commitment of resources that it had previously refused to make. Although Asia was by no means given priority over Europe, and American commitments in the Far East were limited by a consideration of the possible dangers and needs in Western Europe, some shift in short-term objectives seemed to be in the making. However, policies to reach these objectives were lost in the decay of the Western position in Indo-China, the evident ineffectiveness of defense pacts for general Far Eastern policy purposes, and the Chinese Communist threat against Formosa. The United States slowly accommodated itself to a possible necessity for negotiating major issues with Communist China.

With regard to colonial issues, United States policy in general had been to encourage national independence as a matter of principle. As relations with the Soviet Union grew worse and specific colonial issues became hotter, opposition to Communist expansion took precedence over the general principles of self-determination and national independence. However, the shift in priority was never a fixed thing. In Indo-China when it became apparent that unless independent governments were developed, the whole of an area might be lost to communism, the United States gave firm support to their development. But when similar action was apparently called for in North Africa, where the consequences of independence on the maintenance of established American bases could not safely be predicted, the American position remained indeterminate and cautious.

With respect to international organization, the policy of the United States evinced an almost steady shift away from utilizing the United Nations except as a supplementary instrument of national policy, and toward developing new organizations and facilities to deal with foreign policy problems. This development was hedged by continued support of the long-term objective of making the United Nations a key instrument for the conduct of international relations. The United States also found it operationally convenient at times to submit certain aspects of its policies to the judgment of the United Nations in order to obtain support for specific purposes.

For some years these practical adjustments in American objectives and policies had followed step by step actual changes in the structure of the international system. Their value, however, in terms of a capacity to influence the further evolution of the system, depended on their being a genuine reflection of the essential forces at work. Specifically, their usefulness depended on the international system continuing to be as bipolar as it was generally assumed to be by 1950.

It is very difficult, however, to ignore the fact that by 1955 a divergence between United States policies and the direction in which the international system was developing was beginning to show. Initially, the evidence consisted of little more than that some segments of free world opinion, which had once been inclined to accept the strategic estimates of the United States, began to show less confidence in the soundness of American judgment and to regard United States policy as irresponsible and dangerous. These feelings, which frequently ran counter to the official positions of foreign governments, precipitated political demands for independence in policy. Finally, and especially after the appearance of the thermonuclear bomb, it led to a strong and a widespread pressure for an accommodation with the Soviet Union. With this the influence of the United States on the actions of its associates began to diminish in a significant way.

This decline in influence was, however, accompanied by an actual increase in the extent and scope of the United States system of alliances; for more than one process was at work. From 1948 through 1954, the United States was successful in expanding its chain of alliances until it was almost global. But along with this development, it is possible to note a growing independence of action on the part of the states that had been longest and most closely associated with the United States. Western agreement to a Southeast Asia Collective Defense Treaty depended in part on American acquiescence to the Geneva negotiations on Indo-China. The United States was obliged to accept what was, in its view, an inferior substitute for the European Defense Community in order to retain the basic structure of the North Atlantic Treaty Organization. The capacity of the United States to work effectively for its own ends through the United Nations increasingly depended on a willingness to modify those ends to satisfy the judgments of uncommitted states.

Several factors combined to give rise to this growing freedom of action in the free world. Possibly the most important was the success of the American programs of assistance. The initiation and support of genuine processes of economic recovery, or of processes of economic growth, and the development of systems of security in which American power was involved and from which American power could not readily be withdrawn, had the cumulative effect of reviving a desire and restoring a limited capacity for national action to individual states. And this effect was produced before these states had tightly bound themselves in a complex of integrated collective activities. The associations remained and were still valid, but their method of operation had changed considerably by the end of 1955.

It still remained a matter of basic agreement between the United States and the associated states of Western Europe that relations with the Communist bloc and negotiations with the Soviet Union could only be conducted from a base of organized alliances that permitted military and diplomatic action. Within this framework, however, states could differ about the point at which negotiations might begin, about what was or was not negotiable; and they could develop varying degrees of optimism about the possibility of reaching satisfactory adjustments. The associated states no longer felt obliged to accept American guidance in these matters as the final word. They had acquired a capacity for maneuver and were secure enough to differ openly with the United States and to exert pressure on the direction and substance of United States policy.

A number of specific and individual factors reinforced this trend toward an independent foreign policy determination. These factors, distinct from the almost inevitable tendency of partially repressed national objectives to assert themselves whenever American pressure relaxed or domestic considerations became urgent, generated drives and policies that reflected internal political problems. In Great Britain, the Conservative party took office in 1952, headed by a Prime Minister and a Foreign Secretary of unimpeachable repute and experience in the field of foreign affairs. As American aid dwindled and the British economic position improved, this government felt itself free to attempt to modify what it regarded as the rigidities of United States foreign policy. Although forced into temporary retreat with respect to the Prime Minister's plan for a high level four-power meeting, the British Government returned to the charge without hesitation. This time it was the United States that conformed to the domestic political requirements of an ally and to the claims of that ally to an influential voice in joint policy.

In France in 1954, the gap between French opinion and the French Government had widened to the point where a number of the European agreements into which France had entered could not be executed. A new Premier closed the gap by giving voice to popular feeling rather than to official pronouncements. The political result was a sudden short-term capacity of France to affect decisively the course of Western policy in Europe and Southeast Asia. For a brief moment, a purely French policy was developed with heady independence. Although this spasm of free action did not last for long, the fact that it could happen at all and that, when it did, the United States had no ready alternative but to adjust to the situation, revealed the changes that were possible in the relations of the free nations.

Similar signs appeared at many points. A growing independence in the foreign policy of Western Germany was a direct consequence of the mounting German power for which the United States and the North Atlantic Treaty Organization had become suppliants. Although the German Chancellor was in some respects a prisoner of his commitment to United States foreign policy, the United States was correspondingly a prisoner of the necessity for maintaining the authority of the Chancellor. In Japan, the end of the occupation released policy aims that had previously been kept out of sight, such as negotiating a national Japanese position with Communist China and the Soviet Union. The same tendencies came clearly to the fore in the policies of the anticolonial states and achieved a considerable drive as the Asian and African nations tried to group themselves for joint action in the international system.

Finally, certain American techniques for executing policy also worked to encourage freedom of action, although without necessarily intending to do so. The new administration, tending to view the Soviet-Communist threat as long-term, was prepared to experiment with existing policy lines, seeking to reduce economic assistance and to limit specific military commitments. Consequently, the levers by which the United States had obtained acquiescence in the past grew less effective. On the other hand, and in spite of the contradiction involved in seeking quick solutions to long-term problems, the administration sought immediate and positive results from policy. Its spokesmen were inclined to press heavily on other states for supporting action. The combination was one in which freedom of action for other states was possible and one that also gave rise to a kind of irritable opposition to United States policies.

In view of these developments, the American strategy of containment and the pattern of policies by which it had been developed became increasingly hard to implement when, in the course of 1955, a shift took place in the conduct of Soviet foreign relations. The continuing success of the American strategy—and its initial success in relation to the situation to which it was addressed cannot be denied—depended on the structure of the international system remaining much as it had appeared to be in the years 1947 to 1950. This important condition was no longer being obviously fulfilled. Consequently, one of the bases of American strategy—the judgment that the Soviet threat was imminent—lost general acceptance, and a reassertion of independent national interpretations of the significance of Soviet actions followed. The values attached to defensive alliances lost their simple coherence and came more nearly to resemble the diverse claims of individual national security policies. The United States was still the dominating force in the free world, but its capacity to influence the actions of its associates arose more from the fact that it was the only common element in a chain of alliances, and had disposable force and resources, than because its objectives and its policies carried conviction to other states. In a growing number of situations in which the United States found itself committed to acting with others, it was almost as likely to be a follower as a leader.

All of this added up to a considerable change in the position of the United States. The official impulse in 1954 and 1955 was to define the change as highly unfavorable to the American interest and to consider exerting vigorous pressure to check and to reverse the trend. It was too late, however, for such half-way measures. The Soviet tactic of relaxing pressures and breathing sweetness could not be ignored. If the United States were to reject Soviet overtures out of hand, it stood to suffer a considerable further loss of influence in world politics. On the other hand, if it were to accept them, it would be difficult to negotiate without fostering public illusions that would increase the independence of allied policy, soften the allied defensive effort, and thus produce the same effect—a further reduction of American influence. To recognize the significance of the developments in the international system that had brought about this dilemma and to adjust to these developments without providing dangerous opportunities for Soviet policy, became by the end of 1955 one of the most difficult and central problems of American statecraft.

The picture that has been drawn needs, however, one more line to be reasonably complete. It has been one of the theses of this discussion that the alteration in the position of the United States was due in considerable part to a progressive and general alteration in the structure of the international system. It is important to ask whether the position of the Soviet Union was not also affected by this change and whether Soviet policies were not being subjected to critical review.

This question cannot be profitably dealt with primarily in terms of the previous estimates of Soviet intentions and capabilities. If there is any validity in conceptualizing the field of international relations, then a change in the structure of the international system that has not been deliberately brought about by the policies and actions of either of its major components should reasonably suggest that both—not merely one—will be obliged to adjust in some respects to the change. To continue this theoretical exposition one step further, the United States, confronted by a diminishing capacity to influence the actions of other states in ways favorable to its purposes, has two choices before it. It can increase its efforts to shape the international structure it desires, with all that this implies in the way of allocating resources, developing means, and checking dangerous reactions. Or it can rearrange the priorities of its objectives, modify its policies, and temper its techniques of execution to fit the new circumstances. Assuming that Soviet policy is similarly confronted by a development that lies beyond its direct control, the Soviet Union also has before it the same choices.

In addition to this purely abstract analysis, there are some concrete indicators that Soviet policies also approached a momentary dead end in the course of 1954 and early 1955. The components of the Soviet bloc were building up competing claims on Soviet resources. At least one of these components, Communist China, was becoming capable of independent action and hence able to draw Soviet policy into courses that the Soviet Government might not desire. The risks of a policy of piecemeal aggression had, in principle, if not in any given instance, increased. And above all, the uncommitted states were becoming effectively active in international politics in ways that were likely to prove as frustrating and difficult for Soviet policy as for that of the United States. Given the additional factors of internal political and economic problems, it would be very surprising if the Soviet Union had not felt at least the desirability of reviewing its position, rearranging the priorities of its objectives, and tempering its actions to fit demonstrably new circumstances.[3]

Yet the last word here must be to a different effect. The increasing freedom of action of other states has not altered the fundamental fact that the United States and the Soviet Union are still the superpowers of the international system, and that their purposes with respect to each other are still very dominating considerations in the working of that system. All that has essentially altered is the context within which these two powers move to act on their differences of purpose, their relative securities, and their policies of influencing other states to support their purposes. But this context does show signs of having been modified in the course of five years in ways that are bound to increase the complexity of policy formulation and execution for both major states, although probably more so for the United States than for the Soviet Union.

The major impression left is that the international situation has become fluid. Relations that seemed stereotyped began to get

[3] Such evidence as has been provided by Soviet action since the end of 1955 appears to support rather than to weaken this tentative suggestion.

blurred. Policies that seemed firmly knit began to unravel. Because there is no firm evidence that either the United States or the Soviet Union sought as a matter of policy to loosen up state relations, this development can be tentatively attributed to the operation of forces other than the activities of United States or Soviet policy. Observers of the international system will, no doubt, find a variety of explanations of this phenomenon. This study accepts the explanation that it is contrary to the nature of a system of normally dynamic relationships to remain rigid for any length of time. Furthermore, if the policies of some of the major components of the system tend to make it rigid, other components tend to develop policies of resistance. This counteraction, no matter how weak the position of any single participating state, accumulates strength in time and can become a significant influence on the actions of major states merely by confronting them with a changed international system. At this point, major states either adjust their objectives and policies, or exert more positive, intensified, and costly efforts to maintain their objectives and policies.

If at the present time there is a single problem of foreign policy determination that is common to the major powers, it is that of deciding whether they will adjust their objectives and policies, or will make greater efforts to achieve the purposes for which they have been acting. There is little sign of a choice having yet been made. But there is evidence that the problem has been identified and is being explored. However, it is important to realize that while it is being explored both analytically and by tentative actions, past positions are naturally reasserted and previous policies maintained and even advanced. Thus in terms of the present operations of the international system, the "Geneva spirit" of the summit conference of July 1955 is entirely compatible with the "Geneva blues" of the conference of foreign ministers in October and November.

At any rate, the flow of events and the actions of states both before and since these meetings can be interpreted in this light. The multiplication of major power contacts, the scurry of major powers visiting minor powers, the consultations among minor powers, the improvised policy surprises, the rushing out on policy limbs and the creeping back from the ends of policy limbs are the sure signs of uncertainty, reconsideration, and of a search for fresh starting points.

CHAPTER XXIII

The Framework for Policy Review

At the point where the second decade since the Second World War begins, this analytical account could conclude in one of two ways. It could take up, one by one, specific problems of policy—the German settlement, the Far Eastern question, the security of the Middle East, disarmament, and control of atomic energy—and ask what these familiar issues looked like at the start of 1956. Or it could assume that these problems, insistent and important as they are, were less important than the overriding problem of adjusting to possible changes in the structure of the international system, and to the requirements for operating successfully within it.

The second course has been chosen to permit concentration on what may be the key issues and choices of the next few years. It also permits the strategic alternatives in policy formulation and action to be examined without becoming lost in tactical detail. A further justification of this choice is that the United States Government has clearly given signs that its machinery of decision and action was being directed toward a broad and comprehensive review of the American position, the American goals, and the existing ways for approaching those goals.

This kind of review is always a difficult operation for a government to initiate and to carry through, particularly for a modern democratic state in which the power of decision tends to be dispersed. This is inevitably so in a year of national decisions. Previous goals have acquired validity merely because they have been accepted for some time and have become familiar. The policies and programs developed in relation to these goals have also acquired a life, a rationale, and a force of their own. The evidence needed to produce the conviction that change is necessary has to be very persuasive, and even then it is not likely simultaneously to persuade all those who are involved in the policy-making process.

So long as it was possible to regard the international system as essentially bipolar in structure, it was possible to make policy choices in terms of conflict between organized blocs. This basis for judgment remained valid, however, only so long as certain conditions were satisfied. For various reasons that have appeared in the course of this analysis, these conditions have been met less and less as time has gone by. Tension between the major powers, whose conflicting objectives and policies have given rise to the bipolar definition, must seem to continue to increase in order to validate the efforts and sacrifices that their respective policies call for. If not, they will be forced further away from armed conflict by other factors that operate in the international system. This criterion of increasing tension has not been met. In short, in a truly bipolar system each component bloc must be led or dominated by a polar state. Unless conscious, planned, and continuous effort is made to do this, it is only a matter of time before the polar states, in order to maintain their positions with respect to each other, find themselves adjusting their purposes and actions to the requirements of an increasingly diversified system of state relations.

Maximum-Minimum Objectives

For some years it has been assumed that the Soviet Union sought in the simplest and most direct way to dominate and control the world. The strategy of containment and the bipolar concept followed reasonably enough from this assumption. Any review of the situation by the United States inevitably takes this picture of Soviet objectives and capabilities as its starting point.

It is generally agreed that maximum Soviet objectives include the communization of the world. In the same sense, maximum American objectives include the democratization of the world. However, democracy, as we understand the term, would exclude American political domination of the world, whereas Soviet world political domination must be included as part of the process of attaining the final objectives of the Soviet-Communist movement.

Yet this statement of maximum objectives is misleading. It treats as operational what can be no more than verbal formulations of goal values. These may have little direct influence on the formulation of concrete objectives and policies. For example, world democracy is in a sense the maximum objective of United States foreign policy, but it lacks operational relevance, except on very rare occasions and under very special conditions. The same is probably true of the Soviet maximum objective of world communism. It is very doubtful, for instance, that Soviet policy has—at least since the early 1920's—been oriented to driving exclusively and consistently towards this maximum goal.

Maximum objectives, before they can become operational, have to be translated into the more realistic framework of probable world conditions, and in the process they become somewhat less than maximum. In fact, a scale of objectives, ranging from the maximum possible to the minimum acceptable, tends to be set up as a guide to concrete policy choices. Thus maximum objectives are those likely to be pursued if not fully predictable conditions evolve favorably, while minimum objectives are those likely to be pursued if conditions evolve unfavorably. These restrictions, naturally, set the limits for alternative Soviet policies. If the Soviet Union allocates resources to the furtherance of world revolution, that allocation is likely to be on a relatively small scale. However, acquisitions of territory for the sake of strategic, demographic, economic, or political advantages are immediate objectives of Soviet policy that can be interpreted as stages in the pursuit of the most theoretical maximum objectives. To counter such action, planned and costly efforts on the part of the United States may prove necessary. That the converse of this applies equally to United States maximum and minimum objectives needs no underlining. But the analytical task that policy makers perform to determine the point on a maximum-minimum scale of purpose at which they will act, and at which other states are acting, and to bring these two judgments into some sort of operational consonance, is hazardous at best. But the process is certainly at work in the United States and in the Soviet Union.

The immediate American concern is with Soviet intentions. Two concurrent lines of analysis can be noted. The first holds that institutional changes in the Soviet Union are modifying the dictatorship internally and the monolithic character of the Soviet bloc externally. The second argues that economic difficulties and fear of thermonuclear war are leading to modifications of Soviet foreign policy and are increasing the possibility that an accommodation with the Soviet bloc is attainable. In other words, Soviet objectives are, it is held, being acted upon in their minimum forms. This, however, can be confronted by a reaffirmation that the maximum Soviet objective is still operational. This position is supported by reference to Soviet capabilities, especially in nuclear and thermonuclear weapons.

Actually, it is possible for both positions to be maintained at the same time and to be regarded as indicative of possible contingencies. Both may provide accurate judgments of Soviet purposes. Therefore, for practical purposes, United States policy and Soviet intentions and capabilities have to be kept in a flexible relationship. A miscalculation concerning Soviet objectives would be dangerous if the United States were not prepared militarily to meet the most formidable line of action open to the Soviet Union. The same is true in reverse for Soviet policy makers. In addition, for both the United States and the Soviet Union, judgment in these matters cannot be divorced from the need to act on existing concrete issues.

The specific questions of this kind that confront the United States policy makers are, at the start of 1956: Is the Soviet Union prepared to draw back from its forward positions in Central Europe and, if so, under what conditions? Is this a period of general Soviet withdrawal, in which it hopes to gather strength for greater efforts in the future? Has the Soviet Union decided to rely on economic and political competition? How tight a control will the Soviet Union seek to maintain over the world Communist movement? To what extent can the West and the Soviet Union reach agreement on measures for disarmament? Must the West fear a return to localized aggression by conventional means now that the reservations against nuclear and thermonuclear weapons have been so explicitly stated? How long will it be before technological advances remove these reservations? Where, among all these questions, does accommodation lie, and what could be its substance?

Within this general framework of estimate, judgment, specific questions, and concrete issues, any re-examination of the position of the United States must proceed. Such re-examination will be directed: first, to drawing a working picture of Soviet objectives, both maximum and minimum; second, to matching this picture with a view of the way in which the international system is now likely to operate; and third, to a reformulation of American purposes and to a re-examination of American capabilities. From this process will presumably be derived restated policies with restated objectives, adapted to meet Soviet intentions and capabilities in the prevailing circumstances.

In what follows there is no intention of trying to predict the form or the substance of the specific choices that will be made from among the alternatives that now seem available.[1] No more will be attempted than an identification of the key matters on which some sort of choice is likely to be necessary, and a listing of the essential considerations that are most likely to bear on the choice.

Report to the Nation: 1956

Early in January 1956, the President's State of the Union Message was read to the Congress. Under the heading of "The Discharge of Our World Responsibility," the message gave what was presumably a statement of the general conclusions reached in the preliminary official review of the American position. Both theoretical and practical maximum objectives were stated, and by implication, past patterns of purpose and policy were evaluated. The message summarized these as follows:

Our world policy and our actions are dedicated to the achievement of peace with justice for all nations.

With this purpose, we move in a wide variety of ways . . . to remove the pall of fear; to strengthen the ties with our partners and to improve the cooperative cohesion of the free world; to reduce the burden of armaments. . . . These national objectives are fully supported by both our political parties. . . .

[At] the July meeting of heads of government . . . [all] were in agreement that a nuclear war would be an intolerable disaster. . . . But in October, when the Foreign Ministers met again, the results demonstrated conclusively that the Soviet leaders are not yet willing to create the indispensable conditions for a secure and lasting peace.

Nevertheless it is clear that the conflict between international communism and freedom has taken on a new complexion.

. . . Communist tactics . . . have shifted in emphasis from reliance on violence and the threat of violence to reliance on division, enticement, and duplicity. We must be well prepared to meet the current tactics which pose a dangerous though less obvious threat. At the same time, our policy must be dynamic as well as flexible, designed primarily to forward the achievement of our own objectives rather than to meet each shift and change on the Communist front.

. . . We must, of course, continue to maintain an effective system of collective security. This involves two things—a system which gives clear warning that armed aggression will be met by joint action of the free nations, and deterrent military power to make that warning effective.

---

[1] Attention is called to the tentative and qualified nature of this analysis and of Chapter XXIV, below. See also Appendix B, "Contingencies and Choices: 'The Problem Approach.'"

Moreover, the awesome power of the atom would be made to serve as a guardian of the free community and of the peace.

Next the message noted "major gains for the system of collective security" in the form of "security pacts with more than 40 other nations."

. . . We have been steadfast in our support of the United Nations, now entering its second decade with a wider membership and ever-increasing influence and usefulness.

. . . The crucial problem of disarmament has moved to the forefront of practical political endeavor. . . . The issue is placed squarely before the bar of world opinion. . . .

In Asia we shall continue to give help to nations struggling to maintain their freedom against the threat of Communist coercion or subversion. In Europe, we shall endeavor to increase not only the military strength of the North Atlantic Alliance but also its political cohesion and unity of purpose. . . .

In the Near East . . . [the] United States is ready to do its part to assure enduring peace in that area. . . .

Strong economic ties are an essential element in our free world partnership. . . .

This was followed by a request to the Congress to approve United States membership in the Organization for Trade Cooperation as "evidence [of] our continuing desire to cooperate in promoting an expanded trade among the free nations."

Because the conditions of poverty and unrest in less developed areas make their people a special target of international communism, there is a need to help them achieve the economic growth and stability necessary to preserve their independence.

. . . They need assurance of continuity in economic assistance for development projects and programs . . . which require a period of years for planning and completion. Accordingly, I ask Congress to grant limited authority to make longer-term commitments for assistance to such projects. . . .

The various steps will powerfully strengthen the economic foundation of our foreign policy . . . will maintain the present momentum toward general economic progress and vitality of the free world.

Under the heading of "The Constant Improvement of our National Security," a relevant supporting statement was made.

Because peace is the keystone of our national policy, our defense program emphasizes an effective flexible type of power calculated to deter or repulse any aggression and to preserve the peace. . . . The maintenance of this strong military capability for the indefinite future will continue to call for a large share of our national budget. Our military programs must meet the needs of today. To build less would expose the Nation to aggression. To build excessively, under the influence of fear, could defeat our purposes and impair or destroy the very freedom and economic system our military defenses are designed to project.[2]

This message has been quoted at length in order to provide the means of determining the extent to which the United States policy pattern has been relevantly reviewed, or merely reaffirmed. For the purposes of this study, only one or two major points need be singled out. The first is that the essential policy pattern of the past decade is still considered applicable. The second is that the international system still seems to be conceived as tending toward bipolarity. The third is that only very general note is taken of the policy difficulties that would follow if the system were tending to be diversified and if an equilibrium of nuclear weapons were to force major state action into nonmilitary channels.

Key Questions Reopened

The evidence of the years 1955-56 suggests that the last point may turn out to be a major consideration in the design and execution of specific courses of action. The specific problems, at least the specific areas in which the key problems of American-Soviet, or free world-Communist world relations exist, are still much the same. They are Germany and Central Europe, Southeast Asia, and the Middle East. The problems of these areas are still subsumed in the more comprehensive problem of competing security organizations and systems.

Also from the point of view of the accepted approaches of the United States to these problems, the alternatives that have been argued for ten years are to some extent still open for reargument. In this way, it is still possible for the courses that were previously selected to be diverted or distorted. The extent of United States participation in a collective security system; the kind of participation; the geographic range in which policy should operate; and the kind and the degree of accommodation with the Soviet Union that should or can be sought: these are all issues that are certain to be reopened if the existing pattern of purpose and action should run into trouble because the international system has become less

[2] All quotations from *The State of the Union*, Message from the President of the United States, H. Doc. 241, 84 Cong. 2 sess. (Jan. 5, 1956).

receptive to its operation. From these may develop an examination of a very basic question: What kind of structure of the international system is at the maximum desired by, or at the minimum acceptable to, the United States?

The Soviet Union has been comparatively explicit about both its maximum and minimum objectives in this respect. Where does, or where should, the United States stand on the same question?

Some groups in the United States had fully expounded the thesis that these questions had little relevance to the American interest and that the valid course for the United States was to act unilaterally and to participate with other states only to a minimum degree. The highest level of the government, however, as well as the acknowledged leaders of both political parties, had consistently rejected this concept in all of the forms in which it was presented. Consequently, a long period of participation has created patterns of policy, bureaucratic structures, and habits of acceptance that would probably make it extremely difficult to develop alternative answers. Yet the conditions for which the choice to participate was originally made may have been significantly altered. Participation meant, from 1947 to 1955, acting with other states to organize a collective security structure in order to confront another, and a threatening, power bloc. In this sense, it was relatively easy to define a policy of alliances and assistance as a real alternative to nonparticipation and to have it accepted as valid.

If, however, the threatening bloc appears to many to be less immediately threatening, or if the power behind the threat seems to have been negated for the moment by an equivalent power to resist, and if the American security structure seems to be less and less organized because the international system is becoming more and more diversified, participation means something different. Its requirements then become highly diversified also, calling for flexible action in the total field of international relations rather than for co-operative collective action within that part of the field called the free world. The issue becomes one of developing modified patterns of participation to meet changed conditions, without being pressed to the extreme alternative of acting on a decisive policy of nonparticipation.

Where, for example, does a policy of alliances stand? How should the United States define the objective it pursues by means of this policy? This policy has hitherto sought concrete results—

more troops, more equipment, more precise strategic agreements, more infrastructure,[3] more precisely planned and directed assistance programs. It has become rigid and inflexible. It does not readily adapt to a situation in which allied states grow restive in a particular alliance, and uncommitted states become antagonistic to the policy of alliances as a whole. This inherent rigidity has a tendency, if the policy meets with difficulties, to identify the problem of alliances with the issue of American participation in the operation of the free world. And when the part has been taken as the whole, the basic alternatives become to withdraw or to participate unilaterally on an extreme nationalist basis.

On the other hand, where do the policies of economic assistance come out in a re-examination? They have, for some time, been increasingly linked with the policy of alliances, and have tended to become inflexible as that policy has become rigid. The question then comes up for discussion whether their substance can be retained while emphasis and purpose are shifted to gain flexibility. The administration went on record at the start of 1956 as believing that this step was not only possible, but desirable and necessary. However, because the administration simultaneously maintained the necessity for the policy of alliances, this question—as well as the preceding problem and issue—has been thrown into the context of Soviet-Communist intentions and capabilities.

When the review of the American position, objectives, and policies is carried on primarily in this context, a range of continuing issues comes to life again. Many of these are the old familiar ones of the geographical concentration of American action: Is Europe the primary issue? Or Asia? Or should action be taken as required on the global perimeter of the Soviet bloc? Or should the defense perimeter be defined in relation to the Western Hemisphere alone?

Here, again, the questions undergo considerable change of meaning if the conditions in which they had originated are altered. At the start, these questions arose in connection with a strategy of containment based on a bipolar picture of the international system. They reappear in connection with the problem of meeting Soviet-Communist policies and actions in an international system that appears to be moving toward increasing diversification.

---

[3] Infrastructure: airfields, naval bases, warning systems, fixed communications systems, fuel stores, and fuel distribution systems.

The earlier discussion of these questions can be reviewed rapidly. Europe was held to be the pivotal area for a number of reasons. In the first place, its productive capacity was second only to that of the United States, and its man power possessed skills that Asia could not be expected to match within the lifetime of those now living. In addition, through colonial holdings or commercial ties, Europe gave the United States access to a considerable part of the raw materials of the world. Europe also provided strategically disposed bases, internal logistic facilities, and was readily accessible by sea and air from the United States. And in a conflict where ideology played a significant part, the similarity of European and American cultural and political institutions provided a natural basis for alliance and joint action. But above all, European productivity, skills, and control of raw materials had to be denied to the Soviet Union.

With respect to Asia as a competitor for primary American attention, the argument was a blend of the historic theme of "man-power masses of the Orient" and of the fact that communism was taking its most aggressive form in the Far East while the West was losing its earlier dominating position there. Thus Asia was seen as the weak sector of a strategy of containment, requiring more attention than Europe, a more active United States policy, and a greater allocation of American resources. Furthermore, there were the rich resources of Southeast Asia, including Indonesia, to be considered. Because the facts of Communist aggression were undeniable, the pro-Asian argument was met in two ways. One was to reassert the pro-European argument more vigorously. The other was to note that the pro-Asian school was taking the massed man power and the potential resources of Asia and projecting them in terms of national power, without considering problems of logistics, quality of resources, acquisition of skills, and any number of material and cultural factors that both retarded and limited their translation into effective national power.

The dilemma of a choice between Europe and Asia was avoided by the more global-minded who developed the concept of action on a defensive-offensive perimeter that lay on the fringes of Europe and Asia. According to this thesis, United States policy was to be directed to the maintenance of a peripheral position with respect to the Soviet bloc. In Europe this position would consist of Great Britain, Spain, and North Africa. In Asia it would consist of Alaska, Japan, Formosa, the Philippines, and Southeast Asia, including Indonesia. The concept became more vague when applied to South Asia and the Middle East.[4] These positions, while avoiding the dangers of irrevocably committing the United States to action on the continent of Europe or Asia, provided at one and the same time the means of defending the Western Hemisphere and of taking offensive action against aggressions by the Soviet bloc. This concept was opposed on the ground that it met only one contingency: a Soviet-Communist war against the United States. Meanwhile, action on such a line would undermine the concept of collective security and disrupt the policy of alliances, a concept and policy that covered a larger range of intermediate contingencies.

The last of the questions on the geographical focus of American action—concentration on the defense of the Western Hemisphere—was not argued separately from the larger issue of the degree and form of United States participation in the affairs of the international system. The defense of the Western Hemisphere as a sole security policy for the United States existed only as the strategic component of a policy of reducing American participation in the international system to a minimum.

This full range of discussion was largely at an end by 1954. The United States was a participant in the world system. The purpose of participation was to develop collective security action in the free world. The technique of participation was a policy of alliances supported by programs of assistance. The pivotal area was Western Europe. But if the structure of the international system should no longer prove receptive to action along this line, all of these questions might be reopened.

They would be reopened, however, in a context very different from that of a bipolar world. Only the most fundamental difference will be commented on here. It is that in a bipolar system, the American pattern of objectives and policies could be applied universally with some validity. A program of economic assistance leading to political stability, then the support of an alliance, and finally to a system of co-operative defensive action was a valid concept in a world presumed to be tending toward two organized power groupings. With slight modifications for different regions, this course of action could be universally applied because it could be presumed to meet the minimum requirements of all the states concerned.

[4] The Baghdad Pact, based on the "northern tier" of Middle East states, is, however, one fairly specific version.

If, however, the world tended away from bipolarity, a logical progression was no longer possible from a generally applied program of assistance to a single objective of collective security action. Execution across the board would break down first. While economic aid to Western Europe sought to put teeth into the North Atlantic Treaty Organization, economic aid to Southeast Asia, even though defined as putting teeth into the Southeast Asia Collective Defense Treaty, would run into resistance if its aim were thus restricted. Actually, the goal would be economic development. As this goal was approached, the recipient states would in fact become freer to choose whether their next step would be to help to put teeth into the new organization, or to pull away from collective action and to develop national policies to the maximum.

These questions are not the only ones that become subject to re-examination. The United States has formulated positions to support its basic pattern of policy. These include the strategic control of East-West trade and the thesis of massive retaliation. These positions, relevant as they may well have been to a strategy of containment in a bipolar system, are automatically challenged by a diversified and fragmented system.

The control of the movement of strategic materials was a natural derivative from the concept of bloc conflict. While the concept generally prevailed, the corollary of trade control was accepted in principle and was argued only in terms of specific items and particular trading situations. Any questioning of the concept, whether on theoretical grounds or because the bipolar trend was actually reversed, could only reopen the issue of the value of the controls.

The issue has been reopened in two ways. First, as the states of the free world recovered some of their freedom of action, they began to develop independent policies with respect to East-West trade. Without attempting to argue the theory of strategic controls, they have created practical dilemmas for the United States. The dilemma is at its sharpest in the case of Japan, where the stated security requirement for maintaining Japan and the stated security requirement for controlling trade with Communist China conflict with each other as well as with the stated American desire to reduce the costs of maintaining Japan and with current domestic policies of protecting American industry against Japanese competition. The same dilemma, although in a less extreme form, has arisen over and over again in other instances. It is likely to reappear still more frequently as the international system becomes further diversified and an across-the-board application of United States policy becomes less practicable.

Second, the issue has been revived within the United States in the argument that, in principle, a policy of controls runs counter to the long-term foreign economic objectives of the United States and the free world. More concretely, it is argued that the security value of such controls, in terms of the relations of the United States with its associates and with the uncommitted free world, is now of a lower priority than the values to be obtained by the removal of such controls.

It is officially maintained, however, that although much has been and can be done to modify the policy to fit new conditions, the principle of strategic controls should be kept. It is held that there are three general objectives of the Soviet bloc in its economic relations with the free world: to obtain imports that will help the bloc to become more powerful and less dependent on the free world; to drive wedges between the free nations at every opportunity; and to increase the dependence of these nations on the Soviet bloc for markets or supplies, thus making the free world more vulnerable to Communist pressures.

The thesis of massive retaliation is equally called into question. In fact, the policy reactions of other states to this thesis was one of the signs of the extent to which conditions had changed in the international system. While there has been no official repudiation of the thesis, there is little indication that it is seriously relied upon as an instrument of policy. Moreover, reasons have been advanced for giving it very low priority on the scale of action, so low in fact as to make it indistinguishable from the concept of the generally deterrent power of the nuclear and thermonuclear weapons system. These reasons are that massive retaliation can no longer be considered except as a strictly unilateral American action. As such, it is incompatible with a policy of alliances in which the United States seeks to act as a partner. It is also inapplicable in a system of international relations in which a large number of strategically located uncommitted states are acquiring freedom to choose from among alternative courses. Furthermore, it is added, the cost-risk calculations that the thesis was presumed to have forced on the Soviet Union have been nullified by the joint recognition of atomic stalemate. The continued use of the thesis, however, is defended on grounds that, in essence, it has been relegated to the status of a deterrent instrument. As the thesis of deterrence, however, has lost its original meaning of checking the Soviet superiority in man power and conventional weapons, both massive retaliation and deterrence are reduced to the status of reserved instruments against an extreme contingency. The official position continues to rest on the argument that the United States must remain able to employ these instruments in order to cancel out a Soviet capability. This is the sole assurance that the common recognition of thermonuclear war as out of the question will continue to stand.

Accommodation and Disarmament

Two other questions are also reopened. The first is a major one of accommodation between the United States and the Soviet Union, and the other a minor one of disarmament. These are interlocked issues, but they are here defined as major and minor because there is little probability that disarmament proposals will become operative in the absence of persuasive evidence of accommodation.

The issue of the form and substance of an accommodation with the Soviet Union underwent some quiet modification in fact during the course of 1955. This was largely brought about by changes in the international situation in which accommodation would have to be reached. These changes, so far as United States purposes and actions are concerned, have been implicitly responded to and at the same time explicitly denied.[5]

On an assumption of bipolarity, accommodation between the United States and the Soviet Union meant, first, the development of an equilibrium of strength between two power groupings, and second, an adjustment of conflicting interests, objectives, and policies in terms of this equilibrium. This meaning was reflected in the American concept of negotiating only from positions of strength. Inasmuch as these did not always exist, United States policy was directed to their creation rather than to the subsequent end of negotiating an adjustment. Consideration of the form and substance of the accommodation that might then become possible was a

---

[5] The heads of state recognized them by implication at Geneva in July 1955, and the foreign ministers explicitly rejected them at Geneva in November 1955. The indications are, however, that the kind of re-orientation that is showing in both Soviet and United States policies is an adjustment to new conditions.

speculative game played by the theorists of international relations. As a practical measure, however, the United States constructed a system of alliances of varying strengths and restored some of the foundations of power in areas of the free world.

When in the course of 1954 the United States was pressed toward the first steps of negotiation by the states with which it was allied, and when in the course of 1955 these pressures were compounded by the maneuverings of groups of uncommitted states, it was maintained that the pressure need no longer be resisted because the requisite positions of strength had been achieved. Not all observers accepted this judgment. Some held that, because the advantages and disadvantages of the positions of the power groupings were not commensurable, there was no way of determining the relative strength of positions of strength. Others were inclined to say that the United States was forced to adjust to the demands of its allies, or to face the gradual break up of its system of alliances. Still others saw both power groupings being pushed into adjustment by internal difficulties and by pressures from increasingly articulate groups of uncommitted states.

Whatever the final judgment may be, it is clear that accommodation could not have the same meaning in 1955 that it had had in 1948 or 1949. Even though specific accommodation could not be forced—and the second Geneva conference demonstrated that it could not—these accumulating pressures could and did tend to force other considerations, particularly the consideration of third party interests, on the patterns of United States and Soviet policy. The hard cores of the two power groupings might find no basis for accommodation as between themselves, but each might find it necessary or desirable to adjust separately to other factors that were operating in the international system. The direct negotiation of differences is not the only device for making adjustments. The slowly developing pressure of influences that run counter to the objectives and policies of major disputants can also be effective. The issue of accommodation has, in these circumstances, already had some of its substance modified.

The acceptance of war as a solution to the problems of American statecraft has been rejected by both major political parties and is not an active issue in American politics. This shift has been assailed as an "ostrich-like" attitude by those who vigorously maintain that the goal of the Soviet Union is world revolution, and that this goal will be pursued by force whenever conditions are favorable. But as a matter of record, the shift has taken place. It is rationalized by the argument that Soviet institutions and purposes are subject to change, and that Soviet statesmen are as responsive to the dangers of thermonuclear warfare as any other policy makers. Responsible statesmanship, it is added, consequently demands a careful and patient search for alternative modes of action.

On the other hand, both major political parties categorically reject the idea of giving away American positions in order to reach an accommodation. Some bodies of opinion call this view rigid and maintain that only comprehensive modification of the United States position will produce a meaningful relaxation of tension and convert the Soviet Union to taking more flexible positions itself. But American inflexibility is defended, at least so far as the position in Western Europe is involved, by pointing out that an acceptance of the terms offered by the Soviet Union for an accommodation would weaken the principle of freedom, undermine Western security arrangements, and offer up the Western nations individually and collectively. The stakes are too high to run this risk on no better ground than an inference about subsequent Soviet motivations. It is, of course, true that Western bases ring the Soviet Union, but it is maintained that the integrity and peaceful purposes of the Western political systems are effective guarantees against the use of these bases for aggressive purposes. The Soviet system does not provide similar guarantees. And because the West is not free to strike suddenly or to engage in political blackmail, it cannot afford to dismantle its defenses until a substantial demonstration of Soviet good faith has been made.

Both modification and rigidity are in consonance with the changed international situation. The restraint on nuclear and thermonuclear war fits the new modes of action induced by the increased dispersal of power in the international system. The rigidity with respect to a security system for Western Europe is a reasonable tightening up at a key point to compensate for the fragmentation of security policy elsewhere.

Many other substantive aspects of the issue are, however, unsettled. Is the more important first step to establish mutual confidence, or to reach agreement on specific points of conflict? Responsible policy makers were prepared to argue that specific agreements were essential to the creation of confidence because they alone gave concrete evidence of an intent to proceed further in good faith. In this view, the choice—to settle issues, to raise confidence, or to attempt both simultaneously—was a pragmatic matter and not a policy choice. Other equally responsible observers, however, were ready to maintain that few of the really important concrete issues were capable of solution. In this view, the raising of confidence by a mutual recognition of the *status quo* in those areas where the situation had been stabilized by the passage of time was the preferred approach because it could establish sufficient mutual trust to permit the negotiation of other issues over a period of time.

This question is likely to become confused as it is discussed under the pressures from the uncommitted states and under the influence of the forum of the United Nations. In terms of the national policies of such states, a growth of general confidence seems more significant than the adjustment of specific conflicts, for the settlement of particular questions may or may not be pertinent to their individual purposes.

Should the kind of accommodation sought be global, regional, or item-by-item? There have been supporters for each of these approaches in the past, and each is likely to have adherents in the future. The range of arguments is, of course, well-known.

Issue-by-issue negotiation is presumed to increase the possibility that each issue will be settled on its intrinsic merits, and to limit the introduction of contentious or extraneous matters that will stall the process of accommodation. On the other hand, issue-by-issue negotiation increases the possibility that all the specific solutions of a separately presented particular issue will seem to involve costs so high for one of the contending parties that it will feel unable to reach agreement unless these costs are counterbalanced by compensating gains. These gains usually can be had only in connection with some other issue. Thus issue-by-issue negotiation can work to foreclose on all negotiation.

Regional accommodation is favored by those who see the points at issue in various regions as so dissimilar as to make separate negotiations advisable. Furthermore, the relative strength from which the opposing parties negotiate varies considerably from region to region—the American position, for example, is reasonably strong in Europe, demonstrably weak in the Far East, and indeterminate in the Middle East. On the other hand, regional accommodation is opposed by those who consider the points of conflict to be universally distributed and who, consequently, regard anything less than global adjustment as artificial and deceptive. They argue that accommodation is possible only if it represents the settlement of all the major divisive issues.

Generally speaking, the Soviet Union has preferred to negotiate the broadest issues in global terms, probably because global negotiation permits maneuver and possible gains on specific issues behind the screen of an ostensible effort to reduce global tensions. The closest associates of the United States have preferred an item-by-item adjustment, relying for the most part on the use of historic diplomatic techniques. The United States has had no exclusive conviction about either approach and has tended to treat conferences with broad agendas as propaganda struggles and conferences with specific agendas as tests of strength.

In a changed international situation, these attitudes will be hard to maintain. The Soviet preference for broad rather than specific negotiation coincides with the views of the uncommitted states about the need for a general reduction of tensions, and this coincidence of attitudes can be readily carried over into the General Assembly of the United Nations. Consequently, unless the views of the United States on the form and substance of accommodation are modified to fit new conditions, the position of the United States is in danger of being regarded as negative and stubborn. The process of review and modification will, almost certainly, revive the discussions that preceded the formulation of the existing pattern of United States policy. Yet little in these discussions will touch on the question: What adjustments are both possible and acceptable to all the parties involved in concrete major conflicts of interest? This question is reserved for the final chapter.

The general issue of accommodation, however, cannot be dismissed without a word about its poor but articulate relative, disarmament. Disarmament is a goal that, as a general proposition, mankind views with favor. It is widely believed that disarmament will result in savings, which can then be devoted to improving standards of living, and that it will reduce tensions and hence decrease the danger of war. At this level of generalization, all states, large and small, support proposals for disarmament. However, the discussion of disarmament, or even of the reduction of armaments, is misleading when it takes place on this high level of generality. Actually, the presumed general advantages, if indeed they exist, can follow only from an acceptance of specific plans.

Short of universal and total disarmament, the maximum objective for the United States would be to confine armament regulation or reduction to the categories of conventional weapons and armed man power, for it is in these respects that the Soviet bloc is strongest. At the same time, the United States would seek to exclude atomic weapons from arms controls. The maximum objective of the Soviet Union would be exactly the reverse. However, the popular world demand for disarmament has become essentially a demand for restrictions on the possession and use of atomic weapons. It is not politically feasible for a state to advocate a plan that does not link the two issues and that does not contain some plan for restricting the use and reducing the stockpiles of atomic weapons. It is clear that the United States cannot accept proposals in the latter respect unless they are linked with an acceptable plan for the reduction of conventional arms and armed man power. The converse is equally clear in the position of the Soviet Union. The debate turns on the formula for reducing conventional weapons and the formula for controlling unconventional ones. Many such proposals have been made, but their operational insignificance remains the same. Percentage reductions from existing bases continue to be disadvantageous to the United States and the West, and controls acceptable to the United States continue to be disadvantageous to the Soviet Union.

These pragmatic considerations have been understood by professional negotiators, and, so long as the possibility of an accommodation between two power groupings was not in sight, general pressure for fresh disarmament talks did not develop. However, the same increase in the influence of small states that set up a pressure for accommodation generated a fresh demand for action in the field of disarmament. The issue has, consequently, become active once more in its generalized form.

This by no means exhausts the questions that are being reopened at the start of 1956. Nor does it attempt to predict what aspects of these questions will seem more significant. It does suggest, however, that United States objectives and policies were being subjected to review and to reformulation. This process was self-generated in part, as a normal operation of the decision-making machinery of the United States Government and of American political processes. Less obviously, but even more significantly, the process was being forced on policy-making bodies by changes in the structure and operation of the international system of state relations. It was this fact that communicated something of urgency to what might otherwise have gone on in a fairly routine way.

If the tendencies toward diversification and increased national freedom of action can be accepted as of key importance, it will be appreciated that a very basic question lay unanswered at the heart of this process of review. The question was: What did these tendencies signify for the interests and objectives of the United States? What did their presence and their possible further growth require in the way of action by the United States?

The United States could evaluate them as generally favorable and encourage their development. The United States could regard them as unfavorable and take action to check and reverse them. The United States could treat them as minor trends in world affairs, secondary to the confrontation of the Soviet bloc, and could adjust on an *ad hoc* basis by making small changes in its existing pattern of policy operations.

A variety of conclusions can already be noted as having been advanced to those alternative judgments. The situation of the free world has deteriorated, and the policies of the United States have been seriously frustrated. Alternatively, United States policies have forced the Soviet Union to check its course of armed aggression and to turn to tough diplomatic, economic, and ideological competition instead. Both estimates conclude that the United States should carry on with its present pattern of policy: the former calling for greater effort and greater sacrifice, the latter for different emphasis within the pattern. No one has yet suggested all-out action to reverse the trend and to bring the free world firmly into line with American purposes. In the same way, no one has yet suggested that the trend is consonant with American purposes and should be encouraged even at the price of significant shifts in policy. In short, the full scope of the issue has not yet been fully revealed, and the full implications of the basic alternatives have not yet been explored, although there is much in the recent record of events to suggest that a key point of decision may be involved.

CHAPTER XXIV
The Substantive Questions

To WHAT EXTENT can the United States accommodate itself to the claims of the free nations to stand aside from its system of alliances and to develop policies that may run counter to the purposes of that system? This question is being pressed more and more to the front, and the answer that is given to it is likely to be a major guide line for determining choices on many of the key issues that are coming up for re-examination.

The question involves concepts that, while not necessarily contradictory, have tended to become so in United States policy during the past five years. One is the concept of the national independence and juridical equality of states. Another is the concept of organic co-operative relations between states. Both concepts were related without contradiction in the Charter of the United Nations.

But confronted by the threat presented by a Soviet bloc organized on a different basis, the United States, supported by a group of Western democracies, asserted the need for a more tightly organized defensive association than was immediately obtainable from the growth of universal co-operative practices. The process of attempting to construct such defensive associations out of a number of widely scattered nation states, and at the same time to keep the resulting pattern of alliances geared to the requirements of United States security policy, strained both the concept of national independence and the concept of co-operative relations. Because its immediate purpose was to confront the Soviet bloc with a counterforce, the United States sought to co-ordinate the policies and actions of the various groupings of which it was a member and then to focus the action of all on the primary American objective—the effective containment of Soviet-Communist action.

To this end, the United States pressed its associates to recognize that the scope of American responsibilities was greater than theirs and thus to persuade them to make more binding commitments to regional security organizations than the United States was prepared to make. This study has shown how these pressures of United States policy gave rise to strains in the system of alliances by levy-

452

ing demands on traditional national freedoms of choice. It has further shown how the United States had to adjust to the reluctance of Western European countries to support its policy toward the two Chinas, how it was forced to accede to the desire of France to limit its commitments in Indo-China, and to recognize that Great Britain also had world-wide commitments and could not be drawn into collective action against its will.

The Uncommitted States

Limitations such as these have constituted a major problem for United States policy in the recent past. They are not, however, the heart of the issue as it is now being presented. The present substantive problem arises from the fact that many states have stayed beyond the reach of an American principle of organization while coming in various ways within the scope of American programs of assistance. In addition, these states have increasingly shown not only the intention to act but also considerable ability in acting on a concept of sovereign independence. A growing number of states, usually underdeveloped, often occupying strategic geographic locations, have formulated objectives and policies of purely national character, often designed to improve their internal conditions and to create modern social structures. These domestic objectives invariably caused these states to take positions that reflected an assumption that the development of major power groupings and the tensions to which they gave rise impeded the pursuit of their particular interests. Their foreign policies, consequently, took the form of individually resisting efforts to draw them into a major power grouping and of collectively bringing every possible influence to bear on checking a major power conflict.

From the point of view of the United States, this kind of policy was against the best interest of the free world. It was considered to disperse resources, to diffuse power, and to fragment action; in short, by denying the need, to handicap the whole principle of organizing the free world. At the same time, economic assistance was being given to these recalcitrant members of the free world. One of the results was that they were thus enabled to act still more freely. United States policy makers found no sure way of dealing with this situation. Vocal segments of American opinion grew very restive, however, at the spectacle of the objectives of the

United States being effectively resisted by the recipients of American aid.

As of the end of 1955, the uncommitted states in the international system had worked their way into a very favorable position for influencing the actions of the major states. They have become the targets of competitive attention, where hitherto they had been focuses of conflicting pressures.[1] Here lies the problem for the United States. Should it adjust to this change? If so, what does adjustment imply in terms of existing objectives and policies?

As matters now are, strong positions can be developed on both sides of this question. On the one hand, the argument is that in the long-range view, acceptance of diversification and the dispersal of power and influence in the international system are permissible. It can be pointed out that a state such as India has an important function in the international community and may perform useful work by creating restrictions on the actions of major powers. In addition, by limiting physical contact between power blocs, such states reduce potential areas of direct conflict. Finally, in so far as such states co-operate in organizations similar to the United Nations, they force restraining considerations on major power policies.

On the other hand, the argument is that in the short-range view, resistance to diversification is indicated. It is pointed out that to accept the operation of neutral forces interferes with the further effective development of the system of alliances in areas where such a development is important to the security and political objectives of the United States. The principle of organized collective effort is not sufficiently established among the associates of the United States to risk the encouragement of an alternative principle of independence of action. The argument would admit that it might be inexpedient to press the principle of organization in some specific instances, but maintains that the principle should be adhered to as a matter of policy. Only in this way would collective action be developed in fact and situations of strength be built.

[1] Attention is called to the fact that the situation described is unstable. It can be upset if one of the major powers—the United States or the Soviet Union—decides to take positive action to upset it. The uncommitted states do not have the means to resist the application of force. They are, however, protected and encouraged by two considerations. Neither of the major powers seems prepared to use force. And even if one of them were so prepared, its use would be inhibited by the likelihood that the first consequence would be to drive the uncommitted state into the arms of the other major state. Under present conditions this is a fair amount of insurance both ways.

A middle ground can also be developed by assuming that this is not an "either-or" situation; no policy position need be exclusively presented for universal application. The question can be treated in a pragmatic way in terms of relative advantages and disadvantages. Just as the United States recognized the desirability of different degrees of commitment for itself—large and firm in Europe, restricted and flexible in the Far East—so it could accept variable degrees of organization in the free world. Judgments of what would be acceptable depended on a calculation of the effort needed, the concrete benefits sought, and the relative importance to the American interest of the region involved. Thus an organic structure in Western Europe was compatible with a conventional alliance in the Middle East and with no structure of any kind in South Asia. The argument would admit that the situation forced the United States into highly diversified diplomatic activities, but could go on to note that this might actually lead to over-all improvement in American relations with the free world.

This range of positions is based on an assumption that the United States is essentially free to determine its role in the international system. Suppose, however, that this is not quite the case, but that the United States is limited in its choices by the purposes of its associates in much the same way that its purposes have a limiting effect on their choices.

It can be argued that an acceptance of this situation as a basis for policy would place no strain on the American national interest. The United States has always taken the position that all peoples have the right to choose the system of government and the economic and cultural institutions that they prefer. Any recent deviations from this position were the result of an effort to enlist other countries to resist Soviet-Communist expansion only because the Soviet Union sought to impose alien forms of government and social organization on free peoples. And it can be argued that this is an effort that cannot be pushed too far in the face of resistance from non-Communist states without danger of backfiring. In other words, the diversification of the uncommitted sector of the international system along national lines creates problems for the Soviet Union just as it does for the United States.[2] In the absence of the Soviet threat, or perhaps merely with the reduction of the immediacy

[2] This possibility cuts close to the heart of some of the bases of policy: its fixation on the Soviet threat, the uniform and consistent guidance by a strategic concept of containment, the shift to military means as a major instrument of

of that threat, the United States, however, can accept a high degree of diversification of interest and policy in the international system.

From this it could be concluded that there may be no real need for United States policy to strain for ends that can only be achieved by tremendous exertions of power and by an excessive use of resources. If the United States is a participant in a thermonuclear stalemate, so also is the Soviet Union. This situation, even if only temporary, permits resources to be used in other ways by both states. The apparent shift of Soviet action away from the use of force touches United States policy at a sensitive point only so long as the primary aim of that policy is an integrated security alliance of free states. If this objective is given a lower priority, the Soviet Union is involved in nothing more than piecemeal economic-diplomatic competition with the United States in an unstable system of nation-states.

At the same time, an opposite view can be argued. The groundwork of this argument is that because there has been no demonstrable change in Soviet intentions, the conflict between the United States and the Soviet Union remains a clash between democratic and totalitarian concepts of man and society. In such a conflict, there can be no relaxation, no basis for accommodation, no quarter, and no uncommitted states. To lose sight of this would be to open the way for the Soviet-Communists to score the winning point.

From this base, the argument can take many forms and arrive at a variety of conclusions. It can propose a policy of dominating the actions of individual small states in the interest of the entire free world. It can propose a policy of self-sufficiency. It can propose a "realistic" assistance policy, by which American resources are exchanged for commitments to support American purposes. It can, in short, include the whole gamut of earlier judgments made on every occasion when the basic role of the United States in the international system has been up for examination.

There is no way of predicting what is likely to emerge as the chosen American course in connection with this issue. All that can be asserted is that the signs have been multiplying that this issue, or some variant of it, is likely to be a key question for United

---

execution. At the same time, it encourages elements in the pattern of policy to reassert their claims as primary instruments of national action: aid for economic development, collective action through the United Nations.

States policy makers for some time to come. This assertion rests on a considered judgment to the effect that a significant change has been taking place: briefly, that the two major states are now less able effectively to dominate the operation of the international system on terms relevant only to their relations with one another. While the smaller and the uncommitted states certainly did not initiate this change, by making use of the opportunities offered, they have contributed to speeding it up. By the end of 1955, it had reached a point where a return to a previous degree of major power influence was possible only at a price that neither major power seemed willing to pay.

The resulting situation is unstable—but not unique in history—in that the relations of the United States and the Soviet Union, their clashes of interests and purpose, and their specific points of conflict, have not been altered in any essential respect. The difference is that neither seems as free to act directly and exclusively in terms of these relations as was the case earlier. It is possible that the United States, given that one of its objectives was to organize the free world for collective action, is for the moment more hampered by this change than the Soviet Union.

This, it is suggested, means that the American analysis of the situation in which the United States must now act is likely to be laborious and long-drawn out, and that policy and program adjustments will take place slowly. Objectives are likely to be modestly stated, and policies cautious, both because of growing limitations on action and because of the difficulty of realistically judging Soviet intentions. A tremendous sensitivity to contingencies may develop, both in public discussion and in official decisions; for the immediate past is far from dead, and the immediate future is not yet revealed. There is considerable reason to think that much that has guided United States action in the past ten years will have to be reassessed.

This will include not only the major objectives and the broad policies but also positions on outstanding substantive problems.

New Forms for Old Problems

Some of these problems, old familiar ones of the past decade, have already started to be reduced to other forms. Chief among these in the view of the United States and Great Britain, relate to the stability and the security of the Middle East. Positive Soviet action in this region has forced a reconsideration of policy, not so much because Soviet action has been on a large scale as because those steps taken by the Soviet Union have been carefully selected to stimulate more freedom of movement and decision on the part of states of the Middle East. The basis of Anglo-American policy was a capacity to restrain freedom of decision, to hold a check rein, and by this means to prevent minor crises from growing into major conflicts. Soviet policy nibbles at this base. In spite of official protests and appeals to the larger international interest, the United States cannot readily counter this form of Soviet action. As armaments— no matter how few—are sold to Arab states, and support in the United Nations—no matter how trivial or ephemeral—is given to Arab positions, Arab freedom of action is encouraged because Arab policy has been provided with an alternative that looks like an escape from the restraining hands of the West. American and British power to restrain immediately begins to decline because its effective exercise would serve only to drive Arab states to a more exclusive pursuit of this alternative. Nor can the United States and Great Britain unreservedly shift to competition with the Soviet Union to satisfy Arab aims. Not only would this add to the freedom with which the Arab states could maneuver, but it would also force some very unhappy choices on American and British policy makers.

Other problems are keeping their familiar forms. Of these, the settlement of Germany is the most characteristic. Competent ob-servers have long maintained that the partition of Germany was the concrete reality while German unification was the very remote objective. In the face of official statements to the contrary, events have worked to confirm this opinion; a settlement for Germany has become inseparable from the problem of the security of Europe and from the Soviet definition of its own security requirements. Thus although the German problem has remained on the surface, the significant development has been that of a security *status quo* in Europe. This development was clearly recognized in connection with the major power conferences of 1955. At the same time, it was made as explicit as such matters ever are made, that the *status quo*—if not desirable—was nevertheless tolerable to both sides; at least more so than the costs of trying to change it. This acknowledg-ment was plainly made by the Soviet Union, which was in a better position to accept the German problem as indefinitely deadlocked.[3] Having taken this stand, the Soviet Union could await developments.

There were many signs that the Western German Republic was regaining some freedom of action. From the Soviet point of view, the Western powers were committed to a rigid position with respect to a German settlement, while the Soviet Union was not so committed. If, therefore, the Western German Republic sought to use its new freedom to obtain a German settlement, it had no alternative in the long run but to explore the question bilaterally with the Soviet Union, where negotiation was theoretically possible. There were only two ways in which the Western powers could counter such a development. One would be to take a more flexible position. But this was not possible unless they were prepared to divorce the German problem from the Western European security problem at the expense of their present security arrangements. United States policy could not accept this course. The other way would be to drop all talk of German unification and to try to persuade the Western Germans to accept an indefinite partition. This would be an extremely awkward shift to make, and its consequences would be unpredictable. It was, however, a remote possibility, and if acted on, would merely confirm a *status quo* that was acceptable to the Soviet Union.

Thus the German problem also became susceptible to reexamination by the United States in terms of a possible need to devise a new pattern of purpose and action for conducting its foreign relations in a modified international system. But in this case, unlike the situations in other parts of the world, the range within which new and acceptable alternatives are available is very narrow; for in Europe the security *status quo* that has been reached —in great part by American effort—is at least preferred to any changes in it that can now be foreseen.

Although there are changes that could be wished for in this connection, there is nothing here for the United States to seek that it is both willing and able to act to achieve. A review of the position is much more likely to suggest the possibility that the United

[3] The Soviet Union had opened the way for direct negotiations with the two German states at some future time by recognizing the Western German Republic. It also left on the West the onus of continuing to promise unification to the West Germans although making it clear that this could not be carried out under existing conditions.

States might be pressed by its European associates to go along with alternatives that it considered unsatisfactory, but that it would be unable flatly to reject. Among these associates must be included the sovereign German Federal Republic. Consequently, the American review is likely to take the form of designing a policy of rearguard actions to maintain an unstable equilibrium.[4]

The remaining big problem of a Far Eastern settlement is totally different, not only in its substantive issues, but also because it is at a different stage of development. The question here is not one of maintaining an acceptable *status quo,* but of achieving an acceptable *status quo.* Furthermore, from the point of view of the United States, the problem is exposed in nearly all of its aspects to being determined as much, if not more, by the purposes and actions of other states than by the objectives and policies of the United States.

It is no longer possible to doubt that Communist China, for purposes of immediate action in the international system, has adequately consolidated and stabilized its power. There is equally little reason to doubt that the United States cannot challenge this power in the Far East without allocating more of its resources than it is prepared to do and without committing resources on a scale that would limit its capacity to act elsewhere. Furthermore, this would appear to be the case even in the absence of the restraints on such a course that other states have steadily built up ever since the Korean armistice.

Thus as this problem comes up for re-examination, it is likely to involve a very agonizing reappraisal indeed, as it will call into question many positions, proposals, policies, and commitments that have only recently been bitterly debated. To begin with, although it is apparent that an equilibrium is being very tentatively groped for, the basic issue of the kind of *status quo* that would combine acceptability with possibility has not been explored. Nor is it likely to be explored objectively, except over a considerable

---

[4] The possible nature of these pressures is indicated by the proposal made by the British Prime Minister at Geneva in November 1955. Britain suggested a five-power security pact of the four major states and a unified Germany, by which the signatories would agree not to resort to force and to deny assistance to an aggressor. Aside from the immediate and obvious purpose of this kind of proposal, it also initiates a normal progression in international relations from irreconcilable opposition to tolerable *status quo* and from an implicitly accepted *status quo* to a search for a more stable accommodation. However, the American and European estimates of where they stand jointly in this progression plainly do not coincide.

period of time and by a process of feeling out intentions and capabilities.

The re-examination, so far as the United States is concerned, gives every indication of being extremely difficult. It will be accompanied at every step by the necessity for taking action in limited concrete situations. This necessity can be imposed by Communist China, by other states in Asia, by associated states whose interests are involved, and by domestic political considerations. A mere listing of the issues that can be brought to life under these conditions will show the probable complexity of this process of review and adjustment. Should the United States formally recognize the Communist Government of China? What is to be the disposition of the seat in the Security Council of the United Nations that was earmarked for China when the Organization was established? Should two Chinese governments be accepted as sovereign entities in the international system? Can and should the Southeast Asia Collective Defense Treaty be developed into a device for reaching an equilibrium in the Far East, as the North Atlantic Treaty was in Europe? Are the United States security pacts with the National Government of China, the Republic of Korea, and Japan impediments or aids to reaching an equilibrium? Can an equilibrium be reached without stabilizing the situation in Indo-China, in Malaya, and in Indonesia? What is the role of economic and technical assistance programs? What is the role of political action in achieving an equilibrium? Can the United States regain the initiative, has it fallen to Communist China, or is it in course of being taken over by the uncommitted states of the region?

This is more than enough to demonstrate both the need and the difficulty of making a re-examination. The questions also show that the problem of a Far Eastern settlement has become one in which the growing freedom of smaller states to pursue their diversified national objectives is likely to be a determining if confusing influence. This has become a situation in which, while United States policy may continue to propose, other states are more likely to dispose. There is one proviso to this conclusion, however: the United States may also be able to dispose, if its proposals are accompanied by allocations of American power sufficient to accomplish the desired ends. Although this is always a possible solution to a problem of this kind, the evidence of the immediate past—not only the evidence of American decisions, but the development of the impediments to such a choice that have begun to show in the international system—suggests that the choice is an unlikely one.

The pattern of objectives and policies that the United States developed in the first five years after the Second World War was clearly based on a judgment about the nature of the international system in which it was operating. The system was seen as rapidly tending toward a bipolar structure.[5] Purpose and action were consequently focused on developing an organized grouping around an American pole to compensate for the one that existed around a Soviet pole. Other objectives and their related policies, if not explicitly laid aside, were relegated to a lower priority. Policies addressed to this single end, therefore, were designed to be applicable to all areas outside the Soviet bloc, making only practical allowances in operations to fit local conditions. If a policy of defensive alliances was initiated, it was of universal applicability. If a policy of military assistance was determined, it was applicable at all times and in all places so long as it served the overriding purpose of constructing a counterbalance to the Soviet power structure.

It is evident that this pattern was determined by a reasoned view of the international situation as it was then being defined by events. No adverse judgment is intended, nor in fact can one be justifiably brought against the series of linked decisions by which this view was converted into a comprehensive pattern of compensatory action. On the contrary, there are good grounds for concluding that the capacity to do this was a remarkable illustration of the flexibility with which a complex modern democratic society could operate. However, it is equally important to state that this pattern of purposes and action could not be continued into the indefinite future unless the international system continued to conform to the original estimate. This study has been explicit in concluding that this condition has not been met. It concludes, in short, that, at some point in the mid-1950's, a reverse trend, an evolution away from bipolarity, began.

Such a reversal was natural enough, for in a system that is still made up of national states, concentrations of power, unless they

[5] Initially, this concept of bipolarity was more the property of the theorist of international relations than of the operating government official. From the latter's office, neither the problem of policy nor the behavior of states conformed wholly with the concept. There is evidence, however, that the concept was soon picked up and used operationally by policy makers.

are quickly turned into action, create resistances. The resistance is to the fact of power and to the capacity of a concentration of power to inhibit the freedom of action of other states. To seek to whittle down the concentration and to recover some freedom of decision, however slight, becomes a policy goal for every other politically organized society.

Both the Soviet Union and the United States—the latter in spite of the support initially given its purposes—became the objects of these accumulating resistances. If the United States was more specifically resisted, this can be ascribed to the fact that a greater number of states were within reach of the operation of its policies. This did not mean that Soviet purposes were not also meeting with difficulties. Although the detailed evidence is not clear in the case of the Soviet Union, as in the case of the United States, it is reasonable to conclude that both major powers were confronted by problems that were equivalent in kind, if not in degree. Recent Soviet courses of action suggest that there was a recognition of, and an adjustment to, the forces that were creating these problems.

This conclusion leads to an observation about future probabilities. It is that competitive major power adjustments to new conditions may well be one of the essential features of the relations of states over the next five years, and that the American share in this adjustment may become a primary issue for the United States—as significant perhaps for the future as the choice of a new direction that was made in 1947.

This possibility opens up a series of questions about the relative adaptability of the American and Soviet processes for formulating and executing foreign policy, of the relative extent to which both states may be prisoners of their immediate pasts, and of the relative degree to which they can sacrifice present positions without detriment to their future positions with respect to each other. There are indications that these questions are being tested. Already the Soviet Union has shifted to courses of action in the uncommitted, underdeveloped, and intensely nationalistic parts of the world that have strained the capacity of United States policy rapidly to adapt to new considerations.

Although it is impossible to fix the point in time at which the Soviet leaders became expressly aware that the international situation was ripe for a comprehensive review, there can be little doubt that such a review was made long before its American equivalent was undertaken.[6] It would otherwise be hard to explain the precision with which Soviet areas of action were selected, necessary operational details set in motion, and follow-up supporting policies prepared.

The difficulties that the United States experienced in finding a way to respond to the initial impact of the new Soviet courses is partly traceable to the fact that a loosening up of the international system had long been defined as inimical to American aims and hence to be resisted; and partly to the fact that, when put to the test, United States policy had little to refer to in the way of a unifying guideline except a rigid stereotype of national security and defense. The development of a contingent situation to which this guideline was not clearly applicable put the United States at a disadvantage.

On the one hand, a belated re-examination of the international situation had to be made. This inevitably involved a redefinition of the place and role of the United States, as well as a review of the relevance of ten years of firmly established objectives and policies. On the other hand, such a re-examination required as its first step a reorientation of attitudes, a reconsideration of previous judgments, and a release of public opinion from the mold in which it had been set by a decade of direct Soviet threat. Furthermore, both operations coincided with the year of a presidential election and were correspondingly hard to execute with clarity and objectivity.

The immediate advantages of flexibility of judgment and action consequently lay with the Soviet Union. Yet these advantages were not necessarily of indefinite duration. The United States, starting at an equal disadvantage in 1945, nevertheless showed the ability to shift course, to free itself from previous conceptions, and to develop a unifying guideline that was effective for the then existing circumstances.

As of the moment, however, the evolution of the international situation and the rapid adaptation of Soviet policy to some of the more obvious aspects of that evolution are admittedly straining the capacity of the American system to adjust United States priorities, goals, and policies. The serious reality of this strain is clearly vis-

[6] It is equally impossible to separate this review from the simultaneous process of reviving the techniques of "collective leadership" at the apex of the Soviet system and from the process of reducing the internal tensions that had accumulated in the Communist hierarchy during Stalin's regime.

ible, as is also the extent to which the Soviet Union has been able to identify and seize on the opportunity to multiply points of strain to its own advantage. In spite of the obvious difficulties involved, there is no valid ground for assuming that the United States cannot, in the long run, adjust both to changes in the international situation and to the new courses of Soviet action.

There is, nevertheless, a period of danger to be surmounted. This is the period during which the American people and their government will be deciding slowly and confusedly, exactly what adjustments will have to be made. It is during this period, when an element of initiative will almost certainly continue to rest partly in Soviet hands and partly in the diverse hands of the uncommitted states, that American judgments are likely to be categorical and contradictory and United States actions primarily *ad hoc* reactions.

Even for this dangerous stage, one useful point can be made. Soviet action in its present form can represent either of two intentions. The maximum Soviet objective of world communization may have been given the highest operational priority and the new Soviet courses designed simply to disintegrate the capacity of other states—anti-Soviet and uncommitted—collectively to resist a sudden movement toward this goal. On the other hand, a minimum objective of merely stabilizing the relatively secure position and influence of the Soviet Union in a highly diversified system of national states may have been given an overriding operational priority. The new Soviet courses may have been designed simply to ensure the achievement of this end.

There is obviously no basis for making a final judgment between these possibilities. For purposes of a review of United States policy, they can do no more than indicate contingencies. Soviet policy makers probably feel themselves confronted by a set of equally indeterminate contingencies as they attempt to gauge the guidelines of American action.[7]

The significant element in the situation, however, may not be this suspension of judgment on the part of the two major components, but the insistent claims of the minor third parties, to which both

---

[7] Part of the process of competitive adjustment will almost certainly consist of assertions by both the United States and the Soviet Union that the other power has not altered its purposes and is consequently a proper object for continued suspicion and criticism.

major powers will in some respects be continuously and competitively adapting themselves. The longer this process goes on, the more difficult will its abrupt reversal become. If the United States has not been so imprisoned by its past pattern of judgments and policies that it cannot adequately respond to the requirements of the dangerous short term, events may prove it to be better placed than the Soviet Union to maintain a course of competitive adjustment over the long run.

Basic United States objectives, if they can be separated from a direct Soviet threat, do not require a global organization of power. They can be gradually and reasonably pursued in a diversified world; even in a world of multiple conflicting national interests. Basic Soviet objectives appear to be more demanding. Even though Soviet policy shows great flexibility, it is not so clear that Soviet objectives can become more pliable unless the Soviet Union becomes a different kind of state with a considerably changed social base.

Actually, the limits within which the Soviet Union can adapt its policies without calling into question its long-term purposes are narrower than they are for the United States. In the American view, these purposes imply actions in which

> . . . everything includes itself in power,
> Power into will, will into appetite,
> And appetite, a universal wolf,
> So doubly seconded with will and power,
> Must make perforce a universal prey. . . .

Plainly, purposes of this kind cannot remain compatible with any consistent process of adjustment to a diversified world of sovereign states. They are only compatible with efforts to enforce conformity. Yet the Soviet Union is suggesting that it is engaged in a process of adjustment, and that this is a considered policy decision.

It is in these ambiguous circumstances that the United States is being called upon to reach new judgments and decisions that most certainly will greatly alter the existing pattern of policy. But such alteration of policy as these circumstances may impose would not necessarily call for the dispersal of power that the United States now wields. In fact the very ambiguity of the circumstances in which new judgments will have to be made argues for the most careful maintenance of the existing American military establishment, weapons system, and economic base.

Neither will these new judgments and decisions necessarily put an early end to the restiveness and resistance that American leadership now faces. Small states, as well as large states, are never so free that they cannot find grounds for feeling that their needs are being ignored and their aspirations frustrated by the mere existence of a major power. This is an ordinary rather than an unusual condition of things in international relations.

If the period of immediate danger is successfully traversed, with reasonable luck and political skill—and, of course, with the reservation that the thermonuclear stalemate continues to be effective—the United States need not be the loser in a comparison with the Soviet Union. Such a comparison might become very significant during the next decade in determining the courses of the many minor states that with their aspirations and their needs form an increasingly active and influential part of the living reality of the twentieth century world.

APPENDIXES

APPENDIX A

Definition of Terms

THE TERMS *the national interest, national interests, objectives, policies, commitments,* and *principles* are constantly used in the discussion of international relations for analytical, descriptive, persuasive, and even controversial purposes. Even within a given mode of use, the meanings of these terms are likely to vary considerably. These shifts in use and meaning are among the first difficulties that arise when the purpose is strictly analytical. Then, as in the social sciences generally, the handicaps of an inexact terminology are quickly felt. The definitions that follow, while obviously not the only ones that could be developed, are considered to be serviceable for ordinary purposes. In any event, they specify the senses in which these terms are used in this study.

It should first be understood that the terms *the national interest, national interests, objectives, policies, commitments,* and *principles* are used analytically in this volume. They are not used descriptively, persuasively, or controversially. Thus their use should enable an analyst to construct a pattern of decision and action and to locate particular decisions and actions within that pattern.

Take, for example, a particular concrete event—the decision of the United States to engage in lend-lease activities prior to its entrance into the Second World War. The decision was judged by the government to be in *the national interest.* More specifically, the *interest* may have been the strategic security of the United States, the *principle* involved may have been a preference for a peaceful and law-governed international order; while the *objective* was to defeat the Axis powers by increasing the fighting strength of their opponents, the *policy* was to provide military equipment and supplies to secure that *objective;* and particular promises of specified supplies and equipment became *commitments* of the United States Government.

This employment of these terms is analytical in that it makes it possible to organize concrete decisions and actions in a meaningful way, and to relate one decision or action significantly to other decisions or actions. The fact that the United States Executive proposed lend-lease is a raw datum. The analysis of that action and the placing of it within a framework of action leads to information about the purposes of the Roosevelt administration and to a clearer comprehension of the whole series of decisions that was made concurrently and subsequently.

The *national interest* may be defined as the general and continuing end for which a state acts. It embraces such matters as the need of a society to be free from external interference in the maintenance of its identity as an organized state—security from aggression; the desire of a national group to maintain its standard of well-being and cultural cohesion, and the efforts that an organized state, operating politically, makes to achieve the conditions both internally and internationally that will contribute to its security and well-being. This is, of course, a highly generalized definition. But any lower level of generalization tends to lose substantive meaning, and the term becomes increasingly ambiguous. The reason for this is that the requirements of security and well-being not only change with circumstances but are, in addition, matters of judgment and calculation and hence open to varying interpretation by different groups within a nation. In fact, at all lower levels of generalization, it would be preferable to replace the term by *interests,* as this will indicate more precisely particular interpretations for particular conditions.

Interests can then be specifically referred to such diverse motivations as the requirements of physical security, the desire for a higher standard of living, and the wish to transmit a political system to some other society. This use also reveals that *interests* may conflict in any given set of circumstances, and that a choice in terms of priorities and values must be made as a basis for the determination of *objectives* and *policies.*

Take so presumably simple a matter as security. When it is called a *national interest,* there is little room for argument. But then little has been said that is a guide to action. Yet a question of security gives rise to extreme argument, because it is never presented as an abstraction but always in a concrete form. One can say that both isolationalists and interventionists are in agreement about the security of the nation being *the national interest;* they differ about the ways in which *the national interest* is threatened; that is, each interprets *the national interest* as specific *interests* requiring specific supporting actions. Their disagreement may be confined to a factual one about the consequences of various actions. However, it may also, and frequently does, include differing views about involvement in the destiny of one's fellow men, about the nature of man, about values, and even about metaphysical premises concerning the nature of the universe, about the type of action to be undertaken internationally, or about the degree and priority of risk that must be considered before action is determined on. These grounds of difference—and they are real and active in the political sphere—are concealed by an overuse of the term *the national interest,* but are at least opened up for examination by the less generalized term, *interests.*

To avoid confusion in this volume, the term *the national interest* is avoided unless it is clearly used at a high level of generalization. *Interests* is used instead, and is defined as follows: *interests* are what the decision-making group in a government determines is important to the maintenance of the state.

Principles is used to mean the enduring modes of behavior or the relatively established guides to action that characterize nations. A strong sense of proper action and of dismay at action felt to be wrong is constantly revealed in the responses of peoples to the courses prepared or taken by decision-making groups. The decision-making group, concretely concerned with *interests,* tends to think of *principles* as more-or-less subjective and to find them in occasional conflict with *interests.* Nevertheless, *principles* are deeply imbedded in the general culture and political philosophy of a society and are powerful, if intangible and subjective, guides to action. There are real cultural limits on the extent to which *interests* that are in basic conflict with *principles* can be determined and pursued. Thus although *principles* cannot be easily identified and are often modified in action, they represent the underlying patterns of value that guide national action and to which determinations of *interests, objectives,* and *policies* tend over the long run to conform.

Objectives are derived from both *interests* and *principles* and are a specification of previous generalizations for particular circumstances. *Objectives* is thus used to refer to specific goals designed to secure or to support an *interest,* or a *principle,* or some combination of the two. But, it should be noted that the formulation of specific goals is conditioned by the need to come to terms with the *interests* and *principles* of other states. Hence *objectives* must be accommodated to an ability to achieve them against the resistance both of nature and of other states. In consequence of this conditioning, *objectives* generally designate the particular kinds of adjustments in the total international situation sought by a single state. If it were possible, at any given moment, to identify and correlate all the *objectives* of all the *policies* that a state is formulating and implementing, a picture would emerge of how the decision-making group of that state believed the *interests* and *principles* of the state could best be integrated and forwarded under existing circumstances.

Policies is used to refer to specific courses of action designed to achieve *objectives.* As alternative *policies* may be available to achieve an *objective,* there is usually more flexibility in developing *policy* than in defining *objectives.* In common usage *policy* is often made synonymous with *objective,* and even with *interest.* This substitution is avoided in this study. The distinction between *policies* and *objectives* is that between means and ends. But because in the conduct of political affairs, nearly every end is a means to still another end, the *objective* of a particular *policy* tends to be part of a more comprehensive *policy* designed to obtain a more remote *objective.* The distinction between ends and means is consequently analytical and not concrete. Its primary purpose is to permit a series of decisions and actions to be more systematically related.

Commitments denote specific undertakings in support of a particular *policy.* They may be general or precise, depending on circumstances, but in either event they represent fixed points in the application of a *policy.* The term is sometimes used interchangeably for *policy.* In this volume they are differentiated. Thus a *policy* of aid to free nations is distinguished from *commitments* to supply designated amounts of military and financial assistance within a fixed period of time to a particular state. It frequently happens that the *policy* for which a *commitment* has been made ceases to function or falls to a lower priority in the total scheme of action. The extent to which *commitments* continue to be honored in such circumstances is significant. A *principle* of keeping agreements entered into in good faith operates, or the disadvantages of disappointing the created expectations of other states become determining. Both reasons then act as *objectives,* and the maintenance of these *objectives* by keeping agreements becomes a *policy.* The *commitments* continue to be fulfilled, but now in terms of a different *policy.* Thus the analytical structure is still applicable.

By way of final caution, it should be noted that the analytical distinctions employed here are merely tools, which are used only in order to understand and to clarify the relationships of real events.

This leads to the last distinction it is desired to make: the distinction between *the foreign policy of a nation* and *a nation's foreign policies.* The latter term is used only as it has been defined above. The former term is reserved as a shorthand phrase, descriptive of the complex and changing course that a state follows in relation to other states. The *foreign policy of a nation* is, therefore, more than the sum total of its *foreign policies;* for it also includes the *commitments* of a state, the current form of its *interests* and *objectives,* and the *principles* that it professes.

APPENDIX B

Contingencies and Choices: "The Problem Approach"

THE SUBSTANCE of this whole study suggests the general grounds for refusing to take categorical positions or to make final conclusions about problems of foreign policy. The matter can, however, be pressed further.

Recent studies of foreign affairs by the Brookings Institution have followed this same pattern, and its staff has developed a method of attack on problems for the express purpose of bringing its studies into closer correspondence with the process of decision-making in the field of public policy. The controlling assumption was that in this field, problems were not matters to be dealt with in terms of finding the correct answer in the sense of the abstract truth; problems were a continuous flow of specific and concrete situations to be dealt with in terms of taking action-decisions. Furthermore, to take an action-decision was not considered to mean acting on a single hypothesis in order to achieve the goal of a single predetermined result. It was considered to mean choosing among alternative possible courses the one most likely to lead toward the desired goal in view of all the contingencies that could be envisaged.

As the Brookings staff was not in the position of the responsible policy maker and could never be cognizant of all the raw material of information from which the policy maker developed his judgments about the choices that were open and the contingencies that could be identified, the studies were naturally confined to the use of analytical methods that simulated, even if they rationalized, the habits of mind and the approaches used professionally by the policy maker and his aides. The intent was not only to bring the work of nonofficial specialists into consonance with the requirements of policy makers, but also—and perhaps more important—to convey something of the actual nature of problems of public policy and something of the real meaning of the term "decision." This, in essence, was the "problem approach."

Any decision, including those made in the conduct of United States foreign policy, constitutes a problem for the person who must make it. The decision to build the atomic bomb did not follow automatically from the scientific principles that governed its operation. Social conduct was involved, and examinations of social conduct differ from examinations of natural phenomena. The actual decisions that are made can only be understood in terms of the problems they presented to decision-making officials in the situational and historical contexts in which they arose. The history of foreign policy is a history of choices, supplemented by an awareness of choices that were available but were not made.

The earth moves about the sun and not about some other star and man believes that this orbital rotation is independent of conscious choice. In

475

contrast, President Roosevelt's decision to press for lend-lease legislation was made in circumstances that presented alternatives to him, which he could consciously weigh, and from among which he could consciously make his choice. Every situation that calls for conscious decision is one in which man has the problem of choosing from among alternatives. The range of possible alternatives open to the policy maker is usually determined by the resources available for allocation, the evaluation of the objectives or the principles that are involved, and judgments about the reactions of others.

But a decision on the effective use of resources can only be made rationally when there is some system of evaluation that measures the consequences of the alternative choices that might be made. Systems of measurement applicable to equating quantities of things have no use in this connection. What comes into play instead is a system of principles—or values. This leads to the next element in decision making. A decision also involves arranging the applicable principles in an order of preference and evaluating the consequences of action in accordance with this hierarchy of values.

Principles are not static things. They are imbedded in the activity of men, and they change as the conditions of that activity change. The free-movement of labor may have low priority during a war, although it may regain its previous high status following the establishment of peaceful conditions. This would be a case of delayed priority in the hierarchy of values, a situation in which a value is temporarily denied expression in order that its long-range status may be protected. On the other hand, war may produce such drastic changes in the conditions and beliefs of men that a value may not be restored when peace returns. *The decision maker can never substitute some one else's hierarchy of values for his own;* he cannot choose according to any framework of values other than his own. If he is wise and experienced, he will realize that a failure to take account of the values of others will usually result in ineffective action, unless, as is the case with aggressive action, the decision so to act is accompanied by an allocation of resources sufficient to override the resistance to which other systems of value give rise.

Now the third element in the process comes into play: taking account of the claims and possible actions of other nations, and also of domestic groups not directly involved in the process of choice. To what extent must the decision be ensured against the consequences of offsetting decisions by others? Are some choices foreclosed because insurance cannot be taken out against some possible counteractions? How far into the future should the chain of action and reaction be projected? What degree of compromise with an opposition point of view should be sought, and in what circumstances? What adjustments should be made to keep or to acquire sufficient domestic support to carry out the preferred decision?

Seen in terms of these elements, the complexity of decision making is very great. A moment's consideration of what is involved should make it plain that the academic approach—conditioned as it is to the pursuit of absolute truth—is neither similar to nor exchangeable with the approach of the policy maker to problems. At the root of the differences lies the fact that the former need not act or persuade others to act; the latter must. A decision maker is not concerned with the question whether a decision is the right one in the abstract. His concern is: Will the decision be accepted and implemented in the situation that exists here and now? And once the course is initiated, can it be controlled and adjusted to the contingencies that will certainly arise so that the result will be approximately what was desired?

There are two further complicating factors. In the large governmental machinery concerned with the making and execution of foreign policy decisions, the raw data on which decisions are based are almost never seen in their original form by the decision maker. The material has gone through many stages of processing. To an indeterminate extent, the range of possible choices has been reduced, and even the final choice has been partially shaped and predetermined by this chain of collection, analysis, co-ordination, evaluation, re-evaluation, and recommendation.

Secondly, once a decision is made and action on it is started, the problem has changed, and the situation to which the decision was addressed originally cannot be recreated. Despite the talk of statesmen to the effect that such and such conditions are to be restored, previously existing conditions and the alternatives for action that depended on them can never be restored. A country may regain the power to accomplish certain ends, but it always does this in a new context.

Every decision closes some of the alternatives that were available at the time it was made, and action on a decision opens up some new alternatives that were not apparent or perhaps not available before. For example, the decision to maintain the Nationalist Chinese regime when it withdrew to Formosa restricted the opportunities of the United States to cause a cleavage between the Chinese Communists and the Soviet Union. However, it increased the ability of the Nationalists to harass the Communists in the consolidation of their power on the mainland. Although it is possible that the United States may some day find it advisable to change this policy and to attempt to split China and the Soviet Union, that decision would have to be carried out under conditions quite different from those that prevailed in 1949. The specific choices that would be open would be determined by the new, not the old, set of circumstances.

Again, a series of policy decisions may progressively narrow the alternatives open to a nation until in certain large areas, there is virtually no choice in policy determination. This is particularly true when the decisions have led to a number of interlocking commitments. The decision to rearm Germany within the framework of the North Atlantic Treaty Organization in 1950 appears to have been such a decision.

On the other hand, a decision may increase the alternatives that are available to the foreign policy planner. The decision to continue constructing atomic weapons after the close of the Second World War opened to the United States the alternative of a possibly successful preventive war if the Soviet Union were to prove too dangerous a potential threat. Moreover, it did not close off the possibilities of negotiation, accommodation, or the formation of a bloc of free nations.

A decision, consequently, should be thought of as a lever that directs the course of history from a set of present alternatives to a new set of alternatives. Each of the alternative decisions is a pathway to a set of future alternatives. Of course these future alternatives are rarely so distinct and accurately defined as this discussion would seem to indicate. Moreover, many decisions are made within the same period of time, and they mutually influence the future possibilities. The situation is so complex that the human mind can deal with it only by employing the mechanisms of simplification and by considering the situations separately to the fullest extent possible.

At the simplest level, the decision maker requires information concerning the consequences of the alternative policies that are open to his choice. This information cannot be supplied when it is needed unless a good deal of advance work has been consistently done. High on the list of requirements is knowledge of the objectives, policies, and systems of values of other states. This knowledge, it may be noted parenthetically, consists largely of informed guesses that have a way of becoming rigid hypotheses. Judgments must also be available of the various ways in which other states may act in response to United States decisions.

The difficulty of obtaining reliable information about any of these factors has led to rules-of-thumb in policy making. Experienced officials often operate according to unstated rules, which can be termed their operational codes. These codes are statements of the prudent rules of conduct for situations in which not much is known or is likely to be known. For example, it is generally held to be wise to follow a policy that leaves an alternative open should the policy fail. It is generally prudent not to bluff, particularly if a situation can be made worse if the bluff is called. It is generally prudent to be cautious and precise with respect to entering into commitments. Of course, the final rule is that there are exceptions to all rules of prudence. The virtue of being experienced consists in the accumulated professional judgment that permits the exception to be made with confidence.

There are no certainties in international relations, and when the state is scarcely distinguishable from the lives and hopes of countless individuals and from institutions that have developed over centuries, the responsibility of the decision maker consists primarily in making prudent calculations to protect the investment that has already been made in the life of the nation. This is particularly true of an established and mature nation like the United States.

This complex, uncertain, and never-ending process of dealing with policy problems by taking action-decisions responds to analysis only if the method of analysis bears some resemblance to the process itself. Naturally, there can be no hope, and there need be no intention, of reproducing the process. In any case, to reproduce it unrelated to an action responsibility would be to operate it in a vacuum. All that is needed is to employ a formalized representation.

This need not be too complex, as it requires no more than: (1) identifying and describing a problem in the form in which it is actually being presented; (2) collecting, organizing, and presenting the information that is relevant to taking action; and (3) identifying and discussing the alternative solutions that are available in terms of consequences and contingencies. The final step—the decision, the choice of an alternative—can be omitted, leaving the reader in the position of the policy maker with the act of decision still to perform.

Like the policy maker, he will have the problem laid out before him in a relevant context, and he will also have before him the fullest range of choices and the clearest obtainable basis for exercising judgment. Even if he does not wish to make a choice, he will at least have been put in touch with the habit of mind required to approach problems of policy.

In the view of the Brookings staff, as exemplified in their studies of foreign policy, the "problem approach" also furnishes a means of linking the work of the government official with the work of the teacher and the student of international relations and with the public discussion of United States policy. It can provide a common ground for appreciating the difficulties of conducting foreign relations and understanding the limitations on national action in the international system. But above all, it can be used to develop the realistic attitudes toward policy and the minimum analytical skills that are needed if public opinion is to be well-informed.

APPENDIX C

Defense, Foreign Aid, and Other Uses of Output, 1946-1955[1]

IN ORDER to estimate how much of the total physical volume of the production of goods and services has been absorbed by national defense and foreign aid and how much has been available for other purposes, it is necessary to have estimates of national defense and foreign aid that include only expenditures on goods and services and that are also adjusted to eliminate the effects of price changes. The government publishes official estimates of the total value of goods and services produced, adjusted to a constant price basis, but it does not publish correspondingly adjusted estimates for national defense and foreign aid. To estimate the volume of goods and services available for other purposes, therefore, it is necessary to estimate national defense and foreign aid expenditures in constant prices, deflating official estimates of their value in current (*i.e.* prevailing) prices by using the most appropriate of the available price indexes and being sure that military foreign aid is not counted both in defense expenditures and in foreign aid.

The method of estimating national defense expenditures, excluding military grants to foreign countries, at 1947 prices is shown in Table A. The concept of "national defense expenditures" rather than "national security expenditures" was used because the former excludes expenditures for international security and foreign relations (other than military assistance) and, after 1949, for promotion of the merchant marine. "National defense expenditures" include military services, military assistance, civil defense, development and control of atomic energy, promotion of defense production, and economic stabilization, and, before 1950, promotion of the merchant marine.[2] Because military assistance was to be included in foreign aid, it was substracted from national defense expenditures. It should be noted that the removal of all military assistance from national defense expenditures assumes that all military assistance is included in the figures for these expenditures. There is some question about how much of the military aid during the years 1946-50 actually is included in these figures. Because total military aid was small in these years, however, any error involved in subtracting it all must also be small.

No price index exactly appropriate for the deflation of defense expenditures is available. There are official estimates of total federal government expenditures on goods and services, both with and without adjustment for price changes. The ratio of these two series implies a price

[1] By Walter S. Salant.
[2] *Cf. National Income, 1954 Edition*, p. 148.

480

Table A

EXPENDITURES ON GOODS AND SERVICES FOR NATIONAL DEFENSE[a]

(Money figures in billions of dollars)

Year	National Defense Expenditures and Military Grants in Current Prices				National Defense Expenditures, Excluding Military Grants to Foreign Countries (In 1947 prices)
	National Defense Expenditures, Including Military Grants to Foreign Countries	Military Grants to Foreign Counties	National Defense Expenditures, Excluding Military Grants to Foreign Countries	Price Index (1947 = 100)	
	(1)	(2)	(3)	(4)	(5)
1946	19.60	.07	19.53	92.2	21.18
1947	12.25	.04	12.21	100.0	12.21
1948	11.58	.30	11.28	100.8	11.19
1949	13.57	.21	13.36	104.6	12.77
1950	14.26	.53	13.73	108.0	12.71
1951	33.86	1.47	32.39	119.9	27.01
1952	46.41	2.60	43.81	119.0	36.82
1953	49.39	4.25	45.14	116.2	38.85
1954	41.45	3.13	38.32	118.4	32.36
1955	38.8	2.15	36.7	123.1	29.8

[a] Sources: U. S. Department of Commerce, *Survey of Current Business*, various issues as indicated.
Col. 1. 1946 estimated from national security expenditures in 1946 and relation between national defense and national security expenditures in 1947; 1947–54 from "National Income and Product of the United States 1954" (July 1955), Table 2; 1955 from "National Income and Product, 1955" (February 1956), Table 5.
Col. 2. 1946–52 from "Balance of Payments of the United States, 1919–53" (July 1954), Table 1, line 28; 1953–54 from "The First Quarter Balance of Payments" (June 1955), Table 3, line 29; 1955 from "Balance of Payments, Fourth Quarter" (March 1956), Table 3, line 2.
Col. 3. =Col. 1 less Col. 2.
Col. 4. This index is the implicit price deflator for federal government purchases of goods and services, given for 1946–54 in line 14, Table 41, "National Income and Product of the United States 1954" (July 1955); 1955 implicit deflator computed as ratio of federal government purchases of goods and services in current and 1947 prices, shown in Tables 5 and 1 respectively, "National Income and Product, 1955" (February 1956).
Col. 5. =Col. 3 ÷ Col. 4 ×100.

index for total federal government expenditures on goods and services. Inasmuch as national defense expenditures were more than half the total of such federal expenditures in all but two of the postwar years and were much more than half in most of them, this implicit price index was used to convert national defense expenditures from a current to a constant price basis. This index, although not an appropriate one, appears to be the best available.

The derivation of foreign aid expenditures in current prices is shown in

Table B, and the adjustment of it for price changes is shown in Table C. Grants and loans that are authorized but not disbursed are excluded because they involve no use of current goods and services. The grant component is taken to consist of all *net* international transfers by the government for which no goods, services, or assets were received in return,

Table B

UNITED STATES FOREIGN AID EXPENDITURES[a]

(In millions of dollars at current prices)

Year	U.S. Government Net Unilateral Transfers, Excluding Investments in IBRD Pensions, etc. (1)	U.S. Government Net Capital Movements, Including Investments in IBRD and IMF (2)	Total (3)	Adjustment for Investments in IBRD and IMF (4)	Adjusted Total (5)
1946	2343	3024	5367	323	5044
1947	1940	6969	8909	2300	6609
1948	4194	1024	5218	—	5218
1949	5207	652	5859	—	5859
1950	4010	156	4166	—	4166
1951	4505	156	4661	—	4661
1952	4563	420	4983	—	4983
1953	6082	218	6300	—	6300
1954	4710	−93	4617	—	4617
1955[b]	3973	293	4266	—	4266

[a] Sources: U. S. Department of Commerce, *Survey of Current Business*, various issues as indicated.
1946–52: Col. 1. "Balance of Payments of the United States 1919–53" (July 1954), Table 1, lines 28 and 29.
    Col. 2. *Ibid.*, line 39.
    Col. 4. *Balance of Payments of the United States 1949–1951*, Table 3a. Adjustment is second line less fourth line.
1953–54: Col. 1. "The First Quarter Balance of Payments" (June 1955), Table 3, lines 29 and 30.
    Col. 2. *Ibid.*, line 39.
1955:   Col. 1. "Balance of Payments During Fourth Quarter" (March 1956), Table 3, lines 27 and 28.
    Col. 2. *Ibid.*, line 37.
All years: Col. 3 = Col. 1 + Col. 2.
    Col. 5 = Col. 3 − Col. 4.
[b] Preliminary.

except pensions, as shown in statistics of the balance of international payments. The figures are net of receipts such as reverse Lend-Lease and Mutual Security Administration-Economic Cooperation Administration counterpart funds, but the total of receipts deducted from expenditures, through 1951 at least, was never more than $330 million.[3] The loan com-

[3] *Cf. Balance of Payments of the United States 1949-1951*, Table 23.

ponent of foreign aid is the figure shown in the balance of payments for *net* outflow of government capital. This means that repayments of past loans have been deducted from disbursements of new loans.

Foreign aid figures for 1946 and 1947 have been adjusted to remove the large subscription by the United States Government to the capital

Table C

CONVERSION OF FOREIGN AID FROM CURRENT TO 1947 PRICE BASIS[a]

(Money figures in millions of dollars)

	Foreign Aid in Current Prices			Price Indexes (1947 = 100)		Foreign Aid in 1947 Prices		
Year	Total (1)	Military Grants (2)	All Other (3)	For Military Grants (4)	For "All Other" (5)	Military Grants (6)	"All Other" (7)	Total (8)
1946	5044	69	4975	92.2	84.0	75	5923	5998
1947	6609	43	6566	100.0	100.0	43	6566	6609
1948	5218	300	4918	100.8	106.4	298	4622	4920
1949	5859	210	5649	104.6	98.9	201	5712	5913
1950	4166	526	3640	108.0	95.7	487	3804	4291
1951	4661	1470	3191	119.9	109.6	1226	2911	4137
1952	4983	2603	2380	119.0	109.0	2187	2183	4370
1953	6300	4251	2049	116.2	108.5	3658	1888	5546
1954	4617	3132	1485	118.4	106.9	2645	1389	4034
1955[b]	4266	2146	2120	123.1	108.0	1743	1963	3706

[a] Sources:
Col. 1. From Table B, Col. 5.
Col. 2. 1946–52 from "Balance of Payments of the United States 1919–53," *Survey of Current Business* (July 1954), Table 1, line 28; 1953–54 from "The First Quarter Balance of Payments," *Survey of Current Business* (June 1955), Table 3, line 29; 1955 from "Balance of Payments during Fourth Quarter," *Survey of Current Business* (March 1956), Table 3, line 27.
Col. 3. = Col. 1 less Col. 2.
Col. 4. From Table A, Col. 4.
Col. 5. This is the index of the unit value of United States exports on a 1936–38 base, shifted to a 1947 base. 1946–54 index from *Business Statistics* (1955 edition). 1955 from *World Trade Information Service*, January-February 1956, Part 3, "Total Export and Import Trade of the United States."
Col. 6. = Col. 2 ÷ Col. 4 × 100.
Col. 7. = Col. 3 ÷ Col. 5 × 100.
Col. 8. = Col. 6 plus Col. 7.
[b] Preliminary.

stock of the International Bank for Reconstruction and Development and the International Monetary Fund. In these years these two institutions had no immediate use for most of the dollars thus received, so they reinvested most of the proceeds in the United States. To the extent of this reinvestment, the transaction can be regarded as a paper one, an exchange of financial assets that involved no drain of United States goods and services. Consequently, a figure has been deducted representing the difference between the amount of the United States subscription to the capital stock and the disbursements by the two institutions to foreign countries. The effect of this procedure is to treat the payments by the United States Government to the two institutions as not being United States aid and to treat the payments by the two institutions to other countries as though they were United States aid.

It is assumed that the resulting figures do represent a draft on current output of goods and services. It should be noted, however, that some foreign aid took the form of cash and some the form of transfers of goods purchased abroad. There is a question to what extent such aid has resulted in larger exports from the United States. To the extent that it has resulted in the accumulation of foreign reserves or other financial assets by the recipient or other foreign countries, no draft on the real resources of the United States occurs, and the real burden of foreign aid is overstated by these estimates.

In adjusting the resulting foreign aid figures for price changes, the total aid was separated into military grants and all other aid. Military grants in current prices were deflated by the same price index that was used to deflate defense expenditures. Some of this aid consisted of military goods that the United States purchased abroad and transferred to the aid recipient. It was pointed out above that the proceeds of this expenditure might not have been spent in the United States at all. Here it may be noted that if they were spent in the United States, they were probably spent on nonmilitary goods or services and in that case the price index used for deflating this portion of military aid is not an appropriate one. However, the total amount of aid consisting of military goods purchased abroad was negligible before 1952 and has not exceeded approximately $700 million since then, so the error involved in using an inappropriate price index to deflate it is small.

In adjusting all other aid, the Department of Commerce index of the unit value of exports, shifted to a 1947 base, was used. Although objections could be raised to the use of this index, it seemed better than any other available measure of price changes for exports.

The last columns of Tables A and C, derived by the procedures just described, provide the estimates used in the second and third columns of the table in the footnote on page 379. The first column of this table comes from Table 1 of the article "National Income and Product in 1955" (*Survey of Current Business,* February 1956), except for the 1946 figure which comes from Table 40 of "National Income and Product of the United States, 1954" (*Survey of Current Business,* July 1955).

The population figures used to convert the fourth column to a per capita basis were taken from the *1955 Historical and Descriptive Supplement to Economic Indicators* (page 9) and *Economic Indicators* (May 1956, page 6), published by the Joint Committee on the Economic Report (84 Congress).

APPENDIX D

Selected Bibliography

THIS reading list is intended to supplement the general analyses of the volume. The items cover in the main the period from the Second World War to the present time.

Official Publications

The number of official publications in the field of international relations continues to grow so rapidly that it is becoming increasingly difficult for either a student or a general reader to select easily the items he may wish to use. It is the purpose of this bibliographical note to lessen that burden by setting forth some basic guides to official sources.

United States

There are a number of publications issued regularly by government departments that provide current official materials. The *Monthly Catalog of United States Government Publications* is a monthly listing (cumulative annually) by the issuing agency of all publications, printed and processed, that come to the attention of the Superintendent of Documents of the Government Printing Office and that are generally available to the public. Most important among the government publications on foreign affairs is the Department of State *Bulletin,* which is published weekly. It is a primary source of official information on developments in the field of United States foreign relations and on the work of the Department of State and the Foreign Service. It contains selected press releases on foreign policy issued by the White House and the Department of State, statements and addresses by the President and the Secretary of State and other officers of the department, texts of notes and official statements, information concerning treaties and international agreements, and special articles on international affairs and the operations of the department.

The Department of State also publishes other material on general and specific subjects connected with United States foreign relations: treaties, diplomatic correspondence, official analyses of various aspects of United States foreign policy, collections of documents, records of international conferences, and many other useful materials. One such publication is *Foreign Relations of the United States,* an annual volume of state papers. A basic collection of Department of State publications is available in most college and university libraries. There are complete files of all publications in selected libraries designated as government depositories. A cumulative list of Department of State publications for the period October 1, 1929, to January 1, 1953, has been published, as well as one covering the period from January 1, 1953, to December 31, 1954. Cumulative lists of current publications are issued from time to time.

On foreign economic problems, *Foreign Commerce Weekly,* published by the Department of Commerce, *Foreign Agriculture,* published monthly by the Department of Agriculture, the *Treasury Bulletin,* a monthly, and the *Federal Reserve Bulletin,* also a monthly, contain much valuable information.

Congressional documents furnish a wide range of materials both official and nonofficial. Hearings, materials printed as public documents, and the texts of bills can ordinarily be obtained on request from members of Congress. Records of debate in deliberative bodies are another excellent source on the development of foreign policies. The *Congressional Record* is in most libraries.

Two special congressional publications provide useful compilations of foreign policy documents. *A Decade of American Foreign Policy: Basic Documents, 1941-49,* published in 1950 at the request of the Senate Committee on Foreign Relations, contains over three hundred documents relating to problems that are of concern to the United States. *Review of the United Nations Charter: A Collection of Documents,* published in 1954 for the Senate Subcommittee on the United Nations Charter, comprises nearly two hundred documents selected as background for consideration of the review of the Charter of the United Nations.

Atomic Energy Commission. *In the Matter of J. Robert Oppenheimer.* Transcript of Hearing before Personnel Security Board, April 12, 1954, through May 6, 1954. Washington: Government Printing Office, 1954, 993 pp. A source of information on the development of the hydrogen bomb.

Commission on Foreign Economic Policy (The Randall Commission). *Report to the President and the Congress.* Washington: Government Printing Office, 1954, 94 pp. Re-examination of American foreign economic policy in the Eisenhower Administration.

Congress, House Committee on Foreign Affairs. *Background Information on the Soviet Union in International Relations.* Washington: Government Printing Office, 1950, 54 pp. H. Rept. 3135, giving a compilation of material based on published documents, indicating some of the main currents of Soviet policy—such as treaty violations, obstructionism in the solution of international problems, and territorial expansion.

Congress, Joint Committee on the Economic Report. *Trends in Economic Growth: A Comparison of the Western Powers and the Soviet Bloc.* Washington: Government Printing Office, 1955, 339 pp. This study, prepared by the Legislative Reference Service of the Library of Congress, concludes that "the present economic capacity of Western Europe, the United States, and Canada is significantly greater in terms of absolute magnitudes, diversity, and flexibility than the combined strength" of the Soviet Union and the satellite countries of Eastern Europe. This does not, of course, take into account the vast resources of Communist

China. Included in the report are staff papers on population and man power, agriculture, transportation, foreign trade, and other related subjects. There are also useful statistical tables and charts.

Congress, Senate Armed Services and Foreign Relations Committees. *Military Situation in the Far East*. 82 Cong. 1 sess. Washington: Government Printing Office, 1951, 5 vols., including Appendix and Index, 3691 pp. Hearings to conduct an inquiry into the military situation in the Far East following the dismissal of General MacArthur.

Economic Cooperation Administration. Special Mission to the United Kingdom. *The Sterling Area: An American Analysis*. Washington: Government Printing Office, 1952, 672 pp. This volume brings together for reference purposes basic economic information about the sterling area and about the economies and main commodities of the member countries, with particular attention to the period from the end of 1945 to the middle of 1950.

Gray, Gordon, and others. *Report to the President on Foreign Economic Policies*. Washington: Government Printing Office, November 1950, 131 pp. Broad recommendations for an American foreign economic policy.

International Development Advisory Board. *Partners in Progress: A Report to the President* (The Rockefeller Report). Washington: Government Printing Office, March 1951, 120 pp. A report on problems of underdeveloped areas. It concludes that to strengthen the economies of the underdeveloped regions and to improve their living levels must be considered a vital part of the defense mobilization of the United States.

Library of Congress, Legislative Reference Service. *Trends in Russian Foreign Policy Since World War I*, prepared for the use of the Senate Committee on Foreign Relations. Washington: Government Printing Office, 1947, 68 pp. A chronology of events from March 15, 1917, to January 1, 1947.

President's Materials Policy Commission. *Resources for Freedom* (The Paley Report). Washington: Government Printing Office, 1952, 5 vols., 184, 210, 43, 228, and 154 pp. respectively. Volume I—Foundations for Growth and Security; Volume II—The Outlook for Key Commodities; Volume III—The Outlook for Energy Sources; Volume IV—The Promise of Technology; Volume V—Selected Reports to the Commission.

Public Advisory Board for Mutual Security. *A Trade and Tariff Policy in the National Interest: A Report to the President* (The Bell Report). Washington: Government Printing Office, February 1953, 78 pp. Recommendations for a United States trade and tariff policy.

State, Department of. *The Department of State, 1930-1955: Expanding Functions and Responsibilities*. Washington: Government Printing Office, August 1955, 66 pp. A study of the machinery available in the Department of State for the formulation and execution of foreign policy.

———. *East Germany under Soviet Control*. Washington: Government

Printing Office, 1952, 95 pp. Publication 4596. A description of life in the Soviet Zone of Germany as viewed from West Berlin.

———. *Foreign Relations of the United States: The Conferences at Malta and Yalta 1945*. Washington: Government Printing Office, 1955, 1032 pp. Broad documentary coverage of the Malta and Yalta conferences, including background material.

———. *The Geneva Conference of Heads of Government, July 18-23, 1955*. Washington: Government Printing Office, 1955, 88 pp. Publication 6046. Documents showing the kinds of problems discussed at the "summit" conference and United States policy with respect to them.

———. *The Geneva Meeting of Foreign Ministers, October 27-November 16, 1955*. Washington: Government Printing Office, 1955, 306 pp. Publication 6156. Texts of the proposals of the United States, Great Britain, France, and the Soviet Union, together with the principal statements of the four foreign ministers.

———. *Germany 1947-1949: The Story in Documents*. Washington: Government Printing Office, 1950, 631 pp. Publication 3556. The story in documents of American policy toward Germany and of developments in Germany from January 1947 to September 1949. Early documentation on occupation policy respecting Germany was published by the Department of State in the pamphlet *Occupation of Germany: Policy and Progress, 1945-1946*. Publication 2783, released August 1947.

———. *In Quest of Peace and Security: Selected Documents on American Foreign Policy, 1941-1951*. Washington: Government Printing Office, 1951, 120 pp. Publication 4245. The selection includes documents relating to the wartime period, to defeated and occupied areas, and to security against aggression.

———. *International Organizations in Which the United States Participates*. Washington: Government Printing Office, 1949, 335 pp. Publication 3655, released February 1950. Information on the international bodies with which the United States is concerned, with brief accounts of the origins functions, membership, and activities of each.

———. *The Korean Problem at the Geneva Conference, April 26-June 15, 1954*. Washington: Government Printing Office, 1954, 193 pp. Publication 5609. Background and documents on Korean problem.

———. *London and Paris Agreements: September-October 1954*. Washington: Government Printing Office, November 1954, 128 pp. Publication 5659. Texts of documents resulting from nine-power conference held in London September 28-October 3 and Paris conference of October 20-23 on the status of Western Germany. The report of Secretary of State Dulles on these meetings is also included.

———. *Making the Peace Treaties, 1941-1947*. Washington: Government Printing Office, 1947, 150 pp. Publication 2774. A documented history of the making of the peace, beginning with the Atlantic Charter and culminating in the drafting of the Axis satellite peace treaties.

———. *Nazi-Soviet Relations, 1939-1941*. Washington: Government Printing Office, 1948, 362 pp. Publication 3023. Collection of documents from the Archives of the German Foreign Office bearing on German-Soviet relations during these years.

———. *Objectives of U.S. Foreign Policy in Latin America.* Washington: Government Printing Office, 1955, 51 pp. Publication 6131. Five speeches by the Assistant Secretary of State for Inter-American Affairs.

———. *Our Southern Partners: The Story of Our Latin American Relations.* Washington: Government Printing Office, 1954, 48 pp. Publication 5604. A very brief examination of one hundred and fifty years of United States foreign policy in Latin America.

———. *Point Four.* Washington: Government Printing Office, 1950, 107 pp. Publication 3719. A co-operative program for aid in the development of economically underdeveloped areas.

———. *Postwar Foreign Policy Preparation: 1939-1945.* Washington: Government Printing Office, February 1950, 726 pp. Publication 3580. Documented record of the planning and preparation in the Department of State during the Second World War for postwar international organization.

———. *Southeast Asia Treaty Organization: First Annual Report of the Council Representatives March 1956.* Washington: Government Printing Office, March 1956, 27 pp. The texts of the Pacific Charter and the Southeast Asia Collective Defense Treaty are included in this pamphlet.

———. *Treaties of Peace with Italy, Bulgaria, Hungary, Rumania, and Finland.* (English versions). Washington: Government Printing Office, 1947, Publication 2743. Separately paged. The texts of the treaties of peace with the Axis satellites.

———. *The United Nations Conference on International Organization, San Francisco, California, April 25-June 26, 1945: Selected Documents.* Washington: Government Printing Office, 1946, 992 pp. Publication 2490, Conference Series 83. A selection of documents from the full sixteen-volume record.

———. *The United States and Germany 1945-1955.* Washington: Government Printing Office, 1955, 56 pp. Publication 5827. Recapitulation of United States policy for Germany.

———. *United States-Latin American Relations: Report to the President.* Washington: Government Printing Office, December 1953, 23 pp. Publication 5290. Report of Milton S. Eisenhower, who headed a special mission to Latin America in order to make recommendations to the new Republican administration on United States policy for that area.

———. *U. S. Policy in the Near East, South Asia, and Africa, 1954.* Washington: Government Printing Office, 1955, 70 pp. Publication 5801. A compilation of American policy in these areas together with footnote references and tables.

———. *United States Relations with China,* with special reference to the period 1944-49. Washington: Government Printing Office, August 1949, 1054 pp. Publication 3573. The China White Paper, published by the Truman administration to justify United States policy toward China during this period. The annexes contain many documents.

Other

Official state papers of foreign governments are not readily available to American students. However, most foreign governments maintain information services in the United States. They issue English-language publications containing texts of official documents and statements as well as other relevant foreign material. A convenient reference to British official publications is the *Government Publications Monthly List* of Her Majesty's Stationery Office. The record of debates in the United Kingdom Parliament can be found in *Hansard*, which is in most larger American libraries, as is the *Journal Officiel*, which records debates in the French National Assembly. An unofficial publication that is helpful because of the difficulty in obtaining Soviet material is the *Current Digest of the Soviet Press*, published by the Joint Committee on Slavic Studies. It often carries in translation complete texts of important documents.

The use of United Nations documents presents unusual problems because they are so numerous and because they cover so broad a range of subject matter. A special classification system has been developed to facilitate their use. The General Assembly, the Security Council, the Economic and Social Council, and the Trusteeship Council each have separate series of *Official Records*. These record the debates in these organs and in some instances the texts of resolutions passed by them. In addition, the resolutions adopted at each session of the General Assembly, the Economic and Social Council, and the Trusteeship Council are published in collected form. The *Yearbook of the United Nations* contains texts of resolutions, summaries of the deliberations of United Nations organs, and brief discussions of principal developments connected with the United Nations. The specialized agencies and commissions issue bulletins or reviews at stated intervals, as well as annual reports and technical and economic surveys. A *Treaty Series* is published of all treaties and international agreements registered, filed, or recorded with the Secretariat of the United Nations.

Since January 1950 the United Nations has issued a monthly *United Nations Documents Index*. This lists documents and other publications, arranged chronologically under the issuing agencies: General Assembly, Security Council, Economic and Social Council, Trusteeship Council, International Court of Justice, and Secretariat, as well as the specialized agencies. In each issue, which covers one year, there is a general index. In 1955 the United Nations published *Ten Years of United Nations Publications 1945 to 1955*, which is a complete catalogue of official records, publications, and periodicals of the Organization covering the period from the San Francisco Conference in 1945 to December 1954. The specialized agencies are not included in this compendium.

The Pan American Union is the principal central source for official documents concerned with inter-American affairs. It publishes texts of documents, analyses of inter-American problems, and other materials on relations with Latin America.

Council of Europe. *European Yearbook*. Vol. I. The Hague: Martinus Nijhoff, 1955, 584 pp. The first of an annual volume on European institutions and their activities. Various phases of European co-operation are considered by officials in these bodies. Some discussions are in English; others in French. A documentary section contains basic documents on European organizations, including the Brussels Treaty Organization, the OEEC, the Council of Europe, the Coal and Steel Community, and others. There is a bibliographical section on European integration.

————. *Focus on East-West Relations: A Policy for Europe*. Strasbourg: January 1956, 252 pp. The publication in a separate volume of texts relating to debates held by the Consultative Assembly during 1955 on East-West relations. The aim of the debates has been to establish a joint European approach to the East.

International Bank for Reconstruction and Development. *The Economy of Turkey: An Analysis and Recommendations for a Development Program*. Washington: International Bank for Reconstruction and Development, 1951, 87 pp. Report of an economic mission to Turkey in 1950.

Lord Ismay. *NATO, The First Five Years, 1949-1954*. Paris: 1954, 280 pp. The Secretary General of the North Atlantic Treaty Organization discusses the origins of the treaty, the evolution of the civil and military machinery necessary for its execution, and the accomplishments of the Western alliance from 1949 to July 1954. Appendices contain a chronology of developments leading to the treaty, NATO communiqués, and other related documents.

Organization for European Economic Cooperation. *Seventh Report of the OEEC: Economic Expansion and Its Problems*. Paris: February 1956, 298 pp. Part I of this annual report considers Western Europe as a unit. Part II contains country studies.

U.S.S.R. Ministry of Foreign Affairs. *Documents and Materials Relating to the Eve of the Second World War*. New York: International Publisher, 1948, 2 vols. Published by the Soviet Government in reply to the publication of the U. S. State Department on "Nazi-Soviet Relations, 1939-41." Includes English translations of documents from the German Foreign Office and private papers from the estate of the German Ambassador to Great Britain, chiefly covering the period of Munich.

United Nations. *Catalogue of Economic and Social Projects of the United Nations and the Specialized Agencies, 1954,* No. 5, 157 pp. U. N. Sales No. 1954. II D.2. The work of the secretariat of the United Nations and the specialized agencies in the economic and social fields is described.

————. *Documents of the United Nations Conference on International Organization,* San Francisco, 1945. London and New York: U.N. Information Organization, in co-operation with the Library of Congress, 1945-46, 16 vols. The basic documents of the conference that drafted the United Nations Charter.

————. Economic Commission for Europe. *Economic Survey of Europe*

Since the War: A Reappraisal of Problems and Prospects. Geneva: 1953, 385 pp. U.N. Sales No. 1953. II.E.4. A review of the history, problems, policies, and results of economic developments in Europe in the postwar period.

Memoirs and the Like

Out of the Second World War and the last decade has come a group of memoirs, biographies, and autobiographies of government officials, military leaders, and others who have shared in the making of policies and events. Although these volumes are unofficial, they are nonetheless primary sources for much material relating to the period under consideration in the present study.

Adenauer, Konrad. *World Indivisible With Liberty and Justice For All.* (Translated from the German by Richard and Clara Winston.) New York: Harper and Bros., 1955, 128 pp. Selections from Chancellor Adenauer's speeches covering the period from the inception of the Federal Republic in September 1949 to the entrance of Western Germany into the North Atlantic Treaty Organization and Western European Union in May 1955.

Bowles, Chester. *Ambassador's Report.* New York: Harper and Bros., 1954, 415 pp. The former Ambassador to India reports on his mission there in 1951-53. He examines many of the problems common to Southeast Asia.

Bundy, McGeorge (ed.). *The Pattern of Responsibility.* Boston: Houghton Mifflin Co., 1952, 309 pp. The public record of Secretary of State Acheson from January 1949 to August 1951.

Byrnes, James F. *Speaking Frankly.* New York and London: Harper and Bros., 1947, 324 pp. Secretary Byrnes' account of his tenure as Secretary of State, including the negotiation of the Balkan and Italian peace settlements.

Campbell-Johnson, Alan, *Mission with Mountbatten.* New York: E. P. Dutton and Co., 1953, 383 pp. The story of the mission of the last Viceroy and first constitutional Governor-General of India.

Clark, Mark W. *From the Danube to the Yalu.* New York: Harper and Bros., 1954, 369 pp. The experiences of the Commander of the United Nations forces in Korea from May 1952 to the signing of the cease-fire agreement in July 1953. Among other matters, he discusses alternative courses of action open to the United States in connection with the resolution of the Korean War.

Clay, Lucius D. *Decision in Germany.* Garden City, N.Y.: Doubleday and Co., 1950, 522 pp. A record of four years of service (April 1945-May 1949) as deputy military governor and as military governor of the United States zone of Germany.

Connally, Tom (as told to Alfred Steinberg). *My Name is Tom Connally.* New York: Thomas Y. Crowell Co., 1954, 376 pp. The autobiography of the former Democratic Chairman of the Senate Committee on Foreign Relations. Among other subjects of interest to the student of foreign affairs, he discusses the establishment of the United Nations Organization, Greek-Turkish aid, the Marshall Plan, the North Atlantic Treaty, the Korean War, and bipartisan foreign policy.

Churchill, Winston S. *The Second World War:* (Vol. I, *The Gathering Storm;* Vol. II, *Their Finest Hour;* Vol. III, *The Grand Alliance;* Vol. IV, *The Hinge of Fate;* Vol. V, *Closing the Ring;* Vol. VI, *Triumph and Tragedy*). Boston: Houghton Mifflin Co., 1948, 1949, 1950, 1951, and 1953, 784, 751, 903, 1000, 740, and 800 pp., respectively. Both a chronicle and discussion of outstanding political and military events, Vol. I covers the interwar years 1919-39; Vol. II, through the fall of France and the Battle of Britain; Vol. III, blitz and anti-blitz, 1941, Anglo-American relations, and the entrance of the "strange new ally," Russia; Vol. IV, the onslaught of Japan, 1942, and the 1942-43 Africa Campaign; Vol. V, the events of 1943-44, from the invasion of Sicily to the eve of the Normandy invasion; Vol. VI, the remainder of the Second World War and the Potsdam conference.

Deane, John R. *The Strange Alliance: The Story of Our Efforts at Wartime Co-operation with Russia.* New York: Viking Press, 1947, 344 pp. General Deane headed the American Military Mission to Moscow during the war years. He adds to the authoritative published material on the international conferences of the period, ending with Potsdam. His narrative shows the difficulties in the way of United States collaboration with the Soviet Union even in wartime.

Dedijer, Vladimir. *Tito.* New York: Simon and Schuster, 1953, 443 pp. The authorized biography of Tito.

Dulles, John Foster. *War or Peace.* New York: Macmillan Co., 1950, 274 pp. The views of the author on United States foreign policy before he became Secretary of State.

Hiscocks, Richard. *The Rebirth of Austria.* New York: Oxford University Press, 1953, 263 pp. An account of Austria under four-power occupation, by the British Representative on the Allied Control Council from 1946 to 1949. The volume contains background material from the prewar period. There is also a bibliography on postwar Austria and maps.

Hull, Cordell. *The Memoirs of Cordell Hull.* New York: Macmillan Co., 1948, 2 vols. 1804 pp. An account of the major developments and decisions in American foreign relations between 1933 and 1945 while Cordell Hull was Secretary of State.

Jones, Joseph M. *The Fifteen Weeks (February 21-June 5, 1947).* New York: The Viking Press, 1955, 296 pp. The events surrounding the decision to put into force the Truman Doctrine.

King, Ernest J., and Whitehill, Walter Muir. *Fleet Admiral King: A Naval Record.* New York: W. W. Norton and Co., 1952, 674 pp. This volume includes an account of the international conferences in which Admiral King participated as a member of the Combined Chiefs of Staff from August 1941 to Potsdam. It presents authoritative basic data.

Lane, Arthur Bliss, *I Saw Poland Betrayed: An American Ambassador Reports to the American People.* Indianapolis and New York: Bobbs-Merrill Co., 1948, 344 pp. The failure of a mission: to ensure "free and unfettered elections." Ambassador Lane tells how the Communists consolidated their power in Poland.

Langer, William L. *Our Vichy Gamble.* New York: Alfred A. Knopf, 1947, 412 pp. United States policy toward Vichy France examined by an historian at the request of Secretary of State Cordell Hull, with the benefit of official documents and conferences with key officials.

Leahy, William D. *I Was There: The Personal Story of the Chief of Staff to Presidents Roosevelt and Truman Based on His Notes and Diaries Made at the Time.* New York: Whittlesey House, 1950, 527 pp. Personal observations on many historic conversations and events between November 1940 and September 1945, including the Cairo, Teheran, Malta, Yalta, and Potsdam conferences. A source of authoritative unofficial material of the period.

Lie, Trygve. *In the Cause of Peace.* New York: Macmillan Co., 1954, 473 pp. The first Secretary-General of the United Nations reviews the problems that concerned him most during his seven years in office. He examines his efforts to mediate East-West differences.

Mao Tse-Tung. *Selected Works.* Vol. I: 1926-1936, Vol. II: 1937-1938, Vol. III: 1939-1941. New York: International Publishers, 1954, 1955, 336, 296, and 260 pp., respectively. The officially sponsored translation of selections from the writings of the Chinese Communist leader. They give insight into the official doctrines of Chinese communism.

Mikolajczyk, Stanislaw. *The Rape of Poland: Pattern of Soviet Aggression.* New York: Whittlesey House, 1948, 309 pp. An account of the communization of Poland by a leader of the Peasant party who spent the war years with the government-in-exile in London, but who returned to Poland as Deputy Premier after the war. He escaped from the country after the elections of January 1947.

Millis, Walter (ed.). *The Forrestal Diaries.* New York: The Viking Press, 1951, 581 pp. Excerpts from letters, reports, and recorded conversations of James Forrestal from 1944 when he was made the Secretary of the Navy to March 1949 when he resigned as the first Secretary of Defense. An excellent, although often incomplete, source for the student of United States foreign policy during this period.

Nagy, Ferenc. *The Struggle Behind the Iron Curtain.* New York: Macmillan Co., 1948, 471 pp. The story of the communization of Hungary by the leader of the Small Holders party, who was Premier in 1946-47.

Nasser, Gamal Abdul. *Egypt's Liberation: The Philosophy of the Revolution.* Washington: Public Affairs Press, 1955, 119 pp. Impressions of the Premier of Egypt on the revolution of July 23, 1952.

Ridgway, General Matthew B. (as told to Harold H. Martin). *Soldier: the Memoirs of Matthew B. Ridgway.* New York: Harper and Bros., 1956, 371 pp. General Ridgway discusses, among other subjects that relate to American foreign policy, the Korean War, the role of the

Army in the atomic age, and policy on Indo-China, Quemoy, and Matsu.

Rosenman, Samuel I. (ed.). *The Public Papers and Addresses of Franklin D. Roosevelt.* New York: Random House, Macmillan Co., Harper and Bros., 1938-50, 13 v. Edited and annotated addresses and other public papers of President Roosevelt from 1928 to his death in 1944.

Sherwood, Robert E. *Roosevelt and Hopkins: An Intimate History.* New York: Harper and Bros., 1948, 979 pp. A biography of Harry Hopkins, bearing mostly on his important association with the momentous events of the years of the Second World War. It is preceded by a sketch of his earlier career, including his relationship to the New Deal.

Smith, Walter Bedell. *My Three Years in Moscow.* Philadelphia and New York: J. B. Lippincott Co., 1950, 346 pp. Ambassador Smith's account of his service as head of the American mission in Moscow between 1946-49.

Stettinius, Edward R., Jr. *Roosevelt and the Russians: The Yalta Conference.* Garden City, N.Y.: Doubleday and Co., 1949, 367 pp. The Yalta story as seen by the Secretary of State who participated in the conference.

Stimson, Henry L., and Bundy, McGeorge. *On Active Service in Peace and War.* New York: Harper and Bros., 1948, 698 pp. Henry Stimson's years of public service under six Presidents, beginning with Theodore Roosevelt. Over half of the volume is devoted to his term as Secretary of War from July 1940 to September 1945, first under Franklin Roosevelt and then in the cabinet of President Truman.

Stuart, John Leighton. *Fifty Years in China.* New York: Random House, 1954, 346 pp. Dr. Stuart was officially American Ambassador to China from 1946 to 1952. Almost half the volume is devoted to that period.

Truman, Harry S. *Memoirs.* Volume One: *Year of Decision.* Garden City, N.Y.: Doubleday and Co., 1955, 596 pp. President Truman's own record of his first momentous year in office. Volume Two: *Years of Trial and Hope, 1946-1952.* Garden City, N.Y.: Doubleday and Co., 1956, 594 pp. This volume includes the President's story of the major foreign policy developments of the period, among them the Marshall mission to China, the Truman Doctrine, the Marshall Plan, and the Korean War.

Van Aduard, Baron A. J. Lewe. *Japan From Surrender to Peace.* The Hague: Martinus Nijhoff, 1953, 351 pp. A compilation and political analysis of the developments surrounding the occupation of Japan, by the Deputy Chief of the Netherlands Mission in Japan during that period. Foreword by John Foster Dulles.

Vandenberg, Arthur H. *The Private Papers of Senator Vandenberg,* Edited by Arthur H. Vandenberg, Jr., with the collaboration of Joe Alex Morris. Boston: Houghton Mifflin Co., 1952, 599 pp. An account of American foreign policy from 1940 to 1951 from the congressional point of vantage, based upon the letters and diary of the late Senator Vandenberg.

Whitney, Major General Courtney. *MacArthur: His Rendezvous with*

History. New York: Alfred A. Knopf, 1956, 547 pp. A justification of the record of General MacArthur by a close member of his staff.

Wildes, Harry Emerson. *Typhoon in Tokyo.* New York: Macmillan Co., 1954, 356 pp. An account of the occupation of Japan by a former SCAP official, who does not have a high opinion of General MacArthur's administrative procedures and claims to achievement.

Willoughby, Major General Charles A., and Chamberlain, John. *MacArthur: 1941-1951.* New York: McGraw-Hill Book Co., 1954, 441 pp. A decade in the life of General MacArthur, as told by his intelligence chief.

Annual Surveys and Collections of Documents

There are several nonofficial collections of documents containing both original and secondary materials that are easily accessible and very useful to the student of foreign affairs. *Documents on American Foreign Relations,* published annually since 1938, contains much valuable documentation. This volume was issued by the World Peace Foundation until 1953 when the Council on Foreign Relations took over its publication. *International Conciliation,* published monthly except July and August by the Carnegie Endowment for International Peace, presents analyses of problems in foreign relations. Each issue is devoted to a single problem. The *American Journal of International Law,* a quarterly, has a supplement of official documents as well as signed articles. The Royal Institute of International Affairs, Chatham House, London, publishes an annual *Survey of International Affairs* and an annual companion volume, *Documents on International Affairs.*

International Organization, a quarterly published by the World Peace Foundation, contains summaries of the activities of the more important international organizations and a supplement of official documents. Each issue also includes a selected bibliography, giving references to official documents, books, pamphlets, and periodicals. *Vital Speeches,* a semimonthly magazine, reprints the texts of important speeches by government officials. Newspapers with extensive national and international coverage such as the *New York Times* and the *New York Herald Tribune,* are a continuing and current source of information for the student of international affairs. The *New York Times Index,* issued semimonthly (cumulative annually), is a valuable bibliographical tool. The *Christian Science Monitor* is also helpful. All three newspapers publish texts of official documents not otherwise easily obtainable.

Among the more important of the annual surveys and collections of documents are the following.

Calvocoressi, Peter. *Survey of International Affairs, 1951.* London and New York: Oxford University Press for the Royal Institute of International Affairs, 1954, 505 pp. After the interruption caused by the

Second World War, the survey is again published on an annual basis. It includes a section on the Middle East.

Campbell, John C. *The United States in World Affairs.* (Annual). Volumes for 1945-1947, 1947-1948, 1948-1949. New York: Council on Foreign Relations, 1947, 1948, and 1949, 585 pp., 572 pp., and 604 pp., respectively. The first three volumes of the postwar series of annual reviews, resumed in 1947 after a lapse during the war years, by the Council on Foreign Relations. For the subsequent volumes, *see under:* Stebbins, Richard P.

Curl, Peter V. (ed.). *Documents on American Foreign Relations, 1953.* New York: Harper and Bros. for the Council on Foreign Relations, 1954, 458 pp. The fifteenth in this series of selected documents on United States foreign policy. Until 1953, the volume was published under the auspices of the World Peace Foundation.

Degras, Jane (ed.). *Soviet Documents on Foreign Policy,* Vol. I: 1917-24; Vol. II: 1925-32; Vol. III: 1933-41. New York: Oxford University Press, 1951, 1952, and 1953, 501 pp., 560 pp., and 500 pp., respectively. Official documents on Soviet foreign relations and policy between 1917 and 1941.

Eagleton, Clyde, Chamberlin, Waldo, and Swift, Richard N. (eds.). *Annual Review of United Nations Affairs for 1954.* New York: New York University Press, 1955, 253 pp. The sixth volume in an annual series. For earlier volumes, *see under:* Eagleton, Clyde, and Swift, Richard N.

Eagleton, Clyde, and Swift, Richard N. (eds.). *Annual Review of United Nations Affairs for 1949, 1950, 1951, 1952, 1953.* New York: New York University Press, 1950, 1951, 1952, 1953, 1954, 322 pp., 265 pp., 278 pp., 226 pp., and 213 pp., respectively. Developments relating to the United Nations presented annually.

Holborn, Louise W. (ed.). *War and Peace Aims of the United Nations.* Vol. 1, Sept. 1, 1939—Dec. 31, 1942; Vol. 2, Jan. 1, 1943—Sept. 1, 1945. Boston: World Peace Foundation, 1943 and 1948, 730 and 1278 pp. A documentary collection tracing the evolution of the war and peace aims of all the nations participating in the coalition against the Axis.

Stebbins, Richard P. *The United States in World Affairs.* Annual volumes for 1949, 1950, 1951, 1952, and 1953. New York: Harper and Bros., for the Council on Foreign Relations, 1950, 1951, 1952, 1953, 1954, 574 pp., 500 pp., 473 pp., 492 pp., and 512 pp., respectively. The most recent volumes in the annual postwar series of the Council on Foreign Relations. For earlier volumes, *see under:* Campbell, John C.

Toynbee, Arnold, and Ashton-Gwatkin, Frank T. (eds.). *Survey of International Affairs, 1939-1946:* Vol. 2, *The Middle East in the War,* by George Kirk. New York and London: Oxford University Press for the Royal Institute of International Affairs, 1952, 511 pp. This volume discusses those political and economic events and conditions in the Middle East during the Second World War that resulted in the conclusive establishment of the Near and Middle East regions as a geopolitical unity.

Toynbee, Arnold, and Toynbee, Veronica M. *Survey of International Affairs, 1939-1946: Hitler's Europe*. New York and London: Oxford University Press for the Royal Institute of International Affairs, 1954, 730 pp. One of the special war series. In addition to Hitler's Germany, this volume contains chapters on Vichy France and the Free French movement, Italy, the occupied countries of Europe, and the Eastern European satellites.

Background and Current Studies

Innumerable studies have been published, presenting both background material and current treatment of United States foreign policy between 1945 and 1955. The standard basic bibliographic sources are useful for checking such material. Among these studies are the following:

Ackerman, Edward A. *Japan's Natural Resources and Their Relation to Japan's Economic Future*. Chicago: University of Chicago Press, 1953, 655 pp. An extensive examination of the natural resources of Japan. It is based on a study done originally for SCAP. Many photographs, maps, and graphs are included.

Almond, Gabriel A. *The American People and Foreign Policy*. New York: Harcourt, Brace and Co., 1950, 269 pp. An examination of the relation between American public opinion and foreign policy.

Arnold, G. L. *The Pattern of World Conflict*. New York: The Dial Press, 1955, 235 pp. A synthesis of views common to American and European liberal and socialist supporters of public planning, as well as an analysis of recent political trends and a brief examination of long-term processes released by the collapse of the nineteenth century system of world trade.

Beloff, Max. *The Foreign Policy of Soviet Russia, 1929-1941*. London and New York: Oxford University Press, 1947 and 1949, 2 vols. A survey of the aims and policies of the Soviet Union.

———. *Soviet Policy in the Far East, 1944-1951*. New York and London: Oxford University Press for the Royal Institute of International Affairs, 1953, 278 pp. An account of the development of Soviet policies in East and Southeast Asia from the negotiations leading to Soviet entry into the war against Japan to the San Francisco Conference on the Japanese Peace Treaty in September 1951.

Bemis, Samuel Flagg. *The United States as a World Power, a Diplomatic History 1900-1950*. New York: Henry Holt and Co., 1950, 491 pp. A reprint, adapted and revised, of Part III, "The Twentieth Century," *The Diplomatic History of the United States* by the same author.

Betts, R. R. (ed.). *Central and South East Europe, 1945-1948*. London and New York: Royal Institute of International Affairs, 1950, 227 pp. The joint effort of a number of specialists who collaborated in recording the course of events in the Soviet satellite countries.

Lord Birdwood. *A Continent Decides*. London: Robert Hale Ltd., 1953,

315 pp. A British view of India and Pakistan, including their relationships to the Commonwealth.

Borton, Hugh. *Japan's Modern Century*. New York: Ronald Press Co., 1955, 524 pp. A comprehensive political, social, and economic history of Japan from its opening to the West in 1850 to the present. The author has included maps, illustrations, tables, documents, and biographical notes.

Bowles, Chester. *The New Dimensions of Peace*. New York: Harper and Bros., 1955, 391 pp. The author describes this volume as "one man's primer on policy priorities for the days ahead." The final part is especially challenging. Entitled "American Policy in a World of Revolution," it examines such subjects as the uses and limits of military power and economic aid; Europe, America, and colonialism; the poles of power, images of America abroad, and disarmament.

Brinton, Crane. *The United States and Britain*. Cambridge, Mass.: Harvard University Press, 1945, 305 pp. Problems of Anglo-American relations as seen in 1945.

Brooks, Michael. *Oil and Foreign Policy*. London: Lawrence and Wishart, 1949, 142 pp. The role of petroleum in international politics. Consideration is given to the Middle East, especially Azerbaijan, Iraq, and the Arabian desert. Indonesia is discussed, as is the relationship of oil to military installations, including air and naval bases.

Buchanan, Norman S., and Ellis, Howard S. *Approaches to Economic Development*. New York: Twentieth Century Fund, 1955, 494 pp. A general study of the problem of economic development.

Byford-Jones, W. *The Greek Trilogy (Resistance-Liberation-Revolution)*. London: Hutchinson and Co,, 1945, 270 pp. Developments leading to the political situation in Greece in 1944-45.

Caroe, Olaf. *Wells of Power. The Oilfields of South Western Asia*. London: Macmillan Co., 1951, 240 pp. A regional study stressing the strategic importance of the area to the free world. It develops the thesis that the danger of attack by the Soviet Union is greater in the Middle East than in Europe.

Carr, Edward Halett. *A History of Soviet Russia. The Bolshevik Revolution: 1917-1923*. Vols. I-III. New York: Macmillan Co., 1951, 1952, and 1953, 430 pp., 400 pp., and 614 pp., respectively. Vol. I analyzes the political structure of Soviet society from 1917 to 1924. Vol. II discusses the economic policies and problems of the early Soviet regime. Vol. III describes early Soviet policy toward the outside world.

Cheever, Daniel S., and Haviland, H. Field, Jr., *Organizing for Peace: International Organization in World Affairs*. Boston: Houghton Mifflin Co., 1954, 917 pp. The purpose of the authors is to relate international organizations to the total setting of international political, economic, and social relations. Among the subjects considered are a comparison of the structure and authority of the League of Nations and the United Nations, the League and the United Nations at work, and regional and other systems. They conclude with an examination of the fundamental issues involved.

Cole, Taylor (ed.). *European Political Systems.* New York: Alfred A. Knopf, 1953, 699 pp. Political systems of the Soviet Union, the People's Democracies of Eastern Europe, Germany, Italy, Great Britain, and France are described by a group of specialists. An extensive bibliography completes each section.

Cressey, George B. *How Strong is Russia.* Syracuse: Syracuse University Press, 1954, 146 pp. An appraisal by a geographer of the strength of the Soviet Union, with a final chapter on foreign policy, considering, among other aspects, the domestic base, objectives abroad, and the Soviet Union and China.

Dean, Gordon. *Report on the Atom: What You Should Know About the Atomic Energy Program of the United States.* New York: Alfred A. Knopf, 1953, 321 pp. An account of the American atomic energy program by the former Chairman of the Atomic Energy Commission.

Dennett, Raymond, and Johnson, Joseph E. (eds.). *Negotiating with the Russians.* Boston: World Peace Foundation, 1951, 310 pp. A symposium on the record of United States negotiations with the Soviet Union.

Deutscher, Isaac. *Stalin: A Political Biography.* London and New York: Oxford University Press, 1949, 600 pp. An extensive collection of material tracing the course of Soviet political developments, the story of an epoch built around the central figure of Stalin.

Dewar, Margaret. *Soviet Trade with Eastern Europe, 1945-49.* London and New York: Royal Institute of International Affairs, 1951, 123 pp. A summary of postwar economic relations between the Soviet Union and Czechoslovakia, Poland, Bulgaria, Hungary, and Rumania, including extensive statistical material and the texts of several commercial agreements.

Dulles, Foster Rhea. *America's Rise to World Power: 1898-1954.* New York: Harper and Bros., 1955, 314 pp. A volume in the New American Nation Series. It surveys the diplomatic history of the United States from the discovery of the region to 1954.

Elliott, William Y., Chairman of the Study Group. *The Political Economy of American Foreign Policy. Its Concepts, Strategy, and Limits.* Report of a Study Group Sponsored by The Woodrow Wilson Foundation and The National Planning Association. New York: Henry Holt and Company, 1955, 414 pp. An examination of American foreign economic policy that takes into account interdependent political, strategic, and psychological factors, both domestic and international.

———. *United States Foreign Policy: Its Organization and Control.* Report of a Study Group for The Woodrow Wilson Foundation. New York: Columbia University Press, 1953, 288 pp. An analysis of some of the modern problems in the organizational formation and control of United States foreign policy that arise from the basic structure of the government.

Emerson, Rupert. *Representative Government in Southeast Asia.* Cambridge: Harvard University Press, 1955, 197 pp. Issued under the auspices of the Institute of Pacific Relations. A study of the development of representative government in Indonesia, Burma, and Malaya. Indo-China and Thailand are discussed very briefly, and there are chapters on the Philippines and local self-government prepared by Willard H. Elsbree and Virginia Thompson.

Fainsod, Merle. *How Russia is Ruled*. Cambridge: Harvard University Press, 1953, 575 pp. A comprehensive survey of the power organization of Soviet society.

Farley, Miriam S. *United States Relations with Southeast Asia with Special Reference to Indochina*. New York: American Institute of Pacific Relations, 1955, 81 pp. mimeo. Part I discusses the United States and Indo-China, 1950-54. Part II considers United States relations with Burma, Indonesia, and Thailand during the same period. Part III covers the period from the Geneva Conference to October 1955.

Feis, Herbert. *The China Tangle: The American Effort in China from Pearl Harbor to the Marshall Mission*. Princeton: Princeton University Press, 1953, 445 pp. An account of "what the American Government tried to do in and with China during the war and in the critical period of peacemaking."

———. *The Road to Pearl Harbor*. Princeton: Princeton University Press, 1950, 356 pp. A well-documented account of the prolonged and fateful "diplomatic chess game" that led to Pearl Harbor.

Finletter, Thomas K. *Power and Policy: US Foreign Policy and Military Power in the Hydrogen Age*. New York: Harcourt, Brace and Co., 1954, 408 pp. A plea for new national policies to meet absolute Soviet air-atomic power of fission and hydrogen bombs carried mainly by big manned bombers. The author argues that this phase of atomic development will not last long. Science will soon devise new and unforeseeable weapons of destruction. Now is probably the last chance to control these weapons and prevent science from destroying civilization and man.

Florinsky, Michael T. *Integrated Europe?* New York: Macmillan Co., 1955, 182 pp. Examination of the movement for the economic, military, and political integration of Europe. The author concludes that although European co-operation has been substantially increased, integration in the sense of a supranational European government has failed and should not be an objective of American policy.

Ford, Alan W. *The Anglo-Iranian Oil Dispute of 1951-52*. Berkeley and Los Angeles: University of California Press, 1954, 348 pp. An examination of the development of the Anglo-Iranian oil dispute through July 1, 1952, and of the role of law in the relations of states.

Gluckstein, Ygael. *Stalin's Satellites in Europe*. London: George Allen & Unwin Ltd., 1952, 333 pp. A study of economic and political changes in Eastern Europe since the Second World War, based mainly on publications of the Eastern European governments and the Communist parties of these countries.

Goodrich, Leland M., and Hambro, Edvard. *Charter of the United Nations: Commentary and Documents*. Boston: World Peace Foundation, 1949, 2nd and rev. edition, 710 pp. An account of the origins of each provision of the Charter, comparisons with the League of Nations

Covenant, summary of the San Francisco deliberations, and very brief account of United Nations activities to mid-1948. Contains texts of important background documents.

Grindrod, Muriel. *The New Italy.* London and New York: Royal Institute of International Affairs, 1947, 118 pp. The transition from the Second World War to the peace treaty.

Haines, C. Grove (ed.). *Africa Today.* Baltimore: Johns Hopkins Press, 1955, 510 pp. Based on a conference on contemporary Africa, held in Washington, D.C., in 1954, by the Johns Hopkins University School of Advanced International Studies. Among others, such subjects are examined as the position of Africa in world affairs, its strategic significance, recent developments in the African dependencies, an American view of the United States and Africa, and an African view of the same relationship.

————. *The Threat of Soviet Imperialism.* Baltimore: Johns Hopkins Press, 1954, 402 pp. The outcome of a conference held in Washington in 1954 by the Johns Hopkins University School of Advanced International Studies. Part I deals with the broad aspects of Soviet relations with the non-Soviet world. Part II discusses techniques of Soviet subversion and attack. Part III assesses Soviet strength. Parts IV and V contain case studies of Soviet expansionism. A final chapter examines the response of United States foreign policy to the challenge of Soviet imperialism.

Halle, Louis J. *Civilization and Foreign Policy: An Inquiry for Americans.* New York: Harper and Bros., 1955, 277 pp. The thesis of the author is that an effective foreign policy for the United States must be based on "a conceptual scheme that reveals and explains the world in terms that bear the test of practical application." He rejects the alternatives of isolation and dominion and accepts that of coalition as most likely to be successful for the United States.

Hammer, Ellen J. *The Struggle for Indochina.* Stanford: The Stanford University Press, 1954, 342 pp. Published under the auspices of the Institute of Pacific Relations. This volume gives a detailed survey of recent Indo-Chinese history. It discusses the relations of the three Associated States with France, the Viet Minh, and the United States. The issues of colonialism, nationalism, and communism are examined.

Hanson, Simon G. *Economic Development in Latin America: An Introduction to the Economic Problems of Latin America.* Washington: The Inter-American Affairs Press, 1951, 531 pp. An analysis of the development problems of Latin America in terms of public policy, and a guide to the implementation of policy.

Hawtrey, R. G. *Towards the Rescue of Sterling.* London, New York, Toronto: Longmans, Green and Co., 1954, 159 pp. A British view of the balance-of-payments problem.

Herring, Hubert. *A History of Latin America From the Beginnings to the Present.* New York: Alfred A. Knopf, 1955, 772 pp. A history of the twenty nations of Latin America. The final part considers Latin America and the United States.

Hoskins, Halford L. *The Middle East: Problem Area in World Politics.* New York: Macmillan Co., 1954, 311 pp. Consideration of situations in the Middle East that affect Western efforts to establish positions of strength to increase the security of the free world.

Hughes, H. Stuart. *The United States and Italy.* Cambridge, Mass., 1953, 256 pp. United States relations with one of the members of the free world.

Hurewitz, J. C. *Middle East Dilemmas.* New York: Harper and Bros., for the Council on Foreign Relations, 1953, 273 pp. A discussion of the development of American interest and responsibilities in the Middle East.

———. *The Struggle for Palestine.* New York: W. W. Norton and Co., 1950, 404 pp. The Palestine problem from 1936 to the establishment of the state of Israel.

Huszar, George B. de, and associates. *Persistent International Issues.* New York and London: Harper and Bros., 1947, 262 pp. Specialists consider such problems as relief and rehabilitation, displaced persons, food and agriculture, industry and trade, money and finance, and others.

———. *Soviet Power and Policy.* New York: Thomas Y. Crowell Co., 1955, 598 pp. Twenty chapters by specialists setting forth the major factors of Soviet power and aggrandizement.

Issawi, Charles. *Egypt at Mid-Century: An Economic Survey.* New York: Oxford University Press, 1954, 280 pp. Published under the auspices of the Royal Institute of International Affairs. The author, a member of the Department of Economic Affairs of the United Nations, has revised his 1947 study on *Egypt: An Economic and Social Analysis.* He describes the physical and historical background of Egypt, analyzes some of the major branches of the economy, and discusses aspects of the political, social and cultural life of the country.

James, Daniel. *Red Design for the Americas: Guatemalan Prelude.* New York: John Day Co., 1954, 347 pp. The circumstances surrounding the Communist subversion in Guatemala, ending in the anti-Communist revolution of June 1954, as presented by a United States journalist.

Jones, F. C. *Japan's New Order in East Asia: Its Rise and Fall 1937-45.* London: Oxford University Press, 1954, 498 pp. Issued under the joint auspices of the Royal Institute of International Affairs and the Institute of Pacific Relations. The failure of the Japanese to secure the hegemony of East Asia is discussed. The major documents relating to the period are included in the appendix.

Kaufmann, W. W. (ed.). *Military Policy and National Security.* Princeton: Princeton University Press, 1956, 274 pp. Consideration of what the military policy of the United States should be in a time of thermo-nuclear stalemate.

Kelly, Alfred H. (ed.). *American Foreign Policy and American Democracy.* Detroit: Wayne University Press, 1954, 126 pp. The Franklin Memorial Lectures for 1952-53—"American Foreign Policy and the Concept of International Law," "Military and Strategic Aspects of Contemporary

American Foreign Policy," "The United States, the Soviet Union, and Western Nationalism," "American Foreign Policy and Its Critics," and "American Foreign Policy and the Future of American Civilization."

Kennan, George F. *American Diplomacy, 1900-1950*. Chicago: University of Chicago Press, 1951, 146 pp. Six lectures delivered by the author at the University of Chicago that seek to examine the basic concepts and purposes of American foreign policy during the past half century. Two appendixes contain reprints of articles on Russia that first appeared in *Foreign Affairs*.

———. *Realities of American Foreign Policy*. Princeton: Princeton University Press, 1954, 120 pp. A series of lectures delivered at Princeton University. It represents an effort to relate contemporary problems of foreign affairs to certain basic external realities in which United States policy must operate.

Kulski, W. W. *The Soviet Regime: Communism in Practice*. Syracuse: Syracuse University Press, 1954, 807 pp. The study is designed as a reference book, giving indirect access to Soviet sources. No foreign commentaries or secondary accounts have been used by the author in his comprehensive examination of the Soviet system.

Langer, William L., and Gleason, S. Everett. *The World Crisis and American Foreign Policy* (Vol. I, *The Challenge to Isolation, 1937-1940;* Vol. II, *The Undeclared War, 1940-1941*). New York: Harper and Bros., for the Council on Foreign Relations, 1952 and 1953, 794 pp. and 963 pp., respectively. A history of American foreign policy in the period prior to the Second World War. Vol. I ends with the fall of France and the breakdown of American neutrality. Vol. II outlines developments leading up to Pearl Harbor.

Leiss, Amelia C. (ed.). in co-operation with Raymond Dennett. *European Peace Treaties After World War II*. Boston: World Peace Foundation, 1954, 341 pp. The negotiations relating to and the texts of the peace settlements with Italy, Bulgaria, Hungary, Rumania, and Finland. Supplementary to *Documents on American Foreign Relations*, VIII, 1945-1946 and IX, 1947.

Lenczowski, George. *The Middle East in World Affairs*. Ithaca: Cornell University Press, 1952, 459 pp. A study of contemporary politics and diplomacy in the Middle East from 1914 to the present. There is also a chapter on the diplomatic history of the Ottoman and Persian empires, especially in the nineteenth century. The volume contains a bibliography, statistical tables, and maps,

———. *Russia and the West in Iran, 1918-1948: A Study in Big-Power Rivalry*. Ithaca: Cornell University Press, 1949, 383 pp. An examination of modern political developments in Iran, with emphasis on its relations with foreign powers. Documentary appendices are included.

Leonard, L. Larry. *International Organization*. New York: McGraw-Hill Book Co., 1951, 630 pp. A basic text showing how governments use international organizations in the conduct of foreign relations and pointing out the significance of these institutions in the world community.

Levi, Werner. *Free India in Asia*. Minneapolis: University of Minnesota Press, 1952, 161 pp. A well-documented study of India's position in Asia and its relations with each of the countries in the area, with emphasis on developments since 1947.

————. *Modern China's Foreign Policy*. Minneapolis: University of Minnesota Press, 1953, 399 pp. An attempt to analyze Chinese foreign policy. China, not the countries with which it has relations, is the focus of the volume.

Lippmann, Walter. *The Cold War: A Study in U. S. Foreign Policy*. New York and London: Harper and Bros., 1947, 62 pp. A publicist examines critically the containment thesis as presented in "The Sources of Soviet Conduct," which appeared in *Foreign Affairs* for July 1947.

Litchfield, Edward H. and associates. *Governing Postwar Germany*. Ithaca: Cornell University Press, 1955, 661 pp. A reference volume on the governments of postwar Germany, with relevant documentation.

Longrigg, Stephen Hemsley. *Iraq, 1900-1950: A Political, Social, and Economic History*. London, New York, Toronto: Oxford University Press, 1953, 436 pp. Issued under the auspices of the Royal Institute of International Affairs. An exhaustive history of modern Iraq, with an appraisal of its situation as of 1950.

MacMahon, Arthur W. *Administration in Foreign Affairs*. University, Alabama: University of Alabama Press, 1953, 275 pp. A very useful examination of the machinery available for the development and execution of American foreign policy.

Macmichael, Sir Harold. *The Sudan*. New York: Frederick A. Praeger, 1955, 255 pp. The history of the area up to the signature of the Anglo-Egyptian agreement of 1953. The political relationships of Great Britain, Egypt, and the Sudan are considered rather fully.

Madan, B. K. (ed.). *Economic Problems of Underdeveloped Countries in Asia*. New Delhi: Indian Council of World Affairs; London: Oxford University Press, 1953, 290 pp. Examination of the problem of the economic development of Asia by scholars from the interested countries. The volume recognizes that the problem is important for the welfare and stability of these countries and vital for the peace of the world.

McCloy, John J. *The Challenge to American Foreign Policy*. Cambridge: Harvard University Press, 1953, 81 pp. Attention is called to the inadequacies of our foreign policy and to the necessity for reconsidering the related aspects that would constitute an integrated and more effective foreign policy.

McKay, Donald C. *The United States and France*. Cambridge, Mass.: Harvard University Press, 1951, 334 pp. An account of United States relations with France going back as far as Colonial America. This includes discussion of the position of France in the postwar world. Appendices give statistical material and suggested reading.

McNeill, William Hardy. *Survey of International Affairs, 1939-1946. America, Britain, and Russia: Their Co-operation and Conflict, 1941-1946*. London and New York: Oxford University Press for the Royal Institute of International Affairs, 1953, 819 pp. An American historian examines the Grand Alliance of the Second World War from Pearl Harbor through 1946. He discusses the permanent significance of the alliance and its relationship to the cold war. He points out that the co-operation of the great allied powers forwarded changes that could not have come about if each nation had conducted its affairs in isolation.

Marjolin, Robert. *Europe and the United States in the World Economy*. Durham, N.C.: Duke University Press, 1953, 105 pp. Lectures given in the fall of 1951 by the Secretary-General of the Organization for European Economic Cooperation.

Marshall, Charles Burton. *The Limits of Foreign Policy*. New York: Henry Holt and Co., 1954, 128 pp. A series of lectures on the limitations imposed on United States foreign policy goals, by a former member of the Policy Planning Staff of the Department of State.

Mason, Edward S. *Promoting Economic Development: The United States and Southern Asia*. Claremont, Calif.: Claremont College, 1955, 83 pp. This volume is an extension of the Claremont lectures of November 1954. It examines the American concern with the problem of economic development in Southern Asia. Pakistan is examined as a case study. The author has served as consultant to the National Planning Board of the Government of Pakistan.

Mikesell, Raymond F. *Foreign Exchange in the Postwar World*. New York: Twentieth Century Fund, 1954, 658 pp. The purpose of the volume is "to provide a better understanding of foreign exchange practices and policies since World War II."

————. *United States Economic Policy and International Relations*. New York: McGraw-Hill Book Co., Inc., 1952, 341 pp. A brief survey and analysis of the foreign economic policy of the United States.

Mills, Lennox A., and associates. *The New World of Southeast Asia*. Minneapolis: University of Minnesota Press, 1949, 445 pp. Eight experts contribute chapters to this integrated survey of recent political developments and their geographical and historical antecedents in Burma, Indo-China, Indonesia, Malaya, Thailand, and the Philippines.

Moore, Barrington, Jr. *Terror and Progress USSR: Some Sources of Change and Stability in the Soviet Dictatorship*. Cambridge: Harvard University Press, 1954, 261 pp. An attempt to evaluate the sources of stability and the potentialities for change in the Soviet regime.

Morgenthau, Hans J. *In Defense of the National Interest: A Critical Examination of American Foreign Policy*. New York: Alfred A. Knopf, 1951, 283 pp. An analytical study of the national interest in the formation of American foreign policy and of the revolutionary forces that have influenced the course of that policy.

Nettl, J. P. *The Eastern Zone and Soviet Policy in Germany, 1945-50*, New York: Oxford University Press, 1951, 324 pp. A British author examines events and policies during the first five years of Soviet occupation of Eastern Germany. He concludes that unless the *status quo* were to continue for a generation, Eastern Germany "would shed its

Communist superstructure without much difficulty once the direct military control of the Russians was removed to a safe distance."

Northrop, F. S. C. *European Union and United States Foreign Policy. A Study in Sociological Jurisprudence.* New York: Macmillan Co., 1954, 230 pp. A philosophical approach to the movement toward European union.

———. *The Taming of the Nations: A Study of the Cultural Bases of International Policy.* New York: Macmillan Co., 1952, 362 pp. Through an examination of the cultural bases of international policy, the author seeks to show the inadequacy of the power politics theory, and the feasibility of a policy based on common ideals and spiritual values.

Pearson, Lester B. *Democracy in World Politics.* Princeton: Princeton University Press, 1955, 123 pp. The Stafford Little Lectures at Princeton University, 1955. The Canadian Secretary of State for External Affairs discusses problems of political life both within states and in relations between states. He considers "the change in scale with respect to the greatly increased force now available as an instrument of policy, and some of the problems that this has caused or accentuated."

Perkins, Dexter. *The American Approach to Foreign Policy.* Cambridge: Harvard University Press, 1952, 195 pp. An analysis of the moral, political, economic, and social factors that influence American foreign policy and actions.

Pickles, Dorothy. *French Politics: The First Years of the Fourth Republic.* London and New York: Oxford University Press for Royal Institute of International Affairs, 1953, 302 pp. An account of political issues and problems of the French Republic from its liberation to the late summer of 1951.

———. *France: The Fourth Republic.* London: Methuen and Co., 1955, 238 pp. An examination of the postwar French government and political scene. Foreign policy problems and the state of mind of postwar France are discussed.

Possony, Stefan T. *A Century of Conflict: Communist Techniques of World Revolution.* Chicago: Henry Regnery Co., 1953, 439 pp. The author seeks to present the Soviet pattern of conquest by tracing the development of Communist techniques of usurpation and expansion.

Price, Harry Bayard. *The Marshall Plan and Its Meaning.* Ithaca: Cornell University Press, 1955, 424 pp. Published under the auspices of the Governmental Affairs Institute. A history and evaluation of the Marshall Plan. The author had access to government records and interviewed many officials and private citizens in the United States and Europe who had personal knowledge of the working of the program.

Randall, Clarence B. *A Foreign Economic Policy for the United States.* Chicago: University of Chicago Press, 1954, 83 pp. The Chairman of the Commission on Foreign Economic Policy proposes a foreign economy policy for the United States.

Reinhardt, George C. *American Strategy in the Atomic Age.* Norman: University of Oklahoma Press, 1955, 227 pp. An assessment of the strategic impact of nuclear weapons by the Army Colonel who in 1953 wrote with Lt. Col. William R. Kintner, *Atomic Weapons in Land Combat*. The author pleads for the determination of a "cold war strategy."

Roberts, Henry L., and Wilson, Paul A. *Britain and the United States, Problems in Cooperation*. New York: Harper and Bros., 1953, 253 pp. The conclusions of American and British study groups for the Council on Foreign Relations and the Royal Institute of International Relations on relations between the United States and Great Britain.

Rostow, W. W., and others. *The Dynamics of Soviet Society*. New York: W. W. Norton and Co., 1952, 1953, 282 pp. Part One considers the evolution of Soviet rule; Part Two is concerned with cohesive forces, instabilities, and tensions in contemporary Soviet society; Part Three presents the authors' conclusions with respect to the Soviet structure of power.

———. *The Prospect for Communist China*. New York: John Wiley and Sons and Technology Press of Massachusetts Institute of Technology, 1954, 379 pp. An important group study. It examines developments between 1840 and 1949, Communist policy between 1949 and 1954, the Chinese Communist Government and its people, Sino-Soviet relations, and the prospects for Communist China.

Rostow, W. W., with Hatch, Richard W. *An American Policy in Asia*. New York: John Wiley and Sons and Technology Press of Massachusetts Institute of Technology, 1955, 59 pp. A sequel to *The Prospect for Communist China* (1954). American foreign policy problems in Southeast Asia are considered, and policy alternatives are set forth with recommendations.

Royal Institute of International Affairs. *Atlantic Alliance: NATO's Role in the Free World*. London and New York: Royal Institute of International Affairs, 1952, 172 pp. A study of the "growth working, and future development" of the North Atlantic Treaty Organization, and a critical analysis of Western policies after the invasion of Korea.

———. *Britain in Western Europe: WEU and the Atlantic Alliance*. London and New York: Royal Institute of International Affairs, 1956, 121 pp. The examination by a study group of the implications of the London and Paris Agreements for the United Kingdom and Western Europe.

———. *Defense in the Cold War: The Task for the Free World*. London and New York: Royal Institute of International Affairs, 1950, 123 pp. A report by a study group on the problems and objectives of the Western democracies, and an examination of the effectiveness of regional defense arrangements.

———. *The Middle East: A Political and Economic Survey*. London and New York: Royal Institute of International Affairs, 1950, 496 pp. A summary of political, social, and economic information on the region as a whole.

———. *The Soviet-Yugoslav Dispute*. London: Royal Institute of International Affairs, 1948, 79 pp. Texts of published Soviet-Yugoslav correspondence relating to the expulsion of the Yugoslav Communist party from the Cominform.

Schiller, A. Arthur. *The Formation of Federal Indonesia: 1945-1949.* The Hague, Bandung: W. Van Hoeve Ltd., 1955, 472 pp. A description of the steps taken in the formation of the federal state in Indonesia from 1945 through 1949. The study is based on field work as well as on an examination of basic private and public documents.

Sennholz, Hans F. *How Can Europe Survive.* New York: D. Van Nostrand Co., 1955, 336 pp. The author examines doctrines and plans for European economic co-operation and political unity. He supports unification, but opposes "the spread of socialist and welfare ideas and their adoption in the political world" as promoting "impediments to the free movement of men, goods, and capital."

Seton-Watson, Hugh. *The East European Revolution.* London: Methuen and Co., Ltd., 1950, 406 pp. Wartime and postwar developments in Eastern Europe and Greece, including the Axis conquest, the resistance movements, and the Communist seizure of power.

———. *From Lenin to Malenkov: The History of World Communism.* New York: Frederick A. Praeger, 1953, 377 pp. A survey of communism in the world today, emphasizing the relationship of Communist movements to social classes and to the internal balance of power in the states concerned.

Shepley, James R., and Blair, Clay, Jr. *The Hydrogen Bomb.* New York: David McKay Co., 1954, 244 pp. A report by two journalists on the controversy surrounding the development of the hydrogen bomb in the United States.

Slessor, Sir John. *Strategy for the West.* New York: William Morrow and Co., 1954, 180 pp. The former Chief of the British Air Staff presents a strategy for the West. Its objective is—in the age of atomic and thermonuclear weapons—to drive communism behind its own frontiers and keep it there. This means, among other things, "accepting, perhaps for many years, a heavy burden of armaments and not falling for the catch phrase 'an armaments race always leads to war.'"

Staley, Eugene. *The Future of Underdeveloped Countries.* New York: Harper and Bros., for the Council on Foreign Relations, 1954, 410 pp. An examination of the problem of economic development. It shows why the underdeveloped countries have been selected as a primary target by communism. It points out the attitudes and sensitivities of the peoples of these countries that must be taken into consideration in any Western counter measures against Communist infiltration and conquest.

Stuart, Graham H. *The Department of State.* New York: Macmillan Co., 1949, 517 pp. A history of its organization, procedure, and personnel.

Sweet-Escott, Bickham. *Greece: A Political and Economic Survey 1939-1953.* London and New York: Royal Institute of International Affairs, 1954, 207 pp. The history of Greece since 1944 with background material from the years 1941-44. Included in the appendices are a discussion of the problem of Cyprus, as well as statistical tables, maps, and a note on further reading.

Thornburg, Max Weston and others. *Turkey: An Economic Appraisal.* New York: The Twentieth Century Fund, 1949, 324 pp. A comprehensive economic survey. It takes into account the strategic significance of Turkey and attempts to lay the intellectual groundwork for the American assistance program there.

Toynbee, Arnold. *The World and the West.* New York and London: Oxford University Press, 1953, 99 pp. An exposition of the effects of Western culture on the major cultures of the non-Western world, with speculation regarding the future.

Vinacke, Harold M. *The United States and the Far East 1945-1951.* Stanford: Stanford University Press, for the Institute of Pacific Relations, 1952, 144 pp. An examination of the main developments of American policy in the Far East since 1945, as presented against an historical background and in relation to problems of American policy in Europe.

Walker, Richard L. *China Under Communism: The First Five Years.* New Haven: Yale University Press, 1955, 403 pp. A survey of the first five years of Chinese Communist domination of the mainland of China. The author points out that the Chinese Communists "make no secret of their intention to follow the path blazed by the USSR under Stalin as closely as conditions in China permit."

Wallich, Henry C. *Mainsprings of the German Revival.* New Haven: Yale University Press, 1955, 401 pp. The economic revival of Western Germany. The author endeavors to bring into perspective the circumstances and policies that he considers responsible for the rapid growth of the German economy since about 1950.

Ward, Barbara. *The West at Bay.* New York: W. W. Norton and Co., 1948, 288 pp. Western association in light of the Communist challenge.

Webster, Sir Charles; Jacob, Major General Sir Ian; and Robinson, E. A. G. *United Kingdom Policy: Foreign, Strategic, Economic.* London and New York: Royal Institute of International Affairs, 1950, 104 pp. An appraisal of the fundamental factors that govern British policy.

Westerfield, H. Bradford. *Foreign Policy and Party Politics.* New Haven: Yale University Press, 1955, 448 pp. The role of the Congress and the political parties in the administration of foreign affairs. Among the specific problems examined are American relations with the Soviet Union, European recovery, and China.

Whitaker, Arthur P. *The Western Hemisphere Idea: Its Rise and Decline.* Ithaca: Cornell University Press, 1954, 194 pp. The subordination of Latin America in United States foreign policy.

Williams, John H. *Economic Stability in a Changing World.* New York: Oxford University Press, 1953, 284 pp. The central theme is the relation of economic theory to public policy. The volume comprises a series of papers on the Marshall Plan and two essays, concerning economic stability at full employment levels in the United States and the monetary doctrines of Lord Keynes.

Woytinsky, W. S., and Woytinsky, E. S. *World Commerce and Governments: Trends and Outlook.* New York: Twentieth Century Fund,

1955, 907 pp. A comprehensive survey of the population, needs and resources, agriculture, industry, transportation and trade, and governmental systems of all the regions of the world. Sections are included on international co-operation, American foreign assistance, European integration, and other subjects of value to the student of international affairs.

Zimmern, Sir Alfred. *The American Road to World Peace.* New York: E. P. Dutton and Co., 1953, 287 pp. A study of international co-operative attempts to ensure world peace, with emphasis on the role of the United States, and with extended discussion of the background and operation of the United Nations Organization and suggestions for its improvement.

INDEX

Index

220, 310, 392; infrastructure of, 309, 440n; integrated defense plans of, 196, 390, 390n; Italy, relation to, 199; Korean War, relation to, 283, 390; London and Paris Agreements on Western Germany, 405-06; military commands under, 309n;

North Atlantic Council, 308; Defense Committee, 128, 256, 308; Financial and Economic Committee, establishment and purpose of, 128, 308; first session (1949), 128; second session (1949), 128; third session (1950), 128; fourth session (1950), 286; fifth session (1950), 288, 290; Ministerial meeting (December 1953), 401; ministerial meeting (December 1955), 415; ministerial meeting (May 1955), 408, 409; ninth session (1952), 395, 396; standing group, 308

Production Division, 309-10; Purposes of, 362; Secretariat, 309; Strategic concept, development of, 285, 310, 401; Supreme Commander, 284, 291, 309; Underdeveloped countries, relation to, 209; U.S. policy toward, 284-93, 359; Western Europe and Canada, contributions to, 287; West German membership in, 288-93, 320, 394-97, 408, 411; Yugoslavia, relation to, 310, 310n

North Korea. See Korea, north

"Northern tier" alliance, in Middle East, 413, 442n

Norway, postwar economic recovery in, 200; re-establishment of political stability in, 200; U.S. base rights, restrictions on, 415

Objective, definition of term, 9n, 473

One world, concept of, 104, 117

Opie, Redvers, cited 132n

Organization for European Economic Cooperation (OEEC), 121, 215, 249, 250, 309-10; European integration, relation to, 206-07

Organization of American states (OAS) (see also American republics; individual countries; Latin American states; Western Hemisphere), 36n, 81, 313, 362n; charter of, 76; purposes of, 77

Outer Mongolia, U.N., membership in, 416

Pacific security pact. See Far East, Pacific security pact

Pakistan (see also Arab-Asian states; Baghdad Pact; Southeast Asia Collective Defense Treaty); 135, 296, 315, 315n, 331; sovereign state in, 222; India, relations with, 401, 403; Turkey, treaty of mutual defense with, 403; U.S. assistance (see under United States assistance); U.S. policy toward, 403

Palestine (see also Arab League; Israel); Anglo-American Committee of Inquiry, recommendations of, 215; Arab-Israeli armistice agreements (1949), 216; British mandate, 215, 216; British policy toward, 215, 216; economic development of, 215; fighting in, 216; U.N. General Assembly, partition resolution on (1947), 216; U.N. Security Council, decisions on, 216; U.N. Special Committee on Palestine (UNSCOP), report of, 216; U.N. trusteeship, proposal for, 216; U.S. policy toward, 215-18

Paris Peace Conference (1946), 86, 90n

Paris Peace Conference (1919), 18

Pax Brittanica, 17, 17n

Peace settlements, after Second World War (see also individual countries); U.S. plans for, 42-46, 57-75, 141

Peaslee, A. J., cited 171n

Peripheral world. See Economic development

Philippines (see also Southeast Asia Collective Defense Treaty), 296, 315n; Asian states, split with, 392; Pacific pact, proposal for, 311; U.S. assistance (see under United States assistance); U.S. policy toward, 221n; U.S. strategic estimate of, 441; U.S. treaty of mutual assistance with, 312, 391, 393

Point Four Program (see also Economic development; United States assistance, technical), 417; congressional opposition to, 136-37; inception and development of, 134-37; justification for, 136-37; purposes of, 135; colonialism, relation to, 135

Poland, Communist government in, 69,

Schuman Plan. *See* European Coal and Steel Community

Security, national, U.S., as internal problem, 258; choices on, 337-38; collective versus unilateral, 342-44; 426; costs of, 378-79n, 379-82; extension of arrangements for, 320, 330; U.S. position on, 37-40, 88, 259, 332-50

Selective Service Act (1947), 50

Self-determination, principle of, 102, 221, 222, 316, 368-69, 424, 452, 455

Siam. *See* Thailand

Sinkiang, 306

Sino-Soviet bloc, 307, 430

Sino-Soviet Treaty (1945). *See* China, Sino-Soviet Treaty

Situations of strength, development of, by U.S., 321-23, 322n

Sokolovsky, Soviet Marshal, 156

"Sources of Soviet Conduct," article in *Foreign Affairs,* 94

Southeast Asia *(see also* Bandung Conference; Far East; Southeast Asia Collective Defense Treaty); U.S. strategic estimate of, 367

Southeast Asia Collective Defense Treaty (1954) *(see also* Southeast Asia Treaty Organization), 313, 426; conclusion of, 312, 404, 404n; Indian views on, 406

Southeast Asia Treaty Organization (SEATO) *(see also* Southeast Asia Collective Defense Treaty), 443, 461; Burma, rejection of aid through, 411; membership of U.S. in, 367; organization of, 312

Southeast Asian conference (Colombo, 1954), 315-16

South Korea. *See* Korea, south

Soviet bloc *(see also* individual countres; Sino-Soviet bloc; Trade relations, East-West), 66-67, 331, 353-54, 424, 442; Council for Mutual Economic Assistance, establishment of, 254, 305; economic co-ordination of, 305, 307, 386; European Recovery Program, invitation to join, 118-19; international system, place in, 303-08, 329; military co-ordination of, 305, 306, 336; NATO, confrontation of, 286, 306-07, 314; organization of, 95, 161-63, 253-54, 303-08, 319-20, 330, 452; Soviet Union, economic agreements with, 103; treaties of mutual

assistance between members of, 304, 304n, 306-07; U.S. policy, relation to, 161-63, 332-33, 384, 441-42

Soviet-Nazi Pact (1939), 85

Soviet Union *(see also* Containment policy; individual subjects; for relations with other countries, *see* individual country; International system; Sino-Soviet bloc; Soviet bloc), Churchill, Sir Winston, views on, 89-90; collective leadership in, 464n; deflation of currency in, 103; economic strength of, 103-04; expansionism of, 87, 88, 89, 352; Far East, concessions in, 64; five-year plan for, 103; France, treaty of alliance with, 190, 292n; Great Britain, treaty of alliance with, 292n; military capabilities of, 99-101; national Communist parties, use of, 87, 101; NATO assessment of strength (1950), 286; objectives, politico-military, 100-01; political strength of, 101-03; U.S., assessment of capabilities and intentions of, 64, 84-91, 93-96, 99-104, 107, 149, 174, 253-56, 260 *et seq.,* 282-83, 286, 295-96, 320, 353-54, 380-82, 391, 416-17, 428 *et seq.,* 433-34, 456; U.S., negotiations with, as means of reducing international tensions, 320, 321 *et seq.,* 323-24, 370-72, 397-98, 400-02, 407, 422, 423, 425, 426, 445-50; U.S., political relations with, 89-91, 323-24, 325, 354-55, 370-73, 414, 422-23; U.S., wartime relations with, 85; Wallace, Henry A., views on, 89, 90, 90n

Spain, 248, 296; U.S. bases in, 391, 392; U.S. strategic estimate of, 441

Sparrow, John C., cited 49n

Stalin, Josef V., death of, 399

State relations, nature of. *See* International system

Sterling area, 203

Stimson, Henry S., 76

Stockpiling, of critical materials, 334, 346

Stone, Donald C., cited 122n

Strategic concept, NATO, development of, 256

U.S., development of *(see also* Military coalition), 99-112, 113-40, 247-53, 256, 294-95, 310, 321, 332-50, 422-23, 441-42; containment policy as, 105-07, 141, 289; Eastern